The Lost Lawyer

The Lost Lawyer

FAILING IDEALS OF THE LEGAL PROFESSION

Anthony T. Kronman

THE BELKNAP PRESS OF
HARVARD UNIVERSITY PRESS

Cambridge, Massachusetts
London, England

Third Printing, 1995

First Harvard University Press paperback edition, 1995

Library of Congress Cataloging-in-Publication Data
Kronman, Anthony T.
The lost lawyer: failing ideals of the legal profession /
Anthony T. Kronman.
p. cm.
Includes bibliographical references and index.
ISBN 0-674-53926-5 (cloth)
ISBN 0-674-53927-3 (pbk.)
1. Practice of law—United States. 2. Lawyers—United States.
3. Legal ethics—United States. I. Title.
KF300.K76 1993
174'.3' 0973—dc20   93-10685
CIP

For Nancy

Preface

In the spring of 1981, the student editors of the *Yale Law Journal* sponsored a symposium on the nature and purposes of legal scholarship. They invited my colleague Arthur Leff to make some introductory remarks at its opening session, but, weakened by cancer, Art had to withdraw shortly before the event. The *Journal's* editors asked me to take his place and I accepted. In my talk (with which Art surely disagreed, though he was much too kind to say so) I spoke about the difference between scholarship and advocacy. Scholarship, I said, aims at the truth. Advocacy, by contrast, is concerned merely with persuasion. I said that practicing lawyers are interested only in persuasion, whereas law teachers are dedicated mainly to the truth-seeking enterprise of scholarship instead. This I pictured as a higher and better calling than the advocate's (which, I claimed, corrupts the soul by encouraging a studied indifference to the truth). I ended by suggesting that the law teacher's highest responsibility is to convey a scholarly love of truth to his or her students, whose work as practicing lawyers promotes bad habits to which legal academics are happily immune.

Afterward, my colleagues Paul Gewirtz and Barbara Underwood asked me how, if I had such a low opinion of law practice, I could in good conscience go on training students for it. Isn't it true, they asked, that a practicing lawyer needs powers of judgment an academic lawyer does not—a practical wisdom as honorable as the scholar's love of truth but very different from it? Their question disturbed me, and I have been trying to answer it ever since.

It has taken me a long time to do so, and the list of those who have helped has lengthened with the years. I have first to thank all those outside the Yale Law School who gave me their encouragement and support. These include the dean and faculty of the University of Michigan Law School, who invited me to give the Cooley Lectures in 1987, on which the first three chapters of this book are based. I presented later versions of these chapters at workshops at the UCLA, University of California, University of Toronto, and Columbia law schools. Each gave me an opportunity to rethink my views, and I have benefited from the sharp but friendly criticisms of those who participated in these sessions. I also presented an early draft of Chapter 2 to the Society for Ethical and Legal Philosophy. Over the years I have learned much from this extraordinary group; its meetings have been for me a model of what philosophical friendship can be.

Within the Yale Law School, my debts are likewise heavy. To Harry Wellington—during whose deanship this book began—and Guido Calabresi—during whose it was completed—I owe thanks for their support. Many other colleagues have also helped me with their criticisms and suggestions and doubts. I am indebted to them all, and especially to Bo Burt, Mirjan Damaska, Bob Ellickson, Paul Gewirtz, Henry Hansmann, Paul Kahn, Harold Koh, John Langbein, George Priest, Jed Rubenfeld, and Alan Schwartz. Above all I have benefited from the skeptical encouragement of two of my colleagues, Bruce Ackerman and Owen Fiss. I doubt that I shall ever persuade these two good friends that I am right. But the debt I owe them for helping me to know my own mind is immeasurable and can never be discharged.

I also want to thank three of my student research assistants for their help in preparing the manuscript—Steve Garvey and Brett Scharffs, both of the Class of 1992, and Claire Finkelstein, of the Class of 1993. They have checked, corrected, and instructed me and helped me sustain my enthusiasm for the book. To the readers who reviewed the manuscript for Harvard University Press, I must express my thanks as well for their perceptive suggestions and for the supportive spirit in which they were made.

Over the years I have had the good luck to work with two very able secretaries, Diane Hart and Isabel Poludnewycz. Their efforts have been indispensable, and I appreciate all they have done.

Finally, there is my family—my children Emma, Hope, and Matthew and my wife, Nancy. They have borne more of the trauma of the birth of this book than I had any right to ask, and Nancy's wisdom has been my example and guide from the start. Gratitude is too weak a word to describe what I owe them.

Contents

There is nothing to encourage us to believe that what has captured current fancy is the most valuable part of our inheritance, or that the better survives more readily than the worse. And nothing survives in this world which is not cared for by human beings.

Michael Oakeshott

Introduction

This book is about a crisis in the American legal profession. Its message is that the profession now stands in danger of losing its soul.

In material terms, of course, American lawyers hardly seem to be in any danger at all, let alone the serious sort that would justify an apocalyptic claim of this kind. By most outward measures they appear, in fact, to be thriving. There are now nearly a million lawyers in America. As a group, they are very well paid. And they continue to dominate our public life, at all levels of government, exactly as before. The economic downturn of the 1990s has inevitably affected lawyers along with everyone else. But the legal profession remains one of the most prosperous and powerful groups in American society. Tocqueville said, "It is at the bar or the bench that the American aristocracy is found," and judging by the wealth and influence of lawyers in contemporary America, one might conclude that his famous dictum is as true today as when he uttered it a hundred and fifty years ago.[1]

To be sure, there are critics who claim the legal profession has more influence than it should. Dan Quayle and Derek Bok have recently made statements to this effect.[2] And there have always been those who questioned the honesty and trustworthiness of lawyers (an issue that since Watergate has been very conspicuously in the public eye). Every year produces a fresh crop of scoundrels and renewed doubts about the ability of the profession to police itself, along with familiar complaints about the undue power of lawyers (which any democratic society is bound to regard with suspicion). These criticisms are perennial. They reflect recurrent anxieties and concerns,

1

some of which are surely justified. But none touch the crisis that now threatens the collective soul of American lawyers.

People choose a career in the law for many reasons. Some do so for money and others for power and prestige, and a few, at least, become lawyers in order to advance their political ideals. But these are all external reasons for choosing a life in the law. They all portray the practice of law as a means to an end that lies beyond it. There is nothing wrong with any of these reasons. They are all respectable, and the last is genuinely admirable. But whatever external goals they aim to achieve through the practice of law, most lawyers also hope that their work will be a source of satisfaction in itself. Indeed, many hope that the intrinsic satisfactions it affords will be important enough to play a significant role in their fulfillment as human beings. Not everyone who becomes a lawyer looks for this kind of fulfillment in his or her work. But many do, and the professional pride of lawyers as a group has always depended on the belief that what they do has the potential to be rewarding in this way.

It is just that belief, however, which is now faltering and whose enfeeblement has caused the crisis in which the American legal profession is now caught. This crisis is, in essence, a crisis of morale. It is the product of growing doubts about the capacity of a lawyer's life to offer fulfillment to the person who takes it up. Disguised by the material well-being of lawyers, it is a spiritual crisis that strikes at the heart of their professional pride.

This crisis has been brought about by the demise of an older set of values that until quite recently played a vital role in defining the aspirations of American lawyers. At the very center of these values was the belief that the outstanding lawyer—the one who serves as a model for the rest—is not simply an accomplished technician but a person of prudence or practical wisdom as well. It is of course rewarding to become technically proficient in the law. But earlier generations of American lawyers conceived their highest goal to be the attainment of a wisdom that lies beyond technique—a wisdom about human beings and their tangled affairs that anyone who wishes to provide real deliberative counsel must possess. They understood this wisdom to be a trait of character that one acquires only by becoming a person of good judgment, and not just an expert in the law. To those who shared this view it seemed obvious that a lawyer's life could be deeply fulfilling. For the character-virtue of practical wisdom is a central human excellence that has an intrinsic value of its own. So long as the cultivation and exercise of this virtue remained an important professional ideal, lawyers could therefore be confident that their work had intrinsic value too. But in the last generation this ideal has collapsed, and with it the professional self-confidence it once sustained.

I have given this ideal an old-fashioned name to stress its roots in the past and the air of obsolescence that now surrounds it. I call it the ideal of the lawyer-statesman. It is an ideal that has had distinguished representatives in every age of American law. Lincoln, for example, was one. In the years before the Civil War, as he struggled to find a way to save the Union and democracy too, Lincoln had no formula to guide him. He possessed no technical knowledge that could tell him where the solution to America's dilemma lay. He had only his wisdom to rely on—his prudent sense of where the balance between principle and expediency must be struck.[3] A century later Earl Warren needed the same wisdom as he lobbied patiently to produce a unanimous opinion in *Brown v. Board of Education*.[4] When in the midst of the Second World War Robert Jackson reasserted the value of toleration in a case that made its conflict with the most potent forms of patriotism obvious to all, he needed Lincoln's prudence too.[5] And just yesterday we saw this virtue again in the plurality opinion in the Court's most recent abortion decision: an opinion marked by its judicious search for a middle course and wise balancing of principle and precedent.[6] In all these cases it was judgment, not expertise, that counted, and it is this quality of judgment that the ideal of the lawyer-statesman values most.

This ideal is now dying in the American legal profession. As it does, lawyers will find it harder to believe their work provides intrinsic fulfillment of any kind. Of course, the external benefits of law practice remain as obvious as before. But by themselves these are not enough to sustain the pride that lawyers have always taken in their craft; nor are the anemic new ideals that have arisen to replace the failing ideal of the lawyer-statesman. The result is a growing sense, among lawyers generally, that their yearning to be engaged in some lifelong endeavor that has value in its own right can no longer be satisfied in their professional work.

This is a catastrophe for lawyers. Beyond that, it is a disaster for the country as well. A disproportionate number of America's political leaders have always come from the legal profession. If lawyers are especially well equipped to play a leading role in politics, however, it is not because of their technical legal expertise. It is because their training and experience promote the deliberative virtues of the lawyer-statesman ideal. As this ideal fades and these virtues come to seem less important within the profession, they will be less consciously cultivated by lawyers themselves. And as that happens, the ability of lawyers to provide sound political leadership must eventually deteriorate too. In the future, the legal profession will continue to supply a large percentage of the country's political leaders. But the demise of the lawyer-statesman ideal means that the lawyers who lead the country will on the whole be less qualified to do so than before. They will be less likely to possess the traits of character—the prudence or practical wisdom—that made them good leaders in the past. Like ripples on a pond, the crisis of values that has overtaken the legal profession in the last twenty-five years must thus in time spread through the whole of our political life with destructive implications for lawyers and nonlawyers alike.

In this book I have tried to do two things. I have tried, first, to make the ideal of the lawyer-statesman fresh and appealing to a contemporary audience. In the eyes of many, that ideal has grown stale and unconvincing. My first objective has therefore been to make it attractive again by explaining, in new but simple terms, the timeless value of the virtue that it honors and the crucial role this virtue plays in the practice of law. That is the aim of Part One ("Ideals").

Second, I have sought to describe the intellectual and institutional forces that are now arrayed against the ideal of the lawyer-statesman and that together have caused its decline. These include the currently dominant movements in American legal thought, which share a powerful antiprudentialist bias; the explosive growth of the country's leading law firms, which has changed forever the practice of the lawyers in them and created a new, more openly commercial culture in which the lawyer-statesman ideal has only a marginal place; and the bureaucratization of our courts, which has transformed the ancient art of judging into a species of office management whose main virtue is efficiency rather than wisdom. Each of these developments has contributed to the demise of the lawyer-statesman ideal, and in Part Two ("Realities") I discuss them all in detail.

Part One is, as its title implies, deliberately high-minded. It seeks to define and defend a very demanding standard of professional excellence. I am aware, of course, that real human beings with their ordinary flaws do not always live up to their ideals in the real world, with its pitfalls and temptations. But that is no reason to aim lower in defining our ideals. To the contrary: it is important to aim high precisely because events and our imperfect natures drag us down; otherwise the aspirational pull of our ideals is lost, and we are defeated at the start. I understand, too, that lawyers in the past were not giants with extraordinary gifts that dwarfed our own, and on the whole had no more success in living up to their ideals than their counterparts today do. But their ideals were different from those our law schools, firms, and courts now encourage, and in certain ways they were much better. The profession's past had its shameful aspects too, including, most obviously, its racial, religious, and sexual exclusivity. But these failings are so striking, and our sense of rectitude in having overcome them so intense, that we lose sight of what was better in its past and fail to notice how impoverished the ideals of American lawyers have become. It is this better part of the profession's past—the richness and appeal of its lost ideals—that I want to rescue in Part One.

To do so, it is not enough merely to restate these ideals in their original form. If the ideal of the lawyer-statesman is to be more than a historical curiosity—if it is to be a live ideal for us today—what is permanently valuable in it must be identified more explicitly than before. In the past it was enough simply to praise a lawyer for possessing good judgment, without inquiring too deeply into the nature of this complex power. That is no longer true. The belief that prudence is the lawyer's central virtue has lost its credibility, and to restore it a new and more thorough account of practical wisdom is required. Anyone who attempts to provide such an account, however, immediately confronts difficult philosophical questions. Is prudence a form of calculation? How does it differ from intuition? What role does feeling (as opposed to thought) play in it? Is it the same in public and private deliberation? And will the prudent man or woman be disposed to adopt a distinctive political outlook of some kind? To build a foundation on which lawyers may again base their belief in the value of prudence as a professional virtue, I have found it necessary to discuss these questions at some length. This gives the first part of my book a philosophical character—though not in any technical sense, for its argument is presented in simple terms and without the use of specialized jargon. Still, I am aware that there is a kind of tension between the philosophical spirit of my argument and the practical nature of its subject. But this means only that philosophy is not a substitute for prudence. It does not mean it cannot help us understand what prudence is. It can—just as it can help us understand the nature of love and courage and other nonphilosophical dispositions. And more important, it must, for lawyers have lost their faith in the value of practical wisdom, and thought alone now has the power to revive it.

Part Two has a more sociological focus. It is primarily concerned with institutions and their cultural dynamics. In the last quarter-century a scholarly culture has emerged in the country's leading law schools that depreciates the ideal of the lawyer-statesman. The same has happened—for different reasons but with similar effect—in our most influential firms and courts. In each case the result has been the growth of an environment hostile to this ideal. Part Two analyzes the cultural shifts that have occurred in these three areas of professional life and examines their effect on lawyers' expectations and beliefs.

Some readers will find the sociological approach of Part Two a relief after the more abstract discussion that precedes it. Those who are most interested in the changing character of legal education may wish to start with Chapter 4 and then work backward to the book's beginning. Readers who are especially interested in the nature of law practice may want to follow a similar strategy, starting with Chapter 5. Those who are philosophically inclined will find it easiest to read the chapters in the order they appear, though Part Two is likely to be as challenging for them as Part One is for others. But wherever he starts, and whichever aspect of my argument he finds most congenial, any student of the legal profession who wants to understand its current crisis must combine the philosophical and sociological perspectives of the book's two parts. Moving in one direction, he must ask what practical wisdom is, and moving in the other, how the ideal that honors this virtue has come to lose its authority in every branch of professional life. Only when these two approaches are joined, in a venture of philosophical sociology, do the scope and meaning of the crisis that has overtaken the American legal profession come fully into view and the question of its fate force itself upon us with the urgency it merits.

Regarding its fate, I have reached a gloomy conclusion. I do not think the ideal of the lawyer-statesman can be revived, at least at an institutional level. Nor do I think there are any plausible successors to it—new ideals that can provide an equally secure foundation for the lawyer's professional pride. Individuals, perhaps, may find a way to honor this ideal in their own careers. But increasingly, I fear, they will be able to do so only by openly rejecting the announced values of their profession and by searching out the cracks and crevices in which a person devoted to the ideal of the lawyer-statesman may still make a living in the law. To these lawyers I hope my book will give encouragement and support. The continued existence of the lawyer-statesman ideal—even marginally, interstitially, contrapuntally—depends on them. They must nourish this ideal and keep it alive. For in the end, as Oakeshott observed, "nothing survives in this world which is not cared for by human beings."

Part One

IDEALS

1

An Embarrassed Virtue

Some years ago, Chief Justice William Rehnquist gave a talk to students at the University of Chicago Law School that was later published under the title "The Lawyer-Statesman in American History."[1] In his talk he spoke about the role of lawyers in our country's public life. Many of America's earlier leaders, he told his audience, were wise and public-spirited lawyers, and he stressed that these outstanding figures, the lawyer-statesmen of his title, had themselves been regarded by their contemporaries as models to be copied and admired. The chief justice made no effort to define, in abstract terms, the sort of lawyer he had in mind. Instead he sought to illustrate his theme through a series of individual portraits, beginning with Thomas Jefferson and Alexander Hamilton. After sketching the careers of eight representative figures, all from the eighteenth and nineteenth centuries, he concluded his talk by commenting briefly on the demise of the lawyer-statesman as an important professional type and on the diminishing role that such lawyers now play in American politics—a development to be explained, he suggested, by changes in the way that law is practiced as well as taught.

It is possible, of course, to dispute the chief justice's claim that there have been fewer lawyer-statesmen of real consequence in this century than in the previous two. Henry Stimson, Dean Acheson, and John McCloy come immediately to mind, along with Robert Jackson, a great example of the type. And one may also doubt whether he was right to assert that lawyer-statesmen are today a disappearing "breed," and point to men and women like Cyrus Vance,

Paul Warnke, and Carla Hills as contemporary representatives. But whatever one believes the present state or future prospects of the type to be, it is clear that in the past, at least, the figure of the lawyer-statesman played an important role in defining the ideals, and hence identity, of American lawyers as a group.

Indeed, the farther back we go in the period that begins with the establishment of our national independence (the starting point of Chief Justice Rehnquist's talk), the clearer this becomes. Thus for the early-nineteenth-century bar, whose leaders still viewed their work and social function in classically republican terms, the idealized figure of the lawyer-statesman was the embodiment of professional excellence.[2] In him, lawyers of the period could see gathered the entire range of qualities they valued most. And in the greatest advocates and judges of the time—in men like Webster, Choate, and Marshall; Ames, Pinkney, and Kent—they saw the living representatives of this ideal.

To be sure, few lawyers ever reached the level these hero figures occupied, and most understood as clearly then as they do now that the mundane business of earning a living in the law offers little opportunity for the exercise of statesmanship on a grand scale. But however far short of this ideal they fell in their own work, many nineteenth-century lawyers continued to look up to it as a standard of professional excellence and to invoke the lawyer-statesman as a model when they wanted to express, in concrete terms, their common aspirations. The lawyer-statesman—possessed of great practical wisdom and exceptional persuasive powers, devoted to the public good but keenly aware of the limitations of human beings and their political arrangements—is in fact a stock figure in the hortatory literature of the early-nineteenth-century bar, and however sanctimonious or self-congratulatory that literature now seems, it suggests how lawyers of the period wished, at least, to see themselves.[3]

Today the figure of the lawyer-statesman no longer represents a professional ideal. There are, of course, lawyers who still fit the type, but the type itself does not now command, within the profession generally, the authority it once did. Indeed, looking at the matter in a long perspective, one might say that its prestige has been declining for a century or more. This is an accurate perception, for in the latter part of the nineteenth century another very different professional ideal took shape and began to compete with this one, and in the struggle between them (which has continued ever since) the ideal of the lawyer-statesman has steadily lost ground. Still, even in this century it has not been entirely without defenders, though the defenses they have offered have become increasingly weak and incomplete. But in this generation—my generation—the prestige of the lawyer-statesman has reached an all-time low. Today this ideal no longer claims even the nominal respect of lawyers to the same extent it did only a quarter-century ago. The classical figure of the lawyer-statesman has in my generation become a quaint antique with little of the power it once possessed to inspire or excite, and if its invocation as a model of professional excellence continues to stir any feelings at all, for the many contemporary lawyers who believe this model to be not only irrecoverable but dangerously elitist too, these are most likely to be feelings of suspicion or contempt.[4]

The reasons for the demise of the lawyer-statesman ideal are complex and, as Chief Justice Rehnquist rightly supposed, reflect deep structural changes in legal education and law practice, as well as in adjudication (which, revealingly perhaps, he fails to mention). A large part of this book—the whole of Part Two—is devoted to an examination of the role that each of these changes has played in bringing the ideal of the lawyer-statesman into its present state of disrepute. But before one can talk intelligibly about the decline of an ideal, it is first necessary to know what that ideal represents—whether one hopes to rescue it or believes it cannot be restored and wants only to understand the full meaning of its loss. It is to this preliminary task that Part One is addressed.

My aim here is to provide as compelling an account of the lawyer-statesman ideal as I am able—to clarify its content but also, and more important, to make accessible again its original appeal, something lawyers today find difficult to grasp.[5] The attractions of the lawyer-statesman ideal, once so obvious, are now hard to see, and any attempt to measure the meaning of its loss, let alone assess the merits of a campaign to restore it, must begin by recovering some sense of what attracted earlier generations of lawyers to the ideal and gave it such stature within the profession as a whole.

That cannot be done merely by repeating what others have said about the ideal in the past. For it is just this—the traditional portrait of the lawyer-statesman—that has lost its power to inspire. The ethos of belief that sustained the ideal of the lawyer-statesman and was sustained by it in turn, the web of professional attitudes and expectations in which this ideal had a place, has largely disappeared, and in its absence the traditional account of the ideal is likely to seem hollow and unmoving. To regain some sense of its appeal, therefore, we must reconstruct the ideal of the lawyer-statesman from the bottom up, by articulating its intellectual premises more deliberately than its earlier defenders felt required to. For them the value of the ideal went without saying, as did the wisdom of the view of law and human nature it implied. Being confident about its worth, they were never moved to scrutinize their convictions in a philosophical light. But the naive confidence that once surrounded the ideal of the lawyer-statesman is now gone and reflection must take its place.

To reverse a famous image of Hegel's, only philosophy can breathe life back into an ideal when the tradition that sustained it dies away.[6] The recovery of every lost ideal is in that sense a philosophical project, and the model of the lawyer-statesman is no exception. If this conception of professional excellence is to be made credible again, it must be by analysis and argument, for that is now our only path back to it.

LEADERSHIP AND CHARACTER

I want to start by briefly sketching the main elements of the lawyer-statesman ideal in its classical nineteenth-century form. I mean at this point to describe these elements only in rough provisional terms. Each obviously requires a more elaborate explanation and will receive it in due course. But to fix ideas and establish a point of departure, it will help to give the ideal some preliminary content, however incomplete.

The outstanding lawyer, as this ideal presents him, is, to begin with, a devoted citizen. He cares about the public good and is prepared to sacrifice his own well-being for it, unlike those who use the law merely to advance their private ends. The spirit of citizenship that sets the lawyer-statesman apart from the purely self-interested practitioner of law can to that extent be understood in motivational terms. But it is not only his motives that make him a better citizen than most. He is distinguished, too, by his special talent for discovering where the public good lies and for fashioning those arrangements needed to secure it. The lawyer-statesman is a leader in the realm of public life, and other citizens look to him for guidance and advice, as do his private clients.

The help that others seek from him, moreover, is not just instrumental. A lawyer whose only responsibility is to prepare the way for ends that others have already set can never be anything but a deferential servant. The lawyer-statesman is not a servant in this sense. Whether acting as the representative of private interests or as a counselor in matters of state, one important part of what he does is to offer advice about ends. An essential aspect of his work, as he and others see it, is to help those on whose behalf he is deliberating come to a better understanding of their own ambitions, interests, and ideals and to guide their choice among alternative goals.

The ability to do this, however, is not one that all lawyers, or any group of human beings, possess in equal measure. Some deliberate about ends more wisely than others. The lawyer-statesman is distinguished by the exceptional wisdom he displays in this regard. He excels at the art of deliberation as others excel at writing, singing, or chess. The lawyer-statesman is a paragon of judgment, and others look to him for leadership on account of his extraordinary deliberative power.

This power is more than a clever knack or skill. It is, most fundamentally, a trait of character. By character I mean, broadly speaking, an ensemble of settled dispositions—of habitual feelings and desires. To have a character of a certain sort is to possess a set of such dispositions that is identifiable and distinct. The nineteenth-century model of the lawyer-statesman portrayed him as a person with a character in just this sense. Thus in addition to whatever intellectual abilities he might possess, the lawyer-statesman was pictured by writers of the period as having certain temperamental qualities as well: as being, for example, more calm or cautious than most people and better able to sympathize with a wide range of conflicting points of view. Like other practitioners, of course, the lawyer-statesman was assumed to possess a stock of specialized professional knowledge, of esoteric legal know-how. But those nineteenth-century writers who held him up as a model for the profession meant to do more than affirm that the possession of such knowledge is a good. They meant also to hold up as good, and therefore worth striving to attain, the temperamental traits that define the lawyer-statesman's special character.[7]

Preeminent among these was the trait of prudence or practical wisdom, which even today we view as a quality of character. When we attribute good judgment to a person, we imply more than that he has broad knowledge and a quick intelligence. We mean also to suggest that he shows a certain calmness in his deliberations, together with a balanced sympathy toward the various concerns of which his situation (or the situation of his client) requires that he take account. These are qualities as much of feeling as of thought. They are qualities of character, and the role they play in the trait we call good judgment is an essentially important one. Thus even today the claim that someone has good judgment is understood to be a claim about his character and not merely the breadth of his learning or the brilliance of his mind. The classical portrait of the lawyer-statesman as a person of good judgment carried a similar implication, and when those who eulogized him praised his practical wisdom, they meant to praise more than just his learned understanding of the law's arcane requirements. They meant also to commend his character and to suggest that the lawyer-statesman's professional standing is as much to be explained by who he is as what he knows. They meant to praise him for his virtue and not just his expertise.

This last fact helps to explain the appeal of the lawyer-statesman ideal and its wide acceptance within the profession throughout the nineteenth century. For this ideal affirmed that a lawyer can achieve a level of real excellence in his work only by acquiring certain valued traits of character. Though linking professional achievement to character-virtue in this way undoubtedly made the first seem more remote and harder to attain, it also gave it greater value. It put the heroes of the bar high up beyond the point that most practitioners could reach, but at the same time endowed their achievements with a dignity and stature that no amount of technical know-how can confer.

The ideal of the lawyer statesman was an ideal of character. This meant that as one moved toward it, one became not just an accomplished technician but a distinctive and estimable type of human being—a person of practical wisdom. And that was an ennobling thought, even for those who fell short of the ideal or found they had only limited opportunities in their own work to exercise the deliberative virtues that the lawyer-statesman exhibited to an exemplary degree. The ideal of the lawyer-statesman encouraged this thought, and by so doing affirmed the self-worth of lawyers as a group in a way that makes the durability of this ideal as a model of professional excellence easier to understand.

SCIENTIFIC LAW REFORM

This brief sketch of the lawyer-statesman raises more questions than it answers—questions, in particular, about the nature of practical wisdom and the role it plays in the professional work of lawyers. A full statement of the ideal will require that these questions be explored, and the philosophical issues they raise exposed and settled. But first I want to make two points about the historical fate of this ideal within the legal profession itself.

First, toward the end of the nineteenth century a very different model of professional excellence began to take shape and gain acceptance among influential and well-educated lawyers. Though sharing certain features with the lawyer-statesman ideal, this second model also conflicted sharply with it, and in the decades that followed, the competition between them became more focused and intense. For some time the contest remained undecided. In the last generation, however, the tide of battle has swung decisively in favor of the second model, with far-reaching consequences for the profession as a whole. The story of this struggle of ideals is a complex one that I shall tell in more detail in Chapter 4. Here I want only to introduce some of its main themes.

Second, though the lawyer-statesman ideal has continued until quite recently to have powerful defenders of its own, these have tended, increasingly, to view the ideal in limited terms and to ignore, even reject, certain of its central elements. Supporters of the ideal have thus proved to be halfhearted friends at best, whose own support for it betrays a growing lack of confidence in the conception of professional virtue that the figure of the lawyer-statesman once embodied. This tendency is exhibited with particular clarity in the revival of republican ideas that has recently attracted such attention in the field of public law—a movement that has sought to restore certain features of the lawyer-statesman ideal (its insistence on the value of civic-mindedness and the importance of deliberation) while ignoring others (its stress on character and leadership). A closer look at this contemporary movement and the philosophical assumptions that underlie it will help to explain why even the lawyer-statesman's friends have in this century become embarrassed by him, and to clarify the claims that need support if that embarrassment is to be overcome. But first I want to sketch the new conception of professional excellence that, toward the end of the last century, began to compete with the older ideal of the lawyer-statesman and slowly to displace it within the upper reaches of the bar.

I shall call this new ideal that of scientific law reform. In the earliest phase of its development this new ideal was nearly indistinguishable from the classical ideal of the lawyer-statesman (from which, in fact, it emerged in a gradual, almost unnoticed way). Even for some time afterward these two ideals remained closely intertwined, the new ideal being, to begin with, not so much an alternative to the older one as an offshoot of it. At first the differences between them were thus mainly ones of tone and emphasis, and were to a large degree obscured by the ideals' common features. But in this century these differences have widened and become more visible, and the advocates of each have come to see the other in an increasingly antagonistic light.

Like its predecessor, the ideal of scientific law reform stressed the importance of the role that lawyers play in public life. Proponents of the ideal insisted that lawyers not devote themselves entirely to the satisfaction of their clients' private needs, but take an interest in the public good as well and provide leadership in the effort to define and then secure it. The distinctive role of the lawyer, as they saw it, is not merely to "advance the interests of clients pursuing particular ends," but rather to "mediate" between the public order and its requirements, on the one hand, and the self-regarding desires of private individuals, on the other—to serve, in Robert Gordon's illuminating phrase, as "double-agents" working to reduce the inevitable and sometimes dangerous tension between public law and private ambition.[8]

But dangers of this sort arise not only from the excesses of private ambition. They can arise from defects in the legal order too, from the failure of the law to respond with sufficient sensitivity to the changing requirements of social and economic life. If lawyers are to perform their mediating function well, they must therefore make an effort to ensure that the law itself remains in good working order and press for its reform when that is needed. A good lawyer must, on this view, be more than a skillful advocate who uses his energy and learning to promote the private interests of his clients within a framework of public norms whose soundness is taken for granted. He must also be a public-spirited reformer who monitors this framework itself and leads others in campaigning for those repairs that are required to keep it responsive and fair.

The ideal of scientific law reform thus implied a general commitment to the public good. In explicating this commitment, however, its adherents made two further claims that gave their ideal of professional responsibility a novel and distinctive character.

First, they claimed, the appropriate object of the law reformer's concerns is the structural arrangement of the legal order as a whole and not the resolution of particular disputes of the sort that lawsuits and other concrete controversies typically involve. There is, of course, no sharp line between these things, nor can there be, for even the most individualized case must be decided by an appeal to general legal norms. But a large difference remains between the view that disagreements about the legal system are best decided in the focused context of specific cases and the belief that decisions of this sort are better made by examining the broad structure of the law directly. It was in the structural reform of law, and not the argument of great public cases, that the proponents of this new ideal found their model of professional success.

Second, the ideal of scientific law reform enthusiastically proclaimed that the law could be most effectively reformed through the application to it of certain methodical and rigorous techniques—that its problems could be solved in what proponents never tired of insisting was a "scientific" fashion.[9] The inspirations for this belief were several. Most immediately, perhaps, it was suggested by the new, more systematic approach to the study of legal doctrine that began to be employed by law teachers at Harvard and elsewhere in the last decades of the nineteenth century under the influence of Dean Langdell's call for the scientific reform of law school pedagogy. And it was encouraged, too, by the newly emergent social sciences whose practitioners claimed the ability to expound the laws of social and political life with a previously unimaginable discipline and comprehensiveness.[10]

Among those who shared the belief that legal problems could be analyzed and solved in a scientific fashion, there were, of course, differences of opinion concerning the content of that science and its implications for law reform. Some, for example, believed that only the codification of the law could put it in scientifically respectable shape, while others favored the retention of common-law rules, reorganized to bring their latent logic to light. But despite these important disagreements, the champions of the new ideal felt a common commitment to the goal of redesigning the structure of the legal order in a disciplined and systematic way, with a less haphazard understanding of the law than their predecessors had possessed. This confidence in the possibility of a science of law reform was reflected most clearly in the belief (which many defenders of the new ideal shared) that the special wisdom needed to determine what the law's structure ought to be was reducible to rules and hence teachable in an academic setting. Despite their differences regarding its content, they agreed that the science of law reform was a theoretical discipline whose insights could be expressed in a scheme of ordered propositions and thus mastered in the way that all such systems might be: by reading books and listening to formal lectures. It was the optimism implicit in this last assumption that, perhaps more than anything else, gave the ideal of scientific law reform its distinctiveness and wide appeal.

Of course, many of the great lawyers and judges of the classical period had been systematizers too, who believed in the value of organization and clarity, both in established fields (where the historically evolved elements of doctrine were often exceedingly tangled) and in the newer sphere of constitutional law as well. Joseph Story's magisterial treatises and John Marshall's sweeping opinions—the greatest legal documents of their age—are deeply colored by a faith in the importance of system and order.[11] Indeed, throughout the legal literature of the period, one encounters a similar confidence in the power of ideas and the widely shared belief that lawyers must know something about history, literature, and rhetoric as well as law if they are to do their jobs in a properly broad-minded way.

This marks an important point of contact with the ideal of scientific law reform which also urged a systematic approach to legal problems and stressed the contribution that nonlegal disciplines could make to their solution. But missing from this new ideal was any clear endorsement of another value that the ideal of the lawyer-statesman had emphasized as well—the value of prudence or practical wisdom. The lawyer-statesman ideal was partly shaped by an Enlightenment enthusiasm for system and order. But it was also deeply rooted in the common-law tradition that historically had taken a more skeptical view of systematic legal reform and stressed the wisdom of proceeding on a case-by-case basis instead. The common lawyer instinctively mistrusts abstract speculation. He believes that general principles have a role to play in the law but doubts that most serious disputes can be decided by reference to them alone. In addition, he insists, hard cases require the exercise of practical wisdom: a subtle and discriminating sense of how the (often conflicting) generalities of legal doctrine should be applied in concrete disputes. Alongside and in tension with an Enlightenment rationalism of more recent origin, this ancient common-law reverence for the virtue of practical wisdom was incorporated into the ideal of the lawyer-statesman too. Indeed, in one respect at least, it was amplified by that ideal. For to the common lawyer's belief that the chief business of the law is the prudent resolution of individual cases, the ideal of the lawyer-statesman added the claim—which defenders of the common law assumed but rarely stated—that prudence is a trait of character and not just a cognitive skill.

To prudence so conceived the ideal of scientific law reform gave little weight. The outstanding lawyer, as this new ideal portrayed him, is distinguished less by his practical wisdom—his judgment of particular people and situations—than by his theoretical understanding of the basic structure of society, his knowledge of the forces that shape the social and economic order as a whole. This knowledge is abstract. It is more concerned with concepts than with cases. It can be expressed in propositional form and taught by means that produce intellectual competence but no change of temperament or character, in contrast to the virtue of practical wisdom, whose acquisition implies a change of exactly this sort.

For all its Enlightenment rationalism, the lawyer-statesman ideal viewed the work of lawyers through the prism of the common law. It conceived their primary task to be the argument and adjudication of concrete disputes, and it placed a high value on the character-virtue of practical wisdom that this task requires. In Daniel Webster's great speeches before the Supreme Court and on the floor of the Senate, it found a model to admire, and when it urged lawyers to look beyond the law for insight and instruction, it was to the case-centered disciplines of rhetoric and history that it recommended they turn. The ideal of scientific law reform located the lawyer's main responsibilities at a different point. It encouraged lawyers to view themselves as "social engineers" engaged in the structural design of institutions.[12] Individual disputes would of course continue to arise within the institutions they had built. But except in the aggregate—as statistics, patterns, tendencies, and the like—particular cases were no longer to receive the same attention they had been given in the past. The lawyer's interest was henceforth to be focused on more-abstract concerns—on the large-scale construction and repair of institutions—and in contrast to the common lawyer of the past, who built by indirection and without a conscious plan in view, the lawyer of the future must (proponents of the new ideal claimed) work from a blueprint carefully drawn in advance.

For those who embraced this ideal, social scientific disciplines such as criminology, economics, and statistics began to replace the older humane studies of history and rhetoric as the primary nonlegal fields to which lawyers should look for support. Whatever level of philosophical generality the disciplines of history and rhetoric aim to achieve, they remain under the spell of the accidental and unique. They are for this reason well suited to the cultivation of practical judgment. The social sciences are not. For however deeply they enable us to see into the general structure of society, they take no interest in the accidental for its own sake, as history, for example, does. Nor do the social sciences have a character-shaping function like that of history and literature, of which it was often said, by early-nineteenth-century lawyers, that their study is not only informative but essential to the proper training of a lawyer's temperament as well.[13] The champions of scientific law reform made no such claim on behalf of economics and statistics. Indeed, they felt no need to. For in these disciplines they sought a knowledge of the social order whose acquisition and utility do not depend upon the character of those who possess it. They sought a theoretical understanding of society that—unlike the practical wisdom of the lawyer-statesman—is a strictly intellectual achievement. Theoretical understanding and practical wisdom are not incompatible qualities. The same person may possess both. But they differ in important ways and, depending upon which is thought more pertinent to the work that lawyers do, two strikingly different conceptions of professional excellence emerge. The early-nineteenth-century ideal of the lawyer-statesman made prudence a central value, as did the common-law tradition on which that ideal drew. The late-nineteenth-century ideal of scientific law reform demoted the virtue of practical wisdom to a position of marginal importance and put a more abstract form of theoretical understanding in its place instead.

In the beginning the difference between these two ideals was barely noticeable, the second evolving from the first through slight variations of nuance and tone. Indeed, well into the twentieth century one finds combinations of the two ideals that cross all the lines I have drawn. The Progressives, and Louis Brandeis in particular—who was at once a great defender of the classical ideal and a vigorous proponent of the usefulness of social science in the law—offer an especially good example of such syncretism.[14] But gradually these lines became clearer and more fixed, and as this happened those inspired by the ideal of scientific law reform came to see the older ideal of the lawyer-statesman not merely as a different and potentially complementary conception of the lawyer's role but as one antagonistic to their own. They came to see the lawyer-statesman as their enemy, as an obstacle to clear thinking and sound practice, and with increasing energy sought to locate the appeal of their own ideal in its ambition to free lawyers, and the society they serve, from the need for something as imprecise and personal as practical wisdom. In the past hundred years this ambition has exerted a steadily widening influence in American legal thought—first on Langdell and his generation, then on the realists of the 1930s, and today most notably on the law-and-economics movement. And as its influence has grown, the lawyer-statesman ideal, which once played such an important role in defining the aspirations of American lawyers as a group, has lost much of its original plausibility and appeal.

A FALTERING DEFENSE

If the lawyer-statesman ideal has lost ground in this century, it is not only because the champions of scientific law reform have become more articulate in their criticisms of it. It has suffered, too, from a lack of forcefulness on the part of its defenders. Even those who have been its strongest supporters have failed to provide the kind of philosophical defense that the ideal now needs to regain its credibility.

No twentieth-century American lawyer, for example, has defended the proposition that great lawyers and judges are distinguished from less outstanding ones by their superior practical wisdom with more energy than Karl Llewellyn.[15] Indeed, one might reasonably describe this as the central point of all his later work. And in arguing for a return to what he calls the craft-concept of law, with its emphasis on judgment and the allied notions of habit and experience, Llewellyn draws conscious inspiration from the same early-nineteenth-century period in which the ideal of the lawyer-statesman assumed its classic shape—the period of what he calls the Grand Style in American law.

Despite his obvious attraction to this ideal, and his passionate efforts to revive it, Llewellyn's own account of the virtue of practical wisdom is incomplete. What Llewellyn fails to explicate—indeed, never really addresses at all—is the important but obscure connection between character and judgment. If sound judgment is a trait of character, it is not enough merely to point out, as Llewellyn does, that it must be acquired in the way one acquires a habit as opposed to a theoretical insight (though that is a true and important claim). We also want to know what sort of trait it is, what the character of a person with practical wisdom is like. We want to know what combination of dispositional attitudes sets the prudent person apart. On this vital question, however, Llewellyn has little to say, and his silence is damaging because it leaves an essential component of the lawyer-statesman ideal concealed in mystery and therefore vulnerable to attack as a mystical conceit. Once the foundations of that ideal have been challenged, they must be rebuilt from the ground up in a new and more self-critical way. And that is something Karl Llewellyn never attempted to do.

Alexander Bickel is a second case in point.[16] Bickel was the most influential scholar of his generation in the field of constitutional law, as Llewellyn was in those of contracts and commercial law. Like Llewellyn, Bickel stressed the need for prudence in adjudication, and insisted that theoretical analysis alone cannot decide the questions most serious legal controversies present. "Prudence" is in fact the key term in Bickel's jurisprudence (as "craft" and "horse-sense" are in Llewellyn's). By prudence Bickel meant the ability to live and work in what he calls the Lincolnian tension between a society's ideals, on the one hand, and the reality of its present situation, on the other. The main job of the Supreme Court, as Bickel saw it, is to guide the process of societal self-reform through which existing laws and practices are reshaped in the image of our deepest ideals. But to do this job well, he said, one needs more than a theory of these ideals themselves. One must also appreciate the resistance that present realities offer to them; be artful in inventing strategies of reform that gradually increase the society's tolerance for change (like a patient growing accustomed to new medicine); and, most important, possess the strength to endure the slowness with which such change typically occurs—and to accept the fact that it is never finished or complete. These are all essential qualities in a Supreme Court justice. They are not, however, the virtues of a theoretician. They are the virtues of a statesman, a word Bickel himself uses to describe the complex mediating role the justices play in our society's ongoing self-reform. From his account of the qualities that such statesmanship includes, it is clear that he himself viewed them, in part at least, as qualities of character.[17]

In this last respect, in particular, Bickel's defense of prudence, though limited to constitutional adjudication, rests on assumptions close to those that underlay the classical ideal of the lawyer-statesman. Indeed, near the end of his life Bickel himself came to see his own account of constitutional lawmaking as an expression of a much broader tradition in political thought, one he associated primarily with Edmund Burke and that he defined in opposition to the contractarian philosophies of Rousseau and Locke and contemporary writers like John Rawls.[18] Whereas the first tradition has always emphasized the importance of judgment in politics and insisted that the prudence which political life demands cannot be reduced to or replaced by an abstract science of government, proponents of the second have from the beginning insisted on the possibility and value of such a reduction (though disagreeing as to how it might be achieved). The conflict between these two traditions in political theory parallels that between the two ideals of law practice I have sketched. Indeed, as we shall see, the latter conflict is simply a branch or aspect of the former one, a local campaign in a wider war, fought out within the special province of the law. In his last essays, Bickel acknowledged this and began to explore, in a tentative way, the philosophical foundations of his own constitutional jurisprudence, to seek a deeper ground for his prudentialist view of the Supreme Court and its work in a general account of the nature of political action.

How much progress Bickel would have made in this direction, had he lived, no one can say. The sad truth is that by the time of his early death he had made very little. Bickel's final articles are for the most part polemical pieces, and their arguments are largely negative. They do not contain even the beginnings of a positive theory of practical wisdom, and are silent, in particular, on the crucial relationship of prudence to character. However close the affinity between Bickel's prudentialism, on the one hand, and the classical ideal of the lawyer-statesman, on the other, Bickel himself never provided a philosophical account of practical wisdom and its role in the work of lawyers and judges. Like Llewellyn, who was drawn to the ideal too, Bickel thus ultimately left it suspended in midair without a supporting foundation, in sharp contrast to the ideal of scientific law reform, whose foundational premises have in the last century been fortified by its proponents with increasing clarity and vigor.

THE NEW REPUBLICANS

Still, thirty years ago the lawyer-statesman ideal had powerful defenders, and even if the most influential of these failed to provide the kind of self-critical account of their positions that a reflective age demands, they nevertheless represented a significant body of professional opinion. Indeed, they spoke for a point of view that many lawyers at the time would have considered the soul of professional orthodoxy. Today that is no longer true. There is now no one in the legal profession of Bickel's or Llewellyn's stature who could be called a champion of practical wisdom, and few who even feel an allegiance to their views. The ideal of the lawyer-statesman is now without a great defender and nearly without friends.

To this last claim, however, there is an apparent exception that I now want to examine in some detail. I have in mind the recent and influential movement in American public-law scholarship that is generally referred to as the "new republicanism."[19] The new republicans have sought to rehabilitate certain features of the lawyer-statesman ideal, and from this one might infer that their attitude toward it is on the whole a friendly or supportive one. Two components of the ideal play a particularly large role in their thinking. First, the new republicans stress the distinction between private interest and public good and insist that the latter can be an important goal of political action too. And second, they emphasize that politics often involves independent deliberation about the public good, about the content and meaning of a community's ultimate ends. Civic-mindedness and deliberation—practical reasoning about ends—are key concepts in the new republicanism. The prominent place these same ideas occupy in the lawyer-statesman ideal represents, therefore, an important link between it and this contemporary movement, and by drawing as heavily as they have on the literature of classical republicanism, with which the lawyer-statesman ideal was closely entwined, the new republicans have made this link more visible still.

But there are other elements of that ideal which the new republicans seem less willing to endorse—which, in any case, they treat quite cursorily or ignore. They have little to say, for example, about the nature of practical deliberation, and nothing about the qualities that make one person better at it than another (a better judge of political affairs). Nor do they address, in any careful way, the relationship between deliberation and character, a relationship at the heart of the classical ideal of the lawyer-statesman. The most one might claim, therefore, is that the new republicanism represents a partial reassertion of this ideal, less complete even than the truncated versions one finds in the writings of Llewellyn and Bickel.

But even this overstates the closeness of the link between them. For the aspects of the lawyer-statesman ideal that the new republicans omit have not simply been overlooked by them, or temporarily put aside, but rejected because they conflict in a deep if unnoticed way with other philosophical beliefs those in the movement share. The new republicanism is not, in reality, an incomplete version of the lawyer-statesman ideal, to which its other missing features might be easily reattached. It is, in fact, at war with that ideal, and there is no way of reconciling their opposing claims.

To understand why, we must take a closer look at the new republicanism and the intellectual traditions on which it draws. This would be a worthwhile exercise even if its only aim were to make clear how great a distance separates the ideal of the lawyer-statesman from the one contemporary movement in American legal thought that might plausibly be said to be informed by it, however incompletely. But it has another object too. The failure of the new republicans to give an account of practical wisdom—indeed, their discomfort with the very idea—is a consequence of their commitment to a certain view of political equality, or more exactly, a certain view of how the principle of political equality should be defended. It is this commitment that makes the omitted elements of the lawyer-statesman ideal so unpalatable to them. The new republicans are not the only ones who believe that equality is best defended in the way I shall describe. Many others, including most of their opponents, believe it too. Understanding the implications of this belief for the movement that today stands closest to the lawyer-statesman ideal, in appearance at least, can therefore help explain why that ideal is now so widely discredited within the profession as a whole and no longer has champions even of the imperfect sort that still supported it a generation ago.

DELIBERATION AND THE PUBLIC GOOD

The new republicanism is now an established movement in the field of public law. Whole issues of leading journals have been devoted to it, and the expression itself has become a term of art in academic legal writing.[20] Among those in the movement, there are, of course, differences of opinion on various historical and philosophical questions, some quite important. Beneath these differences, however, there is relatively firm agreement on certain fundamental matters, and it is these elementary points of common understanding that I want to pursue here. This can most easily be done by first considering the view of politics that the new republicans reject, for it is largely by attacking this view that they have defined their own position. I shall call the view they oppose the interest-group theory of politics.[21] Those who embrace this theory make three connected claims about the nature of political life, and the new republicans define themselves by their repudiation of all three.

Proponents of the interest-group theory maintain, first, that the interests people pursue in politics are not themselves formed in the political arena but have an antecedent origin. It may be that these interests can be satisfied only through political action. But they would continue to exist in exactly the same form, defenders of this theory claim, were the entire realm of politics dissolved (though of course they would then be unsatisfiable). On this view, politics brings no new interests to light but is entirely dependent for its subject matter on the prepolitical sphere in which the interests that people pursue in politics first arise.

The relation of politics to this sphere of prepolitical concerns—

which we may for convenience call the social realm—is, on the interest-group view, a purely instrumental one. Politics is just one of the tools that people use to get what they already want, and the decision to employ it, in combination with or in place of other tools, is no different from the choice a carpenter makes when he reaches for a hammer rather than a saw. Tools by their nature lack independence or autonomy. We cannot say what they are without explaining what they are for, which in turn requires a reference to something other (and presumably more important) than the tool itself, namely, the aim or object of its employment. Hence if politics is simply a tool we use to satisfy our prepolitical interests, in the way the interest-group theory of politics implies, then it must be an activity that by definition lacks autonomy and has only the dependent sort of existence that any tool or instrument does.

The second assumption on which this theory rests concerns the nature of the interests pursued in politics, as distinguished from their source. Proponents of the interest-group theory conceive these interests to be essentially private in character—the interests that political actors take in their own separate welfare rather than in some common or collective good. It is important to be careful here about the meaning of the term "private." A private interest, in the sense in which I am now using the expression, need not be an interest that individuals form or pursue on their own, in isolation from other people. There are not many interests of this sort—perhaps, in the strictest sense, there are none—and the phrase "interest-*group* theory" in any case implies that the goals people pursue in politics have a social character in the twofold sense that they are formed in a social setting and achieved by collective means. It is therefore neither their origin nor the way in which they are attained that makes all political goals private on this view. What makes them private is something else, namely, the kind of justification that is needed to legitimate their pursuit.

According to the interest-group theory of politics, one can always justify a decision to pursue a particular interest within the political realm simply by stating that one has this interest and wants to satisfy it. Nothing more need be said. There are, of course, many interests whose pursuit can be defended in this way. If someone asks me, for example, to justify my decision to buy a chocolate ice cream cone, it will in most circumstances be enough merely to reply that I have a taste for chocolate and the present desire to indulge it. Psychoanalytic reflection may reveal that my taste has a complex social history, and the ice cream store where I have gone to satisfy it is plainly a social institution. But my justification for pursuing the interest in question is complete when I have said I wish to do so: it is a private interest in the sense that nothing but my own estimate of my own interest need figure in the justification that I give.

This is the sense in which the interest-group theory conceives all political action to be essentially private in nature. A group's interests are likely to have a social origin, and within the group itself may even be viewed as collective interests—interests that belong to the group as a whole rather than to its individual members. But the group's pursuit of its interests in the political realm, where it must compete against other groups and their conflicting claims, can on the interest-group theory of politics be justified with a statement as short and uncomplicated as the one I give in defense of my decision to buy a cone of a certain flavor: "We want what we want and are prepared to spend the resources needed to get it." That may not be enough to explain the group's behavior, but on the theory of politics we are now considering, it is always sufficient to justify it.

The third basic assumption that the interest-group theory of politics makes about the nature of political life is closely connected to the second. If the interests that people pursue in politics are private interests in the sense I have indicated, then reaching agreement with one's adversaries—getting them to adopt one's own interests or at least to see them in a favorable light—will not be an essential feature of the political strategies that competing interest groups adopt. On the interest-group view, political action can have only one aim, and that is to satisfy one's own interests in the most economical way possible. Sometimes, of course, the least-costly way of doing so will be by means of persuasion, but sometimes not, and when the method of persuasion is too expensive or simply unavailing, other methods must be employed—those, for example, of logrolling and agenda manipulation—that do not seek to convert the opposition by argument but to conquer it by force. From an interest-group perspective there is, in fact, no principled distinction to be drawn between these techniques and the method of persuasion, whose entire value depends from this point of view on the added power it gives the group that uses it over those who are persuaded of the goodness or rationality of that group's cause. The interest-group theory of politics views persuasion as simply another mode of power with no greater intrinsic worth than any other. All that matters from this point of view is what works, and the only basis for comparing different political strategies is their cost and likelihood of success. Politics is a theater of power, it consists of nothing but contests of power, and every appearance that suggests otherwise is in reality just a subtler form of power in disguise.

To be sure, what I am calling the interest-group theory of politics does not portray the political process as a ruleless dogfight in which absolutely anything goes. Almost all defenders of the theory maintain that this process is constrained by two important sorts of rights—by the rights of individuals to participate in the political contest and to be free from at least certain burdens that other contestants might wish to impose on them. Together these two sets of rights define the limits beyond which political fighting may not go, and when it does, its outcomes lose legitimacy.

The specification of these political rights is of course a difficult and controversial matter, and even among those who subscribe to the interest-group theory there is substantial disagreement about their scope and content. But despite such disagreement, defenders of the theory all conceive the basic function of these rights in similar terms, as analogous to that performed by the various rights that limit the process of exchange in the sphere of economic life. The function of these rights is in each case to define a bounded arena within which contests of power may proceed without further restriction or supervision, the victory going, in each instance, to the stronger party. Everyone has a right to participate in the (political or economic) contest and to be protected against certain outcomes that a wholly unregulated competition might produce (discriminatory legislation, for example, and the accumulation of monopoly power). But once these threshold rights have been secured, the interest-group theory offers no further grounds on which to challenge the results that flow from the ensuing power struggle. Thus although the rights that I have mentioned do play an important constraining role within the interest-group theory of politics, this role itself is limited by the three basic assumptions about the nature of political life which together give that theory its distinctive shape.

The new republicans reject each of these assumptions. To begin with, they say, the point of political action is not always to obtain

something the actors antecedently want—to satisfy a prepolitical desire—but sometimes to determine, instead, what it is they ought to
want, to decide what their interests shall be, and not merely to pursue
the ones they already have. No one will deny that politics is often a
contest among groups pursuing their prepolitical interests. But it is
not always and entirely that. There is a distinction, the new republicans insist, between acting on a settled preference and deliberating
about which preferences to form or cultivate, a distinction we recognize in our private lives, but one present in the political realm as well.

Political judgments of the latter kind—for which the new republicans suggest the term "deliberation" be reserved—may, it is true, be
motivated by an interest of a certain sort, namely, the higher-order
interest we take in our ideals, the aspirational norms we think should
guide our more immediate preferences even when they do not. But
these judgments still differ in two ways from decisions about how
best to satisfy some preestablished lower-order interest. They are self-
critical (open to revision at every level), and the goal they seek cannot
be satisfactorily described in maximizing terms, which makes them
peculiarly resistant to economic analysis. This distinction, say the new
republicans, is one proponents of the interest-group theory fail to
perceive, thereby missing a crucial fact about the nature of political
action: that its aim is sometimes the formation of new interests rather
than the satisfaction of antecedent ones. On a republican view, those
who enter the political arena do not always do so with their interests
settled in advance, but sometimes with the object of determining
them instead, of fixing their interests in the light of their ideals. To
the extent that political actors have this latter goal, the interests they
form in the give-and-take of political debate are thus themselves political in origin: they have their beginnings in the sphere of politics
and not (as the interest-group theory maintains) in the social world
anterior to it.

The second point on which the new republicans insist is that there
are some political interests that cannot be described as private ones
in the sense suggested earlier. Not all political contests are meant,
they claim, to decide how far each participant's own separate interests
shall be satisfied. Some are meant, instead, to determine the collective
interest of everyone involved, or more exactly, the interest of each as
a member of the political association to which all belong. Of course,
in any such debate different participants will present different and

conflicting interpretations of the common good, of its content and requirements. That is unsurprising, since if everyone agreed in these respects, there would be no need for political deliberation in the first place. But on a republican view of the matter, for one participant to justify his interpretation of the common good to others, it is never enough for him merely to point out that the interpretation in question is his and that he wishes to have it endorsed (in the way, for example, that I might justify my voting for chocolate in an election to determine how a common ice cream fund shall be spent, assuming it must be spent on a single flavor). If it is to be considered a justification of any sort at all—even an unpersuasive one—the argument that each participant offers on behalf of his or her own favored interpretation of the common good must be framed not in terms of private interests, which may diverge from those of the community, but in terms of the interests of the community itself.

No one doubts that appeals to the public good are often only disguised attempts to advance some private interest. The new republicans do not deny this. Nor do they suggest that it is easy, either psychologically or institutionally, to separate these things. But they do claim they are separable in principle, and insist we must distinguish them to understand the special logic of debates about the meaning of the public good (a logic the interest-group theory fails to grasp). In principle, on a republican view, it should be a matter of indifference to the participants in any such debate whether the interpretation that prevails is their own. Indeed, we might go further and say that on this view citizens have a responsibility to decide controversies about the common good in the same way philosophers are expected to approach disagreements about the truth, concerned only that the best account be given of it, regardless of whose account that is. Political debate is of course rarely so self-effacing, but that it should sometimes aim, at least, to be is a fact the new republicans claim only their view of politics can explain.

From a republican point of view, moreover, it is important not only that the best among competing interpretations of the public good prevail, but that it prevail in a certain way—through deliberative debate and the unforced agreement flowing from it. The interest-group theory draws no principled distinction between persuasion, on the one hand, and the manipulative techniques of power politics, on the other. Persuasion, on this view, is merely one of many instruments a group may use to achieve its political goals, and beyond that has no special value of its own. The new republicans insist, on the contrary, that deliberative agreement has intrinsic and not merely instrumental worth. They maintain that political processes which promote deliberation and outcomes that rest upon it are substantively better than processes and outcomes that do not. For them, deliberative agreement is a part of the public good itself. Indeed, some go further and equate the public good with the achievement of free agreement, implying that the special good of politics not only includes but entirely consists in its attainment, whatever the content of the agreement in question happens to be. But whether one takes this strong position or asserts more modestly that deliberative agreement is a component of the public good—one element among several— the claim that such agreement has inherent political value is distinguishable in principle from the view that it has only instrumental worth. The contention that deliberative agreement is an independent good and not just a means for reaching some already given end is the third basic assertion on which the new republicans' conception of politics is based, and like the other two it represents a repudiation of one of the interest-group theory's three main claims.

In summary, then, the new republicanism is defined by its insistence on three distinctions that the interest-group theory of politics either ignores or rejects: the distinctions between social and political interests, public and private values, power and persuasion. In one way or another, each of these distinctions challenges the instrumental view of politics implied by the interest-group theory—the view that politics is in its essence an adjectival process with no internal ends or values of its own. The point of the challenge is in each case to affirm the autonomy of politics, to emphasize that political action does have an independent goal that cannot be reduced to or made the instrument of anything else. In this sense we might say that what the new republicans are most anxious to secure is the realm of politics itself, for their basic criticism of the interest-group theory is that it abolishes this realm entirely.

Two Traditions Joined

The interest-group theory leaves no room for the deliberative pursuit of the public good. Within the realm of politics, as this theory conceives it, there are no citizens but only lobbyists. The new republicans seek to reclaim a space for citizenship and rightly understand that to do so the autonomy of politics must be restored.

There are thus important points of contact between the new republicanism and the older professional ideal of the lawyer-statesman. Both take seriously the concept of the public good and emphasize that political debate is not always instrumental but sometimes deliberative instead. Indeed one might go further and describe the lawyer-statesman as an exemplary citizen in just the sense in which the new republicans also understand that term: as a public-spirited participant in those deliberative debates concerning the meaning of the common good that on a republican view of politics constitute its core. In these respects the new republicanism seems closely linked to the lawyer-statesman ideal—more so at least than any other movement in contemporary legal thought.

But this linkage is plainly incomplete, for the lawyer-statesman ideal has other elements that the new republicans fail to stress, indeed hardly mention at all. Notably missing from their writings is any reference to three other components of the ideal: the claim that some citizens have a superior ability to discern the public good; the belief that this superiority is due to their excellence of judgment; and the assumption that good judgment is a trait of character and not simply an intellectual skill. Each of these is an essential feature of the lawyer-statesman ideal. The new republicans pass over all of them in silence.

This is a striking omission. For since their main aim is to rescue the idea that politics is an autonomous activity with a distinct object of its own, one might have expected them to make some effort at describing the qualities a person needs to practice this activity well. Indeed, their failure to pursue this topic is even more surprising in light of the important place it occupies in the tradition of classical political thought on which the new republicans rely so heavily. Perhaps its omission is simply a consequence of their preoccupation with the preliminary task of reclaiming the autonomy of politics itself. That is a plausible explanation, but it is not, I think, the right one. The new republicans have failed to answer the question of what it means to practice the art of politics well because their own view of politics discourages them from asking it in the first place.

In their writings the new republicans combine ideas drawn from two very different intellectual traditions. From the tradition of classical republicanism, whose roots are to be found in Aristotle and other ancient writers and to which the ideal of the lawyer–statesman is also closely linked, they draw their belief in the autonomy of political life. But onto this they have grafted a form of egalitarianism that has an entirely different source and is, in certain respects, quite foreign to the spirit of classical republicanism itself. The particular conception of equality to which the new republicans subscribe has its foundation not in the political philosophy of Aristotle and his humanist successors, but in the moral philosophy of Kant. Kant's conception of equality contains a deep moral insight. But his elaboration and defense of this conception make the value of prudence problematic. Indeed, they make it difficult to understand what practical wisdom is. They thus obscure the meaning and importance of the very virtue that the lawyer–statesman ideal most forcefully commends. Kant's defense of the principle of equality renders this virtue morally suspect. Like many of their contemporaries, the new republicans follow Kant not merely in affirming the principle of equality but in the justification they give for it as well, and as a result they too tend to see the virtue of practical wisdom—the central virtue of the lawyer-statesman—in a jaundiced light.

The idea that politics is an independent activity with a special aim or object of its own is one of the main themes in the tradition of thought known as civic humanism.[22] The classical expression of this idea is to be found in Aristotle's *Politics*.[23] There is a fundamental distinction, Aristotle claims, between the realm of politics, on the one hand, and the prepolitical realm of the household, on the other. The latter, he says, is a realm of necessity whose unalterable routines are fixed by the metabolic requirements of human life. If politics were merely an extension of the household, its scope and character would be determined by these requirements too. But political action is not simply another branch of household management, like the art of moneymaking, whose sole aim is the satisfaction of prepolitical needs. According to Aristotle, the real goal of politics is something altogether different, the self-government of a community of equals by deliberative means. Unlike the private sphere of household life, the public realm of politics is thus essentially one of freedom or self-rule. Indeed, on Aristotle's view a person begins to lead a fully human life of self-control rather than an animalistic one of dependency and need only when he leaves the household and begins to participate as a citizen in political affairs. For Aristotle, politics is therefore an autonomous activity in two related senses: first, in its independence from the prepolitical domain of private needs; and second, in the freedom of its own deliberative processes, participation in which he portrays as essential to the achievement of the self-rule that our fulfillment as human beings requires. Later writers in the humanist tradition stress the autonomy of politics in both these senses, and to the extent the new republicans do too, they also endorse a view of politics that Aristotle was the first to describe systematically.

But there is another aspect of Aristotle's political philosophy that they emphatically reject—his notorious claim that the human species is divided into several different branches that are by nature unequally fit for political life. Aristotle believed this to be an indisputable fact. Some human beings, for example, he thought unqualified for participation in political affairs on account of their age or sex, and others— whom he called natural slaves—because of their native incapacity for self-government. In fact Aristotle ascribed the capacity for citizenship to only one small group of human beings: the adult male heads of households. All others, he felt, were incapable of the self-rule that politics implies and so had to be ruled despotically, outside the realm of politics, by others.

Crucial to Aristotle's view is the assumption that a person's capacity for self-rule depends on fixed attributes like sex and intelligence in such an obvious, regular, and important way that these may themselves be used as criteria for determining who shall be allowed to participate in the political life of their community. Like nearly everyone else today, the new republicans reject this assumption and the inegalitarian implications flowing from it. Thus while accepting Aristotle's broad description of politics as a process of collective self-rule and the equation of self-rule with freedom, they deny his restrictive understanding of who is eligible to participate in this process and affirm the principle of universal enfranchisement instead.

Aristotle's own naturalistic understanding of the conditions of self-rule makes it difficult to see how these ideas can be combined, however, without first reinterpreting the meaning of self-rule in different, non-Aristotelian terms. To combine them one needs an account of self-rule that dissociates it from membership in any natural class, like that of biological males. The most powerful account of this sort that any philosopher has ever given is the one Kant offers in his moral writings, and it is Kant's profoundly nonnaturalistic conception of self-rule that the new republicans have grafted onto the Aristotelian-humanist view of politics as a realm of freedom and fulfillment in an effort to support their very un-Aristotelian belief that this realm must be open to all.[24]

According to Kant, the power of self-rule has its foundation in the will, a faculty Greek writers hardly recognized at all. Kant defines the will as the capacity for action in accordance with "the conception of laws."[25] The actions of animals, indeed even of inanimate objects, are generally lawlike in the sense that they conform to rules, that is, exhibit a regular pattern of some kind. But only human beings (and other rational creatures, if any exist) possess the power of self-determination. Only they are able to direct their own actions in accordance with the conception of a rule that they hold self-consciously in mind as they are acting. Only they are able to live (as Josiah Royce said) in accordance with a plan.[26] The fact that someone possesses this ability does not by itself, of course, ensure that he will adopt good rules rather than bad ones as his guides. But whatever rules he does choose, he will be his own master in a way no animal can, with all the opportunities and obligations such self-mastery implies.

This special power of self-rule is something only reflective or self-conscious beings possess. Just as important, it is also a power that no such being lacks, including those who employ it in bad or self-destructive ways. Kant's conception of self-rule is therefore much thinner than Aristotle's, and imposes far less stringent limitations on political participation. For if to be a member of the community of self-ruling agents one need only possess the capacity for action in accordance with the conception of a rule, then the community in question will be a very wide one indeed. There can, for example, be no justification for excluding any human being from it on the basis of his or her sex, since the power of self-rule, so understood, is utterly independent of a person's gender. No matter how different men and women may be in other ways, they do not differ in this one, and from a Kantian point of view that is the only thing that matters so far as their status as free agents is concerned. The same holds for racial and ethnic differences, as well as differences of intelligence (though the last do present a special problem, since the severely handicapped, like the very young, may even in Kantian terms possess the power of self-rule only to a limited degree).

Viewed abstractly as wills—as beings capable of action in accordance with the conception of a rule—all persons are the same, regardless of the natural and social distinctions that set them apart. All stand on the same moral plane and are entitled to equal respect, and none can be denied admission to the realm of political self-rule on the naturalistic grounds Aristotle thought appropriate. The abstract conception of personhood that Kant's account of self-rule implies thus leads directly to the principle of universal enfranchisement, which Aristotle rejected out of hand.[27] At the same time, however, it permits one to continue to affirm the equation of self-rule with freedom and even to maintain, with Aristotle, that a complete human existence must include some participation in the collaborative undertakings of political life—in the enterprise of collective (as opposed to personal) self-rule. By joining Kant's interpretation of self-rule as the exercise of will to Aristotle's account of political action, one thus arrives at a view that combines the following three claims: that the realm of politics is one of freedom and deliberation importantly detached from the necessities of metabolic life; that engagement in the activity of political self-rule is an essential component of each individual's full flowering as a human being; and that everyone is equally qualified to participate in political deliberation and hence to experience the special fulfillment it affords. It is this combination of ideas—the union of an ancient belief in the autonomy of politics with a modern commitment to universal equality—that gives the new republicanism its special character and distinguishes it both from the interest-group theory of politics and from all older forms of republicanism as well.

THE CONDITIONS OF SELF-RULE

The motive for combining these ideas is clear enough. By reinterpreting the meaning of self-rule along the lines that Kant suggests, it seems possible to save the most attractive features of Aristotle's political philosophy while avoiding his disturbing claim that certain human beings are by nature unfit for politics and ought to be excluded from it. Hardly anyone now accepts this last idea in the strong form in which Aristotle defended it. The belief that every person possesses a basic moral dignity on account of his or her humanity alone and because of this should be allowed to participate in political decisions on equal terms with everyone else is today one of the most widely held of all ethical beliefs. Like many other ancient writers, Aristotle did not share it. Kant's nonnaturalistic conception of moral personality, on the other hand, offers a uniquely deep and secure foundation for this belief. And it does so without destroying what still seems to many the most appealing aspect of the classical view of political life: its insistence on the irreducibility of public deliberation to private interest or need. To create an egalitarian republicanism that captures the best features of Aristotle's political philosophy but eliminates its worst, all that we must do, it seems, is substitute Kant's abstract understanding of self-rule for Aristotle's more naturalistic one and leave the other elements of Aristotle's account intact.

But matters are not so simple. For Aristotle had a view not only about who should be admitted to the realm of political deliberation but also about the requirements for performing well within this realm itself. Aristotle's understanding of these requirements was naturalistic and inegalitarian too, but despite this not patently objectionable, even today, in the way his limited conception of the franchise is. Indeed I would go further and say that the latter aspect of Aristotle's political philosophy—his analysis of political excellence—remains both valuable and true, its naturalism and inegalitarianism notwithstanding. In any case, it has been of continuing importance in the civic humanist tradition and is the source, more specifically, of the lawyer-statesman ideal's emphasis on character and judgment. But Aristotle's account of political excellence is rendered suspect by the same Kantian conception of self-rule that to many modern writers has seemed the best way of defending their commitment to universal enfranchisement. Perhaps, in a strictly logical sense, there is no necessary connection between these things. Nevertheless, for reasons I shall explain, Kant's view of moral personality tends to throw the propriety and even the intelligibility of Aristotle's analysis of political excellence into doubt. Those who adopt Kant's view are therefore likely to see this aspect of Aristotle's political philosophy, and later expressions of it, in an unfavorable light, if indeed they are able to see it at all. To understand the reason for this is to understand why, despite appearances, the new republicans are so hostile to the lawyer-statesman ideal.

According to Aristotle, politics is a deliberative activity calling for judgments about particular matters "in which an indeterminate element is involved"—matters that are neither governed by necessity nor utterly subject to chance, whose "outcome is unpredictable" but to some degree within our power to control.[28] Indeed, on Aristotle's view, politics is the most important of all deliberative activities, for its end—the good of the political association—is the greatest and most inclusive one that human beings can have.[29]

Aristotle's fullest account of deliberation is to be found not in his treatise on politics but in the *Nicomachean Ethics,* a work more concerned with problems of personal than of political life. In the *Ethics* Aristotle stresses that deliberation is not an activity at which everyone does equally well. The young, he says, are handicapped by their lack of experience and on the whole deliberate less well than those who have seen more of life. And even among adults, some deliberate better than others because of their greater natural abilities and superior education. Those who deliberate well, Aristotle says, we call practically wise, practical wisdom being the excellence appropriate to the activity of deliberation, in the same way, for example, that temperance is appropriate to eating, drinking, and sex, or courage to physical combat.

It seemed obvious to Aristotle that some people possess more practical wisdom than others, and he maintained that in deliberating about personal matters we ought to take those who possess the most of it as our guides. And we should do the same, he insisted, in the political realm as well. Here, too, there are "experts" or "masters" who are distinguished from ordinary citizens by their superior powers of judgment, and it is from them that we must learn what politics involves and how to do it well.[30]

Practical wisdom—the excellence of the person who deliberates well about personal or political affairs—Aristotle repeatedly describes as a virtue of character, a dispositional habit shaped by training or education. The practically wise person is more than merely clever. He also has "the right kind of likes and dislikes."[31] His affects are in order: he knows what he ought to care about and actually cares about it. Hence the education he receives must be a training in sentiment as well as in belief.

The elementary passions of attraction and disgust are the raw materials from which the cultivated likes and dislikes of the practically wise person are formed. But although these passions are universally shared by all human beings, they are more pliant in some than in others—more easily shaped into the feelings a person of practical wisdom must possess. Moreover, whatever their original affective endowment, only some people receive the kind of training that is needed to give their passions the appropriate shape. For both these reasons, there is an unequal distribution of practical wisdom among human beings, some possessing more of it than others, and if one accepts Aristotle's premises, it is difficult to see how this inequality could ever be removed. Surely no educational reform is likely to have this effect, so long as children are raised in separate households, and even if the process of child rearing were completely collectivized (in the way, for example, that Socrates proposes in the *Republic*),[32] differences of affective endowment would remain.

More to the point of our present concerns, no widening of the franchise to include those Aristotle thought unfit for political life can by itself achieve an equal distribution of the practical wisdom that, on his view, politics requires. Let us agree that no one should be excluded from participating in the public affairs of his or her community, and that Aristotle's arguments for doing so are indefensible. Still, there is no reason to think that just because more people participate in politics, the superior ability of some to do it well will disappear. Even in a regime that gave all its members the same formal rights of participation, and that sought to make this formal equality effective with a program of material support, the distinction Aristotle emphasizes, between the master of politics and the ordinary citizen, would remain, and for the reasons that he gives. Repudiating Aristotle's biological elitism (which shapes his conception of the limits of the public realm) thus leaves this other, character-based elitism (which underlies his account of excellence within that realm) in place.

The latter inequality, moreover, can also be described in the same general terms that Aristotle uses to describe the first one: as an inequality in the capacity for self-rule. Aristotle wrongly assumed that only men possess this capacity—wrongly because there is no reason to believe that men are any more capable of self-rule than women. But he also assumed, more reasonably, that a person's capacity for self-rule depends on the character traits that he or she possesses, traits some possess to a greater degree or in a more developed form than others.

A person exercises self-rule by making choices for him- or herself, as opposed to having them made by someone else, and the process that leads to the making of such choices is what, according to Aristotle, we call deliberation. Anyone who is completely unable to deliberate will be incapable of self-rule (in the same way, and for the same reason, that animals are). And to the extent that a person's powers of deliberation are impaired, his capacity for self-rule will be too. Impairments of this sort are not, however, always the result of an intellectual deficiency, of a shortfall in brainpower or intelligence. Indeed, Aristotle has relatively little to say about the consequences of such purely intellectual defects. They can also result from deficiencies of character, and it is on these that Aristotle concentrates in his account of deliberation. If, for example, a person is habitually overcome with fear in the presence even of small dangers, or is paralyzed by strong physical desires, his ability to deliberate will be compromised, as compared with those who possess more courage and moderation. And to that extent so will his capacity for self-rule, as our tendency, even today, to describe such a person as lacking in "self-control" suggests.

Thus, for Aristotle, this capacity is one a person may possess in differing degrees—may have more or less of—depending upon the kind of character he has. Though none, perhaps, lack the capacity for self-rule altogether, those who have the right sort of character will be better at exercising it than those who do not, or whose characters are still unformed. This is clearest, perhaps, in the realm of private life, where it is easy to see that certain character traits—what Aristotle called weakness of will, for example—are an obstacle to freedom.[33] But it is just as true in politics, on Aristotle's view the highest and most inclusive form of deliberative self-rule.

To deliberate well about political matters, a certain measure of what Aristotle called theoretical intelligence is of course often indispensable. But it is not their theoretical intelligence that primarily distinguishes the great statesmen of the public realm. Rather, according to Aristotle, it is their practical wisdom, which here, as in the sphere of personal life, has an essential dispositional component. If he is to deliberate wisely about the affairs of his community, a person must possess certain character traits (sobriety, fair-mindedness, incorruptibility, and so on) as well as raw intelligence, just as he must if he is to govern himself with wisdom, and the absence or weakness or underdevelopment of these traits will necessarily impair his capacity for political self-rule. Those who possess the required traits in extraordinary measure will be the best at exercising this capacity, the wisest citizens with the most to contribute to the governance of their communities, and it is their actions and judgments that, on Aristotle's view, we ought to take as our standard in assessing the conduct of political actors generally.

If we substitute Kant's conception of self-rule for Aristotle's, however, the permissibility—perhaps even the possibility—of using such a standard is thrown into doubt. This is a consequence of the radically abstract way in which Kant defines the power of self-rule and of his insistence that the only thing that can be good without qualification is the will.[34]

According to Kant, a person's capacity for self-rule cannot depend upon his possession of any attribute or quality whose distribution is a function of the accidents of birth and education, for if that were true, he argues, freedom would be hostage to fate and hence no longer be freedom at all. The power of self-rule is defined by its autonomy or independence. Consequently, if we are to conceive it in a way that is faithful to its own essential nature, we must, Kant insists, disentangle it from every aspect of our human condition that is tainted by fatefulness and contingency, from everything about us that Kant terms "heteronomous," including the character traits we possess as a result of our original affective endowment and the family settings in which we happen, quite by accident, to have been raised. But when, by a process of abstraction, all such qualities have been eliminated as conditions to or ingredients in the power of self-rule, all that remains is the bare capacity for choice itself, the ability to say yes to some things and no to others that continues to exist even after reason and feeling have spoken: the independent power of assent (or dissent) that Paul and Augustine discovered and that, following them, we call the faculty of will.[35] It is in the exercise of this faculty, and in it alone, Kant claims, that true self-rule consists.

But if we conceive self-rule in these Kantian terms, what can excellence in ruling oneself—either alone or as a member of a self-governing community—mean? There may, of course, be standards by which to judge the merits of the different choices people make, hence a basis for condemning some and praising others. Kant himself believed that such a standard exists and even thought it could be formulated as a rule, which he called the categorical imperative. Equating self-rule with the exercise of will does not, therefore, lead automatically to nihilism (though a nihilistic conclusion can be drawn from this equation). What it does do is render problematic the claim that one person has greater powers of self-rule than another or possesses a special talent for deploying them. Conceived abstractly, as a power of affirmation or negation only, the will of one person is no different from that of any other. The power it gives its possessor is therefore identical in every case as well. And because the will, so conceived, is like a switch with only two positions—those of assent and denial—there can be no grades or degrees of distinction in its exercise other than these two. Indeed, it is difficult to understand how a person can possess a will in Kant's sense without exercising it, or how he can ever exercise it less than completely, whichever of these two positions he assumes.

Kant maintained, of course, that a person may rule himself in a way that contradicts his own true nature as a free and rational being and that denies his community with other beings of this sort. But by insisting that self-rule is a function of the will alone, Kant undermined the distinction between potency and act that plays such a crucial role in Aristotle's account of self-rule and that allows the latter philosopher to speak, in an intelligible way, of a graduated movement toward it. If to rule himself a person must attain (among other things) a certain level of emotional maturity—if we view self-rule, in the way Aristotle did, as a function not just of intellect but of character—then the condition of self-rule may appropriately be described as an excellence, as a kind of completion or fulfillment that different individuals achieve to differing degrees depending upon their affective constitution and early training. If, however, we say with Kant that the possession of a capacity for action in accordance with the conception of a rule is enough by itself to put a person in this condition, to endow him with the same power of self-rule that every other being of this sort enjoys, then we cannot describe the condition in question as an excellence that some possess and others lack, like the excellence of courage, or musical and athletic virtuosity.

Indeed, the whole subject of excellence in deliberation, which occupies such a prominent place in Aristotle's moral philosophy, is likely on this Kantian view to seem mysterious. It is true that Kant does at points touch upon this subject. In the *Critique of Pure Reason,* for example, he observes that "[a] physician, a judge, or a ruler may have at command many excellent pathological, legal, or political rules, even to the degree that he may become a profound teacher of them, and yet, none the less, may easily stumble in their application. For, although admirable in understanding, he may be wanting in natural power of judgment." Kant calls this power "mother-wit," whose lack, he says, "no school can make good."[36] And in the *Critique of Judgment* Kant offers an extended account of aesthetic judgment and taste, in which Hannah Arendt and others have claimed to find an implicit theory of political deliberation.[37] But in his moral writings Kant makes no effort to describe the "natural power of judgment" that is required to deliberate well about ethical matters of either a personal or a political sort. Indeed, he hardly even recognizes the need for such a power in this sphere at all, let alone conceives it, in the way that Aristotle did, as an affectively conditioned trait of character.

This is unsurprising, given Kant's conception of the will as a power of self-determination independent of external influences and his insistence that even if a "step-motherly nature" has left it bereft of all natural powers, the will remains "a thing which has its whole value in itself," like a jewel shining "by its own light."[38] For it is unclear whether a character-based theory of practical wisdom of the sort Aristotle offered can coherently be joined to this Kantian view of moral personality. Even if there is no logical bar to doing so, the principled antinaturalism of Kant's view inevitably puts the moral value of any such theory in doubt. Those who are drawn to the Kantian conception of self-rule as a way of defending their belief that every human being is entitled to basic moral and political respect are therefore likely to look with a suspicious eye, as Kant himself did, upon any suggestion that the character trait of practical wisdom has an intrinsic value of its own. For the claim that it does—which the lawyer-statesman ideal of the early nineteenth century affirmed—has naturalistic and inegalitarian implications deeply in tension with the view that the bare power of action in accordance with the conception of a rule is the final and exclusive source of every person's moral worth.

EQUALITY AND EXCELLENCE

Aristotle and the humanists who followed him viewed political life as a realm of freedom in which the judgments and actions of those involved are not settled in advance by their antecedent interests. Politics, they claimed, offers its participants an opportunity to experience free self-rule in the most complete sense, as members of a self-ruling community, and they concluded that participation in this realm ought to be viewed as an intrinsic good and an important type (according to some, the most important type) of human fulfillment. With all these claims the new republicans are in agreement and to that extent belong to the tradition of thought that derives from Aristotle's political philosophy.

But Aristotle's politics are also notoriously undemocratic—some human beings, he says, have natural deficiencies or disabilities that make them unfit to participate in political affairs—and this aspect of his views the new republicans flatly reject. To the Aristotelian conception of politics as a realm of freedom and fulfillment they join the egalitarian claim that everyone should be admitted to this realm on equal terms, regardless, for example, of sex or social position (which Aristotle believed to determine a person's fitness for political action).

For two centuries now it has seemed to many that the deepest and most powerful justification for this latter egalitarian claim is the one supplied by Kant. If the capacity for self-rule that politics demands is nothing more than the capacity for action in accordance with the conception of a rule, then all who possess this primordial power will be equally qualified to participate in political life. In comparison with this justification for extending the franchise beyond the limits that Aristotle imposed, other arguments seem anemic and incomplete and appear not to go to the root of the matter. That is why the Kantian defense of political equality has had such a powerful appeal. Indeed, one might go further and say that Kant's conception of self-rule has become, in our contemporary culture, almost a dogma of belief to which the adherents of otherwise quite different political philosophies subscribe.[39] Many new republicans appear to subscribe to this dogma as well.[40] And for that reason, though it is right to call them neo-Aristotelians in one sense, it is equally correct to call them neo-Kantians in another.

Kant's understanding of self-rule not only undermines Aristotle's restrictions on political participation. It also casts suspicion on his claim that self-rule (including political self-rule) is an excellence of character, an activity at which some do better than others because of the affective habits they possess. Those who accept Kant's conception of self-rule are likely to find this latter claim troubling. They are likely to view Aristotle's account of practical wisdom in the way they do

his discussion of natural slavery and the incompetence of women, and
see it, too, as an expression of Aristotle's elitism, which the Kantian
conception of self-rule decisively refutes. Because of this they are
likely to be uninterested in the question, which Aristotle took so
seriously, of what the excellence of practical wisdom *is*. That is why
one finds in the otherwise quite varied writings of those political
theorists who subscribe to the prevailing neo-Kantian consensus—
including the writings of the new republicans—so little attention to
the topic of practical wisdom, a topic that occupied a central place in
the political philosophy of civic humanism. For to the extent they
understand the meaning of self-rule in terms that make this ancient
subject morally dubious, the new republicans break with the humanist tradition they claim to represent.

It must be emphasized that the rejection of this aspect of Aristotle's
political philosophy does not follow from the endorsement of universal enfranchisement alone. There are, in fact, many different arguments that can be made in defense of this political practice: for example, that it counteracts the alienation that develops when
government decisions are formally beyond the power of popular control; that it serves as an obstacle to tyranny; that it ensures the widest
possible pool of talent from which those with a calling for politics
may be drawn; and that there is, in any case, no correlation between
political ability, on the one hand, and easily identifiable natural or
social traits, on the other, that is sufficiently strong to justify the admission of some and the exclusion of others on the basis of the traits
they happen to possess. Each of these is an argument for universal
enfranchisement, but none contradicts the claim that political self-
rule is an excellence that some possess and others lack. (Indeed, far
from contradicting it, certain of these arguments rest upon that very
claim.) What makes the claim difficult to accept is thus not the principle of universal enfranchisement as such, but the Kantian justification
for it. The arguments I have mentioned can all be combined with the
idea that only a few among those eligible to participate in politics
possess the deliberative excellence that political self-rule requires. But
these arguments are all based upon considerations of a sort that Kant
called merely "empirical,"[41] and from the point of view he made seem
mandatory in moral and political philosophy, they are thus incapable
of providing an adequate ground for the universal right of political
participation. One who shares this point of view will therefore feel

compelled to find some other, nonempirical ground on which to rest that right, and if one pursues the search for it in a rigorous way, must come eventually to the idea of a pure power of self-rule that all self-conscious beings share. It is on this idea that one will build a defense of the universal right of political participation, and while there are other justifications for that right to which Aristotle's account of practical wisdom can easily be joined, it cannot easily be joined to this one.

So far as the acceptability of Aristotle's account is concerned, therefore, the important thing is not whether one endorses the principle of universal enfranchisement, but the reasons one gives for endorsing it. Today almost everyone accepts this principle. Beyond its bare acceptance, however, a certain way of justifying the principle, broadly Kantian in form, now dominates as well. This justification for the principle is as much a part of our political culture as the principle itself, and it is the justification, not the principle, that is the source of the embarrassed silence that now surrounds the whole subject of practical wisdom, even, perhaps most surprisingly, among those new republicans for whom the concept of deliberation has such importance.

We can now see why the new republicanism is in reality so hostile to the lawyer-statesman ideal. To be sure, its proponents do want to revive certain elements of that ideal, in particular its emphasis on what I have called the autonomy of politics. But other elements they ignore completely. Excellence, leadership, judgment, wisdom, character—essential terms in defining the lawyer-statesman's role—are all virtually unmentioned in the writings of the new republicans. What explains their silence on this score? Not, I think, mere inattention and neglect, but rather an antipathy to the ideas these terms express. If one starts with a Kantian conception of self-rule, as the new republicans do, the assumption of a differential order of excellence in politics is bound to seem suspect: at best an immoral idea and at worst an unintelligible one. But the lawyer-statesman ideal is founded upon just this assumption, and must therefore look suspicious from the standpoint the new republicans adopt. Except in certain limited ways, the new republicans cannot, in fact, feel any real affection for it at all. Some, like Karl Llewellyn and Alexander Bickel, have been genuinely sympathetic toward the ideal, even though they failed to give their sympathies a solid philosophical defense. But they could still be called its friends. The new republicans, by contrast, are more its enemies than allies, and beneath their rhetorical evocations of it, and limited allegiance to it, one may discern an hostility toward the lawyer-statesman ideal that represents an even more advanced stage in its decline as a professional norm.

RECOVERING AN IDEAL

At mid-century the lawyer-statesman ideal still had powerful defenders. To be sure, it no longer enjoyed the same preeminence it had a hundred years before, and its supporters now found themselves challenged by a different and increasingly influential professional ideal, that of scientific law reform. But as late as 1960 the ideal of the lawyer-statesman still retained much of its old appeal, and the consequences of this challenge to it had not yet been fully felt. Two books published in the early 1960s reflect the prestige that the ideal still possessed. One is Llewellyn's masterwork, *The Common Law Tradition,* which appeared in 1960. The other is Bickel's *The Least Dangerous Branch,* published two years later. Both are indisputably great works—arguably the greatest of their generation in the fields of private and public law, respectively—and each is animated by a respect for the virtue of practical wisdom on which the classical ideal of the lawyer-statesman had been based. In both books that ideal is still clearly visible, if in an incomplete and somewhat muted form, and to the extent that these books reflect the professional culture of their time, they offer evidence of the ideal's continuing appeal.

Only a few years later, however, the prestige of the lawyer-statesman ideal was in a steep decline. In part this was a consequence of the triumph, within legal academic circles, of the ideal of scientific law reform, which acquired a new authority and self-consciousness with the rise of the law-and-economics movement in the late 1960s. There had always been a tension between this ideal and that of the lawyer-statesman. But the existence of the tension and its implications had remained largely concealed, in part because so many defenders of one ideal claimed allegiance to the other too. The law-and-economics movement, however, made the tension manifest, and at the same time strengthened considerably the appeal of scientific law reform, which now seemed finally to have a method adequate to its ambitions. The demise of the lawyer-statesman ideal in the last generation has thus been associated with, and accelerated by, the growing influence of a long-standing counterideal whose distinctiveness and full potential have only recently been grasped.

But the triumph of the ideal of scientific law reform has not been the only reason for the declining vitality of the lawyer–statesman ideal. That ideal is also challenged by a certain form of egalitarianism that has become, in recent years, an element of near-orthodoxy among moral and political philosophers. I have called this now-dominant form of egalitarianism Kantian to emphasize that its adherents are distinguished not by their commitment to political or legal equality as such, but by the justification they offer to defend it, a justification that (with whatever embellishments a given writer adds) always starts with Kant's idea of an abstract power of self-rule that is antecedent to and independent of every accident of character that distinguishes some human beings from others. There is no idea that now has as deep a grip on our moral imagination as this one, and even in the new republicanism, which has in other ways been shaped by a classical conception of politics, its immense influence can be felt. But it is an idea at war with the most central feature of the lawyer–statesman ideal. For to the extent that one accepts Kant's defense of political equality, the claim that practical wisdom is an essential virtue in political deliberation, and a trait of character that human beings display to differing degrees, is bound to seem suspicious, indeed scarcely intelligible at all. The more one looks at things from this Kantian point of view, the more practical wisdom is bound to seem an embarrassed virtue. And that is precisely what it has become even for the new republicans, the most outspoken defenders of civic virtue within the legal profession today.

The aim of the following two chapters is to revivify the ideal of the lawyer–statesman: to restore to it some of the credibility and appeal it has lost. To do that, I must first rescue the virtue of practical wisdom from the embarrassment that now surrounds it. All that I have so far said about the nature of practical wisdom has been either quite vague (for example, that it is a trait of character) or essentially negative (that a certain defense of political equality cannot be joined to it). If the virtue of practical wisdom is to be restored to a position of respectability in the profession—if lawyers are again to understand that it is a virtue, and why—a more detailed and positive account is needed, and in Chapter 2 I make an effort to provide one.

The account of practical wisdom that I shall offer there is meant to be quite general. It is not restricted to lawyers in particular, but is intended to apply to a much broader field, that of politics as a whole. The subject of Chapter 2 is the nature of statesmanship in general. In Chapter 3 I shall return to the ideal of the *lawyer*-statesman and, narrowing my focus once again, attempt to show that lawyers have particularly good grounds for valuing the virtue of practical wisdom, and explain why I think they may reasonably expect their professional experience to promote that virtue in more than ordinary measure.

2

Practical Wisdom and Political Fraternity

MEANS AND ENDS

"Statesman" is a term of praise, a word we use to express our admiration for those men and women who lead their communities with exceptional wisdom and skill. It is also an old-fashioned term that has no special connection to present-day political realities. Unlike the modern bureaucrat, who belongs exclusively to our age, the statesman is a figure that appears in every period. In this sense we might say his virtue is a timeless one, for its essential meaning has remained the same from one political epoch to the next despite the revolutions of thought and practice that divide them.

The circumstances in which statesmanship is practiced do of course change over time and are today, in some respects at least, more complex than in the past. Any modern politician who hopes to comprehend the consequences of his actions must understand these new complexities. He therefore needs a working knowledge of the methods of analysis that have been invented to make the circumstances of modern politics intelligible—methods that, historically speaking, are as novel as the social and political arrangements they describe. But the possession of such knowledge does not by itself make one a statesman. Technical sophistication, whose meaning is forever changing, can never be more than a prerequisite of statesmanship, and if we ask what else is needed to achieve it, a good reply would be: the same qualities that distinguished the great statesmen of the past (who were of course, from our perspective, technical illiterates). There have been statesmen, and a need for the art they practice, as long as there have been political communities, and like the private virtues of courage

53

and moderation, the public virtue of statesmanship has remained recognizably the same from the Greek world to our own. Courage and moderation mean today what they have always meant, and we can still find even in the most remote antiquity models of these virtues to admire. The same is true of statesmanship as well.

What is the nature of the statesman's art? What is the end at which a statesman aims, and how does one achieve it? A reasonable answer might be that a statesman aims at the good of the community to which he or she belongs and that the statesman's special virtue consists in an extraordinary devotion to this good and a superior capacity for discerning where it lies. On this unexceptionable view, two traits set the statesman apart: first, love of the public good, and second, wisdom in deliberating about it. How the first of these should be conceived is a question I shall return to later in the chapter. For the moment I want to concentrate on the second trait, the statesman's superiority of judgment. What sorts of judgments does politics require those engaged in it to make and what is meant by saying that some men and women are especially good at making them?

It is useful to begin with the distinction between means and ends. Many of the questions that arise in the ordinary course of political debate are questions about means. They are questions, that is to say, about the best way of reaching some preestablished goal. Questions of this kind assume agreement regarding the end to be achieved, and the uncertainty they reflect concerns only the comparative costs of the alternative paths by which that end may be attained. The point of deliberating about means is to determine which of these paths entails the fewest costs overall.

To make the judgment that such a choice requires, one obviously needs a common metric of some sort, for without a uniform standard of measurement the costs of different alternatives cannot be compared. People may of course disagree as to what this standard should be: should alternatives be compared, for example, in terms of their monetary cost, their social cost, or their utility (either marginal or average)? But a person cannot make the claim that one way of achieving a goal is less costly than another without employing some such standard, and two people cannot intelligibly debate a question of means without first agreeing on the yardstick they will use to compare alternatives. Questions of this sort have meaning, and are in principle decidable, only within the bounds of comparability.

It follows that every political dispute, insofar as it is a dispute about means, presents what is essentially a problem of counting and calls for a judgment of a calculative kind. Clearly, then, the skill most needed in deliberating about means will be the ability to count costs with accuracy and speed. This is often difficult to do, and not everyone does it equally well. Nor can the ability in question be acquired simply by mastering certain expert techniques (such as modern cost-benefit analysis). For to count costs properly one has first to identify the costs that must be counted, and this demands a perceptual capacity that technical knowledge may facilitate but does not guarantee. Deliberating about means thus requires a degree of imagination as well as technical expertise. But the basic point remains that all such deliberation is in essence a kind of counting, and though this may be a more complex activity than is initially apparent, it is clear what its object is and what it means to do it well.

If we understand the distinction between means and ends in its ordinary sense, however, it is obvious that many political disputes are at least partly about ends—about what goals to pursue and how to rank them, and not just about the best way to achieve those ends on which we already agree. Indeed, many disputes that appear at first to be entirely about means implicate questions of ends and cannot be decided until these have been resolved. Thus, for example, if the pursuit of one goal requires the use of a unique resource that is also needed to achieve some other, achieving less of the latter goal will clearly be a cost of pursuing the former one. Whether it nevertheless makes sense, from a purely calculative point of view, to pursue the first goal must therefore depend (among other things) on just how large we believe this particular cost to be, and that cannot be determined without first deciding the relative importance to us of the goals that here happen to conflict. This raises a question of ends that may not have been settled—or even seen—before we began deliberating about the best means for reaching one or the other of these goals. If that is the case, then we must interrupt our discussion of means to address a question of ends. Or rather, since the costs of achieving a given end, when fully accounted for, may cause us to reassess the strength of our original attachment to it, we must go back and forth from one sort of question to the other, reexamining our judgments about means in the light of our judgments about ends, and vice versa. To the extent that a political debate assumes this more complicated form, the clean line between means and ends breaks down. In fact, few political disputes are about means only. Most, if not all, raise questions about ends too, and many are indeed centrally concerned with issues of this latter sort.

We must therefore ask what it means to show good judgment in choosing among ends. In disputes about means, good judgment might be defined as the ability to calculate well. But is the same true when the members of a community disagree about its ends?

There are some who maintain that it is. Many utilitarians, for example, take this view.[1] Every political community, they say, has one ultimate objective, namely, the maximization of its happiness (aggregate or average). Of course, it is not always clear how this goal is to be achieved. In particular, disagreements often arise as to which intermediate goals are most likely to promote the ultimate one of maximizing happiness itself. But the solution in such cases, utilitarians insist, is always in principle the same. It is to adopt the subultimate goal that will produce the most happiness overall. In their view, the community's final end thus provides a uniform criterion for assessing the merits of all other ones, each of which may be thought of as producing a certain amount of the same basic good in a different shape. From the vantage point of the community's single overriding goal, these other, lesser goals are qualitatively indistinguishable. There is therefore only one ground on which any of them may be preferred to any other, namely, that it yields a greater quantity of the same good that gives each its value and appeal. Thus if the utilitarians are right and this is indeed what deliberating about ends in politics is like, it follows that such deliberation must be a form of counting too and the ability it calls for the same as that which is required when the choice in question is a choice among means only.

Often, perhaps, political disputes about ends are what the utilitarians claim. They are disputes about how to produce the most of some agreed-upon common good. But is this always the case? Uncompromising utilitarians of course say yes. But there are reasons to doubt this answer despite the fact that any debate about ends may be formulated so as to give the appearance of posing a problem decidable by calculation alone. For there are some political disputes that cannot be described in this way without obscuring their most salient feature, namely, the participants' own belief that the alternatives involved appeal to incommensurable values.

It is true that the conflicting values in any political debate can be made commensurable merely by viewing them from a sufficiently distant point of view. This is precisely the strategy utilitarians adopt. But even if one is always able to formulate an abstract standard for comparing different ends, the political actors who must actually choose among them may find the exercise unhelpful in some cases. "It does us no good," they may protest, "to be told that what we all want is happiness or wealth or something else. For what divides us here is our disagreement as to what this *is*—what happiness or wealth consists of—and the suggestion that each of our positions be conceived as an effort to secure this common good doesn't help us settle that dispute."

What makes this suggestion sometimes seem so unhelpful from the parties' point of view is the fact that it abstracts from, and hence implicitly devalues, the special features of their positions that are of greatest significance to the parties themselves. Abstraction is often useful, even necessary, in political debate. But sometimes it is not. For there are controversies about ends whose meaning is too closely tied to certain of their concrete features to be helpfully described (so far as the proponents are concerned) as disagreements about the best way of achieving some higher-order goal, like happiness. In cases of this kind, the ends in question cannot be made commensurable without an unacceptable loss of meaning from the parties' point of view. The point at which fidelity to the experience of incommensurability seems preferable, on balance, to the advantages that comparability affords will vary from case to case and, indeed, from person to person, for this is to some degree a matter of temperament and taste. But some such point exists and may as easily be reached in political as in other debates.

Of course, the fact that two goods are incommensurable in the sense I have described does not mean it is impossible to deliberate rationally about the choice between them. For even if they provide pleasures or fulfillments so different in kind that they cannot meaningfully be described as instances of some more basic common good, it may still be true that one choice is demonstrably better than another. Considerations of timing, for example, and of the harmony or disharmony of fit among different goods often justify such a conclusion. In personal deliberation this is commonly the case. Thus if I enjoy reading books and watching films—two activities, let us assume, that give me deeply different pleasures—I may decide that it makes sense to read the book on which a film is based before seeing the film itself if doing so increases my understanding of the film or, alternatively, leaves my imagination unconstrained by visual images in reading. The goods these activities produce may be incommensurable from my own personal point of view, and yet I still have reason to do one before the other (a question of timing). I may also have reason to do some of each rather than one exclusively, for the sake of variety. And it may be, too, that for me the pleasure of seeing a film is spoiled by reading a review of it, either before or after, so that this particular kind of reading cannot be harmoniously integrated, in my life at least, with the activity of film-going at all.

There are political analogues to these personal judgments. Food and culture are both good, yet the material and spiritual satisfactions they afford are, beyond a certain point, incommensurable. Still, it makes sense for a society to assure that its members have enough to eat before it begins to promote their culture, since the pleasures of culture cannot be enjoyed on an empty stomach. Similarly, freedom and equality are both worthy ideals, though their value cannot be measured in terms of some uniform primitive good (whether happiness or wealth or anything else). Nevertheless, it is almost certainly better to have some of both than to pursue one ideal exclusively. And a society that has made a basic commitment to the principle of free expression is likely to find there are other values (like patriotism and religious feeling) that cannot easily be harmonized with this one. All of these cases may be redescribed in such a way as to become amenable to calculative analysis and judgment. But even if we resist the temptation to do this and insist on the incommensurability of the values involved, there may be a uniquely right choice in each situation for reasons of timing or fit. Where such reasons exist, statesmanship is the art of identifying them and getting others to see their force.

It would be wrong to assume, however, that whenever calculation fails to provide a meaningful basis for choosing among conflicting ends, considerations of timing and fit must do so instead. This is true neither of personal nor of political choices. At the personal level, I sometimes have to choose between activities whose values are to me incomparably different and that have no natural sequential relation to one another or differentially supportive connection to other values that I hold. A trivial example would be the choice I must make between hearing a lecture and going to a concert, when both will occur only once and at the very same time. A more dramatic example is the choice that Jean-Paul Sartre's citizen-son faces between joining the Resistance and staying home to protect his mother.[2]

The same thing happens in politics as well. Here, too, similar choices of varying degrees of seriousness arise. Should a dam be built that will bring power to a region but destroy a species of fish (of no commercial value and only genetically distinguishable from other closely related species)? Should a monument be built to the veterans of a recent, controversial war, and if so, what should it say or represent? Should some crimes be made punishable by death? Should women be given a right to abortion upon demand, and with what restrictions, if any? These are real questions that Americans have recently debated. In each case the disagreement is one that cannot be resolved by calculation alone. Nor do considerations of timing settle the issue in any of these disputes. And although those on both sides have been able in each case to point to other values, precedents, and practices that they claim only their position honors, the disputants have generally failed to agree as to which of these are most important and worthy of respect. In all these cases the values in conflict are too different to be treated as expressions of some single underlying good, and considerations of timing and fit provide no common basis for deciding which to prefer.

Political choices of this kind are not uncommon and, as the examples remind us, often produce a great deal of pain. Of course, even when competing goals are assumed to be commensurable, and everyone agrees on a calculative method for choosing among them, the choice itself may be painful to make. That is because in choosing one goal—the one that yields the most happiness or wealth overall— we are almost always forced to abandon other goals that have value for us too. Were our actions unconstrained by scarcity, we would pursue these other ends as well. In this way, scarcity can make even a rationally justifiable choice among commensurable ends difficult to accept, and the same is true when the ends are incommensurable, but independent reasons of timing and fit make it rational to prefer one of them to another. But where political goals are incommensurable and no such reasons exist, or are themselves the subject of intense controversy, any decision that is made must appear groundless, and its groundlessness can be an added source of pain for those involved.

This will most obviously be true for the losers, who cannot be consoled by the thought that their own ultimate values are in reality best served by the choice that has been made. Not only have they lost, but their defeat must seem to them arbitrary and unjustified as well. The winners, too, are not exempt from this unhappiness. Max Weber once observed that the rich and powerful in every society want not only to protect their privilege but also to believe it has been rightly earned as well, and to believe this, he said, they must persuade others less fortunate than they that their disadvantages are deserved.[3] In a similar way, the winners in any political struggle want not only to enjoy the fruits of victory. They also want the losers to acknowledge the propriety of their defeat. A groundless choice makes this impossible, however, and thus leaves the winners with an anxious sense of their own unearned good luck, just as it leaves the losers with a feeling of unjustifiable misfortune.

Of course, if the decision is a trivial one (like my choice between lecture and concert), the groundlessness of the judgment that is called for is unlikely to be very disturbing. In cases of this sort all may agree that the best way of making the decision is by some arbitrary procedure, like drawing lots. But when a political choice touches important concerns, the special anxieties created by a groundless decision are often substantial. This is most apparent when the choice is one that bears on the identity of a community—on the commitments and goals its members consider basic to their common life. These are among the most important choices a community makes, for choosing one end rather than another amounts, in cases of this sort, to a declaration by the community of its own defining values. By the same token, the closer a political choice comes to such issues of self-definition, the less likely there are to be agreed-upon standards for making it, since the argument in disputes of this kind is often over the content and scope of these standards themselves. The more a choice is seen as self-defining for a community, therefore, the more importance it is likely to have, but at the same time the more groundless any resolution of it is likely to be.

Here my account of statesmanship reaches an apparent impasse. So long as a political question can be answered by calculative means, or settled by reference to agreed-upon considerations of timing and fit, it is clear what sort of deliberative procedure is called for, and what it means to deliberate well. But in just those cases where the importance of the question is greatest for the community involved and the need for statesmanship therefore presumably most acute, the groundlessness of the choices that are made seems to remove any foundation we might have for claiming that some people show better judgment than others do in making them. It seems to deprive us of any basis for defining the statesman's excellence of judgment in this important class of disputes. Just where the need for it is greatest, therefore, the nature of the statesman's art remains obscure.

At this point further progress in the argument becomes quite difficult. Either, it would seem, there are common grounds for settling a political dispute or there are not—as when the values in conflict are incommensurable, timing is irrelevant, and any considerations of fit that bear on the question are as controversial as the values themselves. In the latter case, one might conclude, drawing lots is as good a way of choosing as any other and much less costly to boot. To be sure, drawing lots is not itself a form of deliberation but rather its antithesis, for it requires no judgment at all. One might argue, perhaps, that a statesman is distinguished precisely by his talent for recognizing when further deliberation is futile and a more expeditious method should be preferred. Aristotle says it is a sign of wisdom to see that there is no point in deliberating about impossible things.[4] So, too, it may be thought a mark of statesmanship to see the pointlessness of deliberating about questions to which only groundless answers can be given and to recommend that the decision be made in a cheap but arbitrary way instead.

But this conclusion stands our ordinary conception of statesmanship on its head. For instead of affirming what most people believe— that a statesman is distinguished by his superior talent for deliberating about the thorniest political disputes—it explains his excellence of judgment on the grounds that he knows such disagreements cannot be resolved by deliberative means and stops trying while others foolishly persist. This view not only conflicts with widely held beliefs about the meaning of statesmanship. It also leads to the disturbing conclusion that the most important political debates, those concerning a community's basic commitments and ideals, are best decided by some arbitrary procedure like drawing lots. We feel instinctively that this is wrong, and that it is important to deliberate about such choices even if all the decisions we might make are groundless in the sense I have explained. But is there in fact any point to deliberating in situations of this sort? And what does it mean to do it well? These are the questions to which our inquiry has led us, and that we must answer to understand the statesman's art.

A SOCRATIC TURN

I shall approach these questions indirectly, by postponing for the moment any further inquiry into the nature of political judgment and turning to the realm of personal deliberation instead. By personal deliberation I mean the kind of reflection in which an individual engages when attempting to define his or her own good and to determine how it may be achieved. In most cases an individual's personal good will itself have an important social dimension. Normally, for example, there will be social relationships that one must establish in order to pursue one's objectives, and others—those of friendship and love—that one values for their own sake. But though the personal good of most individuals includes a significant social component, deliberating about one's own good is not the same as deliberating about the good of the community to which one belongs. The vantage point from which I judge disputes concerning the meaning of the public good is different from the point of view I adopt when considering the nature of my personal good and its requirements, even if in the end I conclude that my own fulfillment can be achieved only through devotion to a communal ideal. The fact that some define their personal good in public terms, and that, more generally, only a socialized being with powers of reflection developed through participation in a community of speech can engage in personal deliberation at all, does not show that personal and political deliberation are the same.

In shifting the focus of my argument from political to personal deliberation, I am following a strategy that in a certain sense at least is the opposite of the one Socrates adopts in the *Republic*.[5] Socrates and his interlocutors begin by inquiring into the nature of justice as a personal virtue—the virtue whose possession accounts for the justice of individual souls. To get a better understanding of this virtue, Socrates suggests that he and his companions first explore the meaning of justice on a larger scale, in the political domain, where, he says, its nature can be more easily discerned. Socrates defends this detour in the argument on the grounds that public justice (the justice of cities) and personal justice (the justice of souls) are structurally similar, so that one may be used as a key to understanding the other. My suggestion is that we pursue the meaning of statesmanship, of excellence in political deliberation, by first asking about its personal counterpart, whose outlines, I believe, are easier to discern. In contrast to Socrates, who sought to illuminate the meaning of a personal virtue with a political analogy, I am thus proposing to explain a political virtue by first describing its personal equivalent.

Of course, my method resembles Socrates' in one important respect, for just as he assumed that an analogy might be drawn between the justice of cities, on the one hand, and that of souls, on the other, I too am assuming that wisdom in personal deliberation can be analogized to statesmanship in political debate. I am assuming that these two excellences are alike in structure, and that an understanding of the first (a private virtue) can therefore help us to an understanding of the second (a public one). My claim is not that these two virtues are the same—which, were it true, would mean that everyone who has one must have the other too. That is plainly not the case, for there are some who show great wisdom in political debate but less or none in personal deliberation, and others of whom the reverse is true. This obvious and interesting discrepancy is consistent with the claim that personal and political judgment are analogous, for analogy is a relation not of identity but correspondence. The argument that follows assumes that such a correspondence exists. It also seeks to bring the nature of this correspondence more clearly into view and thereby strengthen the plausibility of its own premise.

What sorts of problems do we confront, then, in the sphere of personal deliberation and how do we deliberate about them? Like their political counterparts, many personal problems raise issues merely of means—of determining how to get the most of what we want with the limited resources at our command. I may have decided, for example, to save for my retirement. But what is the best way of doing this? Of the various investment strategies available to me, which is likely to yield the largest postretirement income at a given level of savings? To the extent that a personal choice presents a question of means and nothing more, it can be settled by calculation, and the person who deliberates ably about such questions will simply be the one who calculates well.

Of course, in the personal realm as in the political, questions of means often implicate questions of ends too. Thus in thinking about how to save for my retirement, I may be forced to consider whether my unknown future interests should be weighed equally with my known present ones, and beyond that to inquire what I want to use my retirement *for,* a question that can easily lead into the reexamination of my entire life. But so long as I regard two conflicting personal goals as qualitatively identical, then even though I value each for its own sake—even though neither is a means to anything else—I am likely to see the conflict between them as a tradeoff with an optimal solution that can be determined by calculation alone. This might be the way, for example, that I view the conflict between my interest in present expenditure, which a program of savings frustrates, and my competing interest in future income, which it is the goal of such a program to secure.

Some personal decisions, however, present me with a choice between incommensurable ends—ends so different in kind that it seems meaningless to treat the conflict between them as a problem of trade-offs with a quantitative solution. Even here, of course, considerations of timing and fit may make one choice more reasonable than another. I have given some examples in the previous section. But in the personal realm too, such considerations are not always conclusive, either because they have no bearing on the choice in question or because they are themselves a part of the dilemma that the choice presents and so cannot be neutrally relied upon to solve it.

Vexing as they may be, not all dilemmas of this sort are equally important. Many, in fact, are relatively trivial. Should I spend my summer vacation in the mountains, for example, or go to the beach instead? The more I think about the pleasures each will afford, the more the two alternatives seem unalike, and it strikes me as silly to insist that I just do what will make me happier on the grounds that both represent the same basic good of pleasure, albeit in different forms. Nor (let us assume) does it make more sense to take one vacation this year and the other the next than to proceed in the opposite order. And as far as my other interests, values, and commitments are concerned, each vacation fits as well or as badly with them as the other. Still, despite the absence of any rational basis for making the choice, I should not become too upset about it. For it does not, after all, touch any really deep concerns of mine, and beyond a certain point it is not worth further worry. Perhaps I should settle the issue by flipping a coin, and under the circumstances this may be a perfectly sensible thing to do.

But there are other personal choices, also groundless, that are far more serious. Should I marry? Should I divorce? Should my spouse and I have a child? Should I sacrifice my professional career to stay home with the children? Should I continue with the career I have or drop it and pursue another? Should I take up the study of a musical instrument, or a foreign language, that will take years of hard work to master? Should I enter psychoanalysis? Should I give my time and money—perhaps even my life—to a political cause or share them with friends and family instead? Should I remain close to my parents or move far away? Should I help my aging father fulfill his wish to die? These are questions, typically, of immense personal importance, and there is often no rational basis on which to decide them. They do not in any meaningful sense have a calculative solution, timing is frequently irrelevant, and it is often unhelpful to ask how the different decisions I might make will fit in with the rest of my life. For these decisions themselves are likely to have too large a transformative effect on my life as a whole to leave a significant reserve of untouched interests and values as a neutral basis for comparing the harmoniousness or fit of the choices that confront me.

Of course, before concluding that this is so, it is sensible to inquire whether the dilemma I face cannot be settled in some rational way. Despite initial appearances, for example, a problem may turn out to have a computational solution, or to be decidable on grounds of timing and fit; or perhaps it can be divided into several smaller problems, some of which, at least, are easily addressed. As a deliberative strategy, it always makes sense to narrow to the greatest extent possible the range of questions for which no rational answer exists. But some questions of this sort are bound to remain, and over the course of a lifetime no one can avoid them completely.

Among the choices that fall within this category are those that bear most directly on the question of personal identity—of who we are and wish to be as individuals. Which choices these are vary from person to person, but the ones I mentioned above are common examples. Choices of this sort are of great importance to us. They are identity-defining choices with far-reaching implications for the whole of our lives, and although we do not face them every day, they possess a significance out of all proportion to their frequency and number. In this respect, they resemble those fundamental decisions that from time to time force every political community to confront the question of its identity. And like their political analogues, these identity-defining personal choices are also the ones most likely to be groundless too, for they put in question the deepest commitments a person has—the very commitments that might otherwise provide a common basis for assessing the alternatives the choice presents (in terms of their utility, timing or fit). In short, the personal choices of which I am now speaking are the exact counterpart of those political dilemmas on which my account of statesmanship ran aground. It is to them that my Socratic turn naturally brings us, and they that we must try to understand.

SYMPATHY AND DETACHMENT

The first thing to observe about this peculiarly important class of personal dilemmas is that most people do not think it appropriate to resolve them by some arbitrary means like drawing lots. Indeed, the more clearly a choice implicates a person's basic interests and ideals, the more likely he is to subject it to prolonged deliberative review, even when he has become convinced that the issue before him is not one of utility-maximization and cannot be settled on grounds of timing or fit. But conceding that this is so, what is the nature and aim of the deliberation in which he engages?

At this point it is tempting to seek refuge in the concept of intuition, a mode of knowledge that, as Kant remarked, is distinguished by the immediacy of its relation to its objects.[6] Intuition is a form of understanding, but one that is incapable of discursive explication. Unlike other forms of knowledge, the sense or content of an intuition cannot be conveyed by arguments alone. To have an intuition is just to see that something is the case, to apprehend its obviousness in the same direct way that I apprehend, for example, the shape and color of the book I happen at the moment to be holding. Intuition is thus, in the most literal sense, a form of insight, the intellectual equivalent of physical vision. It is how we see things with the mind's eye. When a person is required to make a life-defining choice, one might conclude, he or she can do so only on the basis of an intuition, for in such cases there are generally no grounds on which to base an intellectual argument favoring one option over another. To deliberate about such choices is on this view not to maximize or harmonize but to intuit, and the people who are best at doing so will be those whose intuitions are the surest.

The concept of intuition is less helpful than might at first appear, however. To begin with, the equation of deliberation with intuition seems, on its face, a questionable one, for deliberation is a process that takes time, but intuition can be, and often is, instantaneous. Deliberation always has some temporal duration and can therefore be started, stopped, and (as the term itself implies) deliberately pursued; intuition, by contrast, cannot be. Anyone who claims that intuition plays a central role in the process of deliberating about incommensurable personal goods should perhaps be understood, therefore, as saying that deliberation, which takes time, merely prepares the way for a climactic moment of insight in which the person who has been deliberating stops thinking and looks instead. But even this more careful formulation is less helpful than it seems, for in what can such insight consist?

One may be inclined to answer that, like any intuition, the insight in question is a form of immediate understanding—here, an immediate understanding of the superiority of one of the alternatives among which a choice must be made. This formulation makes sense, however, only on the assumption that one alternative (the intuitively preferable one) is indeed superior to the others, which in turn presumes that they are comparable after all. But if that is so, then the intuition by means of which the superiority of the preferred alternative is grasped can itself be understood only as an abbreviated process of reasoning, though one that is too speedy and complex to be recast in discursive form. This conclusion, however, denies the premise of our problem: that the alternatives among which one must choose are really (and not merely apparently) incomparable, and that a rational choice among them therefore cannot be made on calculative or other grounds, even ones we grasp by a mental process so swift that it outruns our capacity for reasoned explication.

At this point, those who argue that deliberation leads to and culminates in intuition have two options. They can assert, against the evidence of experience, that there are no groundless personal choices, just the illusory appearance of them, while insisting that some personal choices can be made only by the more accelerated processes of understanding we call intuition. Or, siding with experience, they can acknowledge that we are from time to time confronted with dilemmas of this sort, in which case it is no longer clear what the intuitive resolution of them can be an intuition *of*. The first of these two views begs the question of what it means to deliberate about incomparable goods, and the second offers us no help in answering it. The concept of intuition thus turns out to be, on either view, an unrewarding guide and leaves us where we were before in our inquiry. Let us make a fresh start in a more promising direction.

The banal observation that important personal choices should be made with an understanding of the alternatives—that choices of this sort should be, as it is commonly said, "informed"—provides us with a point of departure. Clearly, one of the advantages of informed decisionmaking is that it increases the chances of identifying the superior alternative, assuming the options under review can in fact be compared and one of them shown to dominate the others according to some common measure of worth. In this obvious sense, informed choice has an instrumental value that justifies the effort to understand the alternatives more fully despite the fact that they seem at first to represent incomparable goods. But even if one's examination of these values confirms their incomparability, many people would, I think, consider the process of informing oneself about them to be worthwhile nonetheless, not just because they believe it rational *ex ante* to have undertaken the inquiry in question, but also because they perceive the deeper understanding it produces to be a good in its own right, an intrinsic good, quite apart from any instrumental benefits it yields. Being well informed about the alternatives among which one must choose is widely assumed to be independently desirable, a state or condition we value for its own sake, whether there is a rational basis for choosing among them or not. To put the point metaphorically, most people believe it is better to choose with one's eyes open rather than shut, even if enlightenment does nothing to alter the depth or intractability of the conflict, indeed even if it strengthens one's conviction that the alternatives are really incomparable after all. That is why arbitrary methods for deciding, like drawing lots, seem so inappropriate in the context of important personal dilemmas. For however economical in time and other resources, methods of this sort necessarily prevent one from achieving the intrinsic good of enlightened self-understanding.

Why we value such understanding for its own sake is a supremely important question that I shall address at some length later on. For the moment, however, I propose simply to follow popular opinion in assuming that informed choice is an intrinsic as well as instrumental good. Making this assumption helps us take a useful first step away from the idea that deliberating about incomparable goods is necessarily a pointless enterprise. But it immediately raises a host of further questions. What kind of understanding is it that such deliberation yields? What is the nature of the process that produces it? And what constitutes good judgment in circumstances of this sort?

To begin to answer these questions, we must examine more closely the role that imagination plays in deliberative inquiry. Every such inquiry employs imagination in some way. A person who is attempting to choose among commensurable goods must use imagination to anticipate the costs and benefits of each alternative. And the person who is deliberating about incomparably different options, of the sort we face at crucial turning points in life, needs imagination too. He needs it to construct a concrete mental image of the choices he might make. For only by exploring in imagination their different implications and effects can he acquire an adequate understanding of what each option means and so choose with open eyes even when the choice itself is groundless.

Of course part of what one is attempting to anticipate in imagination are the causal consequences of the various choices one might make. It is important to know, for example, what resources each alternative requires and how this is likely to affect one's ability to pursue other ends as well. But that is not all one hopes to learn by means of this imaginative exercise. One hopes also to gain some understanding of the alternatives in another sense, to learn something about the experience of actually committing oneself to them. What would it be like for me to see things from the standpoint of the different commitments they represent? The causal consequences of a choice may be traced from a standpoint external to the choice itself. To do so, one need only assume that the choice in question has been made and then track its (hypothetical) consequences in an (imaginary) chain of factual events. But if one wants to know what it is like to make this choice and how the world looks from the perspective of one who has made it, then it is necessary to put oneself imaginatively in the position of the person who has chosen and make an effort to comprehend his or her experience from an internal point of view.

To do this one must mimic in imagination the evaluative outlook of the person whose choice one is attempting to understand, something the tracking of causal consequences does not require. When we are deliberating about a personal choice, the mimicking in question will of course be of our own possible future commitments. The effort to do this, however, resembles the everyday attempts we make to understand the experience of other people, and it resembles, too, the efforts of historians and anthropologists to understand those who are remote from them in time and cultural attitude. In these latter cases it is other people and not ourselves whose experience we are struggling to comprehend. But the person I will become if, at an important juncture in my life, I choose one path rather than another can easily seem, at the moment of choice, something of a stranger too, a person at once familiar and remote in the way that other people are. Thus if I am to understand the experience that the alternatives before me represent and—even if these are only possible futures of my own—to anticipate the way the world looks from the point of view of each, I must often engage in the same imaginative mimicking of commitments that is required to make sense of the experience of other people.

This mimicking demands, first, a certain measure of sympathy or compassion, in the literal sense of "feeling with." As I review the alternatives before me, I must attempt to feel with each of the selves I might become the special cares and commitments, attachments and aversions, that give the life of that possible future self its own distinctive shape. I must strain to feel the force of those internal norms that are the source of whatever appeal that life possesses, and make an effort to see the values associated with it in their most appealing light, which means from the point of view of one actually committed to them. For obvious reasons, this is often difficult to do. Much in the experience of my imaginary future selves—the selves my different choices represent—is likely to remain opaque, so opaque, in many cases, that I fail even to notice how little about them I really understand. And even though a particular alternative is appealing in the abstract, my present desires may run so strongly in another direction that I am unable to arouse any sympathy for the life it represents. Still, even with these qualifications, our powers of sympathy seem most of the time robust enough to carry us at least part way across the distance that separates us from our own future selves, and to permit us to take up their imaginary commitments and concerns in a spirit of fellow-feeling, in the same way that we are able, within limits, to sympathize with the concerns of other people.

The attitude I have in mind, though familiar to us all, is not an easy one to describe. It might best be characterized as an attitude midway between observation, on the one hand, and identification or endorsement, on the other. To sympathize with the values represented by a particular choice is to do more than observe their association with a given way of life, to take note of the fact that those living the life in question typically affirm values of a certain sort. Taking account of this fact may be a first step toward a sympathetic consideration of these values but is not equivalent to it. Only those who have experienced something of the power and appeal of a value and who understand why others are drawn to it even if they themselves ultimately are not, may be said to have sympathetically considered it—to have *entertained* the value rather than merely noted its existence as an anthropological fact.[7] In that sense, we might say, sympathy goes beyond observation and demands more of those who are determined to achieve it.

But if sympathy goes beyond mere observation, it also falls short of outright acceptance. It is possible to entertain a point of view without making it one's own, in the sense of giving the values associated with that point of view one's full endorsement. Indeed, where one person actually adopts the values of another as his own, in the way that parents, friends, and lovers sometimes do, it is no longer accurate to describe his attitude as one of sympathy, for sympathy—which a person may feel even for those whose values he rejects—does not imply the affirmation of another's commitments and concerns that marks most relationships of this kind. Here, it is more appropriate to speak of love than of sympathy. Love implies a measure of identification, a degree of union, that sympathy does not. Indeed, it is the most complete form of union of which human beings are capable. The more two people are united in love, however, the more difficult it becomes for them to pass judgment on each other's character or conduct. Judgments of this sort demand a detachment that love normally rules out. But when an individual is deliberating about an important personal choice, it is essential that he preserve some distance between his present point of view and those of the alternatives before him. For only by refusing to endorse any of these alternatives can he maintain the independence he needs to pass judgment on their merits. Hence if deliberation demands sympathy—an effort to see the alternatives in their most attractive light—it also requires that one abstain from actually affirming the values they represent. The attitude of sympathy for which the process of personal deliberation calls might therefore be described as one of suspended identification, less disinterested than the attitude of the observer but more detached than love.

As this last remark suggests, the sort of imaginative sympathy that deliberation requires combines two opposite-seeming dispositions, that of compassion, on the one hand, and that of detachment, on the other. A person who is faced, let us say, with a difficult choice between two careers must make an effort to see the claims of each in its best light and to feel for himself their power and appeal. At the same time, he must preserve a certain distance or detachment from them. From each imaginative foray into the possible future lives that his choices represent, he must be able to withdraw to the standpoint of decision, the position he occupies at present. At least he must be able to do this if he is genuinely to choose among the alternatives and not merely be swept along by the tide of feeling that any sympathetic identification with a particular way of life—even an imagined one— can arouse. To ensure that he remains sufficiently detached to survey the alternatives from a vantage point different from any of their own internal points of view, it is necessary that he hold something in reserve even while making a maximum effort at sympathetic understanding.

The attitude of sympathy that is needed in deliberation thus has a peculiarly bifocal character. Through one lens the alternatives are seen not merely at close range but (in contrast to the attitude of observation) from within, from the normative and affective points of view that the alternatives themselves afford. Through the other lens, each of the alternatives appears at an equally great distance. Anyone who has worn bifocal lenses knows that it takes time to learn to shift smoothly between perspectives and to combine them in a single field of vision. The same is true of deliberation. It is difficult to be compassionate, and often just as difficult to be detached, but what is most difficult of all is to be both at once. Compassion and detachment pull in opposite directions and we are not always able to combine them, nor is everyone equally good at doing so. It is, however, just this combination of opposing dispositions that deliberation demands and that accounts for the characteristic mix of conflicting affects that are generally associated with it: on the one hand, warm enthusiasm and a certain generosity of feeling, and, on the other, coolness and re-serve, not in alternating sequence but together and at once.

Through this combination of compassion and detachment a person engaged in deliberation comes as close to actually adopting the choices that confront him as the independence required for judgment will allow. In the process he gains an understanding of something that a knowledge of causal consequences, no matter how detailed, can never yield—an understanding of what the experience of making the choices in question would be like were he in fact to make them. We all recognize that there is a distinctive form of understanding that comes only with experience, and that those who lack it do not pos-sess. Even children and lifelong teetotalers, for example, know that the consumption of alcohol has certain causal consequences and is likely to change a person's behavior in predictable ways. Knowledge of this sort presupposes no firsthand familiarity with intoxication. But only someone who has actually been drunk can have an internal un-derstanding of the attitudes, feelings, and perceptual experiences that distinguish drunkenness from sobriety. When someone begins to de-liberate about an important personal decision, one that touches his basic interests and allegiances, he is likely to begin by tracing the causal consequences of each alternative. In most cases, this will be the natural place for him to start, and the discoveries that he makes in the course of this inquiry may importantly clarify his choice. But the knowledge that such an inquiry yields will always resemble a child's knowledge of drunkenness, and can never by itself produce the different kind of understanding that experience alone provides. It is this latter sort of understanding that a person seeks by imagining himself in the position of one already committed to the alternatives before him and by entertaining with a combination of compassion and detachment the values that define their internal points of view.

Of course, the situation of a person deliberating about future possi-bilities to which his own past experience provides only an incomplete guide is very different from that of someone who is trying to antici-pate what it will be like to repeat, in essentially the same form, an experience he has already had—to be drunk again, for example, as he has been in the past. In the first case, a person must anticipate something he has never before experienced, and there is only one way he can do this: through the imaginative elaboration of whatever past experiences seem relevant to his present choice. The point of

this exercise is to create, in imagination, a surrogate for actual experience. To be sure, the imaginative projection of an experience is
bound to seem shadowy and indefinite by comparison with the recollection of a real one. But though it lacks the robustness and detail of
recollection, the anticipation in imagination of an experience that
one has not yet had shares certain qualities in common with it, most
important, that of being lived through, if only vicariously, rather than
observed from an external point of view. We are thus able to acquire
in imagination a knowledge of unexperienced future possibilities that
resembles the knowledge by acquaintance we have of the experiences
in our past, and though an imaginary experience can never be the
full equivalent of a real one, the understanding it produces is marked
by the same interiority that characterizes the special understanding
that only those who have lived through an experience can possess.

THE SPECTER OF REGRET

Some identity-defining choices present us with incomparable alternatives, and deliberating about them often only makes this clearer
than before. Yet even in these special but important cases deliberation
can produce something of value, namely, a deeper quasi-experiential
understanding of the alternatives themselves. To acquire such an understanding one must be able to sustain the conflicting attitudes of
compassion and detachment on which the imaginative anticipation
of future possibilities depends.

The ability to do this should be viewed not merely or perhaps even
mainly as an intellectual feat but as an affective one too, for the attitudes in question are modes of feeling as well as of thought. In deliberating, one seeks to anticipate the experience of making a certain
choice, and this can be done only by reproducing in oneself in a
provisional form the cares and concerns of someone who has already
made it and then by asking what it would be like to live that person's
life. Because these concerns are dispositions and not just cognitive
beliefs, the attempt to reproduce them in imagination demands a certain capacity for affective mimicry, coupled with the ability to keep
the feelings in question at arm's length. The first of these capacities is
what I mean by compassion—a power of generating feelings. And
the second is what I mean by detachment, a power of moderating or
confining feelings instead. Only through the exercise of this second

power can a person limit the feelings his compassion stimulates and ensure that during his deliberations they remain tentative and reversible. Both powers thus belong to the economy of our affective life and serve to regulate its forces, though in different, indeed opposite, ways. The person who deliberates well excels at combining these two powers. His distinction therefore cannot be located within the realm of thought alone. Perhaps we should describe such a person as a virtuoso of feeling instead, for if his imagination enables him to understand more than others do, it is in large part because he feels what they cannot.[8]

This combination of affective powers is not something natural or innate, a set of feelings we are born with that later needs only to be released. In fact, the compassion and detachment required in deliberation both run against the grain of more elementary dispositions and must therefore be learned through a process of education. At the beginning of their lives most human beings love what is close to them—in blood, appearance, and behavior—and take no interest in, or fear, what is remote. Before a person can feel compassion for an attitude unfamiliar to him or imaginatively detach himself from his own present likes and dislikes, these childish attitudes must be overcome.

When a person's dispositions have been successfully educated in this way, the combination of compassion and detachment needed in deliberation will be for him habitual. In deliberating he will adopt the complex stance this combination of feelings implies not just occasionally but as a routine matter and without much conscious thought. This does not mean that the problems about which he deliberates become easier to solve. But it does mean that in deliberating he habitually adopts an attitude that those whose education has been less successful assume irregularly and with great effort, if at all.

A habit is, in general, a repetitive pattern of behavior that requires no conscious attention to sustain. For most automobile drivers, stopping at red lights is a habit in this sense. An affective habit is simply a habit of a special sort—a feeling one experiences, without deliberate effort, in recurrent situations of some kind. Courage is an example of an affective habit. Courageous acts may of course be performed by those who lack this habit, just as drivers who lack the habit of stopping at red lights may stop nonetheless, though doing so presumably requires greater concentration on their part. But those who possess the habit of courage can be counted on to act in a more reliably courageous way than those who do not. It is therefore only they whom we describe as courageous persons. The combination of affective dispositions that deliberation requires is similar in both respects. Only those who possess these dispositions as stable features of their personality are likely to deliberate well, not just on occasion but consistently in different settings. And only they may be said to be practically wise.[9]

Courage and cowardice are what we call traits of character, a term we use to describe certain peculiarly important habits of feeling. It is not entirely clear where we are to draw the line between those habitual modes of feeling that should be classified as traits of character and the many others that should not. In different cultures, moreover, the line is drawn in different ways (though the amount of disagreement in this regard is often overstated).[10] But though there is no list of necessary and sufficient conditions for distinguishing this subset of affective habits from the rest, the distinction remains an important one. For it represents, in every culture, an implicit answer to the question of what it is about a person that gives him or her a core identity distinct from that of others. If a disposition is too trivial, or widely shared, it is unlikely to be viewed as a constituent of personal identity and classified as a trait of character. Thus we regard courage, for example, as a trait of character because the possession or lack of it so deeply shapes our perception of who a person is, but we do not normally consider his love of brandy (a trivial habit) or fear of death (a universal one) similarly revealing. Seen in this light, it seems obvious that the affective habits of sympathy and detachment one needs to deliberate well should be classified as traits of character too. For their presence or absence in a person also importantly influences our understanding of who that person is, in the same basic way that courage and cowardice do.

The men and women who possess these traits have enlarged imaginative powers. They have wider access to the realm of surrogate experience that imagination offers and are therefore likely to be better informed about the identity-defining choices they must make—something I have assumed to be valuable in its own right even when there are no rational grounds on which a decision may be based. But is this assumption warranted? When deliberation enables me to see that one of my alternatives does indeed dominate the rest, contrary to what I originally thought, the value of deliberating is obvious and indisputable. But if the insight it affords is an intrinsic and not merely instrumental good, then deliberation must have value even when it fails to produce a resolution of this sort. Many people believe that it does. But what is the basis of their belief and is it in fact well founded? I have put off this question for some time and now must try to answer it.

The answer I shall give combines ideas drawn from Greek philosophy, psychoanalytic theory, and the modern tradition of thought called existentialism. Combining, as it does, elements of such diversity, it is unlikely to appeal to those who subscribe more single-mindedly to any of the traditions on which it freely draws. But none of these is sufficient by itself to answer the question I have put—or, more exactly, to answer it in a way that modern men and women can accept—and the eclecticism of my own answer is a reflection of this fact.

My starting point is an observation about the nature of personal choice that I think no one will dispute. Some choices are unavoidable, including some among incomparable goods or values. This is particularly true of the choices that a person faces in moments of self-definition, on those occasions when he must decide which of his interests and attachments are to be the focal ones in his life generally. Often the decisions a person must make on such occasions will be groundless in the sense I have indicated. There will be no common criterion of choice he can apply to make the decision in a way that does not seem to him to beg the most important question that it poses. But this does not mean the decision itself can be avoided. A person with even minimally complex interests cannot have everything he wants, and is also likely to find that certain of the things he wants in life are incompatible with others. That is so not just because any given human being lacks the time and other resources to pursue all the projects he might wish, but also, and more important, because the pursuit of certain projects, the endorsement of certain interests and attachments and the way of life associated with them, frequently means that competing projects cannot also be pursued without jeopardizing the coherence of the life he has endorsed. When this is true, as it must often be, a person will be forced to let go of some things that he cares about for the sake of others. He must do this if his life is to have the coherence it requires to be a life at all. In order to live

a life that has coherence—to live and not merely to exist—it is therefore necessary, for all but a lucky or gifted few, to narrow one's focus
by endorsing certain values and relationships and putting others aside.
Up to a point, the narrowness of our lives is simply the price we pay
for their intelligibility.

When the interests and attachments that a person is forced to put
aside are important to him, however, he is likely to experience their
abandonment or suppression as a loss, and in the most extreme cases
as a kind of amputation in which some valued part of himself is sacrificed so that other parts may grow. The attachments that must be let
go, moreover, do not simply disappear. They tend, instead, to survive
in the secondary and unconscious forms that psychoanalysis has made
familiar, and they continue to enjoy a shadowy sort of existence as
reminders of what one's life might have been had one chosen differently at certain critical moments.

"[I]n mental life," Freud writes, "nothing which has once been
formed can perish," and to make this idea vivid he compares the
mind to an ancient city whose earlier phases of development are still
preserved within it and that remain visible, to a discerning eye, in all
their original vitality.[11] Adopting Freud's image, we might describe
the projects that a person has had to leave behind in order to achieve
a life with some measure of coherence as neighborhoods in the city
of his soul that, having been abandoned, no longer participate in the
business of the city itself, and though still standing, are now excluded
from its ruling councils. How ought we to understand the relationship that exists between these now-abandoned precincts and those
that are at present in possession of the soul's command?

Plato, who also compared the human soul to a city, suggests one
answer.[12] A soul, he says, has different parts with different and conflicting interests in the same way that a city does. But if all these parts
or factions share equally in the rule of a person's soul, that soul is
bound, he claims, to lack even a minimum of order. One part must
be given a controlling voice in the soul's affairs and be allowed to set
its course. It is a matter of supreme importance, however, which part
is assigned this leading role. On Plato's view there is only one proper
scheme of subordination in which the different parts of the soul can
be arranged, so that a soul in which the wrong part leads must, he
insists, be as disorderly as one in which no part leads at all. Only if
each part of a person's soul acknowledges its proper place in relation

to the others and accepts the role associated with its station in the one immutably correct hierarchy of parts or powers will that soul exhibit, Plato says, the unity appropriate to it.

This conclusion, which assumes the possibility of ranking all a person's interests in a single comprehensive scheme, will not be acceptable, however, to anyone who believes that different interests, and the programs of living associated with them, can present the person whose interests they are with the need to make a choice among incommensurable values. Those who believe this to be true will agree with Plato that in the city of the soul the responsibilities of government cannot be shared by all. But they will reject the idea, to which he and other Greek writers were committed, that there is an authoritative order for determining the proper relations of leadership and deference among the soul's different parts.

If the interests and attachments that a person has been required to give up do not simply disappear, however, and if their subordination to other concerns cannot be justified on the Platonic grounds that they are by nature less well qualified to lead the person's soul, their continued existence as reminders of what might have been will constitute an ongoing challenge to the life he has chosen and a threat to his confidence in having chosen well. The more vitality these abandoned interests retain, the more easily they can suggest that one has mismanaged the business of living by making bad choices or unnecessary ones. The feeling that I have done so is the feeling of regret, the feeling (to borrow a phrase of Aristotle's) that I have failed to be a friend to myself.[13] Where this feeling takes hold, and becomes habitual, it has the power to damage or destroy a person's soul.

If we continue to think of the soul as a kind of city, we might describe the condition of regret, which divides a person against himself, as one of civil war. This is of course only a metaphor, but it does express the most distinctive feature of a common if complex experience. The many attempts that have been made since antiquity to describe this very human experience have generally depicted the conflict in question as a conflict between the different parts of a person's soul, one part being associated with his dominant and more self-conscious interests and the other with whatever competing attachments he has abandoned or suppressed. The study of this conflict has in our century become the subject of a separate discipline, and I think it fair to say that we now understand more fully than ever before the processes by which it is initiated and sustained. But the basic idea on which the discipline of psychoanalysis is founded—the idea that the human soul is marked by certain potentially disabling divisions within itself—is an old one, as is the image of civil war that many writers, ancient and modern, have used to convey it.

Aristotle, for example, describes regret as a symptom of the soul's unhappy division against itself, and Plato compares such a soul to a disorderly community, observing that just as the internal division of a city must lead to its disintegration, so too the kind of division in a soul that is evidenced by feelings of regret must eventually result in its destruction as well, in the diminishment of the soul's capacity for thought and action and, in extreme cases, in the limiting form of confusion we call madness.[14] Like most Greeks, Plato identifies the being of a thing—of an animal, a person, or even an institution like a city—with its well-being, and its well-being, in turn, with a certain hierarchical and harmonic order among its parts. To be disorderly is, on this characteristically Greek view, simply not to be at all. Thus a city that is divided by factional disputes must at some point, according to Plato, lose its identity as a city and become instead a mere collection of individuals. And a person whose soul is similarly divided must eventually lose his personality, the distinctive unity that makes him more than just a collection of parts. If we view regret, in the way that Aristotle did, as a symptom of the soul's division against itself, then we may say that on the Greek view (to which both he and Plato subscribed) this feeling represents a loss of being from the soul's own point of view. For the more a soul is compromised by regret, the more, on this view, it is in danger of disintegrating, of ceasing to be what it is and becoming something else instead.

This way of describing the meaning of regret has an archaic sound. But something quite like it is implied by the psychoanalytic theory of neurosis, the name we now most often give to the phenomenon of regret. The neurotic's soul is confined by its illness to a narrower existence than it need be, and though therapy cannot make a person happy (in that respect Freud's views are notably un-Aristotelian) it can help him to a larger life that takes in more of what Freud famously called the ordinary unhappiness of living.[15] The more powerful and persistent its neuroses, the more energy a soul is likely to expend in self-destructive ways that cramp its range of action and experience and lead to a diminished existence that at the limit of psychosis tends toward the dissolution or disappearance of the soul itself. For a person to be all that he is capable of being, his powers of love and creativity must be reclaimed from the dissipating demands of his neuroses. In that sense we might say that psychoanalysis views the struggle against neurosis in the same way that the Greeks conceived the effort to avoid division in the soul, as a struggle for reality itself.[16]

To accept this idea is to acknowledge that regret is a great evil and to see the capacity to resist regret, or to overcome it, as an equally great good. But how exactly is a person to avoid the feelings of regret that once important but now abandoned interests and attachments can provoke? These do not, as I have said, just disappear. They survive as reminders of the choices one has made, of the path by which a person has come to have the life he does and the paths he has not taken, and at moments, especially, of doubt and disappointment, these reminders assault our confidence and rebuke us for decisions that become less and less reversible the longer we live. That, we might say, is the retribution they exact for our earlier abandonment of them, and the more a person feels the force of their rebuke, the more likely his soul is to be in that condition of divided allegiances that Plato analogizes to a civil war.

Of course, if one believes, as Plato did, that there is a single proper way of ordering the different interests that a human soul can have, a person will have reason to regret the choices he has made only in case he has improperly arranged his life by giving certain base interests a priority over those that are by nature superior to them. The mere fact that his plans are upset by some unanticipated turn of events will not cause such a person to feel regret, for as long as he has chosen rightly, he has no reason to concede that he has failed to be a friend to himself, the best friend that he might. If a person accepts this Platonic view of the soul and its competing interests, it is obvious what strategy he will adopt to avoid the evil of regret. He will attempt to identify the uniquely appropriate hierarchy in which all human interests can be fitted, and then make whatever choices that hierarchy commands.

But however appealing, this strategy is unavailable to anyone who takes the idea of incommensurability seriously. One who does—recognizing that many of his most important choices cannot be justified on the grounds they were *ex ante* the objectively correct ones—may be tempted to adopt another and very different strategy for the avoidance of regret, the strategy of forgetting.[17] If the choices that a person made at decisive moments in his life were groundless choices, if there was and is no common standard for weighing the alternatives they presented, then it may seem that the best (indeed the only) way of avoiding the regret to which such choices expose one is to forget they were ever made. And the only way of doing that is to forget that one was ever interested in or attached to anything other than what one now is. Forgetfulness is not something that just happens to us. Within limits, we are able to cause ourselves to forget, and a person can actively apply this uniquely human power (one of our most amazing and contradictory capacities) to his own past interests and attachments. The person who is able to do this with success may still remember, in an abstract way, that he had such interests in the past, yet be utterly unable to recall—in the sense of imaginatively reliving—any of the feelings or attitudes that gave those interests their appeal in the first place. To that extent they will be for him dead letters, and no more capable of arousing regret than the projects of other people in which he takes no interest himself.

Through a strategy of forgetfulness, therefore, a person can deprive his own past of the power to shake his confidence that the life he is now living is the only one he has ever really entertained. But this strategy for combatting regret—though not (unlike the Platonic one) incompatible with an acknowledgment of the fact that important personal choices are often choices among incommensurable goods—has two serious shortcomings.

The first is that it frequently does not succeed, and indeed often has the opposite effect from its intended one. For as Freud has helped us understand, the mechanisms of repression actually work in many cases to increase the vitality and influence of the past rather than reduce it. A second shortcoming is the enormous price that the strategy of forgetfulness exacts even when it succeeds. The person who has managed to forget what he once saw in a certain activity or way of life, or in some other person to whom he was attached, may have a soul that is better protected against the destructive power of regret, but it will also be one that is smaller and simpler than if he retained some feeling for the abandoned interests of his past. From a Greek point of view, perhaps, such simplicity should be regarded as a virtue, but in the existential and psychoanalytic traditions that have so deeply shaped our understanding of the meaning of personal fulfillment, the simplification that forgetfulness produces represents a loss of the very thing that defines the human soul and gives meaning to its experiences—the soul's own contradictoriness. To lose one's sense of this is on either view to become less human, though perhaps more comfortable or calm, and no modern person who shares the view of the soul to which these otherwise very different movements subscribe will be inclined to think the tradeoff a desirable one.

A person experiences regret, Aristotle tells us, when he fails to be a friend to himself. But if we reject the Platonic assumption of an objectively determinable hierarchy of interests or concerns, and with that the idea that the soul's friendship toward itself consists in a certain harmonious ordering of parts, and if we also refuse to sacrifice an honest awareness of the soul's contradictory ambitions merely for the sake of inward peace, as the strategy of forgetfulness invites us to, how are we to conceive the friendship of which Aristotle speaks? The best answer, I believe, is that such friendship consists in the backward-looking counterpart of the attitude of constrained compassion on which I have already placed so much importance in my account of deliberation.

Deliberation is concerned with choice, and therefore with the future, with what shall be or not be, depending on the choice a person makes. I have said that to deliberate well, one must do more than just survey the alternatives under consideration from an external point of view. One must also make an effort to enter, with appreciative feeling, into the different points of view they represent, while at the same time retaining an attitude of detached neutrality toward them. If a person is to avoid the self-condemnation of regret, he needs to adopt this same combination of attitudes, or something very much like it, retrospectively toward the choices he has made, choices that now belong not to his future but to his past and that are therefore always beyond recall and often beyond reversal or even significant change.

If a person is to remain on friendly terms with himself despite the fact that he has had to make a groundless choice among his interests and ambitions and been forced to abandon some for the sake of others, it is essential that he be able to see those he has put aside in their best light and to imaginatively reexperience something of their original appeal, without pretending that their distinctiveness is less

deep than he once thought or that they can, after all, be assimilated
to the life he has chosen for himself. For a person not to depreciate
the projects he has sacrificed requires an immense effort of self-
directed sympathy. But at the same time, to acknowledge honestly
that they are incompatible with those he has affirmed requires a detachment toward his past that is the analogue of the attitude he needs
in deliberating about his future and the choices it presents.

The person who is able to view his past choices—especially those
that have most fatefully defined his core identity—with a combination of compassion and detachment stands a better chance of being
able to endure his past without either a self-imposed forgetfulness or
a false optimism regarding the harmony of his soul's desires. The past
may be repressed or made harmoniously consistent with the present,
but in either case the picture of his soul that a person constructs for
himself will be simpler than the soul he actually has. It will be a work
of self-deception. And, if these two strategies both fail, the abandoned interests of his past will rise up, like a rebellious faction in a
crowded city, and demand retribution for the groundless harm that
has been done them: a state of internal civil war, tending toward the
dissolution of the soul itself. For a person to stand a reasonable chance
of avoiding both these evils—self-deception on the one hand, and
self-destruction on the other—what he needs is compassion for all
the lost causes in his soul, together with a clear-eyed acceptance of
their loss, of its magnitude and permanence. This is the same combination of attitudes that, in the forward-looking context of deliberation, constitutes the character trait of practical wisdom. What I am
now suggesting is that those who can combine these attitudes in the
view they take of their own past will be better prepared than those
who cannot to live, as Aristotle says, on friendly terms with themselves, without pretending to more harmony or simplicity of soul
than they can in reality achieve.

The Greeks believed the integrity of the human soul to be a function of the harmonious arrangement of its parts, and viewed its loss
of harmony as a loss of the soul's being or reality. Anyone who accepts
the modern idea that human beings must sometimes choose among
incommensurable goods can aspire only to a more limited and vulnerable sort of integrity, the kind that comes from being a friend to
oneself in the sense I have suggested, through a detached compassion
for the abandoned interests and ambitions of the past. This is indeed

a more limited form of integrity, but it is the only one in which we can in good conscience still believe, and despite its limitations it remains, for us, a value of supreme importance within the sphere of personal life. Without it, we are in danger of being undone by the past, and a lack of integrity, even in the weaker sense in which that concept must now be understood, can deprive a person's life of much of its vitality and relish, however groundless the choices that have shaped it.

That is why we can continue to appreciate the value of integrity without assuming, as Plato and Aristotle did, that the different concerns to which a person may reasonably devote himself can be rank-ordered in a hierarchy of objective worth. A person may achieve, or fail to achieve, the kind of integrity I have described in a life devoted to any of a number of different ends, and merely knowing what sort of life he has chosen cannot by itself tell us whether he possesses the quality of integrity as well. In that sense, integrity is a characteristic that is independent of the specific projects a person chooses to pursue (as it must be if we assume that the most important choices in our lives are often choices among incommensurable goods). That, of course, is a decidedly un-Greek view, and those who adopt it must reject Plato's portrait of the soul and his attribution of the soul's integrity to the harmonious arrangement of its parts. But they can still accept Plato's more general claim that for a soul to lose its integrity is for it literally to dissolve, to move from being toward nothingness, and on the basis of this general claim to affirm the value of integrity, while continuing to insist that what gives the most important personal decisions their special *pathos* is the incommensurable worth of the different and equally respectable concerns among which we are all, from time to time, compelled to choose.[18]

If we ask, then, what it means for a person who must choose among incommensurable goods to live well, we cannot answer, with the Greeks, that it means to live in accordance with the truth, for if the goods in question are really incommensurable, the truth cannot adjudicate between them or provide the sort of guidance this answer presupposes. For us, living well can only mean living without regret or self-deception in the full light of our predicament. This is a central theme, of course, in the literature of existentialism. But contrary to what some existentialists suggest, it takes more than an act of will to achieve such an attitude and sustain it over time. It also takes a special sort of strength, for only those who can withstand the terrible temptation to forget have any chance of avoiding both dishonesty and regret in their dealings with themselves. Where does such strength come from and in what does it consist?

By characterizing the attitude that is needed to combat regret as the backward-looking counterpart of the one required in deliberation, I have, in effect, already answered this question. For if these two attitudes are the same, then it is reasonable to think that those who are in the habit of deliberating about the future with a combination of compassion and detachment will just for that reason be more likely than those who are not to conceive the past, with its lost loves and abandoned dreams, in a similar spirit too. In deliberation, which is essentially prospective, the combination of these two dispositions produces foresight, the capacity to see ahead, to anticipate in imagination the consequences and actual experience of following each of the different pathways that one might choose. The same combination, when directed toward the past, produces the power of remembrance. By remembrance I mean something more than mere recollection, the autobiographical knowledge that at a certain point in my life I made a choice that decisively shaped its subsequent course. I mean, rather, the power of sympathetic recall, the ability even now, looking back at the past, to appreciate what the projects I have abandoned once meant to me, to entertain them in the same sense that I entertain my future possibilities when I deliberate, without pretending they can be recovered or belittling the magnitude of their loss. Foresight and remembrance, so conceived, are the same power, deployed in different directions.

If we ask who are most likely to possess the strength to face their past with cheerful honesty, the answer therefore must be, those who possess the power of foresight. For it is they who are most likely to view their past, as well as their future, with the combination of compassion and detachment that one needs to avoid the disintegrative influence of regret. We call those who show foresight in deliberation practically wise. What I am now suggesting is that it is the practically wise who also have the greatest chance of achieving the limited but important kind of integrity that represents the greatest good a soul can hope to have once the Greek confidence in its harmony is lost.

Practical wisdom is thus both a procedural and a substantive virtue. Viewed procedurally, it is a method or technique for deliberating whose exercise is consistent with different outcomes, at least when the alternatives among which one must choose cannot be assessed within some common framework of value. But the contrasting dispositions that constitute the core of practical wisdom are also the ones a person needs if he is to live in friendship with himself after whatever choice he makes, and this self-directed friendship, which I call integrity, is a substantive good of general value: a good that everyone wants whatever else he wants, and that is compatible with a broad diversity of different ways of life.

If practical wisdom had value for a person only as a method for discovering which of the alternatives before him is the best—the alternative that scores the highest according to some common criterion of merit—it would be difficult to see what value it could have where "best" makes no sense because the alternatives are incommensurable. But the deeper understanding of his own interests and attachments to which a practically wise person comes as a result of his deliberations has value in its own right, quite apart from whether it shows him the way to a solution. For if it survives the moment of choice itself, this initially prospective understanding of what he might yet be becomes a retrospective understanding of what he might have been and in that form represents his best defense against the evil of regret. Thus even where deliberation fails to uncover a common standard for evaluating the alternatives among which one must choose but instead confirms their incommensurability and hence the groundlessness of whatever choice one makes, the exercise of the affective powers on which deliberation calls and the achievement of the deeper self-knowledge they produce have intrinsic worth, since it is on the development of these powers and the possession of this knowledge that the good of integrity depends. That, ultimately, is what explains the belief—which remains widespread despite our loss of confidence in the rational arbitrability of many of the soul's inner conflicts—that being well informed about a choice is something good in itself and not just when it points to the right result. And it is what explains our admiration for those who excel at deliberation in the sphere of personal choice, for this attitude reflects our sense that the possession of practical wisdom is a human good of more than instrumental worth.

COMMUNITY AND COMPROMISE

I began this chapter by describing statesmanship as a kind of skill or excellence at making judgments about the public good. But in the most divisive political debates—those that touch on questions of communal identity—it is difficult to say what this excellence is, for there is often no common ground on which an answer to these questions can be based. It is here that the need for statesmanship is most intense. But it is also here that the statesman's virtue is hardest to define.

Confronted with this dilemma, I turned away from the sphere of politics to that of private life and asked what it means to show good judgment in deliberating about the problems of personal self-definition that occupy us in the latter sphere. I described this strategy as the reverse of Socrates' but emphasized that mine, like his, also presupposes that these two realms are sufficiently alike to justify using an account of one as a guide to the structure and aims of the other. To say that personal and political deliberation are analogous is not to claim they are the same, nor is it to suggest that those who excel at one must excel at the other too. But it is to assert that they bear a certain structural resemblance to each other and are to that extent homologous. Having completed my account of personal deliberation, I can now return to my main topic—to the statesman and his political concerns—and explain the resemblance or homology I have in mind.

In personal deliberation one is always asking, "What is *my* good? What ought *my* ends to be?" and even if a person concludes that his own good can be achieved only through participation in some common enterprise with others, the focal point of every such inquiry is a concern on the part of the person deliberating for his or her own happiness or well-being. The focus of political deliberation is different. Here the guiding concern is for the preservation or improvement of some collective enterprise. In whatever setting it occurs, political deliberation always aims at the good of a community and not the separate good of the person deliberating. It is this fundamental difference of outlook that distinguishes personal from political deliberation, and that justifies our speaking of them, metaphorically, as two separate realms of thought.

But though the processes of personal and political deliberation address different questions and are motivated by different concerns, there are certain important structural similarities between them. The first is one I have already mentioned, and which now needs only to be restated in a more explicit form. In the political sphere, as in the personal, there are some choices that have what I call identity-defining consequences. To varying degrees, such choices define the community that makes them in the same way that some personal choices define the individual who does. When a question arises as to what the ends of a community should be, different participants are likely to give different answers, each representing a different interpretation of the aims or purposes of the community itself, of the objectives to which the community should be devoted, and of the institutional arrangements needed to attain them. Sometimes these differing conceptions, though apparently in conflict, can be integrated into a single comprehensive view that is acceptable to all. And sometimes the need to choose one can be postponed or otherwise avoided. But sometimes it is impossible to harmonize the alternatives or to evade a choice among them. In such cases, the choice of one alternative necessarily implies the subordination or abandonment of certain values for the sake of others, just as it does in the realm of personal deliberation. It implies—to put the point more positively—the endorsement of a particular conception of what the community is for, an act of self-definition that gives the life of the community a clearer focus by ascribing certain values to it and ruling others out. Communities, like persons, have careers, but also like persons, they cannot have all the careers they might want. There are thus bound to be moments in the lives of most communities, as there are in the lives of most persons, when a choice must be made whose upshot will be to turn the community in one direction rather than another, sometimes irreversibly. Political choices of this kind amount to a choice of communal identity and are the analogue of those personal choices that give the lives of individuals their distinctive shape.

The alternatives among which a community must choose at such moments, moreover, are often incommensurable, as at analogous moments of personal choice. For there may be no common metric by which the value of competing views can be established, no agreed-upon considerations of timing or fit to settle the dispute, no self-evident hierarchy of value in which the positions of the parties can be objectively fixed—hence no rationally determinable answer to the question of which view ought to prevail when only one can be endorsed. At any given moment in the history of a particular community, there will of course be certain opinions whose correctness all, or nearly all, its members take for granted and that they tend to speak of and appeal to as objective truths. I say "of course" because without any such agreement in opinion there can be no community at all. Today, for example, most Americans regard the institution of slavery as an objective evil and think it inconsistent with the truth, both physical and moral, about human beings. But by the same token, those controversies that happen at any moment to be the most lively and important ones in a community—those with the largest implications for its direction and destiny—often present conflicts among values that reflect incomparable visions of what is most worthy in the community's current practices or future possibilities, and though the advocates of different positions in these debates sometimes claim for their favored values the status of demonstrable truths, there is often no common framework within which the competing communal identities associated with them can be compared. In contemporary America, for example, it is just such an incomparability of ultimate values that characterizes the debate between those who think abortion essential to the liberty of the fetus-carrying mother and their opponents who view it as a form of murder; those who consider capital punishment a sad though justified necessity and the abolitionists who believe it morally intolerable under any circumstances; those who see our few remaining ancient forests as sacred groves and those who view them as an economic resource with stumpage value only. These are the sorts of identity-defining issues that today divide the American people, and the questions they present arise from conflicts among values as incommensurable as those that individuals face in their personal lives when trying to decide, for example, which of two occupations to pursue or how to divide their energies between home and work.

What does it mean to resolve such conflicts in a statesmanlike way? At this point some may be tempted to answer that profound disagreements like these can be settled only through compromise, and that statesmanship is simply the art of finding compromises on which the parties can agree. This is a popular and plausible view that has the advantage of not requiring us to assume that the values the statesman compromises are commensurable. The concept of compromise might seem, therefore, to be just what my account of statesmanship needs to overcome the obstacle that blocked it earlier and to which we have returned. But this is not the case, as a closer examination of the concept itself makes clear.

A compromise of any kind is in essence an exchange. Someone

with a talent for discovering potential compromises, political or otherwise, might therefore be described as a kind of entrepreneur who possesses the ability to exploit previously unnoticed opportunities for trade. If we think of a particular community merely as the means by which its members' antecedent interests may be satisfied, it is easy to see how such opportunities might arise and everyone involved be made better off by taking advantage of them, even if the interests motivating different members to participate are not only conflicting but incommensurable. Politics, so conceived, is just a specialized form of economic exchange and its problems the sort that arise among trading partners everywhere.[19] Two people may obviously find it advantageous to transact even though they are motivated to do so by incommensurable interests or ambitions, and generally speaking, each will have to make certain concessions to the other to obtain a contribution in return. Both, in other words, will have to compromise, to give up something of value, to obtain the benefits of the exchange, and the fact that they view these benefits from radically different standpoints does not alter the situation in the least. To the extent we think of politics in economic terms, as an instrument for the pursuit of the participants' preexisting interests, it is obvious that compromise will play as important a role in its processes as in those of every other branch of economic life, and that here too those who can identify opportunities for mutually advantageous compromise will be performing a valuable service even on the assumption that there is no standard or criterion by which the different interests of the participants may be meaningfully compared.

Not all political differences can be so easily compromised, however. Unlike most market transactions—in which the parties simply take their different interests for granted and, without confronting these differences directly, attempt to work out an arrangement that will be satisfactory from everyone's point of view—many political negotiations center on the question of what the parties' interests and values ought to be, and thus raise problems of a kind that generally remain submerged in the struggles of economic life (and in politics, to the extent we view it merely as a branch of economics). In negotiations of this sort, the participants confront a question of ends that the parties to most economic transactions do not face, and it is unclear what role, if any, compromise can play in their attempt to answer it.

The different views of those involved may sometimes, of course, prove to be compatible after all, so that no compromise is needed. And it may also sometimes turn out that one faction thinks important what another regards as trivial, and vice versa, making it possible for the parties to accommodate their conflicting claims through a system of reciprocal indifferences that can itself be viewed as a kind of trade. Where there is any reasonable chance that a solution of this sort exists, it is obviously sensible first to determine whether it does before concluding that the different conceptions of their community's aims and values that set the disputants apart cannot be harmonized or compromised. But there is no guarantee that such a solution exists, and whenever the views in question are not only different but defined in opposition to each other, so that neither can be affirmed without repudiating the other, compromise will be impossible. Here, if one side is to prevail, the other must adopt its opponent's point of view, or at least abandon its own, in contrast to most economic transactions, which require nothing of the kind. Many political controversies, particularly those in which the identity of the community is at stake, have this character. Disputes of this sort are zero-sum games in which there is no room for compromise. To say that a person shows statesmanship in such situations by discovering hidden grounds for compromise is therefore true only in the sense that it is always sensible to look for compromises before concluding that none exist. This common view of statesmanship ignores the fact, however, that some political disputes, including many of the most important ones, are contests in which the gains and losses of the parties are symmetrical. Here there are no opportunities for the sort of mutually advantageous trade that every compromise at bottom represents. But if statesmanship cannot be defined, in cases of this sort, as the art of compromise, how should we understand it?

My answer is that statesmanship can best be understood, in the important class of controversies on which I am now focusing, not as the art of producing compromise but as the ability to help secure a condition I shall call political fraternity instead. Political fraternity is to communities what integrity is to individuals. It is what gives them their unity and preserves them from disintegration. A community without political fraternity is no longer a community at all. It is merely a collection of parts, in the same way that a soul without integrity is just a set of parts with no separate reality of its own. Political fraternity thus represents for communities the same sort of good that integrity does for individuals: the good of existence itself. What I am now suggesting is that we think of the statesman's excellence of judgment—at least in those important cases where the identity of his or her community is at stake—not as an ability to determine what is right (for there may be no neutral standpoint from which the alternatives can be assessed) or to discover opportunities for compromise (since none may exist), but rather as an ability to advance more reliably than others the good of political fraternity. Integrity is a basic good in the realm of personal life, and the men and women whose deliberative habits make them more likely to achieve it are those we call practically wise in matters of personal choice. My claim is that something like this is true in the domain of politics as well. That is the heart of the analogy I wish to draw between personal and political deliberation, and the key to understanding the meaning of practical wisdom in public life.

POLITICAL FRATERNITY

The condition of political fraternity is one in which the members of a community are joined by bonds of sympathy despite the differences of opinion that set them apart on questions concerning the ends, and hence the identity, of their community. The special character of this condition, and the distinctive kind of order it represents, can best be thought of as one standing midway between two others, the first of which is marked by more cohesion than the condition of political fraternity and the second by considerably less.

On the one hand, political fraternity is not to be confused with the unanimity of sentiment and belief that characterizes the most tightly knit human communities (those, for example, that are formed by certain households and religious sects). The members of such communities identify with one another as completely as it is possible for separate human beings to do. They see the values and objectives of their enterprise in the same light, and because of this their communities possess a measure of cohesion that no association whose members view its ends in different ways can match. The attitude of sympathy on which the condition of political fraternity depends does not require the members of a community to identify with one another in this strong sense. Indeed, its existence is compatible with their recognition of deep disagreements regarding the aims of their community and their acceptance of the fact that such disagreements may never disappear. Though a state of political fraternity may be said to exist only where the members of a community are bound to one another by sympathetic fellow-feeling, the sympathy it demands is therefore necessarily less complete than the coincidence of attitude and affect on which the most perfect forms of human union rest.

On the other hand, political fraternity must also be distinguished from mere tolerance as that latter term is now generally understood. Tolerance is the virtue of noninterference. The tolerant are those who believe it wrong to interfere with the legally or conventionally protected activities of others. But this belief, and the commitment to act upon it, presupposes no sympathy for the activities one tolerantly permits. Indeed, as liberal theorists in particular have pointed out, the nature of tolerance and the need for it are clearest in those situations where the members of a community not only feel no sympathy for one another's projects, but view them with outrage and disgust.[20] When its members are divided on matters of great political importance and are incapable of feeling any sympathy for one another's views, a community can survive only by adopting the essentially negative principle of toleration. But the condition of political fraternity, where it exists, entails something more than this. Political fraternity of course implies a commitment to noninterference, in the way that any regime of toleration does, but beyond that it also entails a willingness to entertain the views of others, to make the positive effort that is required to see their values in the best possible light, the light in which they appear to their own defenders, even when one rejects these values and the political consequences flowing from them. Tolerance by itself requires no effort of this sort. Thus if the fellow-feeling that political fraternity demands is weak by comparison with the more complete forms of union that some communities display, if it is compatible with the existence of differences these communities rule out, it also goes beyond anything required by the principle of toleration, whose great appeal is sometimes said to be that it demands no sympathy at all but is consistent with indifference and even contempt. It is in this sense that the condition of political fraternity may aptly be described as an intermediate between extremes.

Where political fraternity is missing, the members of a community are likely to have more difficulty understanding the point of their opponents' concerns and the significance, for them, of political defeat. They will be more likely to discount the importance of resentment and will make fewer efforts to avoid it through conciliatory gestures of their own. Winners will gloat and losers sulk, envious of their adversaries' good fortune. Injured beyond their actual loss by the feeling that values important to them have been treated unsympathetically, the partisans of defeated causes will be forever on the lookout for opportunities to turn the tables and do to their opponents what has been done to them. By contrast, in communities where political fraternity exists, though sharp conflict cannot always be avoided or a fateful choice among alternatives postponed, such feelings of envy and resentment are less likely to take root. The inevitable pain of losing will be tempered by a sense on the part of those who have lost that their claims have been treated with generosity, and by a willingness on the part of those who have won to make real and symbolic concessions to preserve this climate of good will, though strictly speaking such concessions are unnecessary. In this respect, a community that possesses political fraternity will be importantly different from one that lacks it, despite any outward similarity in their stated values and aims.

The value of political fraternity (a condition of communities) may thus be compared to that of personal integrity (a condition of individual souls). Personal integrity is not the absence of internal conflict, nor is it the kind of harmonic ordering of higher and lower parts that Plato envisions in the *Republic*. It is the condition of wholeness that results when the parts of a person's soul are, in Aristotle's phrase, on amicable terms, when one's present attachments are not at war with past ones, or engaged in a subtler contest of repression and revenge, despite the irreconcilable differences that set them apart. Integrity is a good because it holds the soul together, against the centrifuge of regret, in the only way that ordinarily complex souls can hope for, absent a degree of psychic harmony to which no honest person can in good faith still aspire.

Political fraternity is a good of a similar sort. In all but the simplest communities, disagreements are bound to arise concerning its aims and ambitions, and how such disagreements are resolved is often decisive for the community's identity. Disagreements of this sort put great strain on a community. Like powerful conflicts within a person's soul, they exert a centrifugal force that threatens to pull the community apart and destroy its unity. By establishing bonds of fellow-feeling among its members—bonds based upon their willingness to sympathize with each other's interests and concerns—political fraternity helps to counteract the destructive force let loose in these identity-defining moments. It thus works to preserve communities against disintegration, just as personal integrity preserves the souls of individuals through an analogous, though self-directed, form of friendship.[21]

There are other reasons, of course, why communities survive. The members of a community may, for example, share a set of convictions so complete that destructive differences of opinion never arise. Or they may be bound to one another by a system of material dependencies so broad and strong that political disagreements, however deep, can safely be ignored. But these conditions are rarely satisfied. In most communities, political controversy is inevitable and, on occasion at least, likely to test even the strongest material ties. In these banal circumstances, political fraternity offers the best, perhaps the only, hope of survival for communities. Tolerance, unaccompanied by the spirit of sympathetic fellow-feeling that distinguishes the condition of political fraternity, is not enough. Where this spirit is missing, a regime of toleration can be sustained only by self-interest, by the belief that tolerance of others serves one's own advantage, in the long run if not the short. But any regime of this sort is vulnerable both to the advantage-taking of winners (who may conclude that the principle of toleration no longer serves their interest) and to the resentful defection of losers (who will always have grounds for viewing this principle as a fraudulent pretense designed to legitimate their oppression). If the principle of toleration is to possess any real strength and staying power, it must be founded upon something more than mere self-interest, and where it is not, it is likely to degenerate into a brittle formality with little power to unite the parts of a divided community. Only political fraternity can provide such strength. The spirit of affectionate goodwill on which it rests promotes a form of solidarity more durable than any that tolerance alone creates, and gives those communities that have it their best chance of surviving the internal ruptures that accompany every serious political debate, without pretending that the disagreements from which such controversies arise are less deep or more easily compromised than is in fact the case.

For political fraternity to exist, it is not necessary that the different views which the members of a community take of its values and purposes all be assessable from some common point of view. Indeed, the demand for political fraternity is likely to be greatest in just those situations where the competing conceptions of the disputants are not comparable in this way. This suggests that there is, after all, a criterion for evaluating the wisdom of political judgments even where the alternatives among which the community must choose are incommensurable, just as there is a criterion for evaluating the wisdom of the choices an individual makes among incommensurable personal ideals. The mark of a wise judgment in the personal sphere is its tendency to promote the condition of integrity. In the political sphere, we might by analogy say that what makes one judgment wiser than another when the alternatives cannot be measured on any common scale of value is its tendency to promote political fraternity, the public counterpart of personal integrity. When a person engaged in political debate makes choices that encourage this tendency, we have a reason for praising his judgment that is independent of our assessment of the course he recommends and the same independent reason for condemning his judgment when it encourages the opposite tendency, toward a partisanship unsoftened by the spirit of sympathetic generosity that defines the condition of political fraternity.

Anyone who wishes to be a leader in politics, or even a thoughtful member of his or her community, must of course have some conception, however provisional, of its basic aims. Generally speaking, most political actors already possess some such conception, at least in outline form, by the time they begin to participate in their community's deliberative debates. But however well formed one's initial views may be, a commitment to politics and to its deliberative processes implies an acceptance of what in Chapter 1 I called the autonomy of politics. It implies an acknowledgment that one's own views may be subject to revision on the basis of considerations that political deliberation itself first brings to light. And this in turn requires that one make a positive effort to understand the views of others, no matter how foolish or repugnant they may initially appear. To do this it is not enough merely to take note of the fact that others hold the views they do, and to compile a descriptive catalogue of the claims their views entail. It is also necessary that one attempt to see the concerns of others in their best light, an exercise that demands the same imaginative powers personal deliberation does. Political deliberation too requires an ability to combine the opposing attitudes of sympathy and detachment, the ability to place oneself imaginatively in the position of others and to entertain their concerns in the same affirmative spirit they do, while remaining uncommitted to the values and beliefs that give these concerns their force. Only the person who has surveyed, with sympathetic detachment, the conflicting interpretations that different members of his community offer of its goals is in a position to say whether his own preliminary views should be revised and to make an informed choice among the alternatives before him.

Some, of course, will be better able to do this than others, either because their powers of sympathy are stronger or because they have a greater capacity to tolerate the suspension of commitment that detachment entails. Those who possess both dispositions and can join them with habitual ease will have a special appreciation of the strains that controversy places on their community. Advocates who can see things only from a partisan perspective, who are unable to detach themselves in imagination from their own concerns or to entertain the concerns of others, will have difficulty understanding the meaning of defeat from their adversaries' point of view. By contrast, those who can see each conception of their community's objectives from the vantage point that its proponents do while withholding their assent from any, better understand what it will mean, from each party's own perspective, for it to win or lose the struggle to define the character of its community. They are better able to anticipate in imagination the anger and resentment of defeat, and victory's smug indifference, and thus are likely to have a keener sense than others do of the risks and opportunities that each choice presents for the preservation of those bonds of fellow-feeling on which the existence of their community depends.

The statesman who deliberates with sympathetic detachment is likely not only to have a better understanding of the strains of political controversy. He or she is likely to have a stronger interest in reducing them as well. The explanation for this is psychological. When the affective powers on which statesmanship depends become habitual—when they become part of what Aristotle calls a person's second nature—so that they no longer require great effort to sustain, their exercise is almost certain to be a source of pleasure in its own right, for the same reason that those who have mastered the art of reading, or of playing a musical instrument, take pleasure in the active exercise of their acquired talent.[22] Those who possess the deliberative excellence we call statesmanship are likely to find a measure of intrinsic satisfaction in the practice of their art. And just for that reason they are more likely than those to whom this satisfaction is unknown to prefer political milieux in which this excellence is valued and frequent occasions exist for its employment, just as people who enjoy reading favor environments in which literacy is encouraged.

But to say that a statesman will be drawn to those regimes in which the attitude of sympathetic detachment on which his own excellence depends is accorded a larger and more valued role is equivalent to saying that he or she will be drawn to those regimes that cultivate the spirit of political fraternity. For political fraternity is nothing but this attitude itself, diffused through the community as a whole. Indeed, the friendship that the members of a community feel for one another where the condition of political fraternity is present may be thought of as a kind of statesmanship *in pianissimo,* less demanding than the excellence of statesmanship itself, and less extraordinary, but resembling it in the affections it combines. Political fraternity is the form of statesmanship of which every member of a community is capable, and a statesman will be drawn to those ways of public life in which the good of political fraternity is recognized and consciously endorsed because he loves deliberation and the pleasure it affords. In a community held together by the bonds of political fraternity, the virtue of deliberation and the pleasure associated with it will to some extent be common goods in which all participate, and a statesman cannot help but love this larger image of himself. And that, finally, gives us a good way of explaining what is meant by the popular view that a statesman is distinguished from other citizens not just by the acuteness of his judgment but by the strength of his affection for the public good as well. For when a community is divided by a contest among incommensurable values important enough to place its identity in doubt, it is in the preservation of political fraternity that the public good largely consists.

Political questions, like personal ones, sometimes present a conflict among incommensurable values, and if a community is to survive such disagreements, it is reasonable to think that it needs something more than disinterested toleration. What it needs is political fraternity, a condition midway between tolerance and union, and one that is marked by the same combination of sympathy and detachment that characterizes the deliberative art of the statesman himself. Political fraternity is a substantive good of great importance, for the very existence of most communities depends upon it. It is a good that most communities therefore have a reason to affirm, whatever other values they adopt. In this respect, political fraternity resembles the good of personal integrity. Like its personal counterpart, moreover, the good of civic friendship is most likely to be achieved through the efforts of those who deliberate about the problems of politics in a certain way, with sympathy and detachment. Those who deliberate in this statesmanlike way see the threats to fraternity more clearly and value its preservation more highly than others do, recognizing in this public good a generalized expression of a trait they value in themselves. The wisdom of the statesman is thus at once substantive and procedural. He is wise because he deliberates in a certain way, and wise also because his deliberations lead, more reliably than others', to the good of political fraternity. In the statesman's special wisdom these elements are fused, as they are in the wisdom of those who show exceptionally good judgment in matters of personal choice.

To this account of statesmanship one final observation must be added. The account I have given rests upon the claim that political communities depend for their well-being on a condition analogous to that in which an individual's soul must be to possess integrity. But there is one striking difference, which I have not mentioned, between the things my analogy compares. Political communities are made up of separate individuals, and because of this their parts are less intimately connected than the parts of a person's soul. Given their separateness, and the independence of their capacities for judgment and choice, the individual members of a community must typically be persuaded by arguments to join in any political program. It is true that something like this may also occur within the soul of a single person. But the process of personal deliberation is rarely marked by the kind of self-conscious exchange that typifies a debate between two separate people. In personal deliberation, an individual needs only to persuade himself. In political debate he must, as a rule, persuade others as well if his own conception of the community's good is to prevail, and this requires an additional art not needed in the sphere of personal deliberation: the art of rhetoric, as it has been called since the Greeks first described it.

What makes a statesman wise is his special understanding of the aids and obstacles to political fraternity and his own personal desire to achieve it. But if his wisdom is to be a force in the life of his community, if it is to have some actual influence on the community's political affairs, a statesman must accept the fact that he is only one among many and persuade others to adopt his point of view. He cannot force his convictions on them but must win their support by making arguments they will accept.[23] To do this, it is not enough that he merely express his own concerns in an intellectually respectable form. He needs also to awaken in his fellow-citizens, by rhetorical means, some of the same feeling for political fraternity that motivates his own deliberations. Thus to be successful, we might say, a statesman must through rhetoric create the very sentiment of fellow-feeling in which the condition of political fraternity consists. The arguments of a statesman must in this sense have what philosophers call a performative character: they must actually bring about, through a process of affective conversion, the good that they defend (in the same way that the comments of a psychoanalyst must for his therapy to be effective). The statesman sees the value of political fraternity more clearly than others do, and loves it more intensely. But its actual existence is something he must create, and this no one can do so long as he remains a mere observer of political life. If his own love for the public good is to be fulfilled, a statesman must enter the embattled precincts and work to arouse in others a similar, if less intense, devotion to political fraternity. The art of doing this is the art of rhetoric, the art of building communities from resistant human material, and the statesman's wisdom will bear fruit only if he masters this ancient art and uses it effectively.

DIRTY HANDS

But is it possible to be an effective politician without a certain callousness, even ruthlessness, toward others—a quality that is the very opposite of the sympathetic detachment I have described as the statesman's preeminent trait? This is a question that today goes under the name of "dirty hands," and which Machiavelli posed with shocking clarity in *The Prince*. "[M]any," Machiavelli says, "have imagined republics and principalities that have never been seen or known to exist in truth; for it is so far from how one lives to how one should live that he who lets go of what is done for what should be done learns his ruin rather than his preservation. For a man who wants to make a profession of good in all regards must come to ruin among so many who are not good. Hence it is necessary to a prince, if he wants to maintain himself, to learn to be able not to be good, and to use this and not use it according to necessity."[24]

More specifically, if a politician is to acquire power and retain it, he must sometimes do things that weaken rather than support the spirit of political fraternity. Typically, for example, he must win the backing of some faction within his community, and this frequently requires that he slight or even suppress the interests of others in a way more likely to intensify conflict than restrain it. Those who cannot stomach the indifference and occasional ruthlessness this demands will never be successful politicians. They will never come to power. But such ruthlessness, which is needed for political success, is antithetical to the attitude in which I have said true statesmanship consists. Does Machiavelli's realism, then, give us grounds for rejecting my account of what this virtue is?

The answer is no. If anything, in fact, a sober recognition of the realities of political power suggests an additional ground for believing that the statesman's goal must be the preservation of fraternity. The reason is as follows:

Machiavelli's brutal insistence that a prince who wants to survive needs "to be able not to be good" must be troubling to anyone who enters the political realm for the sake of something other than power itself. The politician who seeks power as his final end will of course be undisturbed by the requirement that he be cunning and ruthless to obtain it. But anyone who pursues a political career to achieve some end other than his own self-aggrandizement will be troubled by the fact that he must behave with a measure of indifference and brutality to acquire the power needed to realize his goals. Anyone who has a political ideal in this broad sense must see power as a means to an end rather than an end itself and be worried when the means he uses conflict with the object of his political actions. Such conflict is inevitable, and only those who make power itself their goal do not experience it. To think otherwise is utopian in the strict sense, and it is against utopianism, not idealism, that Machiavelli's argument is directed.

The real question that Machiavelli's observation raises, therefore, is a question about the ability of politicians to keep the ruthlessness their work requires within bounds. Only the politician for whom power is an end in itself will be unconcerned to do so (except, of course, on strategic grounds). Every other politician—every idealistic politician—will concede that some degree of ruthlessness is necessary to achieve his or her ends, but will view this as a sad necessity to be avoided if at all possible. For an idealistic politician, ruthlessness can be justified only as a means to an end whose desirability outweighs whatever indecency and immorality the ruthlessness itself involves.

The chief danger with all such justifications is their expandability. Once one is prepared to accept a little ruthlessness, as every politician must, it becomes easier to accept more. There is a natural tendency for those in politics to become used to acting ruthlessly as an unavoidable condition of their work and thus to tolerate such actions on an ever-widening scale. This is the greatest danger to which politics exposes its practitioners and all whose lives they affect. Only those who are too saintly or too squeamish to enter the political realm are completely immune from it.

But it does not follow that all politicians are equally at risk. The politician whose ideals are shaped by a conception of human life that affirms a specific view of fulfillment to which only some subscribe and that portrays other views as false or evil is particularly vulnerable. For if one believes there is a single way of living that is demonstrably the best, then the fact that others disagree and follow different paths can only be explained as a consequence of error or sin. And if one makes this favored way of life a political as well as personal ideal, the correction by educational or punitive means of those who see things differently is likely to be an important part of one's program. From this point of view the diversity of belief and practice that exists in most communities must be regarded as a defect to be cured or overcome.

Initially, perhaps, the therapy needed to effect a cure may be administered with gentleness and charity. But built into every program of this sort is the danger that its goals will be pursued with increasing ruthlessness instead. For sooner or later those who resist, who refuse to give up their misguided ways of life, must lose stature in the eyes of their frustrated benefactors. If they continue to resist, it must be because they are willfully stubborn or blindly obtuse, and in either case their reasons for resisting are likely to seem increasingly less deserving of respect to those who would liberate them from ignorance and sin. And as this happens, whatever hesitation their liberators once felt about forcibly suppressing such persistence in evil and error is likely to diminish as well. In this way, the moral barrier to ruthlessness is lowered and its human costs obscured. At the limit, these costs simply disappear: the loss of the way of life that is suppressed is no longer perceived to be a loss of any sort at all. In our century—the most terrible, Isaiah Berlin has said, in European history—we have seen the limiting case of political ruthlessness realized on a scale that still seems unimaginable.[25] But the danger of such ruthlessness is present, to a more than ordinary degree, in every political program that starts with an idealistic commitment to some narrow and exclusive conception of the human good, no matter how noble that conception may be, and not just in the totalitarian movements of the twentieth century. Even Plato's magnificent republic, it is sobering to recall, could be established only on the condition that an entire of generation of children first be banished or destroyed.[26]

The dangers of ruthlessness will be lower, by contrast, if one starts by acknowledging the incommensurable diversity of human goods. The politician who believes there are different paths to fulfillment and no overriding criterion by which they may be definitively ranked will not view diversity itself as the symptom of a moral or cognitive failing that needs to be corrected. Even if he himself favors one of these paths, he will not think it proper to compel those who feel otherwise into sharing his beliefs. And if, in addition to acknowledging the absence of any rational grounds for insisting that his view of the good is superior to those of others, he is also able to see the point of their commitments, to feel the force of their interests and values—if he is able to sympathize with the concerns that animate their ways of life however different from his own—then he is likely to view the forced suppression of their beliefs and practices not merely as illegitimate but as entailing the loss of something humanly valuable too. He will be more sensitive to the human costs of such a program than those who see the suppressed beliefs and practices merely as the product of error or crime. Indeed, rather than weakening whatever natural hesitation he feels to behave in a ruthless way, the empathic pluralism that informs his view of politics is likely to have just the opposite effect. When a course of action would offend the deeply held convictions of others, his own values will make him more reluctant to proceed. They will act as a barrier against ruthlessness and not an invitation to it, unlike the values of a politician who sees nothing of worth in any vision of the good except the one that he supports.

Political fraternity is the idealized expression of the value of empathic pluralism, the pursuit of that value conceived as an end in itself. We thus have reason to think that of all politicians, those who pursue this goal are the ones best protected against the risk of ruthlessness that all political action entails. To believe this risk can be eliminated is utopian. "He who seeks the salvation of the soul, of his own and of others, should not seek it along the avenue of politics, for the quite different tasks of politics can only be solved by violence."[27] The risk that I will have to act ruthlessly toward my opponents is a danger that arises whenever I enter the political realm, and every conception of political leadership, including my own, must honestly face this fact. The real question—the only question—is how well protected I will be in my political life against the seductions of force, whose very destructiveness (as Freud brilliantly perceived) has an erotic appeal of its own.[28] My claim is that some political ideals offer more protection than others and that the ideal of political fraternity offers most of all. The politician who embraces this ideal, with its insistence on what Weber called the ultimate "polytheism" of values,[29] is more likely than any other to reach a point where he feels compelled to abstain from the violence that politics necessarily involves and to say, "This is more than I can stomach, more than I can bring myself to do." The revulsion he feels at that point is rooted in his character, in the habitual combination of sympathy and detachment with which he views the wide range of conflicting human goods, and precisely for this reason provides the most reliable protection against the inevitable expansionary tendency of ruthlessness in politics. Some ruthlessness of this sort is unavoidable; it comes with territory. But my statesman, who takes the preservation of political fraternity as his master goal, is peculiarly well equipped to meet this demon and do battle with it in the spirit we have reason to hope all our politicians will. The realities of political power, which Machiavelli described with brutal candor, thus do not give us grounds for rejecting the ideal of political fraternity as an otherworldly fantasy that only the naive can endorse. Quite the contrary: an unflinching acknowledgment of these realities makes the need to hold onto this ideal clearer still.

To be sure, there is a greater tension between the end of political fraternity and the ruthless means that must occasionally be employed on its behalf than there is between some other ends and the force used to secure them. A statesman loves fraternity but to be effective must sometimes do unfraternal things—must, in Machiavelli's words, "be able not to be good." Thus here again we meet a combination of opposite-seeming qualities, as we did in our attempt to understand the meaning of political fraternity itself. It is just this combination, however, that a politician must possess if he is neither to give up on politics as a hopelessly corrupting enterprise, on the one hand, nor be swept away by the "diabolic forces lurking in all violence," on the other.[30] This is not an easy combination to achieve: no easier than the combination of sympathy and detachment in which practical wisdom consists. But it is what every politician who hopes to be a statesman must aim at as his goal, and if it is objected that far fewer succeed in this effort than fail, a good reply would be Spinoza's famous observation that "all noble things are as difficult as they are rare."[31]

THE POLITICS OF PRESERVATION

In my account of statesmanship I have placed great weight on the value of political fraternity. Without political fraternity, I have said, no moderately complicated community can survive, just as no soul complex enough to be at all interesting can survive without the self-directed friendship that constitutes the core of personal integrity. Political fraternity is thus a preeminent good that in most circumstances exceeds all others in importance.

Some may object to assigning political fraternity such value on the grounds that it gives the existing structure of a community greater dignity than it deserves. Surely, they will insist, there are situations in which the harmonious order, even the continued existence, of a particular political system must be sacrificed for the sake of some greater good, such as liberty or justice. Indeed, to many it may seem that political fraternity can never be more than a secondary value parasitic upon these others. The question of whether it is desirable to preserve a particular community by promoting a spirit of friendship among its members cannot be answered, they will say, until we know what kind of community it is, whether it is free or unfree, just or unjust, and so on. I shall conclude this chapter by offering two responses to these predictable objections.

First, no one will deny that there are communities so irreversibly corrupt that efforts to sustain them through the cultivation of political fraternity are indefensible, and others so hopelessly divided that all efforts of this kind are bound to fail. There is no room in these communities for civic friendship or the statesman's art. But that is because they stand at the boundaries of political life, and if they lead anywhere at all, it can only be to revolution—to a fundamental change in the nature of the regime itself.[32]

The normal situation in politics is not, however, a revolutionary one, and it would be a terrible mistake to think that the ordinary processes of political deliberation should be measured against those typical of revolutionary episodes or refashioned in their image. There are some, of course, who maintain that revolutions offer the greatest—perhaps the only really meaningful—opportunity for authentic political action. Born with the French Revolution, this view still has its defenders.[33] In fact, however, revolutions tend not to be, as the defenders of this view maintain, the most political of events, but the least political instead. For in them, as in war, deliberation is commonly replaced by strategy and force, and the sheltering scheme of institutions that enables political opponents to live with one another despite their disagreements is dissolved. Revolutions can in fact have only one aim, and that is to bring themselves to an end in the establishment of a new, nonrevolutionary regime. They are in this sense inherently self-liquidating, in contrast to ordinary politics, whose preservative work resumes whenever revolutions end.[34] When they do, political fraternity once again becomes an important good and statesmanship a valued art, whatever the nature of the new regime and however unfraternal the revolution that preceded it.

Second, in response to those who maintain that political fraternity can never be more than a subordinate or parasitic good, I would point out that the primary goods on which in their view it depends—the goods, for example, of liberty and justice—are themselves intractably controversial and that one may entertain any of a wide range of beliefs about them without transgressing what are today considered the limits of responsible opinion. To decide whether political fraternity is a good it is unnecessary first to decide what liberty and justice mean and whether the community of which one happens to be a member is free or fair. Indeed, it is precisely because these concepts are so controversial that the need for political fraternity is both obvious and

great. To be sure, there are limits beyond which one may not responsibly go, conceptions of freedom and justice that must be rejected
out of hand rather than treated merely as positions in a debate. But
these limits are wide, and while it is important to recognize them, it
is equally important to acknowledge that an awareness of their existence provides little guidance in resolving the endless controversies
that arise within the broad field they define. Only those who believe
that the proper explication of a community's most basic values can
provide a common standard by which to judge every political dispute
among its members will be tempted to deny that this is so.

In a certain sense, of course, a knowledge of the limits of an activity is always prior to the art that is required to perform it well. Thus
a knowledge of the rules of baseball, which define the limits of the
game, is prior (both conceptually and chronologically) to the player's
or the coach's art. But the knowledge in question is thinner, more
abstract, and easier to acquire than the corresponding art, which is
why there are many people who understand the rules of baseball but
few who play it well. The same is true in politics. It is easier to see
what defines its limits, to know which arguments are at any given
moment beyond the bounds of respectability, than to master the art
of statesmanship, the art of deliberating wisely about the problems
that politics presents. This is an art that only some possess. It is not
distributed equally, like the franchise in democratic states.

The good that the statesman seeks to secure is the good of political
fraternity. In most ordinarily complex communities, this is a good
not of secondary but of primary and independent worth. It is, in an
elementary sense, the good of politics itself. Those who deny this and
celebrate instead the liberating worldlessness of revolution fail to see
that politics is always the pursuit of order, and that its inherent conservatism implies a continuing affirmation of the value of political
fraternity, in all but those transitional episodes of birth and death that
mark the limits of political life. In this sense it is right to say that my
account of statesmanship, with its emphasis on the value of political
fraternity, entails a commitment to order and the status quo. But that
is because it entails a commitment to politics itself, to the existence
of the realm of values that the statesman serves and political fraternity
sustains against the forces of disorder that threaten all our fragile human works.

3

The Good Lawyer

The Case Method of Teaching

The ideal of the lawyer-statesman stands for the value of public service and the virtue of civic-mindedness associated with it. And it stands, too, for the virtue of prudence, or practical wisdom. But this ideal implies more than that prudence and public-spiritedness are traits of a generally admirable kind. In addition it suggests that they are qualities of special importance to lawyers. It suggests that the experience of lawyers promotes these traits, and their professional duties require them, in some regular and important way. The lawyer-statesman ideal points to a connection between the virtue of statesmanship, on the one hand, and the ordinary circumstances of law practice, on the other, and implies that this basic human excellence has special meaning for lawyers as a group. In that sense the figure of the lawyer-statesman may be said to embody not merely a generalized conception of political virtue but a distinctive professional ideal, as the hyphenated term *lawyer*-statesman suggests. What does this ideal come to? Let us begin by considering its implications for legal education.

A lawyer's professional life begins the day that he or she starts law school. This has not always been the case, of course, but today the first phase of almost every lawyer's career consists of a period of time spent studying law in a formal academic program under the supervision of university professors. However diverse their professional experiences may be in other respects, therefore, lawyers still share at least one thing in common: they have all been law students at one time or another, and it is as students that their professional habits first take shape.

109

The single most prominent feature of twentieth-century American legal education is its heavy reliance on the so-called case method of instruction. By the case method I mean two things: first, the study of law through the medium of judicial opinions, mainly appellate opinions, that have been rendered in actual disputes; and second, the examination of these opinions in a spirit that has often, and aptly, been described as "Socratic." Though this latter term is sometimes used to denote a distinctive style of law teaching—one marked by an extreme of bullying and intimidation—it is the term's wider meaning that I have in mind. By Socratic I mean both an unwillingness to take the soundness of any judicial opinion for granted, no matter how elevated the tribunal or how popular the result, and a commitment to place the conflicting positions that each lawsuit presents in their most attractive light, regardless of how well they have been treated in the opinion itself. Most American law teachers today employ the case method of instruction in the broad sense just defined.

It would be possible, of course, to teach the law by studying its operation at the trial and pretrial levels rather than concentrating as exclusively as American law teachers do on the decisions of appellate courts. But appellate opinions have the great advantage of bringing out the legal issues in a case with an economy and a precision that trial transcripts, for example, rarely do. To be sure, appellate opinions also have a characteristic deficiency that most law teachers recognize: they are typically mere distillates that leave out much of a dispute's original complexity and present its facts in an incomplete and stylized way. But the usefulness of appellate opinions as a vehicle for teaching the broad structure of the law outweighs this deficiency and explains why they are used instead of transcripts and briefs as the chief means for introducing students to the doctrine in most fields.

This explanation for the heavy reliance on appellate opinions in American law teaching immediately raises a question of an opposite sort, however. For if their main pedagogical advantage lies in the perspicuousness with which they bring the elements of legal doctrine to the fore, what explains the fact that most American law teachers do not teach from treatises and textbooks instead? If the aim is to familiarize students with the doctrine in a certain field, why isn't a textbook that sets out the relevant rules in a clear and systematic way the best vehicle for doing so? What advantage is there in making students study these rules obliquely, by means of judicial opinions rendered in specific cases, rather than giving them the rules directly? There are three familiar answers to this question.

First, since class time is scarce, it seems reasonable to concentrate on those problems likely to give students the greatest difficulty when they enter practice, and these will by definition be the problems that arise at the unsettled boundaries of a field, not those more routine ones that can be decided by already well-established principles. Boundary problems of this sort necessarily involve a clash of principles in which as much, or nearly as much, may be said on one side as on the other. The evenness of such contests means that at the margin of a field there are, in fact, no controlling principles at all, but only cases—controversies in which principles of roughly equal weight compete for precedence. The case method is certainly the most economical and perhaps the only way of giving students a feel for these controversies, for the boundary conflicts that define, at any given moment, the margins of a field. And from these conflicts it is easier for a student to construct an understanding of the field's settled interior than the other way around.

Second, in addition to a knowledge of legal rules, practicing lawyers obviously also need skill in applying these rules to problems of a concrete kind. A lawyer must be able to apply the law to the complex, real-life dilemmas of clients. And the case method of instruction, which buffets students with a steady stream of such dilemmas, seems better adapted to the cultivation of this skill than textbook expositions do.

A third justification for the case method is that it promotes rhetorical abilities needed in law practice. Lawyers are regularly called upon to defend their clients' interests before strangers in a public setting, often with little opportunity for advance preparation. To be effective a lawyer must therefore be skilled at spontaneous public speaking, and the case method of instruction—in which students are given no advance notice of the positions they will be required to defend before their classmates and under Socratic interrogation—seems the one best suited to teach this skill: better suited, in any case, than an abstract discussion of rules or principles that presents only familiar considerations of a general sort and no new facts that students must incorporate into their extemporaneous arguments.

Each of these three justifications has merit, but each is also incomplete. The first justification, for example, tells us nothing about the way that boundary contests in the law should be resolved. A knowledge of general principles is clearly insufficient by itself to settle such disputes, for by definition they present dilemmas that existing principles do not straightforwardly decide. Is their decision therefore arbitrary? If not, what else must one know, what other skills must one possess, to decide them? And how does the case method teach these skills or convey the required sort of knowledge?

The second justification is incomplete as well. No one will deny that the practice of law involves the application of general rules to specific cases. But the same may also be said of other disciplines, like medicine. The cases that doctors study differ, however, from those that constitute the subject matter of the lawyer's art. A law case is a fight or a contest; to say what it is, is necessarily to describe a disagreement. By contrast, to state a medical case—a patient's presenting symptoms—is not in the same way to report a controversy, though doctors may of course disagree in their diagnosis of a patient's problem. We might express this idea by saying that the problems with which lawyers deal are *constitutively* argumentative, at least in comparison with those of medicine. How is this distinctive feature of the cases they confront reflected in the method that is used to teach lawyers their craft? The claim that the case method teaches law students how to apply general rules to particular problems raises this question and brings it into focus, but by itself provides no answer.

The third justification misses something too. A good lawyer must of course be an effective advocate, and it is reasonable to assume that this requires some skill at public speaking. But effective advocacy demands more than the ability to speak extemporaneously in front of strangers. It also requires that one be able to distinguish persuasive arguments from unpersuasive ones, and the third justification for the case method of law teaching has nothing to say about the meaning of this distinction or the way in which the study of cases helps students to discern it. And it ignores a basic feature of the method itself. For while it is true that the case method forces students to practice the art of advocacy by making arguments on behalf of imaginary clients, it also compels them to reflect on the soundness of these same arguments from a judicial point of view and thus, some of the time at least, to adopt an attitude more neutral and inclusive than that of a committed advocate.

LOSING ONE'S SOUL

These three justifications for the case method all lack one thing: an appreciation of the way in which it functions as an instrument for the development of moral imagination. It is this aspect of the method I now want to examine.

The case method of law teaching presents students with a series of concrete disputes and compels them to reenact these disputes by playing the roles of the original contestants or their lawyers. It thus forces them to see things from a range of different points of view and to entertain the claims associated with each, broadening their capacity for sympathy by taxing it in unexpected ways. But it also works in the opposite direction. For the student who has been assigned a partisan position and required to defend it is likely to be asked a moment later for his views regarding the wisdom of the judge's decision in the case. To answer, he must disengage himself from the sympathetic attachments he may have formed as a committed, if imaginary, participant and reexamine the case from a disinterested judicial point of view. The case method thus works simultaneously to strengthen both the student's powers of sympathetic understanding and his ability to suppress all sympathies in favor of a judge's scrupulous neutrality. Most important, it increases his tolerance for the disorientation that movement back and forth between these different attitudes occasions. In this way the case method serves as a forcing ground for the moral imagination by cultivating that peculiar bifocality that I earlier described as its most essential property.

One aim of this complex exercise in advocacy and detachment is the cultivation of those perceptual habits that lawyers need in practice. Forcing students to defend positions they do not believe in or that they consider morally offensive may seem arbitrary and insensitive, but it serves an important goal. The student who is put in this position must strain to see the claim he has been given to defend in its most attractive light. He must work to discover its strengths and to articulate them, and this he cannot do unless he temporarily puts his earlier convictions to one side. In this way students get used to looking with a friendly eye even at those positions they personally reject, and before long they acquire some skill at identifying the strengths and weaknesses of whatever claim is presented to them, those that are unfamiliar or morally distasteful as well as those they recognize and endorse. Gradually, much of this becomes habitual. One comes to see that the arguments for and against most positions fall into certain stylized patterns, and to recognize which argument forms are most appropriate to which causes. Over time these insights come to shape the increasingly instinctive scheme within which law students view the cases they are given. The gradual acceptance of this scheme marks a change in perception, in the way one sees legal conflict as well as thinks about it. Or more precisely, since this distinction is to some extent an artificial one, the way a law student learns to think about cases comes eventually to affect how he perceives them, below the level of reflective thought. This perceptual adjustment forms the core of the student's nascent professional persona, and is reflected in the habits and reflexes that increasingly distinguish his approach to legal problems from that of a layperson uneducated in the law.

Along with this perceptual adjustment, the case method tends to promote a second change as well, a change in temperament or disposition. The role-playing and Socratic interrogation that are its central features force students to make the most of the conflicting claims presented by the cases. It forces them to entertain these claims in the sense described in Chapter 2. This means more than granting that their proponents have the right to assert them and accepting that they are not irrational to do so. To entertain a claim, one must make an effort to see its sense or value from the point of view of those who actually endorse it: to sympathize with their perspective and not simply tolerate it. The effort to entertain unfamiliar and disagreeable positions may at first cause some awkwardness and pain. But in time it increases a person's powers of empathic understanding and relaxes the boundaries that initially restrict his sympathies to what he knows and likes.

Some students find this experience disturbing and complain that the case method, which makes every position respectable, undermines their sense of integrity and personal self-worth.[1] It is easy to understand why. For the discovery in oneself of a developing capacity to see the point of positions that previously seemed thoughtless or unfair is often accompanied by a corresponding sense of more critical detachment from one's earlier commitments, and this can lead to the feeling of being unmoored with no secure convictions and hence no identity at all.

This experience, which law students sometimes describe, not inappropriately, as the experience of losing one's soul, strongly suggests that the process of legal education does more than impart knowledge and promote new perceptual habits. In addition it works—is meant to work—upon the students' dispositions by strengthening their capacity for sympathetic understanding. The strengthening of this capacity often brings with it the dulling or displacement of earlier convictions and a growing appreciation of the incommensurability of values, changes of attitude that many experience as personally transforming. It is this unsettling experience that underlies the law student's concern that his professional education threatens to rob him of his soul—an anxiety no mere increment in knowledge or refinement of perception can explain.

It may seem implausible that the reading of appellate opinions can bring such a transformation about. Appellate opinions, after all, are typically rather dry documents that contain only an abbreviated statement of the facts; that commonly avoid decision on the merits but focus on the jurisdiction and procedure of lower courts instead; and that frequently fail to present the losing side in its most attractive light (for the obvious reason that doing so makes it easier for the court to justify its decision in the case). These characteristics might appear to make appellate opinions a poor vehicle for stimulating the moral imagination of law students by forcing them to sympathize with a diversity of points of view and to confront the impossibility of framing a comprehensive scheme of values within which all conflicting claims may be compared. If that is our goal, would it not be better to focus, say, on the parties' briefs and closing arguments at trial, where the facts are likely to be presented more fully and the positions of the contestants stated with maximum force?

The answer is no, for several reasons. First, however incomplete the statement of facts in an appellate opinion, it almost always contains some details embarrassing to the winning party. These, so to speak, peep through the opinion and remind readers that the losing party had some facts on its side too. Second, the law teacher who teaches Socratically does not simply say, "On the facts as reported the court held thus and such," and let it go at that. Rather, using the court's selective but manageable statement of facts as a starting point, he invites his students to replay the case by considering whether the losing party might have put its position in a more compelling form and then imagining what could have been said in response. Often this means teaching against the grain of the court's opinion—by taking seriously facts it downplays and arguments it rejects. But many American law teachers teach this way, and since the appellate opinions that are selected for inclusion in student casebooks are often chosen precisely because they invite contrapuntal treatment of this sort, there is even a bias in favor of such teaching. Third, if it is objected that this can all be accomplished more easily by using other materials (a dubious claim in any case, given the length and disorderliness of most trial transcripts and the poor quality of many briefs), the response must be that this objection misses the point. For the students' imaginative powers are most likely to be strengthened if they are forced to work at reconstructing positions only partially visible to them rather than being presented with these positions in already finished form. The moral-educative function of law training requires that this work be strenuous; that it be possible but challenging. And the appellate opinion seems a particularly good instrument for this because it is rich enough in facts to give students something concrete to work with, but sufficiently schematic to make them struggle to reimagine fully the parties' conflicting claims.

These considerations help explain why appellate opinions are more likely than treatises and textbooks, on the one hand, or briefs and transcripts, on the other, to encourage the growth of deliberative imagination, as well as being uniquely well adapted to conveying an understanding of legal doctrine. But there is another element to the moral education law students receive that is also linked to the study of judicial opinions and that would be missing if their reading consisted of academic synopses or partisan statements instead. Once we take this other element into account, moreover, reasons emerge for viewing the negative, belief- and commitment-threatening side of the case method in a more positive light.

THE JUDICIAL POINT OF VIEW AND ITS PRIORITY

The task of an appellate judge is twofold: first, to decide the controversy before him, and second, to provide a set of supporting reasons for the decision that he gives. Both his decision and the rationale for it are set forth in the opinion the judge issues at the conclusion of the case. Of course, the parties to a legal dispute also often prepare documents of their own stating their version of the case. But it is the judge who has the final word, and his opinion enjoys priority over theirs. It establishes the point of view from which every other viewpoint must be assessed. Thus while it may in one sense be correct to describe the judge merely as another actor in the drama of the case, within the structure of this drama his perspective occupies a dominant place.

In the case method of instruction, the priority of the judge's point of view is reflected in the disproportionate amount of class time typically devoted to questioning whether the case at hand was rightly decided, a question that must by definition be approached from the perspective of a judge whether one agrees with the decision or not. The case method is largely an exercise in forced role-playing. But it is important to remember that among the roles students are invited to play is that of a judge, and to recognize that the priority of this role over others is embedded in the method itself.

If the effort to entertain the claims of the parties to a lawsuit demands enlarged powers of sympathy and leads to a loss of ideological conviction, to a blurring of the distinction between right and wrong, and to a diminished faith in the commensurability of values generally, the case method's emphasis on the priority of the judicial point of view underscores the need to conclude the dispute despite these uncertainties and to do so not by *fiat* but in a reasoned and publicly justifiable manner instead. In this way the case method provides its own counterweight to the student's growing acceptance of complexity and pluralism in the realm of values, and blocks the slide to what might otherwise become the cynical celebration of arbitrariness. It does this by habituating students to the need for reasoned judgment under conditions of maximum moral ambiguity, and by giving them practice at rendering such judgments themselves. The result is a combination of attitudes in tension with one another: an expanded capacity for sympathetic understanding coupled with the ability to see every claim with the coldest and most distant, most judicial, eye; a broad familiarity with diverse and irreconcilable human goods coupled with an indefatigable willingness to enter the fray, hear the arguments, render judgment, and articulate the reasons that support it, even when all hope of moral certainty is gone. At war with itself, this complex set of attitudes nonetheless describes a recognizable moral ideal, an ideal closest, perhaps, to the public-spirited stoicism implied by the Roman term *gravitas,* but in any event distinguishable from the indifferent cynicism that some believe the case method of instruction tends inevitably to produce.[2] No doubt it sometimes does, and the fear that a person may lose his soul in the process is to that extent justified. But the aim of the case method is otherwise. For what it seeks to produce, ideally at least, are stoics rather than cynics, a distinction that becomes clear only when the priority of the judicial point of view and its function as a counterweight to relativism are recognized to be essential features of the method itself.

The privileged position that the case method assigns the judicial point of view has another important consequence. Judges are expected to decide cases in a disinterested manner, meaning without concern for their own personal advantage. This does not mean, however, that a judge approaches his task without interests of any kind at all. There is one interest that all judges are allowed and whose absence in a judge is indeed considered a deficiency. That is the judge's interest in the administration of justice, in the integrity or well-being of the legal system as a whole. The judge's interest in the well-being of the law encompasses a variety of concerns—the concern for doctrinal coherence, for example, and for the responsiveness of doctrine to social and economic circumstances. It also includes a concern for the bonds of fellowship that legal conflict strains but that must be preserved to avoid other, more destructive conflicts. The judge's interest in all these things—which, far from compromising his authority, helps to constitute it—might be characterized, in general terms, as an interest in the good of the community represented by the laws. The judge's interest is thus broader or more inclusive than the interests of the parties. They are interested in their own separate welfare. He, by contrast, is concerned with the well-being of the larger community of which they are members, the community constituted by the laws the parties have invoked to settle their dispute. The judge's attitude is in this sense more public-spirited than theirs and his point of view more communitarian.

When law students play-act at being judges, as the case method requires them to do, it is this public-spirited attitude they must assume. To begin with, the attitude is likely to be one most students merely "put on," in the way an actor puts on a mask. It is too disinterested, too remote from most students' own partisan convictions, to be an attitude they experience as their own. But the built-in priority the case method gives the role of judge and constant practice at playing it tend in time to blur the line between what a student puts on and what belongs to him in his own right. By a process of transference that the case method deliberately exploits, the judicial attitude that a student begins by mimicking becomes to some degree his own, and the student himself takes on a measure of the public-spiritedness that distinguishes the judge's view of legal conflict. The student to whom this has happened tends instinctively to look at the law and to argue about its meaning in the same way that a judge would, and even more important, to care with new intensity about the good of the legal system and the community it represents.

One could of course devise a system of legal education in which the judicial point of view did not play the central organizing role it now does. Law students might be made, for example, to consider problems from the point of view of a legislator rather than a judge. But a program of this sort would be less well suited to the cultivation of civic-mindedness. No one doubts that legislators sometimes act for the sake of the public good, the good of the whole community whose laws they are empowered to enact, repeal, and adjust. But the actions of legislators are also often directed toward private ends, toward the advancement of the partisan interests of their constituents, the small groups of citizens that elect them and whose frequently parochial points of view they have pledged to represent. Public-spiritedness and partisanship are thus tangled up in legislation. In adjudication, by contrast, the civic-minded attitude appears in purer form.[3] Unlike legislators, judges are expected to attend to the public good alone, and any deviation from this attitude, though acceptable in the sphere of legislation, is generally considered a failing in a judge. Without denying that civic-mindedness plays some part in the work of legislation, we may therefore say that it *defines* the judge's point of view in a more exclusive way. The priority that the case method gives to this point of view reflects the belief that it is part of what lawyers must be taught. It confirms that one purpose of their professional education is to acquaint lawyers with the attitude of civic-mindedness most perfectly exemplified in the work of judging and through repeated mimicry to inculcate this attitude in them as a dispositional trait. (The cynical view that lawyers must be taught to think like judges in order to manipulate the law for private ends is a view I shall consider later in the chapter.)

It is worth observing that this same purpose cannot be ascribed to every scheme of professional education that employs some form of case method as the vehicle for studying human conflict. Many business school programs, for example, use a version of the case method to study problems of entrepreneurship and management.[4] The business school "case" resembles its law school counterpart in several respects. It, too, presents a concrete situation involving different actors with partly conflicting and partly cooperative interests, and challenges the student to discover or invent an appropriate solution to the problem. But the case that business school students study is simply a set of facts and not, as in law school, a judicial opinion. The business school case is not a problem conceived and articulated from the point of view of one who is expected by virtue of his office to be single-mindedly concerned with the promotion of the common good. Though it also involves considerable role-playing, the business school case thus lacks the one role to which the case method as it is practiced in law schools gives the greatest emphasis, the role of the judge, and hence it cannot be said to teach, as directly or insistently, the attitude that distinguishes this role from others. The dominant perspective in business school cases is that of a manager, not of a judge, and while a manager may more than others be concerned with the overall well-being of his firm, because the firm is situated in a competitive environment populated by other firms, managers must also be partisans in a way that judges are not. The managerial perspective mixes communitarian and self-interested attitudes, and to that extent encourages less forcefully than the judicial point of view the spirit of civic-mindedness that the latter exemplifies in an unmixed form.

The prominence that the case method of instruction gives to the judicial point of view raises an interesting question. Of those who go to law school, only a few ever actually become judges and thus eventually play the part for which their legal training would appear to have prepared them most directly. In this respect, the fit between business education and business practice seems closer, for many more business school students become managers than law students become judges. What explains this puzzling discrepancy between the point of view that predominates in law school and the careers of most lawyers—between the primary role their academic training forces them to assume and the very different roles most lawyers play in practice? The apparent discrepancy would be explained if the judicial attitude that law students learn by habit to adopt could be shown to be essential to the successful practice of law in all its phases. I believe this is in fact the case. But the argument that is required to justify this belief is a long and complex one and must overcome certain deeply ingrained misconceptions about the work that lawyers do.

LAW JOBS

Most law school programs conform to a common pattern. There is a standard list of courses that nearly every law school offers, and these tend to be taught in a broadly similar way. It is therefore easy to generalize about the nature of legal education. But once they graduate from law school, lawyers do many different things, and this makes it harder to speak in general terms about law practice as a whole.

There are, in fact, three quite different "law jobs," as Karl Llewellyn called them, that practicing lawyers perform: those of judging, counseling, and advocacy.[5] Within these categories further distinctions can be drawn. One can distinguish, for example, between the lawyer who counsels private clients (individual or corporate) and the one who is employed to give advice to a legislative body; between advocates who specialize in civil lawsuits and those whose work is limited to criminal proceedings; and within this last group, between the criminal defense lawyer and his adversary, the public prosecutor. And one can divide lawyers by subject-matter area as well. But I shall ignore these finer distinctions and concentrate on the broad divisions represented by Llewellyn's three categories instead. For it is these that separate most fundamentally the main tasks that lawyers in our society perform.

The general nature of these tasks is familiar enough. A *judge* is someone who decides disputes. He does not take sides and has no clients, but stands above the parties that appear before him and resolves their controversy from an impartial point of view. A *counselor,* by contrast, has clients and is expected to be partial to their concerns. It is the counselor's job to help his clients plan for the future, more specifically, to help them identify and control the legal consequences of their actions. In its purest form, counseling does not involve the representation of a client's interests to third parties but only their identification and the formulation of a plan for their pursuit. When a lawyer is acting as a counselor, he must of course speak to his client, but need not speak to anyone else on the client's behalf. That is the job of an *advocate*. An advocate represents his client's interests to others: to the judge presiding over a lawsuit in which the client is involved, to the government official empowered to grant or withhold some desired benefit, to the other party in a contract negotiation. In each of these settings an advocate performs essentially the same task: he speaks to another person as his client's representative. Counseling and advocacy are in reality often intertwined, and the same lawyer who acts in one capacity may soon afterward be required to act in the other or find himself oscillating back and forth between the two. Nevertheless, it is important to separate these two functions analytically, for reasons that will become clearer as we proceed.

The question I have raised about the aims of legal education does not apply to the first of these three law jobs, that of judging. For judging clearly requires the combination of sympathy and detachment and the attitude of public-spiritedness that the case method is meant to promote. There is, therefore, a direct fit between our system of legal education and the work of the judge—enough of a fit, in any case, to make the one seem a natural preparation for the other. But when we turn to the law jobs of counseling and advocacy, the appearance of fit disappears. For counselors and advocates are expected to take sides and act with zealous partiality, and it is unclear how the case method, with its emphasis on the priority of the judicial point of view, equips lawyers for these tasks. What is it that one needs to do these jobs well and how, if at all, does the case method of teaching prepare lawyers to perform them?

There is a familiar answer to these questions that is very much at odds with the account I have given of legal education. The answer reflects a particularly narrow view of what counselors and advocates do—a view that rests upon a constricted understanding of the functions they perform. I shall begin my own account of their work by sketching this narrow view and tracing its deficiencies. This will in turn suggest a better view that is more idealistic—one in which notions of virtue and character predominate—and more realistic too, that is, truer to the actual experience of counselors and advocates when they are doing their jobs well. Deliberative wisdom and civic-mindedness are, on the better view I shall propose, essential to success in these two branches of law practice. Despite what the narrow view suggests, one cannot be a good lawyer without them. And once we understand why this is so, the relationship between a system of legal education that aims to cultivate these qualities and the professional activities of counseling and advocacy will no longer be obscure.

The narrow view insists that a lawyer is merely a specialized tool for effecting his client's desires. It assumes that the client comes to his lawyer with a fixed objective in mind. The lawyer then has two, and only two, responsibilities: first, to supply his client with information concerning the legal consequences of his actions, and second, to implement whatever decision the client makes, so long as it is lawful. The client, by contrast, does all of the real deliberating. He decides what the goal shall be, and whether it is worth pursuing given the legal costs his lawyer has identified. The result is a neat division between ends (which it is the client's prerogative to adopt, alter, or abandon) and means (which it is the lawyer's responsibility to describe and then provide). In this respect the narrow view does not distinguish between counseling and advocacy. Advocacy may require skills that counseling does not (skill at public speaking, for example), but on this narrow view the nature of the lawyer's role is essentially the same in both activities.

The instrumental help that the narrow view implies is the only sort that lawyers give their clients takes many different forms. It includes advising clients about the lawfulness of contemplated actions; describing the legal formalities that must be satisfied once an action is begun; seeing to it that these formalities are observed; suing on behalf of clients; and defending them in suits and prosecutions others bring. It also includes informing clients about the litigation costs they and their potential adversaries face (information that may have the most diverse strategic implications). In all these cases, however, it is the same thing that makes the lawyer's help of value to his client, namely, his expert knowledge of the law.

To some extent this is a knowledge of what many laypeople believe all law to be: rules and procedures collected in esoteric texts like statute books. But these rules are not self-executing. They must be applied by human beings. When and how will this be done? That is the question in which the lawyer's client is most interested, and about which he expects his lawyer to provide expert advice. From the client's point of view, therefore, the most important part of his lawyer's expertise is his knowledge of a certain sort of human behavior: the behavior of those who play a role in determining how the law shall be applied.

In part, all such behavior is shaped by factors external to the law. A government agency that is responsible for enforcing certain rules may do so only selectively, for example, if its budget is inadequate to enforce them all. And a company that has purchased goods that prove defective may decide not to sue for breach of contract, even when it is clearly in the right, because the costs of suing are too great. A lawyer's knowledge of how the law will affect his clients therefore requires an understanding of the extralegal factors that influence those who have it in their power to invoke the law or not. But it also requires an understanding of forces internal to the law. Legal rules are often ambiguous or incomplete. As a result, their application frequently requires an interpretive judgment on someone's part regarding their purpose and scope. To know how the law will be applied in any given case, one needs to understand how judgments of this sort are made. And that in turn requires a knowledge of the ideas, habits, values, precedents, and traditions that belong to the legal order itself. For these constitute the field within which the interpretation of the law proceeds and provide the materials it employs.

There are many people whose decisions have some bearing on how the law is applied. In principle, therefore, the lawyer's expertise relates to an enormous realm of behavior—one that includes the behavior of other private individuals who have the power to deploy the law for or against the client's benefit; of administrators, inspectors, policemen, and prosecutors; and of judges. But within this vast domain it is the behavior of the last group in which lawyers are most interested. That is because judges occupy a position of preeminence among those who have a say in determining the application of the law. For whenever a question arises as to whether anyone else has properly applied the law, that question must, if pressed far enough, be settled by a judge. Judges are the final arbiters of all such questions, the princes, in Ronald Dworkin's phrase, of law's sprawling empire.[6] To be sure, the preeminence of judges is something we tend to forget, since most of the time we have no need to ask how a judge would view our conduct. It is enough to know how the tax assessor, OSHA inspector, arresting officer, or opposing counsel sees it. Very often matters stop there. But the more uncertain or controversial the legal judgments of these other actors become, the more reason one has to ask what a judge would say—the more judicial behavior becomes a focus of concern. And as doubts of this sort grow, the need for a lawyer is likely to become increasingly great. Hence although lawyers are interested in the behavior of many different people, in those situations where their services are most urgently required they often have special reason to be particularly interested in the behavior of judges. For in these situations the decisive role that judges play in the administration of the law, a role usually hidden in the background, tends to be at once more visible and important. The lawyer's expert knowledge of the law is thus above all else a knowledge of judicial behavior, of what judges are likely to do when called upon to say how the law should be applied. This is reflected in the fact that not all lawyers need to be familiar with the operation of the local zoning board or police department or the rules of the government contract office. Only specialists must know these things. But every lawyer, regardless of field, needs to understand the behavior of judges. A knowledge of this sort is the one kind all lawyers must possess: it is the core of their common professional expertise.

But precisely what sort of knowledge is this? On the narrow view, it may be likened to a farmer's knowledge of the weather. A farmer wants to grow crops. The weather, among other factors, affects his ability to do so. Obviously, the better a farmer can predict the weather, the more control he gains over his environment and the greater his chances of success. The fortunes of many public and private ventures depend, in a similar way, on events in the legal environment. Suppose, for example, that a person wants to write a will. A question then arises as to how the different forms of expression he might adopt are likely to affect the validity of his instrument in the event of a challenge to it. The more accurately a person can predict how this question will be answered by the judge who has the ultimate responsibility for deciding it, the more control he acquires over his environment. Skill at making such predictions is therefore as clear an advantage to the person drafting a will as skill at predicting the weather is to farmers. For, other things being equal, each increases the actor's power and likelihood of success.

There is, of course, an important difference between predicting the weather, on the one hand, and the result of a will contest, on the other. Droughts and thunderstorms are not intentional acts. There are no motives, reasons, or beliefs that lie behind them to which one can point as causes to explain their occurrence. A judge's decision to invalidate a will is, by contrast, an intentional act motivated by identifiable concerns and supported by specific beliefs, usually set forth in the judge's own opinion. The judge's reasons and beliefs are among the causes of his or her decision, and must therefore be taken into account by anyone wishing to explain it or to predict it in advance.[7]

Although an understanding of reasons and beliefs plays an important role in the prediction of judicial behavior, proponents of the narrow view insist that a person may acquire such an understanding without subscribing to these reasons and beliefs himself. To predict when a serial killer will strike next, for example, it may be necessary to have some understanding of his motives, but it is generally assumed that a detective investigating the case can make predictions of this sort without actually possessing the killer's motives.[8] Many believe the same is true of lawyers. Like the detective, they say, lawyers are experts at predicting the behavior of certain other human beings, namely judges, and their expertise too rests upon a knowledge of their subjects' motives. But also like the detective, lawyers are able to understand these motives without being similarly moved themselves.

The classic expression of this idea is Oliver Wendell Holmes's famous attempt to define the law from what he termed the "bad man's" point of view.[9] The bad man, Holmes said, is not at all concerned about justice or the well-being of the legal system—unlike judges, who presumably do care about these things. For purely selfish reasons, though, the bad man is very interested in being able to predict how judges will behave, and if he must study judicial psychology in order to make accurate predictions of this sort, that is what he will do. A bad man may become an expert in this regard, however, without ceasing to be bad, that is, without acquiring any of the public-spirited concerns that motivate judges. Holmes assumed that a person can possess an expert understanding of judicial behavior but continue to be bad himself. He assumed, to put it differently, that the acquisition of such expertise does not require that one be, or have the effect of turning one into, a good man motivated by the unselfish concerns of a judge. On Holmes's view there is simply no link between a person's understanding of judicial behavior, on the one hand, and the character of his own motives, on the other. Holmes believed that good motives are not a condition of such understanding, nor bad ones a bar to it.

The narrow view of law practice rests upon the same assumption. A lawyer, on this view, is merely someone who has studied judicial psychology with special care and, by acquiring a deeper knowledge of the motives and beliefs that cause judges to act as they do, has become an expert at predicting their future behavior. It is this expertise that distinguishes a lawyer from his client. But one cannot infer from the lawyer's expertise that he is himself more committed to the public-spirited concerns of the judges whom he studies than his client is—just as one cannot infer a commitment to the beliefs of the tribe that is the subject of his research from the special knowledge an anthropologist possesses. A given client may or may not be concerned about the public good, as opposed to his private interest. In the same way, a particular lawyer may or may not be a public-spirited person. This is certainly of relevance from a general moral point of view. But on the narrow conception of law practice, there is no connection between a lawyer's public-spiritedness and his professional competence, his ability to do his job well by giving clients the most accurate predictions of judicial behavior that he can. For a lawyer's ability to do this, defenders of the narrow view maintain, is not conditioned upon his own acceptance of the judicial attitudes whose influence he has learned to predict. As a result, they claim, it is possible to be both a successful lawyer and a bad man in Holmes's sense.

Those who accept this view of the lawyer's role are likely to see the case method of teaching as an appropriate means of professional training, as I do, though for very different reasons. Given the preeminence of the judge's role within the realm of law, the heavy use this method makes of judicial opinions must seem sensible from their perspective too. But the point of relying so heavily on judicial decisions will not in their view be to promote an attitude of civic-mindedness among the students. Rather it will be to increase the stock of data on which students can draw in making predictions about judicial behavior and to give them practice at formulating predictions of this sort. Seen in this light, the case method is the equivalent of anthropological field work; indeed, it *is* such work in concentrated form. And nothing in the narrow view implies that for this exercise to be successful, law students must themselves assimilate, by a process of transference, the motives and beliefs of the judges they are studying.

Nor does the narrow view attach any importance to what I have claimed is the case method's other central goal: the cultivation of deliberative wisdom. The narrow view attaches no importance to the union of sympathy and detachment in which this capacity consists because, at bottom, it attaches no importance to deliberation itself. If a lawyer is simply an instrument for effecting his client's desires, as the narrow view suggests, then there is no need for him to deliberate at all. The client does whatever deliberating is required. It only remains for his lawyer to calculate the consequences of the client's decisions and to construct an efficient path to the end that he selects. This may require great technical skill, but it does not demand either practical wisdom or civic-mindedness. Whether a lawyer happens to possess the kind of character that one acquires with these traits is thus, on the narrow view, of no significance so far as his success as a counselor or advocate is concerned. Indeed, from this perspective it is hard to see how a lawyer's character can have any bearing on his performance in either role. To be successful, a lawyer must know more than his client does. He must be an expert in his chosen field of behavioral research. But he need not be particularly wise or civic-minded. It is this assumption—that a lawyer's character is irrelevant to his professional performance—that separates the narrow view of law practice most fundamentally from my own, which joins character more closely to success.

SERVING THE CLIENT

The narrow view of what lawyers do has an appealing simplicity and is supported by the arguments of many prominent philosophers of law. It is nevertheless a mistaken view that misrepresents the nature both of counseling and of advocacy. To see why, we must take a closer look at the services a lawyer is expected to provide.

In some cases, of course, a lawyer's main task is simply to inform his client about the legal consequences of pursuing a particular objective that the client has already identified and chosen. But often the client's objective is hazy, or in conflict with other objectives, or clear but impetuously conceived. What is the lawyer's job then? Most lawyers I think would say that at a minimum it is part of their job in such cases to help clarify the client's goal by pointing out ambiguities in its conception and by identifying latent conflicts between it and other of the client's ends.[10] I say such advice is *minimally* required because it is hard to see how a lawyer can give intelligent counsel even of a purely instrumental sort until his client's aims have been clarified in this way. Of course, a lawyer might see such clarification as something he is obligated to provide, but not consider it appropriate to give his client any advice concerning the worthiness or desirability of his ends beyond the "thin" advice that is implicit in the elaboration of their meaning and consequences (the advice to choose an end that is consistent with the client's overall scheme of values, and to choose it only if the client believes the benefits of pursuing that end are worth the costs of doing so when all these costs, including hidden ones, have been taken into account). I believe that on reflection, however, most lawyers would reject such a narrow conception of their role and agree that their responsibilities to a client go beyond the preliminary clarification of his goals and include helping him to make a deliberatively wise choice among them.

That this is so may be seen most clearly in the case of what I shall call the "impetuous" client—the client who, in the grip of some domineering passion like anger or erotic love, has made a quick decision to change his life in an important way, for example, by dissolving a long-standing partnership or rewriting his will for a lover's benefit. Let us suppose the client states his objective with lucidity and insists there is no need for a further clarification of his goals. He merely wants his lawyer's help in implementing the decision he has made. Most lawyers will agree, I think, that under these circumstances it would be irresponsible simply to do what the client asks without first assuring oneself that his decision is a well-considered one. In determining whether it is, a lawyer is likely to begin by asking his client if he has thought the matter through and really wants to do what he now says he does. It may not always be clear that the client's decision is impetuous, but when surrounding circumstances suggest that it is, a responsible lawyer will test his client's judgment before accepting it, recognizing that in such situations the danger of regret is large and that a lawyer must protect his client from this familiar species of self-inflicted harm as well as the harms caused by others.

But it is not enough for a lawyer simply to ask his client whether, on reflection, he wishes to stick by his original decision, for the client's answer to this question may be as impetuous as the decision itself. If the lawyer's effort to determine whether the decision is impetuous or well-considered is to be at all meaningful, he cannot just accept his client's answer at face value. He must have some independent means of evaluating it. But from what vantage point is the lawyer to conduct such an independent inquiry? This is a difficult question, but one thing at least seems clear. It would be inappropriate for the lawyer to conduct this inquiry from the perspective of his own personal desires by asking whether *he* would want to do what the client has proposed, and to conclude that the client's decision is impetuous if the lawyer would not have made it for himself. After all, the client's desires may simply be different from those of his lawyer, and the fact that they differ in their wants is not itself a sign that the client is acting in a foolish or self-destructive way.

It is from the perspective of the client's own interests that his judgment must be assessed. To do this, a lawyer needs to place himself in the client's position by provisionally accepting his ends and then imaginatively considering the consequences of pursuing them, with the same combination of sympathy and detachment the lawyer would employ if he were deliberating on his own account. The kind of deliberation that is required in such cases might be termed "third personal," for it takes as its starting point not the ends of the person deliberating, but someone else's, and hence requires an additional, preliminary act of imagination that first-personal deliberation does not—the imaginative assumption of this foreign starting point itself. In every other respect, however, third-personal deliberation resembles its first-personal counterpart.

The lawyer's third-personal deliberations yield an independent judgment concerning the soundness of the client's decision, a judgment that is in principle distinguishable both from the client's declared views and the conclusion the lawyer would reach starting from his own personal values instead (though obviously in any given case these judgments may coincide). Of course, the lawyer's third-personal judgment is open to revision as the client presents new facts and elaborates his objectives. And by the same token, the client may change his own mind when he hears what his lawyer has to say. The process might thus best be described as one of cooperative deliberation, with the lawyer attempting to see things from the client's point of view, only more clearly, and each party being prepared to revise his or her initial judgment in light of arguments and insights the other presents. Of course, if a lawyer continues to believe that his client is acting impetuously, but is unable to persuade the client of this, a time will come when he must decide whether to do the client's bidding nonetheless. A lawyer may elect to do so, assuming the client's objective is a legal one, without violating any norm of professional responsibility as these are at present defined. But he is likely to experience the decision as a difficult one, and to feel that he has not served his client as fully as he might. The lawyer who feels this way testifies by his feeling to the fact that he considers it his duty not merely to implement the client's decision, no matter how impetuous it is, but also to help him assess its wisdom through a process of cooperative deliberation in which the lawyer examines the decision with sympathy and detachment from the client's point of view.

The lawyer with an impetuous client must consider matters from the standpoint of the client's interests and desires. Once he has assumed this standpoint, however, he proceeds just as if he were attempting to answer a personal question for himself. To do this part of his job well, therefore, a lawyer needs the same capacities that he does in deliberations of a first-personal sort. Indeed, if anything, he needs them more. For, on the one hand, he may have to make a special effort at sympathy to take his client's interests with the seriousness the client rightfully expects. And on the other hand, he must work particularly hard to sustain an attitude of detachment when deliberating on the client's behalf, since this is just what an impetuous client cannot do. The detachment he brings to their cooperative inquiry is one of the main benefits a lawyer can offer such a client, and while it may be true that the client is paying for sympathy, it is also true that he is paying for calmness and distance as well. Only those lawyers who are able to combine the qualities of sympathy and detachment are thus able to give an impetuous client the advice he needs, even if it is not always the advice he wants.

These last remarks help explain the sense in which a lawyer may sometimes be said to act as his client's friend.[11] Friends take each other's interests seriously and wish to see them advanced; it is part of the meaning of friendship that they do. It does not follow, however, that friends always accept uncritically each other's accounts of their own needs. Indeed, friends often exercise a large degree of independent judgment in assessing each other's interests, and the feeling that one sometimes has an obligation to do so is also an important part of what the relation of friendship means. What makes such independence possible is the ability of friends to exercise greater detachment when reflecting on each other's needs than they are often able to achieve when reflecting on their own. A friend's independence can be of immense value, and is frequently the reason why one friend turns to another for advice. Friends of course expect sympathy from each other: it is the expectation of sympathy that distinguishes a friend from a stranger. But they also want detachment, and those who lack either quality are likely to be poor friends.

To put the point in Aristotelian terms, friendship exists in a mean between sympathy and detachment, and requires their combination in third-personal deliberation. The same is true of the lawyer's relation to impetuous clients, and this is why in such cases his role may properly be analogized to that of a friend (not, as some have claimed, because he is prepared to stand by his client no matter what, uncritically making the client's cause his own).[12] There are, of course, obvious and important differences between the professional relation of lawyer to client, on the one hand, and most friendships, on the other. The lawyer-client relation, for example, is not reciprocal—the client is not expected to take an interest in his lawyer's affairs, as the lawyer is in his—nor do friends generally pay each other for their advice. The claim that lawyers sometimes act as friends on their clients' behalf therefore cannot be pressed too far, and it must be acknowledged that the lawyer-client relation is less complete and more one-sided than friendships generally are. But the claim does have a core of truth, for the trait that distinguishes a good lawyer is, in certain situations, one that also characterizes a good friend: an ability to combine the opposing attitudes of sympathy and detachment and to employ them in deliberating on another person's behalf.

That the lawyer's job is not merely to supply whatever means are needed to achieve the client's goals but also to deliberate with the client and on his behalf about these goals is clearest in the case of the impetuous client. But that is not the only situation in which lawyers are called upon to give the sort of deliberative advice I have described. Consider the client whose goals, though not impetuously chosen, are ambiguous or confused (surely a much larger group). At the very least, the lawyer who is presented with such a client must first clarify his goals by identifying the conflict or confusion latent in them. This is a minimal requirement because until the client's aims have been clarified, a lawyer cannot give him even the most limited sort of instrumental advice. But often this minimal requirement itself cannot be satisfied without the lawyer engaging in some third-personal deliberation on the client's behalf. Suppose, for example, that the client sets a goal—one his lawyer believes to be in conflict with another of the client's ends—and then asks what the legal costs and benefits of pursuing it will be. This is a seemingly narrow question. But to answer it a lawyer must first have some understanding of what the ends in question mean to the client and why they are important to him. For without this it will be difficult for the lawyer to say where these ends lead or what they entail and thus hard, or even impossible, to identify the costs and benefits associated with the various legal actions that might affect them. When ends are conflicting or ambiguous, identifying the consequences of pursuing them can never be a matter merely of tracing certain causal connections and making predictions based upon them. In cases of this sort, it is also often necessary to elaborate the ends involved, for the costs and benefits of the pathways to them depend upon their scope and content. To know where and at what cost the law is likely to affect a client's project, one must have an adequately clear understanding of the project itself, and merely being told by a client that he wishes to pursue a certain goal is no more guaranteed to yield such an understanding when the client is confused or ill-informed than it is when he is acting impetuously under the influence of some distorting passion.

In many cases, it is only through a process of joint deliberation, in which the lawyer imaginatively assumes his client's position and with sympathetic detachment begins to examine the alternatives for himself, that the necessary understanding can emerge. Thus even when a client is not impetuous, but merely uncertain or unclear about his ends, some measure of third-personal deliberation will often be required, and the lawyer's nominally narrow job of giving technical advice will be unperformable without it. In all these cases—of impetuosity, conflict, vagueness, and self-doubt—lawyers must regularly do something that the narrow view ignores. They must deliberate, for and with their clients, about the wisdom of their clients' ends, as opposed simply to supplying them with the legal means for realizing their desires. Such situations are by no means marginal or eccentric in the practice of law but together constitute a significant portion of the problems with which lawyers deal, including some of the most interesting and important ones. In his approach to problems of this sort, whether as counselor or advocate, a lawyer cannot be the mere minister to ambition that the narrow view portrays him as being. Here it is necessary that he exercise deliberative judgment. To perform this part of his job competently, a lawyer needs more than technical knowledge. He needs practical wisdom as well. And to have this he must possess certain traits of character, for it is in these that practical wisdom consists.

THE CONNOISSEUR OF LAW

Lawyers are not the only ones, of course, who are paid to give deliberative advice. Other professionals often give advice of this sort too. But no one except a lawyer is professionally competent to advise clients about the law. For lawyers not only know more about the law than their clients do; they know more about it than their clients' other advisors do. The law is their forte, and no other group can claim to have as much knowledge of it as they.

The narrow view of counseling and advocacy rightly emphasizes this fact and also properly points out that the distinctive knowledge lawyers possess is, above all else, a knowledge of judicial behavior. More debatably, however, proponents of this view maintain that the lawyer's superior understanding of judicial behavior is a form of anthropological expertise that, though requiring a broad familiarity with its subject, neither presupposes nor tends to instill in lawyers themselves the same attitudes and dispositions that a judge needs to do his or her own work well. To predict what a judge will do, they say, it is no more necessary that a lawyer possess the dispositions of a judge than that an anthropologist believe in totemism to forecast the behavior of the tribe he is studying. This claim is certainly plausible, but is it true?

We may start by noting one obvious respect in which the relationship of lawyer to judge differs from that of anthropologist to subject. When a lawyer gives advice to a client based upon his prediction of the future course of judicial behavior, he is engaged in an enterprise that, broadly speaking, includes the work of judges too, namely, the maintenance of the rule of law in the political society to which lawyer, judge, and client all belong. This clearly requires the creation and interpretation of public norms, something that is primarily the judge's responsibility. But it also requires the constant adjustment of private behavior to these public norms, a process in which lawyers perform an essential mediating function. Lawyers and judges play different roles within this enterprise, but their roles are nevertheless cooperative ones. For lawyers supply judges with cases to decide, and judges reciprocate by providing lawyers and their clients with decisions. We might even think of the interaction between them as a joint activity directed at producing a common product. The product that lawyers and judges together produce is the rule of law itself.

No cooperative relationship of this sort exists between an anthropologist and the members of the tribe that he is studying. The anthropologist and his subjects are not participants in a common enterprise. Their behavior is not subject to the same norms, nor can their actions plausibly be viewed as contributing to the production of some joint product. There is, to put the point differently, no internal connection between the anthropologist's project and his subjects'; an anthropologist always stands outside the practices he studies. Lawyer and judge are, by contrast, both inside a common practice, though one that is internally divided into different roles.

But even if lawyers and judges are in some broad sense engaged in a cooperative activity, this by itself does not establish that a lawyer must possess the dispositions of a judge in order to perform his own distinctive role in that activity with competence. Baseball players and umpires might also, for example, be described as participants in a common enterprise that requires their cooperation and produces a joint product (the game itself, which would be impossible without both players and officials). It does not follow, however, that baseball players must be dispassionate and coolly objective to perform their own parts well. Players and umpires have different roles with different requirements, and there is no reason to think that the temperamental qualities necessary to one are required for the other too. By analogy, even if lawyers and judges are engaged in a cooperative endeavor, the sharp differentiation between the roles they play within it would appear to support the claim that one can be a good lawyer without possessing any of a judge's traits. But this sensible-seeming conclusion is wrong, for reasons that become apparent when we reflect on a second, less obvious difference between the work of lawyers and that of anthropologists.

In the case of anthropology, and every other behavioral science, a distinction may be drawn between the evaluative judgments of the scientist himself (his beliefs concerning the right or rational response to certain occurrences) and the judgments of his subjects regarding these same events. Indeed, it is precisely this disjunction of internal and external evaluations that makes the idea of a value-free science of human behavior thinkable.[13] For if an anthropologist were unable to separate his own personal view of what is right and wrong, reasonable and unreasonable, from the view of those he is studying, he could not even aim to explain their behavior from an internal point of view—which is the only one that anthropologists with conflicting personal values can ever hope to have in common, hence the only perspective that is neutral between their different normative judgments.

But a lawyer's study of judicial behavior is not characterized by a similarly sharp distinction between his own view of what is right and wrong and the view of the judge whose behavior he wants to predict. That is because a lawyer must often make his predictions without knowing the identity of the judge or, if he knows it, without being able to rely very heavily on what information he possesses about the judge's peculiarities. Obviously, when a lawyer puts a hypothetical question to himself—how would a judge view my client's claim if we were to bring an action on it?—he cannot answer that question by determining how judge so-and-so, a specific individual with known beliefs and a record of decisions in past cases, would view it. For the lawyer's hypothetical judge has as yet no concrete identity. The sorts of predictions that counselors must make are therefore almost always about the behavior of anonymous judges.

More revealingly, perhaps, the same is true of advocates. There are several reasons for this. First, an advocate may be required to make many decisions on his client's behalf before the client's case is brought to court and a judge assigned to hear it, and with respect to these he is in the same position as a counselor who can ask only about hypothetical behavior. Second, even after a judge has been assigned, too little may be known of his or her distinctive biases for an advocate to confidently base a prediction of the judge's conduct on them; here, too, an advocate often has no choice but to proceed as if the judge's identity had not yet been revealed. And finally, even in the extreme case where a judge has idiosyncrasies that are known to influence his decisions, advocates will be constrained in their ability to tailor their arguments accordingly by the ever-present possibility of appeal and the pressure of opposing counsel (who will be quick to object whenever they feel their adversary is exploiting a prejudice the judge may not legitimately indulge). Even here, therefore, an advocate must frequently proceed *as if* the judge's identity were not known by disregarding his peculiar traits and treating him as a blank sheet instead, as if he were a hypothetical judge rather than the real one that he is. Here, also, the question that a lawyer must often ask is not, "What will Judge Jones, a known individual, say about my client's case?" but rather, "What would a judge—or judges in general—say about it?" The point is not that an advocate must view the judge before whom he appears as more intelligent or virtuous than he is, as a paragon of judicial integrity rather than an ideologue or a hack. The point is that the conditions of advocacy commonly compel him to treat the judge as if he were an anonymity, so that in attempting to predict what the judge will do, he has no choice but to guess at the behavior of someone about whom he knows only that he is a legal officer charged with certain responsibilities (which is exactly the position a counselor is in when deliberating hypothetically). How, in these circumstances, is a lawyer to decide what counsel to give his client or what argument to make on his behalf?

When a lawyer does not know the identity of the judge who will decide his case, there is only one way he can predict its outcome. That is by asking how he would decide it himself were he empowered to do so. To answer this question, a lawyer must rely on his own view of what the law requires. There will, of course, be situations in which a lawyer believes the tendency of doctrine in a certain area to be unsound (meaning not in accord with what he considers the best approach) but nevertheless likely to prevail in the thinking of most judges, and in such situations the prediction he makes regarding the decision of the case will not be based upon his own view of the law's requirements but upon someone else's. But where there is no clear doctrinal tendency, or competing precedents of roughly equal weight, a lawyer has no choice but to decide for himself what the legally correct decision would be and to base his prediction of judicial behavior on the judgment that he reaches. In situations of this sort—which are most likely to arise when a case is either new or controversial, and hence just when a lawyer's help is most required—the only way a lawyer can predict how his case will be decided is by determining what his own judgment would be were he sitting on the bench. This judgment is itself, of course, a valuable piece of information to the client, for a lawyer's view of how a case should be decided has greater predictive value than a layperson's, the lawyer being an insider who understands the goals and requirements of the legal system more thoroughly than noninitiates. But it is important to recognize that in supplying such information, a lawyer is reporting his or her own judgment regarding the proper resolution of the case and not simply describing what someone else's judgment would be. In this respect the practice of law differs fundamentally from that of anthropology and every other behavioral science.

Proponents of the narrow view are again likely to respond by granting the truth of what I say while denying that it supports the claim I have put forward—that to predict the behavior of judges accurately, a lawyer must possess, in some measure, the traits or dispositions that define the judicial attitude itself. It is true, they will say, that a lawyer often has no choice except to ask how he would decide his client's case were he sitting in judgment on it. But this is a hypothetical question that does not assume that the lawyer asking it is himself imbued with a judge's public-spirited concern for the well-being of the legal order as a whole, as opposed to an exclusively partisan zeal for his client's separate welfare. Nor is it apparent why a lawyer who shares this concern should be any better at answering the question than one who lacks it entirely.

Defenders of the narrow view thus ask us to imagine what might, at first, seem easily imaginable: a lawyer who tells his client to expect a certain outcome because in the lawyer's considered judgment the law requires this result, but who simultaneously denies any interest in the law's well-being. Having asserted that a particular decision is the legally correct one—the one that most closely fits and best promotes the good of law—why should a lawyer not be free to place whatever value he chooses on this good or to treat it with indifference, just as a person who affirms that the good of the body requires a particular regimen of exercise and diet remains free to ignore that good or even to condemn it?

The correct decision in a case may in general be defined as the one that most effectively advances the law's overall well-being. Often, however, the meaning of the law's well-being will itself be controversial, especially in close cases, and when he gives advice in cases of this sort, a lawyer cannot avoid taking a position in the interpretive debate that such controversies occasion. To take a position of this sort means, essentially, to affirm a particular conception of the law's own internal good and its requirements, to assert that the good of the law is one thing rather than another. And typically it means to assert this not just for the case at hand but across a broader field of conflict. For it is only against the background of some general conception of the law's internal good that more-specific disputes as to its meaning can usually be settled. The lawyer who wishes to decide for himself how his case should be resolved must form and then apply some conception of this sort.

Now it is possible to express an opinion in a debate concerning the good of an activity without taking an interest in that good itself. One may, for example, have an opinion about the good of cooking (is it nutritional sustenance or pleasure? how important to its achievement are senses other than that of taste? what defines a cuisine and how should the plan of a meal be arranged?) but take no interest in the activity of cooking or even view it with disgust. Typically, however—cooking again is an example—those whose opinions regarding the good of an activity are most respected and sought-after tend also to be devoted to the good in question, to care about and place a positive value on its attainment, whatever form they imagine it to take. I shall call such persons *connoisseurs*. A closer look at the phenomenon of connoisseurship, which the narrow view of law ignores, can help us understand why the good lawyer—the lawyer who excels at predicting judicial outcomes—must himself care, like a civic-minded judge, about the law's well-being, and why the accuracy of his predictions is in part a function of his own interest in the good of the law itself.

Within his or her field, the judgments of a connoisseur are generally regarded as a benchmark for the opinions of others. They are assumed to be more reliable and on the whole to reflect a better and more informed view of the aims of the enterprise in question. Thus, for example, it is connoisseurs of cooking (great chefs and gourmets) whose judgments about food generally carry the most weight. But connoisseurs are not distinguished merely by the fact that their judgments tend to be more accurate than those of others. They also typically have a keener appreciation of the objects and actions within their area of special competence. Their enjoyment of outstanding works and great performances is sharper and more refined than the enjoyment others experience, and they take a particular pleasure—one more developed and intense—in the whole field of activity that defines the limits of their connoisseurship. Thus while it may be true that a person's judgment regarding the good of a particular activity is in some cases accompanied by a personal disinterest in the realization of that good itself, the same cannot be said of connoisseurs, for the special pleasure that connoisseurs take in their field of expertise implies an interest in that field and its internal goods, whatever they may be. To say of a person that he is a connoisseur of some activity or class of objects (of cooking or gardening or nineteenth-century novels) but that he takes no interest in it or in the realization of its distinctive goods comes very close to saying something contradictory, given the ordinary meaning of the term "connoisseur" itself.

The connection between a connoisseur's more intense enjoyment of an activity and the greater reliability of his or her judgments about it is not, moreover, an accidental or fortuitous one. Indeed, the fact that a person takes special pleasure in an activity is typically (even if not invariably) a condition of acquiring the perceptual acuteness that distinguishes the judgments of a connoisseur from those of others. This is so for understandable reasons. Those who care about an activity and take an interest in it—who value the goods that are produced by the activity or are associated with its pursuit—will in general be motivated to spend the time and energy normally needed to acquire a capacity for discriminating judgment in any field of human endeavor where such judgment is required. Because they care about the activity, they will be motivated to study it more diligently. They are also likely to find it easier—less awkward or burdensome—to accept and follow, as every student must, the authoritative standards of evaluation internal to the activity that he or she is studying. The mastery of any complex activity requires discipline—the subordination of one's own initial opinions and observations to established guidelines—and the patience and humility this requires are likely to come more naturally to those who see the activity as a source of valued goods than to those who are disinterested in it.

For both these reasons, the person who values an activity and cares about it will tend, in the long run and on average, to form more solid and reliable opinions regarding the good of the activity, where this is a matter of controversy, than the person who studies it but places no value on the activity or its ends. And of course the more refined a person's judgments become—the more expert he becomes in debates about the meaning of an activity's internal goods—the more pleasure he is likely to experience in the process of judgment itself and hence in the whole activity, for in its upper reaches every interestingly complex activity consists mainly of just such a process of judgment and debate. Thus if delight in an activity tends to strengthen a person's capacity to make discriminating judgments regarding its ends or aims, it is equally true that the capacity to make such judgments tends in turn to amplify the pleasure that the activity itself affords and to reinforce the interest one takes in it. This circular process, through which a person's interest in an activity and his capacity to make the judgments it requires grow together, providing a kind of mutual support, constitutes the heart of connoisseurship as I understand it.

Activities like reading and cooking, in which we commonly speak of connoisseurs, confirm that this is so. What I am now suggesting is that the same is true of law as well, that the notion of connoisseurship, which fuses interest and judgment in the idea of taste, is equally appropriate to the work that lawyers do.

The lawyer who is asked for help either as a counselor or as an advocate will often be required, as I have said, to decide how he would view his client's situation were he himself a judge, and to do this he must form an opinion of his own as to the meaning of the good with which judges are by virtue of their office exclusively concerned—the good of the legal order as a whole, the good of the community that the laws establish and affirm. Anyone can of course offer an opinion as to the meaning of this good, whether or not he cares about or takes an interest in it. But not every opinion of this sort is equally sound, and it is plausible to think, for the reasons I have given, that those lawyers who care about the good that judges seek to realize and who thus share to some extent the public-spiritedness that defines the judicial point of view, will form judgments as to what this good requires that are on the whole sounder and more reliable than the judgments of those who are indifferent to the end adjudication serves.

The activity of adjudication imposes on all who engage in it—even lawyers merely pretending to be judges in order to evaluate their clients' claims—a discipline of argument, a set of restraints that limit the justifications that may be offered in defense of whatever decision is reached. The judgment that an ambiguous law should be interpreted in a particular way cannot be justified from an adjudicative point of view on the grounds, for example, that this interpretation is advantageous to one's client. It may be to the client's advantage, but from the standpoint of a judge—and hence from that of a lawyer attempting to determine how he would decide the case were he a judge—this fact is utterly irrelevant. All that ought to matter, from a judicial point of view, is whether the proposed interpretation best serves the whole community represented by the laws, and it is in these terms, and these alone, that the argument for any particular decision must be cast. The discipline of argument that adjudication imposes thus compels the lawyer who has imaginatively assumed the position of a judge to neutralize the value he places on his client's own welfare separately conceived. This discipline is essential to the enterprise of judging. Still, lawyers sometimes find it hard to accept. For it is at war with the partisan devotion to his client's cause that a lawyer is also expected to maintain. But those lawyers who place a value on the good of adjudication and take a personal interest in it will find it easier than those who do not to accept this discipline and to evaluate their clients' self-interested positions with the neutrality inherent in the judge's civic-minded point of view.

A lawyer may, of course, submit to the discipline of adjudication for purely external reasons, for reasons of self-interest having nothing to do with the internal good of adjudication itself, just as one may, for example, submit to the discipline of physical exercise for the sake of acquiring a healthy appearance without placing any intrinsic value on health. But however powerful the external interests that motivate a person to discipline himself in this way, his acceptance of its requirements is bound to be less wholehearted—more qualified, tentative, conditional, and easily reversed—than the commitment of the person who regards the ends of the activity in question as worthy in themselves, as producing goods that are valuable for their own sake and not merely as a means to something else. The person who views the discipline that an activity imposes simply as a means will always be on the lookout for less strenuous methods of achieving his or her ends and will be prepared to cut corners when the opportunity arises. If, for example, one exercises for the sake of appearances only, cosmetics will always be a competitive alternative. The person whose commitment to the discipline of an activity is conditional in this way will be less likely to give himself over to it with the same steadiness and concentration that he would if his commitment were supported by a belief in the value of the activity's internal goals. And because of this he will be less likely to achieve a mastery of the discipline sufficient to enable him to participate with expertness and authority in debates about the meaning of these goals themselves, when the goals are controversial.

That this is true in the case of physical exercise seems obvious and is confirmed by the fact that those who are at first motivated to exercise for appearance's sake often work quite deliberately to cultivate an appreciation of the good of health itself, believing, correctly, that the latter is more likely to supply a sufficiently strong motive to sustain their commitment to exercise over the long term. Something similar is true in law. Those lawyers who value the internal aims of judging are more likely than those who do not to accept its discipline and eventually to master it, acquiring the kind of understanding that distinguishes the opinions of an expert from other less authoritative views. The lawyer who wishes to give his client the best advice he can, who wishes to do the best possible job of determining how he would decide his client's case were he himself a judge, therefore has reason to acquire an interest in the aims of adjudication. He has reason to cultivate the attitude of civic-mindedness that defines the judicial point of view. And, like an advancing connoisseur in any field, he has reason to hope that his appreciation of the good of judging will be strengthened by the exercise of his own developing capacity for judgment in close cases.

It follows that a lawyer's ability to predict the course of judicial behavior cannot be separated, as the narrow view assumes, from the dispositional attitude he himself takes toward the activity of adjudication and its own internal good. To be a successful lawyer, one must care about this good and take an interest in it, and though such an attitude is not the only condition of success in the practice of law, it is close to being an essential one. Because the narrow view denies this, it presents an essentially false picture of law practice, one that obscures the contribution that legal education, conceived as a form of moral habituation, makes to the work not only of judges but of counselors and advocates too. The narrow view makes this conception of legal education appear absurd. But when the phenomenon of connoisseurship is rightly understood, it is the narrow view that begins to seem implausible. The narrow view fails to take account of the connection between judgment and disposition that the connoisseur exemplifies. Once one acknowledges this connection to be as important in the law as in other fields, however, one is forced also to accept that the cultivation of the required dispositions is a legitimate, indeed necessary, part of legal education and thus to affirm what the narrow view denies: that to practice his craft well, a lawyer needs character as well as intelligence and information.

This does not mean that in practicing his craft a good lawyer must always advise his client to behave in the way that best comports with the lawyer's own perception of the law's well-being. Sometimes even a good lawyer feels bound, out of loyalty to his client, to recommend an action at odds with the assessment he would make of the client's position from a judicial point of view. A lawyer may recommend, for example, that his client bring a lawsuit that, though not frivolous, is one the lawyer thinks should lose, if the action has sufficient nuisance value. Or he may advise his client to breach a contract that the other party, though in the right, will find too expensive to enforce. There are limits on a lawyer's freedom to offer such advice. He cannot, for example, encourage a client to commit embezzlement even if he is certain the crime will never be detected; nor can he prepare fraudulent tax documents on the client's behalf in the belief that the IRS is too busy with other matters to inspect them closely. These are actions that go beyond the limits of the loyalty lawyers may show their clients, and even the first two recommendations skate quite close to the edge. Still, the fact remains that within the bounds of what lawyers are ethically permitted to do cases arise in which there is a divergence between the client's well-being and that of the law itself.

Situations of this sort present a dilemma for the lawyer involved. If lawyers were required to act with the same wholehearted devotion to the law that judges must show, no dilemma would exist. Nor would it exist if lawyers were free to do whatever they could to achieve their clients' aims. But lawyers in our legal system have divided allegiances. On the one hand, they are expected to be partisan champions of their clients' interests, and on the other, impartial officers of the court, duty-bound to uphold the law's integrity. When these allegiances conflict, a lawyer cannot fulfill all of his responsibilities at once. He must choose between them, and this creates a moral dilemma for the lawyer involved. Only if he allots his two responsibilities to separate spheres, divided by the limits of ethical permissibility, and insists that within these limits the interests of the client must be given absolute priority but beyond them none at all—only then will his sense of moral difficulty vanish. But this is a mechanical solution to a complex problem that no simple jurisdictional rule can solve (as the endless debate about the meaning of professional responsibility within the bounds of permissible conduct attests). Everyone who enters the practice of law must grapple with this dilemma, just as every politician must confront the problem of dirty hands.

Here, too, the real challenge is not to overcome the dilemma (for that cannot be done), but to resist the temptation to resolve it by always putting the client's well-being before the law's. There are many pressures pushing in this direction. There is, to begin with, the money a lawyer will lose if he refuses to do his client's bidding. There is the understandable desire not to appear a hopelessly high-minded prig, always talking down to others and giving them Polonian advice. And finally, there is the lawyer's professional duty of zealous representation, which provides a moral foundation for these other, more selfish concerns. It is not that lawyers must never prefer the interests of their clients to those of the legal system as a whole. In the situations of which I am now speaking it is always permissible and often appropriate to do exactly that. But the forces pressing in this direction are very strong, and the lawyer who cannot resist them will eventually cease to see his situation as morally problematic at all. He will end up doing what his client wants in every case and feeling no qualms about it, comforted by the thought that his conflicting loyalties belong to separate spheres instead of struggling to remain faithful to both in every aspect of his professional life.

The capacity to resist these pressures is in part a matter of courage. A courageous lawyer is prepared to take risks for what he or she believes is right—to risk anger, contempt, and a lower income for the sake of the law's own good—and nothing can be a substitute for the fortitude this requires. But the more a lawyer values the well-being of the law, the more likely he is to be able to summon such courage when needed. The good lawyer does care about the soundness of the legal order. Contrary to what the narrow view suggests, he shares the judge's public-spirited devotion to it. This is in fact a condition for his being successful at his work. The good lawyer's public-spiritedness is not, moreover, something tacked onto his professional skills, a kind of moralistic addendum to his craft. Rather, it is an essential component of that craft and cannot be separated from it. This internal anchorage of his devotion to the law in the good lawyer's craft gives it a strength and resilience it would not otherwise have. And while the strength of his commitment to the law's well-being does not free the good lawyer from the moral dilemma created by his competing loyalties to client and court, it does intensify his awareness of this dilemma and thus makes it harder for him to slide into the easy habit of resolving all such conflicts in the client's favor. It makes it harder for him to accept the reassuring idea that any action he may perform for the client is one he must. In the end, a heightened awareness of this sort is the greatest asset a lawyer has in attempting to meet the moral conflicts his work presents with a measure of courage and responsibility. The lawyer who takes Holmes's bad man as a model is poorly equipped to do this because he does not even notice that a conflict exists. The good lawyer, by contrast, enjoys all of the advantages that any practitioner who candidly acknowledges the dilemma created by competing allegiances may reasonably hope to possess.

ADVOCACY

Though often intertwined in practice, counseling and advocacy are distinct activities. As an advocate, a lawyer speaks to others on his client's behalf and does not—cannot—show any of the ambivalence or uncertainty about the client's position that a counselor must acknowledge to do his own job well. Up to this point, however, I have treated these two activities indifferently. I have said that all practicing lawyers must deliberate about their clients' ends and not just about the means for reaching them. And I have claimed they must be connoisseurs of judging moved by a concern for the good of the law itself. But it may be objected that even if these claims have some validity so far as counseling is concerned, they are clearly inapplicable to advocacy. This objection is a serious one and deserves a careful answer.

Two things give it plausibility. First, the lawyer who is acting as an advocate begins work only after his client's objectives have been set. In his capacity as counselor, speaking privately as a friend, a lawyer is free to criticize his client's ends. But when he acts as an advocate, speaking to others on the client's behalf, a lawyer must accept the client's goals as fixed and pursue them unswervingly. An advocate thus appears to have no need for the wisdom in deliberating about as-yet unsettled ends that counseling requires.

Second, it is hard to understand why civic-mindedness should be a condition of success in advocacy even if it is in counseling. An advocate is the representative of one particular interest in actual or potential conflict with others, and it is not his duty to define the collective well-being of those involved or to determine how it can be achieved. The advocate's job, as most people see it, is simply to get as much as he can for his client, and a judicial disposition seems not only unnecessary for this job but perhaps even a hindrance of sorts, an obstacle to the deployment of that maximum of preferential zeal that an advocate is paid to exert on his client's behalf.

Thus neither deliberative wisdom nor civic-mindedness appears to play as important a role in advocacy as in counseling. However inappropriate the term "hired gun" may seem when applied to counselors, it is therefore likely to strike many as an accurate description of the advocate's function. And if one assumes, in addition, that advocacy is the most characteristic activity of lawyers generally, then the image of the hired gun and the narrow view of law practice associated with it can easily become the dominant image of lawyers as a group. The persistence of the narrow view is in fact largely a consequence of this. For once we assume that advocates are hired guns and advocacy the most important part of what most lawyers do, the conclusions of the narrow view follow irresistibly.[14]

The first point to be made about this conception of advocacy is that its implications are more limited than they appear. Advocacy and counseling are, it is true, distinct activities. But among those lawyers who function primarily in the first capacity, there are few who do not occasionally act in the second as well. The giving of advice to one's client (as distinguished from the representation of the client's interests to third parties) is a routine part of the practice of most advocates and though lawyers tend to specialize in either counseling or advocacy, it is rare and perhaps impossible to practice the latter exclusively. Thus even if we assume, for the sake of argument, that the capacities required for success in counseling are not also needed by an advocate, the lawyer who plans to specialize in advocacy has reason to acquire these capacities too, for even his work demands that he function as a counselor from time to time. For the many advocates whose work requires them to perform both sorts of tasks, a proper professional training must therefore include, as one of its components, the cultivation of those traits of prudence and public-spiritedness that are essential to success in counseling. The fact that most law students do not yet know what sort of practice they will have reinforces this conclusion.

It must be admitted, however, that this first point is a weak one. For it accepts what the narrow view asserts about the advocate's role and attempts merely to contain the implications of this view by restricting the number of cases to which it applies. It is also something of a double-edged response: if most lawyers have mixed practices, then the capacities and attitudes of the advocate will be as much needed by a specialist in counseling as the counselor's traits are needed by a specialist in advocacy. But the narrow view of advocacy suffers from a second and more serious deficiency, for the picture it presents of advocacy itself is undeveloped and misleading. A closer look at what advocates do reveals an important similarity between their work and the activity of counseling, and makes it plain that the civic-mindedness that characterizes the connoisseur of judging is as necessary to success in one branch of practice as in the other.

Advocates are sometimes described as champions chosen to fight on their clients' behalf, like the medieval champions whose duty it was to represent their sponsors in a public contest of arms. There is, of course, a sense in which this comparison is justified. But there is also a clear difference between a legal advocate and an armed champion, for an advocate uses arguments rather than instruments of physical violence to promote his client's cause. It is sometimes said that arguments can be weapons of violence too.[15] Perhaps there is some truth in this. Still, arguments achieve their effect in a way fundamentally different from that of a club or a gun. To be effective, an argument must persuade the person to whom it is addressed; the addressee must himself assent to the truth or wisdom of whatever claims the argument advances. Holding a gun to someone's head may also, in a sense, be persuasive, but here compliance with the gunman's wishes is not motivated by the victim's own assent to the soundness of whatever arguments the gunman makes to justify his conduct. Indeed, the victim's compliance in cases of this kind is usually accompanied by his unspoken rejection of all such arguments, which is why we speak of his being persuaded only in an ironic sense. By contrast, when an argument is genuinely persuasive, its acceptance supplies the addressee's motive to comply. A legal advocate, whose weapons are words, must win such acceptance for his or her arguments in order to get the person to whom they are directed to do what the advocate wants. Unlike a gladiator, an advocate cannot prevail through physical force alone.

This obvious fact means that a lawyer arguing before a judge must persuade the judge that his client's position is the legally correct one. And that means he must take account of the judge's own conception of what is right and wrong from a legal point of view, for this conception forms the framework within which the lawyer's arguments will be assessed, and therefore determines whether or not the judge finds them persuasive. To be successful in any situation, an advocate must understand the concerns of the person he is addressing and modify his arguments accordingly. It follows that a lawyer arguing before a judge who is responsible for maintaining the well-being of the law must himself become a master of analysis from the judicial point of view, for otherwise he will not know what to say to advance his client's cause.

In the absence of reliable information about the eccentricities of the particular judge before whom he is arguing—information that is often unavailable and in any case cannot be made the basis for a general training in the art of advocacy—the lawyer most likely to possess the required mastery of judicial argument will be the one who is a connoisseur of judging in the sense suggested earlier. The requirements for success in advocacy are in this respect quite similar to those for success in counseling. In both branches of law practice a lawyer must ask himself how he would view his client's case were he the judge responsible for deciding it. It makes no difference whether the client is already involved in a controversy or is merely contemplating an action that may lead him into one. In either case, this question is the first that a lawyer must address, and everything he subsequently does depends upon his answer to it.

Not all lawyers, however, are equally competent in this regard. In particular, those who are connoisseurs of judging are more likely to give consistently better answers than those who are not. If they are counselors, they are therefore likely to give their clients better advice, and if they are advocates, to be more effective in representing their clients' interests before judges. But to be a connoisseur of judging is not simply to know more about adjudication than others do. It is also to be positively disposed toward its internal good, to possess in some measure a judicial concern for the good the law aims to secure. In the law as elsewhere this disposition is a condition of the connoisseur's discernment. An advocate who hopes to make persuasive arguments to judges must thus himself share, to some degree, the civic-minded concerns of the judges before whom he speaks. He must have a judicial temperament of his own. Plato says that an orator who speaks before public assemblies needs a democratic soul, one that shares the interests and ambitions of its audience.[16] My point is that the soul of an advocate who argues before judges requires the ambitions of its audience too—the judicial ambition to preserve and perfect the community of law.

Sometimes, however, an advocate must make his arguments to a jury rather than to a judge. Jurors are laypersons untrained in the law. Unlike judges, their task is not to promote the well-being of the legal system as a whole but merely to find the facts in a particular dispute. A lawyer arguing before a jury might therefore seem to have less need for the public-spiritedness he requires in arguing to judges. What is really vital here, one might suppose, is showmanship, rhetoric, and, above all, an ability to move the jurors by playing on their prejudices, which the process of jury selection can help an advocate identify and (through the careful use of *voir dire* challenges) even shape in advance.

But there are two reasons why the arguments that lawyers make to juries are less sharply distinguished from those they make to judges than this common view suggests. First, in the courtroom as elsewhere, it is a judge who decides the limits within which the actions of other officials (police and prosecutors, for example) are permitted to determine the outcome in any particular case. This applies to juries too. Jurors are officials *pro tempore,* and disputes about the boundaries of their competence must in the end be settled by judicial decision as well. In arguing to a jury, an advocate must keep these boundary issues and their likely resolution in mind. He must ask himself whether he is urging the jury to weigh evidence, draw inferences, and reach conclusions that a judge will disallow. Even in moments of impassioned advocacy, therefore, he must keep one eye on the proceedings from a judicial point of view, and the flow of legal objections, responses, and side-bar conversations that punctuates most jury trials helps to ensure that he does.

Second, and more important, the empanelment of a jury imposes on its members a special duty of fair-mindedness much like that incumbent on a judge. This is an aspirational ideal, but it influences the deliberations of the jurors themselves. In deliberating, jurors are called upon to be more balanced than they are outside the courtroom, and most strive to live up to the responsibilities of their temporary office—to be judicious in considering the evidence and evaluating the parties' claims.[17] A desire to sustain this attitude is in fact a defining feature of the juror's role (as Tocqueville emphasized when he praised the institution of jury service as a training ground for citizenship).[18] To be successful, a lawyer who argues before juries must take this aspiration into account and shape his arguments to suit it. He must make his arguments persuasive to someone who *wants* to be fair-minded. He must learn, therefore, to view the disputes in which his clients are involved from the vantage point a judicious person would assume. And the lawyers best able to do this will on the whole be those for whom judiciousness is itself a value, for the same psychological reasons that explain why those who care about the good of adjudication are more likely to succeed in arguing to judges.

To be sure, the known identities of jurors may suggest ways in which an advocate can tailor his appeal to their biases and beliefs. But despite the exaggerated claims that are sometimes made on behalf of the "science" of jury selection, such knowledge remains severely limited, and there is, in addition, the pressure of opposing counsel to constrain its use where it exists.[19] This means that in arguing to juries, an advocate must often proceed on the same counterfactual assumption as when arguing to a judge, by treating his audience as if it were composed of anonymous officials clothed with certain powers and responsibilities but lacking known attributes of a more personal kind. Both sorts of advocacy are similarly constrained, and both therefore depend, in the end, on the advocate's own devotion to the law's internal good to achieve their intended effect.

The fact that arguments to judges and juries take place in a courtroom helps explain why public-spiritedness is essential to their success. For in a courtroom the well-being of the law is not only a subject of explicit concern; it is a value superior to all others. But advocacy is not restricted to the courtroom. Lawyers also make arguments on their clients' behalf in a wide variety of private settings. They make arguments not only to judges and juries but to partners, agents, employees, spouses, and other lawyers as well. Here, too, the advocate's job is to persuade, but in situations of this sort his arguments are typically addressed to someone who cares only about his or her own well-being, or the well-being of a client, and not the good of the law as such. I have said that an advocate must always take his audience's interests seriously. Does this mean that when trying to persuade a private individual motivated solely by self-interest, an advocate can do without the public-spiritedness he needs in arguments to judge and jury?

Let us consider the matter more carefully. In private negotiations the person to whom an advocate addresses his arguments is indeed often concerned only with his own advantage. To persuade such a person, one must convince him that his own welfare favors the decision he is being urged to make. But an advocate also has a responsibility to his client and must be careful to ensure that any proposals he puts forward promote the client's interests too. In the situations I am now considering, it is therefore necessary for an advocate to search out arrangements that advance the interests of the client and some third party simultaneously. For only these permit him to secure his client's goals while providing the basis for an effective appeal to the self-interest of the other party too. Put differently, an advocate representing either of the parties to a private negotiation must make an effort to identify opportunities for improving the welfare of both and then persuade them to go along.

To be sure, opportunities of this sort normally yield a surplus that can be divided in different ways, and an advocate will want to engross as much of this surplus as he can for his own client's benefit, using cajolery, threats, and bluffing to do so. But the use of these techniques has limits, for no third party will agree to terms from which he does not profit. Consequently, if an advocate is to know the limits beyond which his own client's advantage cannot be pressed—an essential condition of effective bargaining—he must understand the other party's interests at least as well as the latter does, and grasp the cooperative dimension of the situation along with its competitive side. If there are no opportunities for joint improvement through cooperation, there is nothing for the parties to negotiate. In that sense, we might say, the cooperative possibilities of a relationship define the boundaries within which either party can pursue his own advantage at the other's expense.

Even in private negotiations, therefore, an advocate must be more than a ruthlessly partisan competitor. He must also be an expert in cooperation, and be able to discern where opportunities for cooperation lie. For the same reasons that I have stressed throughout, it is plausible to think that those who have a taste for cooperation—who value cooperative arrangements and take pleasure in their discovery and explanation to others—will be more likely than those who do not to possess the required discernment. It is the connoisseur of cooperation who has the best chance of acquiring an aptitude for identifying the cooperative possibilities that limit the competition for resources most private negotiations involve. To be an effective advocate in such settings, one must of course relish a good fight. But in the outstanding advocate—the one who is exceptionally good at his or her job—this pleasure will be offset by the very different satisfaction afforded by the achievement of cooperation itself.

This last achievement amounts to the creation of a certain type of community—one we might call transactional to distinguish it from other sorts of cooperative arrangements—and the pleasure a lawyer takes in the establishment of such communities resembles the attitude of public-spiritedness that defines the judicial point of view.[20] These sentiments belong to a common family of feelings. There is much in the ceremony of the courtroom and in the formal rules of professional conduct to remind even the most zealous advocate that he too is an officer of the court, a public official expected to share the judge's civic-minded devotion to the law.[21] In the privacy of a negotiating session, where the symbols of this devotion are absent and there is no discipline of argument requiring a lawyer to ground his position in some conception of the public good, it might seem that the spirit of civic-mindedness is out of place and in any case irrelevant to an advocate's success. Yet even here, where his arguments are most openly self-serving, an advocate needs something that resembles the judge's concern for the good of the community he serves. He needs a love of cooperation, and of the arrangements that encourage it, to do his own job well. To advance his client's interests in negotiations of this sort, a lawyer must not only understand what his adversary wants. He must also see more clearly than either party often does what opportunities exist for their collaboration, and the lawyer who enjoys creating transactional communities is most likely to spy them out. Even where it seems least public-spirited, therefore, the work of a successful advocate possesses a communitarian dimension—one it displays less openly, perhaps, than do other forms of advocacy, but still shares in common with them.

THE CONSERVATISM OF LAWYERS

A legal education must do more than impart information and technical skills. It must also inculcate the character-virtues of prudence and public-spiritedness. For contrary to what the narrow view implies, a lawyer needs these virtues to succeed both as counselor and as advocate. Together they form the core of his or her professional character, and one important function of the case method of law teaching is to prepare students for practice by nourishing these traits.

The case method is not, of course, the only means for doing so. Long before it was invented as a technique for training lawyers— long before the emergence of the modern law school as we know it—prudence and public-spiritedness were extolled as virtues for lawyers and instilled by a blend of apprenticeship and broad humanistic learning. The ideal of the lawyer-statesman is much older than the case method and for a long time drew its vitality from other sources. But in this century these other sources have disappeared. Apprenticeship training under the supervision of practicing lawyers has been replaced by a program of graduate-level university instruction that has itself become increasingly specialized, losing much of the intermixture with history and literature that characterized the formal legal education of the early-nineteenth-century bar. These changes have altered fundamentally the way that lawyers learn their craft. They have not, however, caused the virtues of the lawyer-statesman to become professionally irrelevant or impossible to teach. These virtues are as much required by lawyers today as they were two centuries ago—they are perennial necessities—and the greatness of the case method is that it provides for their continuing cultivation within the limits of the more specialized academic training lawyers now receive. Whatever other ends it serves, the case method of law teaching also promotes the character traits of prudence and public-spiritedness that the ideal of the lawyer-statesman stressed, and long after the disappearance of the conditions that originally sustained it, helps to keep that ideal alive in the habit-forming classroom experiences to which all beginning lawyers are exposed.

In addition to these two traits, the case method encourages another, the tendency to take a conservative view of law and politics, in a sense I shall explain. The conservatism of lawyers is a further feature of their professional character and belongs, along with the others I have mentioned, to the ensemble of dispositional attitudes that the lawyer-statesman ideal endorses.

The observation that American lawyers tend to be conservative on account of their training and experience has of course been made before, most famously by Tocqueville.[22] According to Tocqueville, two factors explain the conservatism of the American bar. First, lawyers in America (like their English counterparts) are closely connected to the propertied class. Many lawyers make their living by defending the interests of this class and thus naturally sympathize with them. Because of this, lawyers tend to oppose as vigorously as their wealthy clients do the destabilization of property rights that accompanies every rapid change in the legal order, especially revolutionary ones.

The second factor that Tocqueville mentions is internal to the legal profession itself. The ceremonial trappings of the law and, above all, the discipline of legal reasoning, with its requirements of orderliness and precision, encourage a love of intellectual regularity in the American lawyer and a contempt, he says, for the unruly proceedings of democratic assemblies. Tocqueville describes this contempt as an "aristocratic" sentiment and claims that it produces a generalized hostility to popular political reform.

Without denying the validity of Tocqueville's observations, I would explain the conservatism of modern-day American lawyers in a somewhat different way, as a product of the case method of teaching through which law students in America are inducted into their profession. For this method tends inevitably to promote a certain skepticism regarding the power of abstract ideas and to encourage a kind of pragmatic gradualism that constitutes the core of one familiar species of legal and political conservatism.

Law cases worthy of appeal (those, in any event, that are selected for inclusion in the casebooks students use) generally present a contest between principles more or less balanced in their plausibility, and when they do not, law teachers work hard to invent hypothetical variants that do. Even in the closest case, of course, one or the other of these principles must yield and a justification be constructed to support the prevailing point of view, for without such a justification any decision is bound to seem lawless and arbitrary. But the attractions of the losing principle—which, by assumption, came very close to winning—typically exert a counterpressure against the interpretive expansion of its victorious adversary. To be sure, some such expansion is implicit merely in the claim that the winning principle controls the case at hand, for if the case is a close or novel one, this claim itself extends the reach of the prevailing principle beyond its previous limits. The closer the case, however, the smaller this expansion is likely to be. Because the cases selected for study by law students typically present a conflict between principles at the boundary of their respective fields of application, the victory of one principle over the other usually implies only a marginal adjustment in their relationship. The more abstract the explanation one offers in defense of this adjustment, however, the larger the territory that must be added to one principle and subtracted from its competitor. Consequently, if the near-equipoise of the principles in conflict in a close case generally makes a marginal adjustment in their relationship preferable to a wholesale one, then those defenses of the winning principle that are narrow and concrete will generally be better fitted to the outcome of the case than those whose abstractness necessarily entails some more far-reaching change. Because it systematically selects for marginal conflicts of this kind, the case method tends to encourage a preference for narrow justifications over broad ones, and to discourage the belief that hard cases—the cases of greatest professional interest to lawyers—can be decided on the basis of abstract principles that sweep too broadly and omit too much of the peculiarities that distinguish the specific case at hand.

The case method thus undermines students' faith in the power of abstract ideas as instruments of analysis and control and focuses their attention on the details of specific cases instead, encouraging them to search in these details for some small distinguishing mark, some marginal qualification, that will permit them to decide a particular case one way or another without compromising too greatly the losing principle the case involves. The student who is given a steady diet of hard cases and is trained to look for small distinctions grows used to the idea that the sorts of conflicts with which he is professionally concerned cannot, in most instances, be sensibly resolved merely by adopting some scheme of general principles and then sticking to it unwaveringly, using the principles he has chosen as a kind of solvent to decide every conflict in which they play a part. Whether or not this is a good way of proceeding in philosophy, it is almost always a very bad way of proceeding in the law, a point the case method drives home by confronting students with a series of closely balanced contests whose resolution, on the basis of the most marginal distinctions, typically produces not the clean line one would expect if they had been decided according to some single scheme of abstract principles, but a set of irregularly connected dots instead.

Of course, law school casebooks are more than collections of appellate opinions. Modern casebooks all include a variety of other materials as well. Some of these are meant to give students a better understanding of the concrete setting in which a particular case arose and to make their mental picture of the parties more vivid and detailed—to help students see the human beings behind an opinion's abstractions. Materials of this sort (of which Richard Danzig's elaborate case studies are a good example) seek to put additional flesh on what would otherwise be too skeletal a treatment of the issues.[23] They encourage students to demand more facts, to insist on a further specification of the parties and their claims, and to be suspicious about overly broad categories of analysis. The aim of such materials is to turn the student's attention from the general to the particular, and because of this they tend inevitably to reinforce the doubts about abstraction that the study of closely balanced cases already creates.

But other materials have the opposite aim, for they seek to draw the student's attention to broad structural regularities that the details of individual cases hide from view, to turn the eye from the particular to the general. Most of the economic and philosophical materials that are included in casebooks today fall into this second category. The point of giving law students some acquaintance with these disciplines is not, however, to equip them with a comprehensive scheme into which the opinions that they read may then be fit. It is, more modestly, to give them a few additional tools for thinking and talking about cases—tools that belong to a grab bag of techniques, none of which exhausts the cases' meaning or settles all the conflicts they present. Indeed, the purpose of introducing law students to the methods of philosophy and economics is as much to demonstrate their limits as to display their power, to make it clear that the study of specific cases demands a type of judgment no such method can supply. In this respect the role these methods play in legal argument is very different from the one they play in their own home disciplines.

Philosophers and economists use cases to illustrate general principles and to test their reach. The importance of a case, for them, depends upon its contribution to the theoretical inquiry in which they are engaged. It is from the standpoint of that inquiry and its objectives that the value of particular cases must be assessed. In law it is the other way around: the value of every theory must be measured from the perspective of the cases that provide the focal subject of debate.

There is always more to a case—both in the law and out—than any theory can explain; that is a consequence of abstraction itself. But whether we treat this inexplicable residue as an irrelevant detail or as a telling reminder of the limits of theoretical explanation depends upon which perspective we adopt. It depends upon whether we think about cases from the standpoint of theories, or theories from the perspective of cases. Generally speaking, it is the former point of view that prevails in disciplines such as philosophy and economics and the latter that governs in law. Hence when methods from these other disciplines are introduced into legal studies, they are put to a use that inverts their ordinary relationship to cases. They are brought within a discipline that puts cases before theories and whose dominant mood is therefore one of skepticism and doubt rather than the optimistic faith in abstraction that animates every genuinely scientific branch of study. Indeed, they are made to serve, in a way quite foreign to their native spirit, as instruments for the advancement of skepticism by having their inability to explain specific cases constantly pointed out. Hence even these methods, when they are employed in the manner the case method invites, tend more to weaken the law student's confidence in the power of ideas than to give it (as we might expect) additional support.

Many law students find this disturbing. That is because they begin their careers with idealistic expectations, in a twofold sense. First, they believe a career in the law will enable them to serve the public good. It is essential that the education lawyers receive strengthen this belief, and I have tried to show that the case method does so by assigning a priority to the judicial point of view, thereby encouraging a civic-minded devotion to the good of the law as a whole. But beginning law students are often idealistic in a second sense as well, for they tend to place greater confidence than more-experienced lawyers do in the power of abstract ideas to provide needed guidance amid the complexities of political and legal life. This side of their idealism is the product, in part, of youth and inexperience and, in part, of the education they have received as undergraduates. The case method is designed to break down this second kind of idealism, and when it succeeds, its results are bound to be disillusioning.

The experience of such disillusionment is familiar to most law students, many of whom complain that the study of law threatens to rob them of their souls. But what the case method really robs them of is their faith in large ideas, and what it puts in place of this faith is a form of skepticism—the tendency to look with suspicion on broad generalizations, to search for the qualifying exception to every abstraction, to insist on the importance of details.[24] Students who become skeptics in this sense are likely, in time, to find complexity more congenial than simplicity, and though their skepticism may at first extend only to the usefulness of abstractions in the law, there will be a natural tendency for their doubts to grow into a generalized pragmatism that views with suspicion any political program inspired by their old faith in the power of ideas. Those who still possess this faith will be less likely than those who have lost it to see—or, if they see, to feel constrained by—the obstacles that the world puts in the path of every project of reform. They will be more willing to turn the world upside down for the sake of an idea. Skeptics who view abstractions with distrust will tend to have a different attitude toward politics in general, one that prefers small changes to large ones, and slow, tentative adjustments to those that are fast or irreversible. They will believe in the value of caution and the second look, and will give more credit than their idealistic counterparts do to what, from the latter's point of view, seem only like the world's stupidities.

By encouraging a certain skepticism toward the usefulness of abstract ideas as instruments of legal judgment, the case method thus promotes a preference for gradualism in politics generally. This is one way in which it works to inculcate a conservative outlook among lawyers. A second and even more important way in which it does so is by cultivating an attitude of moral cosmopolitanism that is best expressed, perhaps, by the old Roman motto *nihil humanorum alienum meum est,* "nothing human is foreign to me."[25]

Many law students do not, initially at least, share the sentiment this saying expresses, and indeed anyone who believes (as young people often do) that human values are not ultimately plural and conflicting will be likely to reject it out of hand. The latter view is marked by an optimism and self-confidence about the reconcilability of human values that all moral cosmopolitanism of the Roman variety lacks. The case method attacks this youthful confidence by cultivating a combination of sympathy and detachment whose natural effect is to make the differences among human goods more patent and to weaken the belief that conflicts among them can be settled in a principled way.

By multiplying moral perspectives and compelling students to adopt them as their own while at the same time encouraging an attitude of judicial dispassion remote from any interested point of view, the case method of law teaching fosters a cosmopolitanism that is marked by its breadth of sympathy, on the one hand, and by a coolness to the whole range of interests that human beings pursue with such passionate intensity, on the other. This attitude can of course degenerate into indifference and apathy, as it did for many stoics.[26] For if values are plural and the tensions among them ineliminable, then doubts are bound to arise regarding the point of morality itself, and of law to the extent its purposes are conceived in moral terms. The case method, which inevitably stimulates such doubts, cannot avoid the dangers they present and must, if it is to be more than an engine of stoical apathy, attempt in some fashion to mitigate them.

This it does in the only way it can: not by means of abstract argument, but through the presentation of what must frankly be admitted are inspirational examples, the examples of lawyers and judges who have made for themselves a meaningful life, or at least meaningful moments, amid the law's moral ambiguities. To acknowledge that human goods conflict and that nothing in the end can be done to harmonize them, while continuing to believe in the value and dignity of moral argument and of law conceived as a process of such argument—while resolving, in fact, to devote the whole of one's professional life to the administration and refinement of the law so understood—is a very great achievement. It is, indeed, an ideal, and not everyone who undertakes the study of law attains it. Some, instead, hold on to their simplifying faith in abstract ideas, and others give in to the temptation of indifference. But the case method, when it works as it is meant to, sets students on a middle course, strengthening their moral imagination and encouraging them to take a more cosmopolitan view of the diversity of human goods, while also reinforcing, through its insistence on the priority of the judicial point of view, the habit of civic-mindedness that is the only reliable antidote to the cynicism into which all cosmopolitanism threatens to decline.

This combination of cosmopolitanism and civic-mindedness is a key element in the lawyer's professional character and helps to define the particular human type represented by the idealized figure of the lawyer-statesman. This ideal is an essentially conservative one. For however deep a lawyer's devotion to the public good, one who possesses the traits I have described also accepts, to a degree no moral zealot can, the irreconcilable diversity of human goods, and therefore tends to see in every controversial alteration of his society's arrangements some loss as well as an opportunity for gain. As a result, such a lawyer is unlikely to be moved by that passion for purity which motivates the adherents of every great political simplification and to be more comfortable with strategies of compromise and delay. Recognizing the moral imperative for change, the lawyer who embraces this ideal will nevertheless prefer to move slowly and by small degrees. He or she will be repelled by all programs of utopian ambition, whether Platonic or Kantian or Benthamite in inspiration, and in the quirks and absurdities of the *status quo* will be likely to see what no utopian can: a whole series of unthought-out local compromises and adjustments that reflect the plurality of human goods and soften the consequences of their inevitable conflict.

The lawyer-statesman whose portrait I have sketched is not a mindless defender of the status quo, but is tempermentally inclined to see a value in the irregularities of the existing order and to proceed with caution in leveling them out. The lawyer-statesman sees more in these arrangements than others do and tends to be less optimistic about reform than those for whom only a narrower range of moral experience is imaginatively accessible. In this sense it is appropriate to call such a person a conservative. If his or her practical wisdom were merely an instrumental talent for getting things done, there would be no reason to associate it with any particular political position. But my aim has been to show that practical wisdom is not just a technical facility at moving from a goal to its attainment. Practical wisdom is excellence in deliberating about ends, and this excellence presupposes specific traits of character. To be practically wise is to possess certain dispositions, certain feelings and concerns, and among these must be included the disposition to conserve, an affective attitude that grows from the one form of reverence to which a moral cosmopolite may feel authentically entitled: a reverence for the variety of irreconcilable human goods and for the genius of unprincipled invention that has made it possible for people to live together despite the incomparability of their conceptions of what is valuable in life. This reverence implies a humanism that provides the motive for one ancient form of conservatism, and in all societies, including our own, such humanism has been the distinguishing mark of the practically wise. Of them, and of the lawyer-statesman who traditionally has stood at the head of their ranks, it may truly be said that nothing human is foreign.

Part Two

REALITIES

4

Law Schools

THE PRESENT IN PERSPECTIVE

In the preceding three chapters I have sketched a professional ideal for lawyers. I have tried to clarify the content of this ideal and to make its central values as attractive as possible. But however appealing in the abstract, these values no longer possess the authority they once did. The ideal of the lawyer-statesman is today under attack from a variety of quarters, and in recent years its prestige has slipped dramatically. The qualities of character that the lawyer-statesman was traditionally thought to exemplify today play a diminishing role in the way that lawyers understand themselves and the nature of their work. Indeed, the most important of these, the virtue of practical wisdom, has lost so much prestige that its current position in the thinking of the profession can only be described as one of suspicion and even contempt.

This chapter and the following two explore some of the reasons for this development. My account emphasizes three factors in particular, each reflecting important changes in a different branch of the profession—changes (to list them in the order I shall take them up) in the way that law is taught in schools, practiced in firms, and made by judges in courts. Together these developments mark a sea change in the profession as a whole, a realignment of experience and expectations that has discredited the ideal of the lawyer-statesman in a range of different settings. To the question, why is the life of a lawyer worth living, this ideal supplied an answer. But various intellectual and institutional developments have put that answer in doubt, and the result has been a deepening crisis of self-confidence within the profession

165

generally. My aim in this chapter and the next two is to diagnose the causes of this crisis and to convey some sense of its magnitude and meaning. I begin with the crisis in legal education.

Many of the themes stressed in the first part of this book have in recent years been sounded by other academic legal writers too. The new republicans, for example, have also drawn attention to the distinction between deliberative and instrumental reasoning and insisted on the need for public-spiritedness in law. Others, worried by the dangers of an overly abstract approach to legal questions, have urged the use of narratives that stress the historical uniqueness of each case as a counterweight to generalizing theories.[1] And some feminist writers have argued that there is a closer connection between feeling and judgment than is commonly supposed—a connection they claim any sound view of adjudication must recognize and value.[2]

With all of these I feel a certain kinship, though I view none— and none are likely to view me—uncritically. But however great the differences that separate my own conception of the lawyer-statesman from the positions of these other writers, our disagreements are like family quarrels when compared to the gulf that separates us all from the intellectual movement that has had the greatest influence on American academic law in the past quarter-century. I am speaking of law and economics. In the years since 1965 no other approach to the study of law has had a comparable effect on the way that academic lawyers write and teach.[3] Law and economics is today a permanent, institutionalized feature of American legal education. Specialized journals are devoted to it, and its presence is pervasive in the older law reviews as well; faculty positions at many law schools are explicitly reserved for its adherents; and it is now represented by a professional organization of its own, the American Association of Law and Economics.[4] Even these external markers of success do not fully measure the movement's influence, which is nearly unrivaled in some fields (corporations and commercial law) and dominant in others (torts, contracts, and property).[5] The law-and-economics movement has transformed the way that teachers in these fields think about their subject and present it to their students.[6] And in almost every area of law a working knowledge of economics is now required to keep abreast of scholarly developments, whether one is sympathetic to the movement or not.

This is the single most important change in American legal education in the last twenty-five years, and for reasons I shall explain, it has done much to undermine the ideal of the lawyer-statesman in our country's law schools. For in deep and essential ways the discipline of economics is hostile to this ideal. It is incapable of acknowledging the phenomenon of moral incommensurability. It equates judgment with calculation. And it has no room for the notions of character and prudence that lie at the ideal's heart. Those who embrace the methods of economics as the best ones for thinking about law and who acquire the intellectual habits these methods encourage are therefore likely to be blinded to the value of practical wisdom and to the conditions of moral life that make the need for it imperative. In the end, they are likely to view the ideal of the lawyer-statesman as a fiction or superstition. More than anything else, the law-and-economics movement has helped to create a climate of opinion in American law schools that now makes it difficult to take this ideal seriously—the dominant climate that pragmatists, feminists, new republicans, and I all challenge from the margin.

Law and economics has not been the only force contributing to this development, however. The critical legal studies movement, which emerged in the 1970s and during the past two decades exerted an influence on American law teaching second only to that of law and economics, has also helped establish the atmosphere of mistrust that now surrounds the virtue of practical wisdom.

To some this will seem implausible. After all, many of those in the critical legal studies movement view themselves as opponents of law and economics and make a regular practice of debunking its scientific claims. The movement's leading writers repeatedly insist that they are suspicious of grand theoretical programs and in favor of small-scale, interstitial change instead. And some of those associated with critical legal studies (William Simon and Robert Gordon, for example) defend a conception of professionalism that emphasizes the need for deliberative judgment and a public-spirited concern for the good of the law as a whole—crucial elements in the lawyer-statesman ideal.[7]

But the writings of the movement's most philosophical proponents reflect an antiprudentialist outlook that is in tension with their affirmation of the value of practical judgment. This is particularly true of Roberto Unger's well-known book on critical legal studies and of Duncan Kennedy's early articles, which did so much to define the movement's substance and style.[8] A similar outlook may be found in the work of James Boyle, Claire Dalton, Gary Peller, Jack Balkin, and others.[9] All these writers display a preference for theories that explain the busy and disordered surface of the law in terms of some single abstraction: Kennedy's "fundamental contradiction," Unger's "negative capability," Balkin's "crystalline structure," Dalton's "boundary between self and other." All offer this abstraction as a key to understanding the hidden order of the law, whose deep uniformity is concealed (they maintain) by the superficial variety of its doctrines and principles. In their insistence on the need to look beneath the surface of the law to the structures that underlie it, in their emphasis on the simplicity and ubiquity of these structures, and in their belief that only a theory of the highest possible abstraction can describe them, the leading theoreticians of the critical legal studies movement have encouraged an outlook hostile to the prudentialism on which the lawyer-statesman ideal is based. The proponents of law and economics have done this more directly. But many of those in the critical legal studies movement have played a part in promoting this outlook as well. Together these two movements have had a large influence on American legal scholarship during the past twenty years, and despite the differences between them, both have fostered a style of thought that depreciates the value of practical wisdom.

The hostility that the law-and-economics and critical legal studies movements show toward this virtue is not original with them. Indeed, as we shall see, it is centuries old. Most immediately it derives from an earlier movement in American legal thought known as legal realism. Or more precisely it derives from one of the two branches into which legal realism was divided. Others have noted the connection between these contemporary movements and the realist program of the 1930s, and few would deny that some such connection exists.[10] But what has not been adequately appreciated is that legal realism itself encompassed two very different tendencies and that both law and economics and critical legal studies are allied to one of them only—to what I shall call the *scientific* branch of legal realism. To the other, the *prudentialist* branch, both are profoundly opposed. The issue that most deeply divided the adherents of these two approaches was whether practical wisdom is needed in the study and administration of law. Prudential realists said yes and scientific realists no. At their core, both law and economics and critical legal studies are imbued with the spirit of scientific realism. They share its aspirations and methodological beliefs, and because of this their proponents take the latter, negative view of prudence too. To understand the source of their antiprudentialism, we must therefore return to this earlier movement and to the battle of ideas in which the scientific realists' disdain for the virtue of practical wisdom came to be articulated with such clarity and force.

But if we want to comprehend fully the present situation in American legal scholarship, a still longer perspective is needed. For scientific realism itself represents the continuation of an even older tradition of thought, one that every realist rejected in certain respects but whose fundamental aim the scientific realists endorsed and sought in a modified way to achieve. Jerome Frank derisively termed this older tradition that of "Bealism" (after Joseph Beale, a member of the Harvard Law School faculty from 1890 to 1937, best known for his work on the conflict of laws).[11] It is easy to see that the scientific realists subscribed to a theory of law different from Beale's own. What is equally important, though less obvious, is that they also shared his principal goal: that of constructing a science of law capable of determining with a high degree of precision both what the law is and what it ought to be. In this respect, the scientific realists of the 1930s were as much Beale's heirs as the contemporary proponents of law and economics and critical legal studies are theirs, each movement being linked to its predecessor by a common contempt for the virtue of practical wisdom.

Together these movements form a single tradition of ideas. To understand this tradition, we must go back to the movement with which it began, to Bealism, though not to Beale himself. Beale was an articulate defender of the view that Frank named after him, but he did not invent it. The invention of Bealism must be credited instead to Christopher Columbus Langdell, Beale's colleague at Harvard and dean of the law school from 1870 to 1895. Grant Gilmore once remarked that, like his namesake, Langdell was a discoverer of new worlds too, and there is truth in Gilmore's pun, for it was under Langdell's leadership that the Harvard Law School assumed its modern form and through the model of his own research and writing that a conception of scholarship was first defined that still dominates the study of law today.[12] For all their fashionableness and novelty, the law-and-economics and critical legal studies movements are essentially Langdellian in spirit. It is with Langdell's own efforts to give the aca-

demic study of law a respectably scientific form that my account of
these two movements properly starts.

LANGDELL'S GEOMETRY OF LAW

Langdell's position in the history of American legal thought is a curious one. Though his views regarding the teaching and study of law
have been enormously influential, he never presented them with precision or detail. We must infer his views, instead, from a few casual
remarks that he made regarding his method of study and from his
own doctrinal writings in the field of contracts.[13] Langdell is generally
credited with the introduction of the case method of instruction at
Harvard—a method that nearly all American law teachers still employ. And he and his academic followers established a model for legal
scholarship that remained the dominant one for fifty years, until its
repudiation by the realists in the 1930s. But because Langdell never
offered a full account of the methodological assumptions that lay behind these innovations, it is difficult to identify the influences that
shaped his own thinking and even, to some extent, the precise conception of law he endorsed.

One thing, however, is clear. Langdell was firmly convinced that
the study of law must be made rigorously scientific if law schools
were ever to become as intellectually respectable as other university
departments. Previously lawyers had been educated, for the most
part, in law offices under the supervision of practicing attorneys. This
older regime—as old as the common law itself—Langdell thought
haphazard and inexact; his ambition was to replace it with a new
system of legal education, one in which the primary forum of instruction would be not the law office but the academic classroom and
library, and whose masters would be professors rather than practitioners. To the establishment of this new system Langdell devoted
his career.

When Langdell declared that the study of law must be put on a
scientific footing, what did he have in mind and which science did
he look to as a model? To some extent it would seem his model
was biology—in the late nineteenth century still mainly a taxonomic
discipline—for he appears to have conceived the aim of legal science
to be the construction of a comprehensive scheme of classification in
which every individual case might be fit under its controlling rule in

much the same way that a biologist fits individual birds, fish, and so on under their appropriate species-types. Langdell also seems to have viewed this classificatory system as the product of a process of historical development in which the latent logic of the common law had gradually unfolded as its rules were refined and conflicts among them resolved. Langdell's suggestion that legal science seeks to grasp in thought the conceptual relationships that this historical process brings to light reflects, perhaps, some acceptance on his part of the evolutionary theories that were then beginning to reshape biology (though his views in this respect seem more Hegelian than Darwinian).[14]

But whatever the influence of biology on Langdell's thinking, his conception of legal science was also clearly inspired by a mathematical, or more precisely a geometrical, model of scientific method. To understand a given branch of legal doctrine in a scientific fashion, one must begin, according to Langdell, by first identifying the elementary principles on which that field of law is based (for example, in the case of contract law, the principles that the minds of the parties must meet for a contract to be formed and that each must give or promise to give something of value to the other in return). These elementary principles are to be discovered by surveying the case law in the area. Once they have been identified, it is then the task of scholars to work out, in an analytically rigorous manner, the subordinate principles entailed by them. When these subordinate principles have all been stated in propositional form and the relations of entailment among them clarified, they will, Langdell believed, together constitute a well-ordered system of rules that offers the best possible description of that particular branch of law—the best answer to the question of what the law in that area *is*. Langdell also believed that individual cases that cannot be fit within this system must be rejected as mistakes. He thought of the system, in other words, as performing a normative function too. More precisely, he thought of it as performing both functions at once and without distinction, for though we have grown used to the idea that description and evaluation must be kept carefully apart, Langdell's conception of legal science makes sense only on the assumption that he understood them to be essentially the same.

The procedure I have just described shares two features with the method of geometry. The first concerns the nature of the starting points with which it begins. Geometry, too, must of course begin somewhere, and it is tempting to think that its starting points, the basic axioms on which the discipline of geometry is built, are logically true, true by necessity, in contrast to the contingent starting points of legal science. But this is not in fact the case. The proposition that parallel lines never meet, for example, is an essential premise of classical (Euclidian) geometry, but the truth of this claim is not a necessary one in the strictly logical sense that its denial would violate the law of noncontradiction.

Still, even though they cannot be logically derived, the starting points of geometry are easy to grasp. One does not need great experience to understand them. Indeed, even those whose acquaintance with the world is least lengthy and refined are able to comprehend the axioms on which geometry is based (which is perhaps why in the *Meno* Socrates chooses a slave boy as his interlocutor when he wants to demonstrate that the truths of geometry are intelligible to everyone, including the inexperienced).[15] The immense power of geometry is in part a consequence of this.

Something similar may be said about the starting points of Langdell's new science of law. The elementary principles of Anglo-American contract law, for example, cannot be derived by logical means alone; there are other legal systems in which certain of these principles (such as the consideration requirement) do not exist at all, just as there are alternative geometries that start from non-Euclidian assumptions. To grasp the basic premises on which our law of contracts rests, one therefore needs something more than a capacity for logical thought. One needs experience too, which Langdell suggests can best be gotten by reading a certain number of reported cases involving contractual disputes. But Langdell believed that the experience in question, though longer and more specialized than that required to begin the study of geometry, is also easy to obtain and that even a cursory glance at the relevant case law will provide it. He believed, in other words, that a rigorous science of law may be built upon a very thin fund of experience, like the discipline of geometry itself.

The assumption that it can be is indeed an essential premise of Langdell's program. For were the starting points of the new science he envisioned accessible only to those with a thicker kind of experience—the kind that comes with years of immersion in the practice of law—it would be difficult to understand how this science could, as Langdell claimed, be made intelligible to beginning students, or why, as he insisted, its development should be viewed as being peculiarly within the province of university intellectuals rather than that of seasoned practitioners. The apprenticeship system that Langdell sought to uproot rested on the assumption that the experienced practitioner is the best teacher of law and treated his experience as a prerequisite to the kind of understanding law teachers convey to their students. To compete successfully with this older regime, the new university-based system of legal education that Langdell championed had to make the experience of the law teacher less important, less relevant to the activity of teaching itself, and the easiest way to do this was to assume that the starting points of legal science are intelligible even to the young and inexperienced.

The second respect in which Langdell's new science of law resembles that of geometry has been more often noticed in the past. The beginning points of geometry cannot, it is true, be established by logical means. They are postulates with which one becomes acquainted through experience (albeit experience of an exceedingly thin kind). But once these have been grasped, the derivation of the rest of geometry is a matter merely of drawing out the implications they contain. The science of geometry does nothing more than unfold the meaning of its own starting points by a process of reasoned analysis. This is difficult to do. It is a task that requires great patience and disciplined reflection, and sometimes the conclusions at which one arrives are surprisingly counterintuitive. But however difficult its pursuit or surprising its results, the process of geometrical analysis does not draw in any way upon experience. The only resources it employs are those to be found within reason itself; the method of geometry is in this sense rationally self-contained.

The same is true of the method that Langdell recommends for the scientific study of law. Once the basic premises of a particular branch of law have been established, the remaining task is one of ratiocination only. The many subrules that fill out the doctrinal detail of any legal subject can all, Langdell assumes, be drawn by implication from its foundational principles, whatever these may be. On this view, for example, it is possible to produce a full and accurate account of the law of contracts merely by analyzing the elementary notions of mutuality, intention, and consideration on which it rests. Here, as in geometry, clearheadedness is essential and much time and patience are required, but experience is equally irrelevant. As he labors to unravel analytically the implications of his subject's basic premises, the academic lawyer is thus at no disadvantage compared to the worldly practitioner whose greater experience has no role to play in the work of legal science. At the end of this process of analysis, what one possesses is a system of ordered propositions like those that appear in a textbook of geometry. Together these exhaustively describe the law. There is nothing more to the law than what they state, nothing in the law that cannot be stated in their terms, and if a case should arise that appears to present a novel issue, that is only because the relevant propositions have not yet been worked out in sufficient detail. On Langdell's view, the proper way of deciding such a case is simply to carry the process of analysis further, until one reaches an implied subrule specific enough to resolve it. Thus even in cases of first impression, Langdell's method offers a procedure for determining what the law is and hence how the case should be decided—these two judgments, one descriptive and the other evaluative, being in fact the same, as they are in geometry itself. By applying this method to the study of law, Langdell believed one might arrive at an understanding of legal rules more comprehensive and exact than the practicing lawyer's. And he thought it possible to construct such a science of law without relying on the practitioner's worldly wisdom either for the establishment of its premises or for the derivation of its details.

THOMAS HOBBES AND THE PRUDENTIALIST TRADITION

Langdell's immediate motive for embracing a geometrical model of legal science may well have been his desire to avoid a contest with the old apprenticeship system of law training on its own strongest ground. In doing so, however, he placed himself—whether knowingly or not—in a well-established intellectual tradition reaching back to the threshold of the modern age. The two most forceful representatives of this tradition in nineteenth-century Anglo-American jurisprudence were John Austin and Jeremy Bentham, and it seems likely that Langdell's own thinking was influenced by theirs, though this is difficult to document. But the aspiration to construct a geometry of law was by no means limited to these two. Countless expressions of this same ideal appear in the writings of other thinkers throughout the eighteenth and nineteenth centuries.[16] The clearest statement of it is contained, however, in the writings of Thomas Hobbes, who more than anyone else may be credited with the invention of the tradition to which Austin, Bentham, and Langdell all belonged. It is in Hobbes's revolutionary theory of politics that the origins of the contest between Langdell's program and the older apprenticeship system of legal education may be found.

Hobbes sought to establish a new science of politics consciously modeled on that of geometry. In Hobbes's scheme certain basic truths about human beings—or, more precisely, about the passions that motivate them—play a role analogous to Euclid's elementary axioms. From these truths, which Hobbes believed any person could verify from his own experience, he thought it possible to derive by analysis a system of corollary propositions powerful enough to explain the origin of political communities, to account for the legitimacy of their laws, and to define with precision the scope and content of the most important political relationship, that of ruler to subject. Hobbes's method, like the geometer's, begins with assumptions that even the least experienced can grasp. For the rest, it is a product entirely of reason. Because of its minimal dependence on experience and near-total reliance on the method of analysis, Hobbes believed his new science capable of achieving a level of precision never before attained in the study of politics—one previously thought possible only in mathematics, the most rationally self-contained form of human understanding. "The skill of making, and maintaining commonwealths," he says in a famous passage, "consisteth in certain rules, as doth arithmetic and geometry; not, as tennis-play, in practice only: which rules, neither poor men have the leisure, nor men that have had the leisure, have hitherto had the curiosity or the method to find out."[17]

In comparing the study of politics to the science of geometry, Hobbes knew, of course, that he was repudiating an ancient tradition of thought reaching back to Aristotle.[18] Aristotle makes three basic claims about the study of politics, each of which Hobbes rejects. First, he insists that an understanding of political affairs can be gained only through long experience. The facts of political life are in Aristotle's view too complex and disorderly to be derived by reason alone from some simple set of axioms. Political judgment requires a familiarity with these facts and hence a measure of worldliness or maturity, for it is only by living, as opposed to thinking, that a person becomes acquainted with them—in contrast to the truths of mathematics, which can be grasped in thought even by the young and inexperienced.[19]

Second, Aristotle maintains that in the study of politics one ought not to aspire to the kind of precision that is attainable in mathematics, for the same disorderliness that makes experience a condition of political wisdom also rules out the exactness of mathematics as a sensible standard or goal. Those who study political matters "must be satisfied," he says, "to indicate the truth with a rough and general sketch." Indeed it is the sign of what Aristotle calls a "well-schooled man" that he "searches for that degree of precision in each kind of study which the nature of the subject at hand permits," and a person of this sort will recognize that "[i]t is obviously just as foolish to accept arguments of probability from a mathematician as to demand strict demonstrations from an orator."[20]

Hobbes emphatically rejects both of these claims. Indeed, the very point of his geometrically inspired method is to liberate the study of politics from its dependence on experience and to demonstrate the possibility of achieving in political theory a degree of exactness that Aristotle thought it foolish to pursue. But Hobbes's rejection of Aristotle is more thoroughgoing still, for there is a third assumption of Aristotle's that he repudiates as well. Aristotle believed that to make sound judgments regarding political matters, a person must possess not only theoretical understanding but also a trait of character he called prudence or practical wisdom. More exactly, he believed that it is the person of practical wisdom who has the greatest—perhaps the only—chance of acquiring the necessary understanding. He therefore considered the training of a student's character to be an essential part of his preparation for political life. By contrast, such training plays no role in a person's mathematical education, for the obvious reason that an understanding of mathematics is not similarly conditioned on the possession of any particular character trait. The truths of mathematics are intelligible to those with every kind of character, as they would be, indeed, to those with no character at all, if such a thing were possible. In taking geometry as the model for his new science of politics, Hobbes thus also rejects Aristotle's third methodological premise, the assumption of a link between character and political understanding. There is no specific trait of character that Hobbes's political scientist requires to proceed. Like the geometer, he seeks a kind of understanding on which the constitution of his character has no bearing. Or rather, like the geometer, he possesses a method that makes the need for character—for any character at all—superfluous.

In the *Leviathan* Hobbes applies his geometrical method to the most basic questions of politics. Here he is mainly concerned to explain why political societies come into existence in the first place and what justifies the claim to authority of those that rule within them. But it is clear that Hobbes believed this same method capable of answering even very detailed questions about the specific legal structure of political societies, questions normally viewed as being more within the province of lawyers than of philosophers. The *Leviathan* itself suggests this, but the most compelling evidence of Hobbes's faith in the power of his method as an instrument of legal analysis is a curious essay, written toward the end of his life, entitled *A Dialogue between a Philosopher and a Student of the Common Laws of England.*[21]

Hobbes's *Dialogue* is in form a debate between an unnamed "philosopher" (who clearly speaks for Hobbes himself) and a "student," who represents the community of common lawyers and in particular their chief spokesman, Sir Edward Coke. Much of the debate concerns issues of an exceedingly technical kind, for example, the definition of specific crimes and the jurisdiction of various courts. But one general point that Hobbes's *Dialogue* makes clear is that his new science of politics and the geometrical method on which it rests are at war with the common-law method of reasoning the student in the *Dialogue* defends.

The philosopher in Hobbes's *Dialogue* insists that the technical legal issues under discussion be resolved by an appeal to what he calls natural reason, that is, the universal powers of ratiocination that every human being possesses. It is this natural reason, he maintains, that provides the sole standard of right judgment in the law. The student disagrees. Those who judge legal matters rightly do so, he claims, by virtue of their "artificial reason," a mode of understanding that only those who have been professionally trained in the study of law possess. In contrast to its natural counterpart—a product of thought alone—the artificial reason of the professional lawyer must be acquired through experience (like Aristotelian prudence, to which it bears a close resemblance).

The nature of law itself, as the student understands it, explains why this is so. The student in Hobbes's *Dialogue* equates law with precedent, with the body of judicial decisions that make up the common law. These decisions have been rendered over many years by many different judges. Together they form a vast historical accumulation that, though not utterly chaotic, lacks the orderliness and rational clarity that a body of rules would possess had it been formed by a single intelligence concerned with the arrangement of the legal order as a whole rather than by many separate ones each attending to some question of a narrower kind. Furthermore, many of the concepts around which this mass of case law has evolved have themselves been fortuitously determined by the historical circumstances in which they originally took shape: thus they often appear arbitrary or even irrational to later generations (England's feudally determined land law being perhaps the most famous example of this).[22] For these reasons it is impossible to reproduce by means of thought alone the set of rules for which English case law stands (in the way, for example, that every student of geometry may be said to reproduce the entire system of Euclid out of the resources of his or her own intelligence). To understand the law of England, Hobbes's student argues, it is not enough merely to think out the implications of a few fundamental axioms, proceeding as a geometer might. It is necessary in addition to know what the precedents actually say, and this one can discover only by looking at the law as opposed to thinking about it. Experience in the study of law is thus on the student's view a condition of sound judgment in legal disputes. The philosopher's natural reason—which precedes all such experience and remains uninformed by it—is by contrast incompetent to make reliable judgments of this kind.

The judgment an experienced lawyer possesses, moreover, can never attain the level of precision to which one properly aspires in geometry for the simple reason that the complexity and contradictoriness of the relevant precedents often leave room for disagreement as to how specific cases should be decided. Even the most skilled lawyers acknowledge that there may be reasonable differences of opinion regarding the resolution of particular disputes. While each believes his own position is the one that best meets the law's requirements, he nevertheless concedes that other positions may reasonably be defended on the basis of the same ambiguous precedents. In geometry this attitude is out of place. Two geometers may of course disagree about the soundness of a particular proof, but as both admit, one of them is certainly right and the other just as certainly wrong. There is simply no room in geometry for *reasonable* disagreement. But this is a common phenomenon in law, for the judgments it requires—being based upon experience and not (as in geometry) upon the dictates of reason alone—are necessarily inexact and therefore inherently controversial.

The artificial reason of the common lawyer thus resembles the kind of understanding Aristotle thought appropriate to politics in two respects. Neither can be acquired except through "long study and experience," and each aspires only to a middling level of precision that always leaves room for reasonable disagreement. Aristotle also believed that political understanding requires sound character as well as intellectual acuity. The student in Hobbes's *Dialogue* does not endorse this last idea explicitly. But there are other texts from the same period and before that suggest a coincidence even in this third respect between the tradition of common-law thinking and the ancient Aristotelian view of politics. Hobbes's attack on the common-law tradition and on the artificial reason that it celebrates is therefore in reality merely an extension of his more generalized assault on the assumptions underlying Aristotle's political philosophy, a philosophy whose most forceful contemporary proponents Hobbes rightly understood to be not the scholastic writers he ridicules in the *Leviathan* but the guild of common lawyers represented by the student in his *Dialogue*.

Perhaps the clearest evidence of Hobbes's antipathy to the common-law tradition is his rejection of its most fundamental principle, that of *stare decisis,* or respect for past decisions. The student's defense of the lawyers' artificial reason begins, as I have said, by equating law with precedent, and this equation itself implies the principle of *stare decisis,* for if the decisions of judges in past cases actually constitute the law, then the only way to honor or respect the law is to honor these decisions themselves. By challenging the equation of law with precedent and insisting that it be identified with the dictates of natural reason instead, Hobbes's philosopher thus implicitly rejects the principle of *stare decisis* as well. This implication is in fact explicitly drawn in the *Leviathan,* where Hobbes makes it clear that he considers arguments from precedent to be absurd: the "sentence" of a judge in one case, he asserts, though "a law to the party pleading," is "no law to any judge that shall succeed him in office."[23]

Given his adoption of geometry as a model for political and legal analysis, Hobbes's rejection of *stare decisis* is entirely understandable. In geometry, after all, precedent counts for nothing. The past judgments of geometers have no authority of their own, and everyone who engages in geometry has an absolute right—indeed, duty—to review in the light of his or her own natural reason what others have said about the subject before. Hobbes's open rejection of the principle of *stare decisis* thus follows directly from his own commitment to the project of constructing a new science of politics *more geometrico* and reflects his faith in an independent rationality radically opposed to the common lawyer's characteristic deference to the past.

This same faith leads Hobbes to favor a shift in emphasis from adjudication to legislation and to recharacterize the first as a subordinate department of the second.[24] The legislator asks simply, "What is right?" meaning, for Hobbes, "What conforms to natural reason?" and in answering this question gives no more weight to past decisions than a geometer would. For the legislator the vast storehouse of accumulated precedent, to the extent that it conflicts with the requirements of natural reason, is nonsense to be discarded with impunity. And this same attitude, Hobbes implies, ought also to be adopted by those lower-order officials we call judges since they too play a role in the creation of law (albeit a more constrained one, given the jurisdictional limits on their powers). As deputized lawmakers, they too have an obligation to put the dictates of natural reason before those of precedent, and they act irresponsibly when they do not. Hobbes acknowledges that this attitude is at odds with the spirit and outlook of the common law. But he is prepared and indeed quite eager to admit this, for as his *Dialogue* makes plain, it is simply one more consequence of the decision to take geometry as a model for law and politics.

THE CAPTURE OF THE COMMON LAW

Two centuries later the same constellation of ideas may be seen still powerfully at work in the jurisprudential writings of Austin and Bentham. These two of course differed from each other in important ways, and each held views that conflicted at certain points with Hobbes's own. But they shared in common with Hobbes the ambition of constructing a rigorous science of law and like Hobbes felt nothing but contempt for the common-law tradition (giving their views what H. L. A. Hart calls an "un-English" appearance that makes the immense influence they have had on Anglo-American jurisprudence somewhat paradoxical).[25] Like Hobbes, Austin and Bentham attacked the principle of *stare decisis* and insisted on the need for comprehensive legislation as the only alternative to what they claimed was an absurdly fortuitous case law that had grown without planning or rational control. And like Hobbes they believed the professional lawyer's artificial reason wholly inadequate to this task. Hobbes saw the common lawyer as a powerful opponent, and both Austin and Bentham shared this view.[26] For them too, the outlook of the common lawyer represented an obstacle to reform that had to be surmounted if the study and administration of law were ever to be put on a scientific footing.

The claim that Langdell also belonged to this Hobbesian tradition may at first appear implausible. For unlike these others, Langdell did not regard the common law with suspicion or contempt but instead embraced it, claiming to find in its precedents the material for his new science of law. Unlike Hobbes, and in contrast to both Austin and Bentham, Langdell was not a self-declared enemy of the common law. Indeed, it might seem more accurate to describe him as its admiring friend.

But this appearance of friendship is misleading. For what Langdell actually sought to do was reorganize the common law in the spirit of geometry. Hobbes thought that questions of law might be resolved with geometrical exactness, but only in case the common law were scrapped and a new system of comprehensive legislation substituted for it. He believed that a science of law could be constructed only from a standpoint external to the common law itself. Langdell did not accept this last conclusion, but he did share Hobbes's desire to create a legal science whose truths would be as transparent as geometrical proofs. Where Langdell differed from Hobbes was in thinking that a science of this sort could be established by rearranging the common law from within. Langdell believed he could achieve within the common law something that Hobbes, Austin, and Bentham had thought possible only outside it. And to that extent his project was not only similar to theirs but even more ambitious, for what Langdell hoped to do was build a science of law on the very territory, and using the very materials, that his predecessors had considered least amenable to it.

Langdell sought to prove that the common law already contained within it a latent geometry of its own. By bringing this to light he hoped to show that the common law was not, in fact, what its defenders had always claimed: a collection of precedents that fit no rational pattern and hence could be known through experience only. Langdell insisted, on the contrary, that the cases already fit such a pattern—one that earlier proponents of legal science had believed must be imposed by legislative *fiat*—and in making this claim he not only attacked the common-law tradition (as they had) but carried the campaign for a geometry of law into the enemy's camp.

One feature of Langdell's program reflects his hostility to the common-law tradition with particular clarity. Langdell's goal was to construct a rational scheme for the arrangement of legal doctrine by analytically unfolding the implications of a few foundational ideas. But it was obvious to him that there would always be some cases that could not be fit within this scheme, and he concluded that these anomalies must be rejected as mistakes that did not constitute good law and therefore had no precedential value. To take this position, however, is to deny just what the principle of *stare decisis* presupposes: that there is more to the law than can possibly be captured by the propositions at which a rational intelligence would arrive by proceeding *more geometrico*. By denying the status of law to any decision that could not be independently derived by reason alone, Langdell limited the authority of what is actual in the law to what is rational in it, and declared, as Hobbes had done, his hostility to the principle of precedent on which the common law is based.

What influenced Langdell to embrace the idea of a Hobbesian geometry of law and to seek its fulfillment not in some scheme of comprehensive legislation but in the implicit logic of a historically evolved case law instead? About these influences we can only speculate. But it seems reasonable to assume that several factors contributed to the development of Langdell's thinking and the formulation of his own distinctive program for a science of law.

One such factor, almost surely, was the ubiquitous influence of Austin and Bentham, and the partially—but only partially—successful movement for law reform they had inspired. Austin and Bentham were strong proponents of legal rationalization, and their work contributed importantly to the revolution in civil procedure that was accomplished in the middle years of the nineteenth century by the abolition of the ancient writ system of common-law pleading. To contemporaries, the destruction of the writ system seemed to make possible a rational reorganization of common-law doctrine that had been unthinkable even fifty years before, and this attitude undoubtedly prepared the way for Langdell's own ambitious project. But by the same token, the codification movement that Austin and Bentham championed as an alternative to the common law had by the mid-nineteenth century begun to stall.[27] Other proponents of rationalization, like Langdell, therefore had reason to believe that large areas of common-law doctrine would never be displaced by newly minted codes and could therefore be codified, if at all, only from within (one way of describing Langdell's project). The destruction of the writ system, coupled with the frustrations of the codification movement, thus opened the way to a more substantive rationalization of common-law doctrine but at the same time suggested that it could not be legislatively imposed and would have to be achieved through an internal purification of the common law instead.

The rise of Darwinism, and its application to the study of human institutions, was in all likelihood a second, reinforcing influence on the development of Langdell's thought. Darwin's views were themselves influenced by Adam Smith's,[28] and both he and Smith shared an important methodological premise: that order may exist in a field of events (whether the roughly simultaneous events that constitute a market or the temporally sequential ones that form the life of a biological species), though this order is due not to the foresight of a single organizing intelligence but to the innumerable adjustments of separate individuals, each pursuing some local goal of its own. Darwin, and Smith before him, thus raised the hope that an intelligible order might be found even in those areas of human life that are not the product of a plan. To those impressed by the possibilities of applying Darwinian ideas to social and political problems, the pointillist world of common-law decisions must have seemed a perfect field for their employment, and it is reasonable to think that these ideas encouraged Langdell's hope of finding the materials for a legal science in the common law itself—that they provided him, in effect, with the means for decoupling the goal of building a rigorous science of law from the earlier belief that this could be done through legislative codification only.

It was not these two factors, however, but a third that seems to have had the greatest influence on Langdell's thinking: his desire to show the superiority of a university-based system of legal education to the old regime of apprenticeship training that had dominated the common law from its beginning. To show this, Langdell had to establish that university professors were better teachers of the law than their counterparts in practice. If one views the law as a scheme of axioms and analytical entailments, however, this conclusion follows naturally. For it is the academic lawyer, who has time to think and can proceed methodically, who is best equipped to master such a scheme—better equipped, in any case, than the practicing lawyer who must rush breathlessly from one client to the next. It was the attractiveness of this conclusion that undoubtedly made the view of legal science from which it flows so appealing to Langdell.

A common lawyer will of course protest that there is more to the law than Langdell's scheme allows, and that it is he—not an academic scientist—who is in the best position to teach this important, if non-rationalizable, remainder. But Langdell's new science of law challenged the premise on which this claim is based, for it denied that cases which cannot be fit into the scheme are to count as law at all. If Langdell is right, there is nothing left for a practitioner to teach— nothing, in any case, that a full-time academic with the time and inclination to pursue his subject scientifically cannot teach more ably. In the battle for pedagogical supremacy, it is the practicing lawyer's experience that constitutes his chief advantage. Langdell's view of law as a system of axioms and corollaries makes experience of any but the simplest and least-developed kind irrelevant to the understanding of law and thus depreciates the practitioner's main competitive resource. If it is in fact possible, as Langdell thought, to construct a geometry of law, then the assumption underlying the old apprenticeship system of legal education must be rejected and the pedagogical function which that system assigned to experienced practitioners must be transferred to university professors instead.

Hobbes despised the common-law tradition—as did Austin and Bentham—but opposed it from without. Langdell, by contrast, invented a method for attacking the common law from within. Whatever his motives, this was Langdell's chief contribution to legal thought. The method he invented made it possible to pursue the idea of a science of law in the one direction that would have seemed least promising to earlier proponents of it and to defeat the common lawyers on their own home ground. Twentieth-century American legal thought, whose initial orientation Langdell helped importantly to define, thus begins with a victory for Hobbesian ideas in the heartland of the common law.

FRANK'S THERAPEUTIC PROGRAM

Langdell's call for a new science of law had an enormous influence on American law teaching in the last two decades of the nineteenth century and first three of the twentieth. Still, there were those who opposed it from the start. These included, understandably enough, defenders of the older common-law tradition that Langdell's conception of legal science sharply challenged. But among his early critics were also some who shared Langdell's disdain for this tradition yet thought the law could never be a strictly deductive discipline like geometry. The greatest of these, unquestionably, was Oliver Wendell Holmes. Indeed, in Holmes's jurisprudential writings we can discern the outlines of a view that the legal realists were later to embrace and that contains the gist of their attack on Langdell's program. Here we find already adumbrated many of the elements of their own critical counterassault: the recognition of judicial creativity; the insistence that law is not a self-contained and self-serving realm of norms, but a tool to be used for the advancement of social ends; and a confidence in the power of the nascent social sciences, and in particular of economics, to settle the issues of policy that judges must address.[29] Holmes was the first to express many of these ideas, which is one reason why he impresses us as such a genius. But he did not draw them together in an organized way. It remained for the legal realists to do this—to turn Holmes's brilliant but scattered insights into a school of thought and transform his attack on Langdell's program into a program of its own. The realists were Holmes's heirs. But it was they who first shaped the conception of law he bequeathed them into a polished and self-conscious view. In the writings of the master himself this conception is still inchoate. Its elements are there but unconnected. The realists drew these connections and defended them, and by so doing fixed the framework of ideas within which much of American legal thought has since unfolded.

The movement we call legal realism, which began at the Columbia Law School in the late 1920s and achieved full self-expression at Yale a few years later, encompassed a variety of intellectual types.[30] Some were extreme skeptics and others were positive, programmatic thinkers. Some had philosophical concerns and others viewed themselves mainly as empirical social scientists. Some were interested in questions of pedagogy and others in the reform of legal institutions. And though many believed in the value of interdisciplinary research, different realists looked to different nonlegal disciplines for inspiration. The realists were thus a heterogeneous group, with a number of concerns and a variety of strategies for pursuing them. Still, as a movement realism had an identifiable character, though one defined less by what its adherents supported than by what they all opposed. The solidarity that the realists felt was to a large degree a solidarity of opposition, and it was this, more than anything else, that gave those who identified with the movement the sense of belonging to a common endeavor.

What the realists all opposed was the conception of legal science that Langdell had offered as a model for the work of the new law school professoriate that he himself did so much to create. Langdell's conception of legal science was flawed, the realists said, and incapable of providing the basis for a true understanding of what the law either is or ought to be. This negative claim was a rallying point for all who associated themselves with the realist movement and represented the shared premise from which their otherwise diverse endeavors began. It was the soul of realist orthodoxy, and anyone who wants to understand the meaning of legal realism, and of the intellectual problems to which it gave rise, must begin by reexamining the realists' attack on Langdellian legal science.

The basic lines of this attack may be reconstructed from any of several sources. But it will be easiest to focus on a single text, Jerome Frank's *Law and the Modern Mind*.[31] Published in 1930, during the earliest phase of the movement, Frank's influential book is distinguished by its keen appreciation of the relationship between Langdell's program, on the one hand, and the long tradition of belief in a geometry of politics and law, on the other—a tradition that Frank associated with the nineteenth-century legal positivists and whose ultimate origins he located in the mathematizing philosophy of Plato. Frank hated this tradition, of which he considered Langdell and his colleague Joseph Beale only the most recent representatives, and attacked it with unmatched brilliance and ferocity, helping, in this way, to discredit Langdellianism once and for all as a serious jurisprudential theory. But Frank's attack on the Langdellian idea of legal science raised new questions to which other realists felt some answer must be given. As we shall see, the answers they gave led in two very different directions. One sought to revive the idea of a science of law different from Langdell's in certain respects but resembling it in others, whereas the second led back to the common-law tradition that Langdell and his predecessors had repudiated. To follow these later developments, we need first to understand the point of Frank's attack, for it was this that set the agenda of the realist movement by posing problems that henceforth had to be met one way or another.

The gist of Frank's attack can be grasped most easily if we keep in mind two features of the geometrical method on which Langdell modeled his new science of law. The first is its independence or self-sufficiency. In a very general sense, geometry is a constructive activity like any other, for the proofs that a geometer fashions owe their existence to his efforts in the same way, for example, that a chair owes its existence to the carpenter's. Both proof and chair are artifacts. But unlike other craftsmen, a geometer works on material that comes from the storehouse of his own soul. He works on his own ideas, in contrast, for example, to a carpenter, who works on wood and other materials that only the world outside him can provide. The constructive work of the geometer is for this reason more independent than that of other artisans, since their efforts may be interrupted or frustrated by the world's failure to provide the materials they require, whereas the geometer's work cannot be. Because the geometer provides his own materials, he always has what he needs. The builder who works with real boards (boards that cannot be brought into existence by the power of thought alone) must learn to deal, moveover, with the peculiarities that real boards present—with their idiosyncratic knots and bumps—and the understanding this requires can be gained only through experience. Geometry, by contrast, does not require such experience. For a geometer works only on ideas that he himself produces, and the abstractness that distinguishes ideas from things means that his materials can never exhibit the kind of idiosyncratic variation whose effects experience alone reveals. The first characteristic of geometry is thus its twofold independence—of the world, on which it does not depend for materials, and of experience, from which it has nothing to learn.

Its second characteristic is the limitedness of the opportunities it offers for choice. Once the starting points of geometry have been established—whether these be Euclidian or not—all that remains is to unfold their implications by an analytic process that offers no occasions for meaningful choice. There are no decisions to be made in geometry analogous to those that a carpenter must make, for example, between working around a knothole and incorporating it into his design. A carpenter must also, of course, accept the limits that his materials, his own abilities, and the design he has selected all impose upon his work. But within these limits there are many choices to be made, and different artisans will make them in different ways. Geometry, by contrast, imposes on its practitioners a stricter discipline that leaves no room for choices of this kind. At the most, a geometer is free to substitute other starting points for Euclidian ones and in that sense to choose among alternatives. But whatever starting points he chooses, the geometer's art requires no further choices of the sort that must be made in the construction of a chair or table even after a blueprint is selected and indeed up to the moment the carpenter's work is done. Geometry is in this sense marked by an absence of choice that, together with its independence of experience, distinguishes it from constructive activities of other kinds.

The method Langdell recommends for the study of law resembles that of geometry in both respects. It is a method in which the worldly wisdom of practicing lawyers plays no role and only the most limited opportunities for choice exist. To be sure, a person may choose to study a system of rules other than the common law, just as a geometer may elect to begin with non-Euclidean assumptions. But any legal scientist who makes the common law his subject must, according to Langdell, take as his starting point the few easily discoverable axioms on which its various doctrinal branches rest. Once these foundational principles are in place, the Langdellian lawyer will proceed by employing a method of analysis that leaves him nothing more to choose than the method of geometry leaves its practitioners. Only a method of this sort is capable, Langdell believed, of producing the rationally objective judgments that distinguish a true science from a handicraft or an art.

Frank's attack on the geometrical model of law challenges just those features of it that made the model most attractive to Langdell and his followers. His argument focuses on the phenomenon of adjudication—the heart, he believed, of every legal system—and seeks above all else to show that the activity of judging lacks the very two characteristics that distinguish geometry from other forms of human creativity. First, Frank argues, the decisions of a judge inevitably draw upon his experience in a way that the judgments of a geometer do not. And second, they are always the result of a series of discretionary choices that have no counterpart in the science of geometry. Indeed, for Frank, experience and choice are not merely compatible with the activity of judging; they are among its essential conditions. The role that Frank assigns to choice is particularly important. Let us consider it first.

A judge's task is to apply the law to the facts of particular cases. But to do this he obviously needs to find the law and define the case to which he must apply it, and these preliminary tasks require, in Frank's view, a number of choices whose existence the geometrical model of law denies. There is to begin with—in difficult cases at least—a choice to be made among the various starting points from which a legal analysis of the case might reasonably proceed. In every branch of law one finds, according to Frank, a plurality of basic rules, rules that pull in different and sometimes contradictory directions and whose priority cannot be established by any procedure less controversial than these rules themselves. The more broadly one attempts to formulate the basic axioms of any particular field of law, the more obvious this becomes. Thus, for example, if we declare it to be a basic principle of contract law that no promise is enforceable without consideration, we must immediately add that a promise will nevertheless be enforced if the promisor clearly intends to be bound by it, even when no consideration has been given, for the latter rule is the only one on which many decided cases can be explained. Langdell was wrong to think, Frank claims, that a review of the cases in any given field must yield a small number of uncontroversial and internally consistent principles. It is far more likely, he says, that such a review will produce a set of conflicting principles that are the subject of continuing debate. To the extent that such conflicts exist, a controversial choice among competing premises cannot be avoided, and different judges will adopt different premises, no single choice being, as Langdell assumed, the demonstrably correct one.[32]

Nor, on Frank's view, is this the only choice that judges need to make. Langdell conceived the process of analysis by which one moves from fundamental legal axioms to a rule sufficiently detailed to decide the case at hand as one in which no discretionary choices are required. Frank, by contrast, insists that the process of deciding cases not only begins with a controversial choice of starting points but is marked at each additional stage by further choices of an equally uncompelled kind. If legal reasoning, as Langdell envisioned it, resembles the mechanical unfolding of a series of Chinese boxes, each already contained within the ones that came before, the image that best fits Frank's very different conception is that of a decision tree—a branching series of choices, each representing the decision to adopt one of a pair of increasingly specific options. As a judge moves down this tree, attempting to derive a rule specific enough to resolve the dispute before him, he encounters at each level new alternatives whose relative claims have no more been decided in advance than the basic alternatives he confronted at the outset, so that in applying the law to the case at hand, he must make a series of choices as discretionary as the one that was needed to fix the starting point from which he began. The process of law-finding is thus on Frank's view characterized by a certain ubiquity of choice, the very thing most noticeably absent in geometry.

But even this does not fully describe the role that choice plays in adjudication. The decision of a case occurs at the point where the law and the facts meet, and if choices must be made in the derivation of a rule specific enough to decide the case, they must also be made in the construction of the case itself from a set of more primitive facts. A case comes to the judge who has the initial responsibility for deciding it as a complex collection of facts, and out of these, according to Frank, the judge must select some as the legally relevant ones and disregard the others. Different cases may be constructed from the same facts, and there is nothing in the facts themselves that dictates their organization into one case pattern rather than another. It is up to the judge to decide how to arrange them, and his choices in this regard, though typically less self-conscious, are as unconstrained as the choices he makes in finding the applicable law.[33] Thus if we imagine a judge working down through a series of discretionary choices to reach a rule that closely fits the case at hand, we should also think of him as working up through a series of equally discretionary choices to reach a case that is sufficiently well defined to be decided. Both the facts of a case and the legal rules applicable to it are thus products of choice and not, as Langdell assumed, of observation and thought alone. For Langdell, the administration of law, when properly pursued, engages only the reasoning part of the judge's soul. For Frank, it necessarily engages the choosing part as well, the part we call the will. Frank's attack on Langdell's science of law thus begins by substituting will for reason as the key faculty in adjudication.

The role he assigns to will in the activity of judging leads Frank to conclude that adjudication necessarily lacks internal constraints of the sort that exist in the science of geometry, constraints that in the latter case ensure that those who begin with the same assumptions will reach identical conclusions so long as they reason soundly. For a science of the kind that Langdell envisioned to be possible at all, the process of legal reasoning must be comparably constrained, and in denying that it is or ever can be, Frank challenges the premise on which Langdellianism rests. The vision of a system of law that confines its administrators to judgments as uniform as those of geometry may, Frank says, have an understandable appeal to human beings who passionately desire a greater certainty in the arrangement of their affairs than is humanly attainable. But it should not be taken as a true picture of what the law is actually like, or treated as an ideal in adjudication and scholarship. For if choice is inescapable, then it makes no sense to postulate as the goal of either enterprise the establishment of a science from which all meaningful choice has been purged.

To say, as Frank does, that adjudication lacks internal constraints of the sort found in geometry is not, of course, to claim that the choices a judge makes are completely undetermined. It is only to say that the law itself does not determine them. Indeed, Frank himself presents what might fairly be described as a deterministic picture of the adjudicative process, one in which judges are portrayed as moving along tracks often rigidly fixed in advance. But the factors to which he assigns a determining role are external to the law.[34] A judge forced to choose among legal or factual alternatives will invariably be influenced, according to Frank, by his personal values and perceptual habits, values and habits that he has acquired in the course of living and that the judge brings with him to the bench. These "biases," as Frank calls them, tip the scale in favor of one alternative or another. And since it seems necessary, on Frank's view, that something do so, we may properly describe them as a constituent feature of adjudication, even though they have nothing to do with the law but owe their existence to the judge's personal experience instead.

It is in this sense that experience may be said to play, for Frank, an essential role in adjudication. A geometer requires no experience to form his judgments, but only a capacity for clear and patient thought. A judge, by contrast, must make choices for which experience is a prerequisite, since it alone supplies the biases needed to motivate a choice among alternatives otherwise in equipoise. This is, to be sure, a different role from the one that Aristotle assigns to experience in his account of political judgment, and different too from the one emphasized by defenders of the common-law tradition. It is nonetheless a necessary role, and in making the activity of judging so dependent upon experience, Frank challenges the second main premise of the geometrical model of law.

The personal biases that cause judges to decide cases as they do are not, however, on Frank's view, common to them all but vary from one to the next. A judge may of course share certain prejudices with other members of his class, religious community, and so on. But it is the entire set of such prejudices that directs his judgment in specific cases, and taken as a whole this set is his own and no one else's. It is the product of his singular life history. The external factors that determine the course of adjudication are thus, according to Frank, highly idiosyncratic, and though every judge is influenced by his biases, these tend to be so personal in character that their effects cannot be fit into a pattern.[35] It follows that the law not only lacks internal constraints stringent enough to guarantee a convergence of judgments on the part of those engaged in its administration; the personal prejudices of judges are themselves too variable to supply a convergence of this kind by means of an external surrogate. Given the first assumption, we must abandon as absurd the idea of a geometry of law. And given the second, we must also reject the notion of a behavioral science of law aimed at discovering the hidden regularities of adjudication, those that are the product of external forces. For however pervasive their influence, the effect of these forces is on Frank's view too uneven to produce regularities of a meaningful sort.[36] Many realists came, as we shall see, to accept the latter goal and found in it the basis for a renewed commitment to the idea of a science of law. But this path was closed to Frank by his belief in the idiosyncracy of judicial behavior, which he thought must preclude its scientific understanding.

What program does Frank recommend, then, to those who accept the implications of his critical attack on Langdell's geometry of law? The answer is, an essentially personal and therapeutic one.[37]

According to Frank, the challenge that a judge must meet is two-fold. First, he must honestly confront the awful indeterminacy of his own judgments and accept the fact that nothing in the law compels him to decide the cases that come before him one way or the other. He must acknowledge that each of his decisions is a choice for which he alone is responsible, and work to liberate himself from the seductive appeal of the Langdellian view of law, which the thoughtful judge will come in time to see as a response to a psychic need rather than as a true picture of reality.

Second, Frank tells us, every judge must struggle toward a more self-conscious understanding of the prejudices that inevitably shape his own perceptions and deliberations, the habits unreflectively acquired in his lifelong search for something that will satisfy his infantile yearning for authoritative certainty. Once a person understands the origins of this yearning, sees the ways in which it has uniquely shaped his own development, and resigns himself to the impossibility of ever satisfying it, he will no longer be the hostage of his own unconscious needs. For him, the myth of certainty, as Frank calls it, will have lost its mythic power. Self-understanding of this sort in turn enhances one's ability to tolerate the painful indeterminacies of adult life, and of adjudication in particular, and leads to greater spiritual maturity (Holmes being, for Frank, a model of the truly adult judge who has overcome his childish need for certainty and now faces the world without illusions). Liberated by his self-understanding, the mature judge stands ready to meet the real, and unavoidable, tragedies of life. According to Frank, this is all that one may hope for, and all that human responsibility can ever mean, for judges or for anyone else.

This is a hard teaching. Indeed, there is some reason to believe that Frank himself found it too hard to accept. For there are passages in which he suggests that a liberated judiciary—one made up of judges who have seen through their own prejudices in the way Frank recommends—will be characterized by a convergence of judgment greater than that which now exists, and by a consequent increase in the "actual legal certainty" of the adjudicative process as a whole.[38] The assumption underlying this claim, which reflects Frank's own lingering attachment to the ideal of certainty in law, is that many legal questions do in fact have demonstrably right answers, but that these are obscured by prejudice, whose effects can be dispelled by becoming consciously aware of their existence.

There is nothing inherently absurd about this claim. But it runs against the grain of Frank's iconoclastic argument, and he offers no convincing support for it. Frank makes self-consciousness his central value and argues that a self-conscious judge will recognize his own prejudices to a degree an unself-conscious one cannot. This may be true. It does not follow, though, that an enlightened judge no longer has the biases he now acknowledges. Enlightenment may bring greater tolerance, both toward oneself and toward others. But Frank offers no reason for thinking that it also promotes a greater uniformity of judgment among those who have attained it (which would be the case only if self-consciousness brought freedom from one's prejudices and not simply an accepting recognition of them). Indeed, Frank's insistence on the depth of the biases that color judicial perception, and on their variability from one judge to the next, makes it unlikely that even a judiciary whose members have achieved the maturity he celebrates will converge in its judgments to any great extent. In the absence of such convergence, which Langdell believed the very discipline of legal reasoning ensures, no dramatic increase in the certainty of adjudication is likely to result.

The passages in which Frank suggests that a more self-conscious judiciary means greater legal certainty therefore express what can only be described as an article of faith. However understandable, they represent a kind of intellectual backsliding whose implications cannot be accepted without altering the whole tenor of Frank's book. For if it is to be consistent, his argument can lead to one conclusion only, and that is the purely personal conclusion that self-understanding represents the sole form of salvation available to the Holmesian judge who has outgrown his need for certainty but whose views continue to be shaped, as they must, by prejudices accumulated in the course of his distinctive life experience. The aim of *Law and the Modern Mind* is thus essentially therapeutic. Frank's primary intention is to force each reader back into himself and the subjective privacy of his own experience; for the hopeful claim that such introspection leads to an objective convergence of judgment among the enlightened, his book offers no support.

A REALIST SCIENCE OF LAW: DESCRIBING JUDICIAL BEHAVIOR

Unsurprisingly, many of Frank's fellow-realists found his personalistic conclusions hard to accept. Academic lawyers are not particularly well qualified to lead others through the therapy he recommends, and the implications of such a program for law teaching and legal scholarship are hazy at best. Frank's book placed Langdell's conception of the mission of the academic lawyer in doubt but offered no new one to take its place, and during the decade that followed many realists struggled to find some new foundation on which the work of academic lawyers might again be securely based.

To all who shared this goal, one thing, at least, seemed clear. The old, Langdellian account of the work of academic lawyers could not be revived. Langdell's geometry of law had been impeached, once and for all, by Frank's powerful criticisms of it and, in particular, by his insistence on what everyone who followed simply took for granted: the central role that choice plays in adjudication. All agreed that a new account of the aims of legal scholarship had to be constructed. But from this common starting point, those who attempted to provide such an account moved in two quite different directions, and the result was not one theory of law and legal scholarship but two, very different in their aims and assumptions.

The first—which I call scientific realism and whose lineaments I shall describe in this section and the next—represented an attempt to revitalize the idea of a science of law, though in a way that avoided the embarrassments of Langdell's legal geometry. The proponents of scientific realism acknowledged that adjudication involves not only analysis but choice, and they accepted Frank's claim that the various decisions a judge must make are often controversial. They acknowledged, too, the role that external factors play in the adjudicative process. But they nevertheless insisted that it is possible to answer both the descriptive question of what law is and the normative question of what it ought to be in a comprehensive fashion and with a high degree of rigor, and they further maintained that the techniques for doing so are available only to academic specialists. In these respects the scientific realists, though rejecting the geometrical pretensions of

Langdell's program, continued to embrace his central goal, that of constructing a systematic theory of law by means of methods acquired not through experience but academic study.

To understand the premises of scientific realism, we must begin by examining an argument that Karl Llewellyn first presented in the early 1930s in a series of articles written in defense of the realist program.[39] There is an irony in this, for Llewellyn himself later became the most articulate spokesman for a very different conception of law and legal scholarship—one based upon assumptions drawn from the common-law tradition that the scientific realists, like Langdell before them, were united in rejecting. It is a testimony to Llewellyn's genius that he not only laid the foundation for the first branch of legal realism, but almost singlehandedly established the second one as well. Llewellyn's mature convictions clearly lay in the latter direction. But it is in his own early writings that the premises of scientific realism come most clearly into view.

Llewellyn's argument for a new, non-Langdellian science of law begins with an acceptance of Frank's principal critical claim. Like Frank, Llewellyn stresses that cases cannot be decided merely by identifying the controlling rules of law, the "paper" rules, as he dismissively describes them.[40] The decision of a case always requires a choice among alternatives, hence an exercise of will. The law therefore cannot be defined in the way Langdell proposes, as a system of rules *simpliciter.* Legal rules are of course ingredients in adjudication. They are among the factors influencing judges to decide cases as they do. But though they are in this sense a source of law, legal rules are not the law itself. Indeed, once the role of choice in adjudication is acknowledged, it is no longer possible to equate the law with any of the factors that go into the decisions judges make. The law must be defined, instead, as the product or outcome of these decisions, a view classically expressed by Holmes's dictum that the law is what the judges say it is, and nothing more.[41] For anyone who believes in the possibility of a geometry of law, this view will seem absurd—as absurd as the suggestion that the content of geometry depends upon what particular individuals have to say about it, rather than the other way around. On the Langdellian view, a judicial decision may or may not conform to the law (and whether it does will determine whether the decision is a sound one). But it cannot in any sense be said to constitute the law itself. The latter view, which equates the law not with what goes into adjudication but with what comes out of it instead, follows directly from Frank's insistence on the centrality of choice in judging and represents the starting point of Llewellyn's own argument.

This change in viewpoint in turn forces the recognition of a distinction that Langdell ignores and Llewellyn by contrast treats as fundamental: the distinction between "is" and "ought."[42] Asking whether a case has been rightly decided is for Langdell equivalent to asking whether the decision conforms to the relevant rules of law, rules that serve as a standard for evaluating the decision's correctness in the same way that the truths of geometry function as a standard for assessing the judgments of particular geometers. On this view, the question of what a judge *ought* to do in a specific case cannot be disentangled from the question of what the law governing that case *is*. Indeed, any answer to the latter question is also necessarily an answer to the former one as well. But if we define the law instead, in the way Llewellyn does, as the product of judicial choices, as something constituted by them, then it becomes emptily circular to say that the rightness of a decision depends upon its conformity to law, for since the decision constitutes the law (of that case, at least), it must conform to it by definition. Conformity to law can be a meaningful criterion for assessing the rightness of judicial decisions only on the assumption that law exists antecedently to these decisions themselves, which is precisely what Llewellyn denies. On Llewellyn's view, it is of course still perfectly sensible to ask what the law is. (The law is simply the sum of a series of judicial choices.) But unless one is prepared to say that every such decision is correct—which would make any normative discussion of them pointless—an answer to this descriptive question can no longer be assumed to settle by itself the question of the rightness of those decisions that have actually been rendered. What the law is, and what it ought to be, become questions that must now be answered separately.

Putting aside for a moment the second question of how we are to evaluate the decisions judges make, is there any reason to believe that these decisions themselves exhibit an intelligible order of some sort? Llewellyn claims there is and indeed insists it can be described with scientific rigor. The decisions of judges, he says, constitute a discrete area of human behavior, and we understand the structure or order of this area, as we do that of any other, when we grasp the relationship between it and its determining causes. The causes of judicial behavior are many and varied. Among them must be included the so-called paper rules of the legal system; since judges are motivated to conform their conduct to these rules, the rules themselves may rightly be described as one of the factors causing them to behave in the way they do. But Llewellyn also emphasizes that other, nonlegal factors influence judicial behavior too. The causal effect of all these factors, and not just those we consider right or proper from a normative point of view, must, according to Llewellyn, be described and analyzed if we are to understand the body of judicial decisions that is the product of their combined operation.

Llewellyn's account of judicial behavior resembles Frank's in its emphasis on the causal influence of factors other than strictly legal ones. It differs from Frank's account, however, in one critical respect. Frank claimed that the causes of judicial behavior are so idiosyncratic as to elude meaningful generalization. Llewellyn, by contrast, insists that these same causes display a patterned regularity that can be described in lawlike terms and is subject to empirical confirmation.[43] These regularities lie hidden beneath the chaotic surface of the law, and the judges whose behavior they describe are themselves often unaware of them. But they exist, and according to Llewellyn it is the task of legal scholars to formulate and by empirical research to verify their content.

In his early articles, Llewellyn expresses confidence that the regularities in question can be precisely defined and rigorously tested, though he concedes that legal scholars have so far made only a small start in this direction. He speaks, in this connection, of the "backwardness" of law as a science of observation, and stresses its intellectual immaturity as compared with other social sciences, especially economics.[44] These other disciplines are the models for Llewellyn's descriptive science of law, and there is no reason, he claims, why such a science cannot attain as high a level of precision as they. What has held back the study of law, Llewellyn argues, is the confusion of "is" and "ought" that marred the scholarship of Langdell's followers; once the description of law has been disentangled from its evaluation, legal scholarship will, he predicts, take its place alongside the other sciences of human behavior.

The most exact of these sciences is economics. Llewellyn acknowledges that the laws of legal science must for the most part be formulated in probabilistic terms, unlike those of economics. But despite this he maintains that it is appropriate for legal scholars to aim at the same level of exactness that economists have so far been the only social scientists to attain. And just as the exactness of economics depends upon the use of methods more precise than the pragmatic techniques of those whose behavior it studies, so too a science of law must, Llewellyn says, use statistical and other methods less casual than the ones judges employ in deciding cases. The methods of legal science need to be more systematic and exact than those of sitting judges. Moreover, experience alone is incapable of teaching them. They can be learned only through a course of academic study. They are the tools of academic specialists, and the distinctive task of legal scholars—their vocation, so to speak—is to master these methods and then apply them to the study of judicial behavior.

Llewellyn's insistence that legal scholarship be viewed as a branch of social science, that it seek to formulate behavioral laws comparable in rigor to those of economics, and that it do so by adopting methods learned through academic study rather than practical experience, lays the foundation for a new science of law, one similar to the old Langdellian program in its aspiration to exactness and independence from the world of practice, though freed from the now-untenable assumptions on which that program had been based. It was on this foundation that many realists, at Yale and elsewhere, sought in the early 1930s to build a post–critical social science of law. Their extraordinary efforts, which John Schlegel has described in an interesting pair of articles,[45] testify to the renewed confidence in legal science that Llewellyn's methodological argument helped to encourage and legitimate. To many his argument showed that a science of law was possible after all, even in the wake of Frank's radical attack on Langdell's geometry of law, and proved that Langdell's goal, or part of it at least, might be reached by a route very different from the one that Langdell himself had followed.

The Normative Aims of Scientific Realism

The program of research that Llewellyn outlines in his early articles is not a full substitute for Langdell's legal science, for it lacks a normative component. It is a purely descriptive enterprise whose aim is to explain judicial behavior without assessing its correctness or merit.

Langdell's program was by contrast both a descriptive and a normative one. Its goal was to establish a system of propositions that would function simultaneously as statements of the law and as standards for the evaluation of judicial conduct. But this goal seemed attainable, Llewellyn says, only because Langdell and his followers failed to acknowledge the distinction between "is" and "ought"—a distinction that must be rigorously respected if a descriptive science of law is ever to be established. It is one thing to study the behavioral regularities that inform the body of judicial decisions that on Llewellyn's view constitute the law. But it is something quite different, he insists, to inquire into the rightness of these same decisions, and only when the would-be legal scientist accepts the distinction between these two inquiries can he approach the first in a scientific manner. For until then he cannot take account of all the causal factors that influence judicial behavior but only the narrower set he thinks right or proper. The separation or "postponement" of all normative questions is thus on Llewellyn's view essential to the establishment of a truly unbiased descriptive legal science.[46]

When he returns to the normative questions that must be postponed for the sake of establishing such a science, however, Llewellyn makes it clear, in his early articles at least, that he believes these questions do not have similarly scientific answers. He acknowledges that the desire to evaluate is irrepressible, and says that anyone who wants merely to know, and not to judge, is a kind of "freak."[47] But when we come to the realm of value judgments, we leave the "solid sphere of objective observation" and enter what he calls the "airy sphere of individual ideals and subjectivity" instead.[48] Here people have "preferences and hunches," and though we distinguish between the informed hunch and the uninformed one, it is utterly mistaken, he insists, to portray even the most educated value judgment as a "scientific truth."[49] A descriptive science of law cannot answer the question of how judges should behave. This is a question that each of us must answer for ourselves, and we ought never to pretend that the answers we give have objective validity. In the realm of values, Llewellyn claims, the most we can aspire to is a clarification of the meaning and implications of different norms, and thus a greater self-consciousness regarding the value choices they entail. But these choices themselves must always be personal ones, and their subjectivity bars forever the establishment of a normative science of law. In this respect Llewellyn's position remains quite close to Frank's. For though (unlike Frank) he defends the possibility of a descriptive science of law, he too adopts a personalistic view of value judgments that rules out their scientific treatment.

Llewellyn's overall position may thus be summarized as follows: Langdell and his disciples believed in the possibility of a legal science that would be at once descriptive and normative. But this belief depended upon their conflation of "is" and "ought." To rescue the first part of Langdell's program—the descriptive part—these two realms must be carefully disentangled. But when they are, it becomes clear that the second, normative part has to be abandoned. According to Llewellyn, a descriptive science of law can be rebuilt on realist assumptions and given a sounder foundation than the one Langdell provided. But this can be done only if the goal of establishing a normative science of law is surrendered, the renunciation of this second goal being the price that we must pay for the attainment of the first one.

Among the realists there were, however, some who found this halfway position unsatisfying and who—building on Llewellyn's argument for a descriptive science of law—sought to show that a normative legal science compatible with the critical claims of realism was possible as well. Their aim was to restore the dimension of legal science that Llewellyn had eliminated and thus to provide a full substitute, rather than a partial one, for Langdell's program. It is in their work that scientific realism achieves its most complete expression and assumes a form that makes manifest its link to the Hobbesian tradition of thought in which Langdell's own project was embedded.

The effort to establish a normative science of law on realist assumptions comes to a climax in the writing of Harold Lasswell and Myres McDougal. A classic statement of this enterprise is to be found in their 1943 article "Legal Education and Public Policy: Professional Training in the Public Interest."[50] This article is today no longer widely read, and those academic lawyers who consider themselves followers of the approach outlined by Lasswell and McDougal are few in number. The specialized terminology they invented has for the most part been forgotten, and the approach they recommend is now regarded, by many, as obsolete. But this conclusion, though widely shared, is mistaken. For though the details of their approach and their idiosyncratic vocabulary have indeed disappeared from the mainstream of American legal theory, the general position that Lass-well and McDougal defend describes the unspoken common ground on which both the law-and-economics and the critical legal studies movements rest. Their 1943 article defines more clearly than any other document the spirit of American legal scholarship today. It is a forgotten classic, and its argument deserves close study.

The subject of Lasswell and McDougal's article is legal education. What, they ask, are the aims of law teaching and how should it be organized in order to achieve them? The traditional approach to legal education—the approach favored by Langdell and his followers—leads, they say, to a curriculum organized "in terms of legal technical-ity," one based on the assumption that "the body of conventional legal doctrine at once provides comprehensive and well-ordered cov-erage of the important problems of our society and embodies our preferred values for the handling of such problems." On this view, "[w]hat is commonly called 'the law' can . . . be defined as a syntactic system of propositions composed of terms that are supposedly de-fined, plus some admittedly undefinable terms, whose modes of com-bination are governed by certain postulates and rules." The law, so conceived, constitutes "a closed, automatic syntactical system."[51]

Lasswell and McDougal maintain that this Langdellian view of law is "too obviously belied by the facts for many to give it conscious credence today," and they reiterate the familiar realist reasons for re-jecting it:

> The terms and propositions of the legal syntax are neither inter-
> nally consistent nor comprehensive in their reference. They are,
> on the contrary, inconsistent, ambiguous, and full of omissions . . .
> A judge who must choose between [legal] principles can only offer
> in justification for his choice a proliferation of other such principles
> in infinite regress or else arbitrarily take a stand and state his prefer-
> ence; and what he prefers or what he regards as "authoritative" is
> likely to be a product of his whole biography . . . Consciously or
> unconsciously, if [a judge] keeps within the legal syntax, he must
> beg the very question that he has to decide.[52]

Influenced by this critique, they say, legal scholars have now "aban-doned the once prestigeful effort to reduce the vast coruscation of traditional legal learning to beautifully terraced unified statements, geometrically laid out with no overlapping, erosion, or gaps."[53]

In insisting that choice plays a determining role in adjudication, Lasswell and McDougal are of course simply repeating the main point of Frank's attack on the Langdellian view of law. But they emphatically reject the iconoclastic conclusion that certain realists, including Frank himself, drew from this critical argument. Some realists, they say, believe the argument demonstrates that any effort to study the law in a scientific fashion is absurd. Having abandoned all pretense of scientific rigor, the members of this group "content themselves with rather fruitless exposés of existing imperfections and present the law as a chaotic mass of confused and more or less meaningless statements."[54] But Lasswell and McDougal insist that this approach is misguided, that the study of law can and ought to be put on a scientific footing, and that legal education should be reformed with this in mind.

Others before them, they acknowledge, have sought to establish a descriptive science of law on realist assumptions by "attempting to determine what courts and other decisionmaking bodies do as opposed to what they *say* they do." The aim of these scholars has been to advance the "legitimate scientific goal of predicting" judicial and other behavior. Lasswell and McDougal praise their efforts, stressing that the development of any descriptive legal science depends upon the separation of "is" from "ought," and underscoring the need for such a science to take account of the full range of factors, both legal and nonlegal, that have some causal influence on judicial behavior. The more a legal scholar pursues studies of this sort, they say, the less "he continues in the role of logician to the state and the more he must become a man of science." As a descriptive scientist, "his task [is] to account for the occurrence of a selected category of events— to wit: judicial conduct," and to do this he "must take into consideration all variables that may significantly determine it." Descriptive research of this sort in turn requires specialized training, and Lasswell and McDougal emphasize that any "legal scholar who would predict the future course of decision must equip himself with skills appropriate to the task of evaluating variables, and this means that to his traditional knowledge of legal technicality it is imperative to add naturalistic skills of observation and analysis."[55]

But though they endorse the aims of this new descriptive science of law, Lasswell and McDougal insist that its development demonstrates the need for a second branch of scientific inquiry without which this first one must remain permanently incomplete. "In predicting decisions, as in explaining any response, there is no end to the number of factors that may be taken into account, or the degree of technical refinement to which the gathering and processing of data may be carried." Hence if "prediction studies" of this sort are to have a focus, the researcher must begin with a clear understanding of the values or goals he wants to realize in and through the legal order. According to Lasswell and McDougal, only an understanding of this kind can provide the "criteria" needed to give shape and direction to a program of descriptive research. But questions concerning the goals of law have so far been neglected in the field of prediction studies and must now be addressed, they say, if the descriptive branch of legal science is itself to be placed on a more solid foundation.[56]

By their nature such questions belong to the domain of values and thus cannot be answered by an appeal to facts alone. It is only in the sphere of values that one discovers the "social goals" necessary to give descriptive research a "proper orientation." Without such an orientation, which value judgments alone can supply, "what appear to be promising ventures into 'fact research' produce relatively isolated and trivial results,"[57] often degenerating into a formalism "as sterile" as the traditional Langdellian approach. "Unless some such values are chosen, carefully defined, explicitly made the organizing foci of the law school curriculum, and kept so constantly at the student's focus of attention that he automatically applies them to every conceivable practical and theoretical situation, all talk of integrating 'law' and 'social science,' or of making law a more effective instrument of social control is twaddling futility."[58]

How exactly is this to be done? Langdell's syntactical legal science had, of course, a normative component, but his basic values were simply "legal concepts of highest order abstraction," and concepts of this sort cannot serve, Lasswell and McDougal argue, as foundational principles for a normative policy science of the kind they claim all descriptive research presupposes. Even the most basic legal concepts, they insist, are indeterminate in scope and meaning and must therefore be interpreted to be applied. Because of this they lack the clarity and simplicity—the finality—that the elementary norms of any rigorous policy science must possess. If the policy goals of law are to be formulated with rigor and precision, they must therefore be founded upon normative principles even more basic than the legal abstractions that Langdell takes as the starting points for his geometry of law. Since these abstractions occupy the highest position in the hierarchy of legal norms, any principles more basic than they must thus of necessity be anterior to the legal order as a whole and therefore extrinsic to its own internal requirements. "If he is not to choke on triviality," Lasswell and McDougal conclude, a student of the law must have "extrinsic criteria of relevance."[59]

The selection and elaboration of such criteria carry the legal scholar beyond the realm of law, strictly defined, into the sphere of moral and political theory, where questions of ultimate values must be addressed. Some, Lasswell and McDougal observe, have contrasted questions of this sort with those that may properly be treated by a "science disinfected of all preference,"[60] implying that questions of ultimate values can be decided only by subjective *fiat* and are therefore incapable of scientific analysis or resolution. This is of course precisely the position that Llewellyn takes in his early articles. Lasswell and McDougal reject it with a vehemence approaching contempt. It is true, they admit, that we cannot construct a policy science of law on the model of geometry, but they insist that the extrinsic principles on which such a science must be based can nevertheless be identified with a high degree of objectivity and the implications of these principles worked out in a rigorous and systematic fashion, down even to a level of great technical detail. Four related considerations support this claim.

First, they assert, the ultimate values on which any normative assessment of the law might plausibly be based are not nearly as numerous as the subjectivist view suggests. This view implies that there are as many ultimate values, potentially at least, as people making value judgments. But according to Lasswell and McDougal, almost all political and moral controversies can be reduced to a few elementary disagreements and explained in terms of the differences among a handful of competing philosophies. Thus the range of choices one encounters in the domain of values is in fact much narrower than subjectivist views, like Llewellyn's, seem to assume. At a minimum this makes the task of describing the structure of the normative realm simpler than it might appear.

Second, Lasswell and McDougal insist that the choice a person makes among the small number of ultimate values to which nearly all moral and political disputes can be reduced should not itself be viewed as an arbitrary act of will, based upon nothing but the person's idiosyncratic preferences and hence beyond the power of reason either to explain or to justify. On the contrary, they claim, arguments can be constructed for and against the few competing norms that must be treated as serious candidates for the role of ultimate value in any normative theory of law, and they stress that a choice among these values can and should be made on the basis of such argumentative considerations. It is the job of the law teacher, they say, to elaborate these considerations and by doing so to rationalize the value choices that his students make.

Third, Lasswell and McDougal maintain that there are compelling reasons for a modern American law student to adopt one value in particular as his normative starting point and to endorse the political system associated with it. This is the value of individualism, a value that in their view only democratic government can fully realize. There are, of course, other values on the basis of which it is logically possible to construct a comprehensive political philosophy. But according to Lasswell and McDougal only individualism, which assigns a supreme value to personal autonomy, provides a defensible premise for normative theory under the political and cultural conditions that exist in the modern West. While other premises are thinkable, none but individualism can in their view be acceptable to anyone who regards even the most basic features of Western civilization in a positive light. Individualism—and the democratic system of government needed to secure it—thus provides, they claim, the most appropriate foundation on which to build a policy science of law today.

Fourth, and most important, Lasswell and McDougal insist that each of the small number of ultimate values one confronts in the sphere of normative choice can be unfolded in a systematic way and applied with exactness through a range of increasingly specific settings. Once he has established the superiority of democratic individualism as an ultimate value, the main task of the legal educator thus becomes to "amplify" the meaning of this value and to develop in detail its implications for political and legal issues of a concrete kind. This is to be done, they say, through "rules of interpretation, of varying degrees of generality, that show how observers of specific situations can validly use the terms [that define the value of democratic individualism] in describing concrete reality and [by] promoting the occurrence of relatively specific events in harmony with the definition." The process is admittedly a "long and arduous" one. But its end result—"indispensable to clarity and, hence, to the education of policymakers"—is a set of "consistent propositions of varying degrees of generality" that together define the institutional, psychological, and other consequences of adopting democratic individualism as one's fundamental value.[61]

Such an elaboration of ultimate values should not be confused, of course, with the method employed by Langdell, with the "logical derivation of values by philosophers," a procedure in which one "take[s] sentences that define moral standards and deduce[s] from them more inclusive propositions or vice versa." To avoid the sterility of this approach, it is essential that the would-be policy scientist supplement his most basic values with what Lasswell and McDougal call "operational rules"—rules that specify how one's highest-order norms bear on more-specific goals that can be described only in "statement[s] of low-level abstraction."[62] The formulation of such rules requires, above all, careful attention to what they term the "conditioning variables"[63] of one's chosen value system: the conditions that must be satisfied if one's ultimate values are to be realized in practice. These conditioning variables provide the linkage needed to connect very general moral and political values, like that of democratic individualism, with the specific problems of practicing lawyers. Lasswell and McDougal express confidence that the variables in question can be identified and their operation defined in a sufficiently rigorous way to permit students of policy science to move with smoothness and precision from the highest level of normative abstraction to much lower ones.

To recapitulate: a descriptive science of law can have focus and direction only if it is accompanied by a normative theory that specifies the ends the law should serve. The discovery and elaboration of these ends is not a matter of mere taste or preference, as some maintain, but a task to be pursued with as much rigor and objectivity as we demand in the case of its descriptive counterpart. The aim of this pursuit is to establish a normative science of law, and the student who would become a master of this science must proceed in a disciplined way. First, he must consider the arguments for and against the few ultimate values that compete for our allegiance in the realm of norms, and on the basis of these considerations pick the one that is rationally preferable (which in the modern West, at least, means the value of democratic individualism). He must then amplify the basic value he has chosen by elaborating its specific institutional and other implications, using "operational rules" that state the effect of certain "conditioning variables" to do so.

Having gotten this far, the student of policy science must then also become skilled at identifying "trends" in the law and in society, and acquire an expert knowledge of the causal factors that determine judicial behavior. It is the function of the descriptive branch of legal science to supply all knowledge of this latter sort, and though it cannot by itself provide the normative guidance he requires, a policymaker needs such knowledge in order to determine the most effective strategy for implementing the value judgments he has made. The descriptive science of law thus becomes an important, though subordinate, component in a more comprehensive legal science that purports to answer questions of value with the same methodical exactness it displays in answering questions of fact.

This new science establishes a "policy-potent framework"[64] within which traditional legal issues may be reexamined "with insight for the express purpose of problem solving." In the past, Lasswell and McDougal say, lawyers placed too much reliance on the "unanalyzed and unexplored hunch."[65] The aim of their new science of law is to replace judgments based on hunch with a disciplined procedure for defining social goals and for managing the human beings engaged in their pursuit. Those who approach legal questions in the spirit recommended by defenders of the common law, believing that such questions can be answered on the basis of what Lasswell and McDougal derisively call one's "judgment of men,"[66] proceed without order, exactness, or direction. Only a policy science of law possesses these attributes, and it does so not in virtue of any worldly wisdom drawn from an acquaintance with human affairs, but because of its reliance upon intellectual and observational techniques foreign to the practicing lawyer—techniques that can be learned only in a university setting under the supervision of academic specialists and whose mastery owes little, if anything, to experience.

Langdell hoped to achieve exactness in the study of the law by using methods that do not rely upon experience and, like earlier enemies of the common-law tradition, challenged in the name of legal science the claims of prudence and precedent on which that tradition rests. Lasswell and McDougal do the same. Accepting the core of

Frank's attack on Langdellianism, but rejecting his iconoclastic conclusions, they too insist that the law should be a science, not a handicraft—a science of values as well as of facts. In this respect their program resembles Langdell's own and is equally at war with the common-law attitudes he attacked. For while rejecting his naive equation of science with geometry and his precritical confusion of "is" with "ought," they too uphold an ideal of legal science that is antithetical to the common lawyer's conception of his craft and find in it, as Langdell did, the meaning of the legal educator's special task.

Habits and Horse-Sense

Jerome Frank criticized the Langdellian view of law for its failure to acknowledge the role of choice in adjudication, a failure made inevitable by Langdell's adoption of the choiceless science of geometry as his model. Every legal realist accepted this criticism. It represented the one negative proposition to which they all assented. But from the claim that judges make choices in deciding cases, Frank himself drew the antinomian conclusion that their behavior cannot be described with scientific rigor nor the correctness of their choices evaluated in a disciplined and objective manner. Most realists rejected this conclusion, and some of those who did sought to overcome Frank's iconoclasm by attempting to build a rigorous science of law on non-Langdellian assumptions. This effort culminated in the work of Harold Lasswell and Myres McDougal, whose policy science of law represents a kind of critical Langdellianism, a program purged of the most embarrassing features of Langdell's own but colored by a similar contempt for the common law and the claims of practical wisdom.

There is, however, another strand of thought in legal realism that represents a second and quite different response to Frank's antinomianism. Unlike its scientific counterpart, this second strand—which I call prudential realism—was not animated by the Hobbesian ambition to construct a rigorous science of law independent of experience and precedent. Instead it drew inspiration from the even older understanding of law embodied in the common-law tradition, a tradition based on ideas classically associated with Aristotle and attacked by Hobbes and all his followers, Langdell included. The heart of this tradition lay in a certain conception of prudence or practical wisdom, and it was around this same conception that the second branch of realism wove its argument. If scientific realism reflects a Hobbesian conception of law, prudential realism may therefore be said to embody an Aristotelian one, so that in the difference between these two strands of realist thought, each of which sought in its own way to transcend Frank's celebration of mature despair, we see enacted once again an ancient contest of ideas.

In contrast to the scientific branch of legal realism, however, the prudentialist branch was not a group creation and never became an organized school of thought. Prudential realism was the invention, in fact, of a single man, Karl Llewellyn, a supremely talented but isolated thinker who had no followers in the conventional sense.

Llewellyn's early articles on the meaning and goals of legal realism were motivated by a desire to make the study of law as methodically exact as other, less backward social sciences. In this phase of his thinking, Llewellyn drew a sharp contrast between what he called the "realm of science," on the one hand, and that of "craft," on the other. While acknowledging that adjudication is an "art" that requires "the intangible something we know as hunching-power, or skill, or judgment," he insisted that "skillful work in the art" of deciding cases "is no sign of the existence of a science that will satisfy the observer."[67] Although "loose, inaccurate and partial summations of much experience are valuable in an art even though no one of them is complete, even though their totality is never self-consistent," craft knowledge of this sort cannot, he stressed, be "put into a consistent arrangement which describes human action" and can therefore never provide the basis for a genuine science of judicial behavior. According to Llewellyn—the early Llewellyn—"[w]e are presented in law, as in every other discipline, with the fierce distinction between a science and an art," and the very possibility of a behavioral science of law depends upon our respecting this distinction and making the former point of view our primary one.[68]

But soon after the publication of his early articles on legal realism, the notion of an art or craft begins to play a larger role in Llewellyn's thinking and within a few years has become the central organizing concept of his jurisprudence. Simultaneously, the idea of a legal science starts to recede in importance and in time comes to be viewed by Llewellyn with intense suspicion. In this sense, we might say, the notions of science and craft change places in Llewellyn's understanding of law, the latter moving to the center of his thought and the former to the periphery. When, precisely, this change occurs and what provokes it are difficult questions. According to Llewellyn's own testimony,[69] several experiences together pushed him in this new direction, and there are intimations even in his earliest work of his later fascination with the craft-concept of judging. In any case, by 1940 the transformation was complete. In that year Llewellyn delivered the Storrs Lectures at Yale, and it was from these that his masterwork, *The Common Law Tradition,* eventually grew. *The Common Law Tradition* is a quirky book, both in its style (which some find charming and others hate) and in its peculiar methods of proof. Nevertheless, Llewellyn's book contains the best account of common-law adjudication that any American has ever offered, and in it we find, worked out in some detail, an alternative to scientific realism and indeed to the whole tradition of thought, so contemptuous of common-law attitudes, that runs from Hobbes three centuries before to Lasswell and McDougal.

The Common Law Tradition bears the subtitle *Deciding Appeals,* and it is with the process of appellate adjudication that Llewellyn is principally concerned. The book begins with an emotional account of what he claims is a deepening "crisis in confidence" concerning the "reckonability" of appellate litigation. According to Llewellyn, the concern that appellate courts do not work in a reckonable way has reached epidemic proportions among practicing lawyers, and this concern, he warns, produces a "novel corrosiveness" because "it goes to whether there is . . . any real stability of footing for the lawyer, be it in appellate litigation or in counselling, whether therefore there is any effective craftsmanship for him to bring to bear to serve his client and justify his being." Lacking confidence in the work of our appellate courts, today's lawyer is in danger, Llewellyn says, "of feeling his own sustaining faith in his craft, in his craftsmanship, in his very office and utility as a lawyer . . . ooze and seep away from him until he stands naked and hollow, helpless and worthless, a nithing, or a medicine man who has discovered his medicine to be a cheat."[70]

How has this crisis of professional self-confidence come about? Llewellyn offers the following diagnosis. At the turn of the century, he says, it was the "ingrained practice" to "write an appellate opinion as if the conclusion had followed of necessity from the authorities at hand and as if it had been the only possible correct conclusion." Opinions written in this fashion reflected the belief that judges can indeed decide cases with the geometrical precision to which Langdell aspired. This belief was psychologically reassuring because it confirmed the comforting view that the process of deciding cases is "reasoned and rational"—Frank's seductive myth of certainty.[71]

Beginning in the late 1920s and early 1930s, however, a group of "attackers and destroyers"[72] set out to show that Langdellianism is false and that appellate decisions which appear to rest solely on considerations of legal logic cannot in fact be logically derived from the available precedents alone. One critical element in this iconoclastic assault on the Langdellian view of law was the claim that precedent never, or almost never, controls the decision of a case—that it is too loose, too ambiguous, too conflicting to do so, and that judges must therefore choose among alternative interpretations of precedent, unavoidably exercising their own creative powers in the process. An opinion that conceals its own creativity, the iconoclasts insisted, must be either a disguise or a deceit.

From the relatively uncontroversial claim that adjudication is a creative act, Llewellyn tells us, some drew the conclusion that the process of deciding appeals must therefore be completely arbitrary, assuming, in effect, that "if the outcome of an appeal is not foredoomed in logic it therefore is the product of uncontrolled will." This cynical conclusion—which some insisted follows merely from acknowledging that adjudication is "a process of creative choice"—undermines the doctrine of *stare decisis* and, "[w]orse and more terrifying," our conviction that "'[i]t is the law, not the court, the judge, that decides the case'" (that ours is a government of laws and not of men).[73] The result of this way of thinking is a view of law that makes it impossible to believe that the outcome of cases can be meaningfully predicted in advance and denies that there are standards for evaluating the soundness of individual decisions. From these doubts and denials have come, Llewellyn claims, the bar's skepticism about the reckonability of appellate litigation and its dwindling self-esteem. To combat this skepticism, lawyers must regain their confidence in a twofold sense. They must again become confident both in their ability to predict how courts will decide cases and in their capacity to distinguish good decisions from bad ones. *The Common Law Tradition* is Llewellyn's attempt to show why such a renewal of confidence is justified.

Broadly speaking, this was of course Lasswell and McDougal's goal as well. For they too wanted to establish a new basis for belief in the reckonability of law. Llewellyn also assumes, as they did, that legal rules cannot provide such reckonability on their own—the source of which must therefore be located in something other than these rules themselves. But agreement on these general points marks the limit of any similarity between their two approaches. Whereas Lasswell and McDougal sought to restore reckonability to the prediction of judicial conduct by employing techniques of social scientific analysis remote from the methods used by sitting judges and to stabilize the normative assessment of the law by placing it within a larger framework of more-basic values extrinsic to the legal order, Llewellyn insists that confidence in the reckonability of adjudication can be restored without going outside the law in either of these ways. To persuade oneself that the outcome of future cases can be predicted with tolerable accuracy and to discover criteria adequate to assess the soundness of individual decisions, one need only look more closely, he says, at the methods of interpretation judges actually employ. Built into these methods are constraints that guide the process of adjudication and make it reckonable in both a descriptive and a normative sense. These constraints are different from, and stronger than, those that legal rules impose. They supplement the weaker limitations that doctrine by itself establishes and discipline the choices these limitations leave open. But they are nevertheless constraints internal to the law and to the methods of judging, and thus provide a solution to the problem of reckonability different in kind from the one proposed by Lasswell and McDougal, whose solution requires the employment of extralegal values and techniques. According to Llewellyn, once we recognize the existence of these internal constraints and appreciate their power, Frank's iconoclasm loses its plausibility, and the search for constraints outside the law no longer appears the only strategy for avoiding his disheartening conclusions.

If legal rules alone are insufficiently constraining to ensure that the process of adjudication retains its reckonability, what other internal features of the process can supply the necessary discipline? Llewellyn's answer is that judges are constrained not only by doctrinal rules but also, and more importantly, by specific traditions of work and by the habits of thought and perception that an immersion in these traditions typically produces. Adjudication is of course a creative process—through the pages of the law reports "there swirls a constant current of creation"—and the iconoclastic realists were right to emphasize this element of creativity in their attack on Langdell's "moribund and misleading orthodoxy."[74] What they failed to appreciate, according to Llewellyn, is that judicial creativity is almost always constrained by traditions and habits as well as by rules. No matter how many choices the rules leave open, a judge whose task is to apply the law will be guided in his deliberations by what might be called the *ethos* of his office, by a certain ideal of judicial craftsmanship, and by the habits that a devotion to this ideal and long experience in attempting to achieve it tend to instill. Llewellyn elaborates these claims in a passage worth quoting at length:

> [B]asic to most of both the misconceptions and the cross-purposings of the realist controversy, was an absence everywhere of the concept of craft, of craft-tradition, of craft-responsibility, and of craftsmanship not as meaning merely the high artistry of God's gifted, but as including the uninspired but reliable work of the plain and ordinary citizen of the craft. The existence of a craft means the existence of some significant body of working know-how, centered on the doing of some perceptible kind of job. This working knowhow is in some material degree transmissible and transmitted to the incomer, it is in some material degree conscious, it is to some degree articulate in principles and rules of art or of thumb, in practices and dodges or contrivances which can be noticed and learned for the easing and the furtherance of the work. A healthy craft, moreover, elicits ideals, pride, and responsibility in its craftsmen. And every live craft has much more to it than any rules describe; the rules not only fail to tell the full tale, taken literally they tell much of it wrong; and while words can set forth such facts and needs as ideals, craft-conscience, and morale, these things are bodied forth, they live and work, primarily in ways and attitudes which are much more and better felt and done than they are said. Now appellate judging is a distinct and (along with spokesmanship) a central craft of the law side of the great institution of Law-Government. Every aspect of the work and of the man at work is informed and infiltrated by the craft. It is a tough craft, too; over a whole era it has survived a drift away into formalistic thinking and even believing. More, it has then also survived a degree of neglect of its conscious philosophy which could have choked a less hardy plant, and which remains a peril in the current crisis.[75]

Both Langdell, who sought to construct a transparently rational science of law, and his iconoclastic critics, who believed that judges decide cases in whatever way "seems good to them," assumed that adjudication must be either an "intellectual process" or an exercise of arbitrary power, differing only as to which branch of this dichotomy they grasped.[76] In this respect, Llewellyn says, the proponents of both positions were in error. For each failed to recognize the existence of an aspect of adjudication that significantly limits the judge's will, giving his decisions a steadiness and reckonability they would not otherwise possess—though not intellectually, through the medium of ideas. This missing element is the craft tradition in appellate judging, which Llewellyn calls the "human" element and characterizes as a connected body of habits acquired through experience:

> The place to begin is with the fact that the men of our appellate bench are human beings. I have never understood why the cynics talk and think as if this were not so. For it is so. And one of the more obvious and obstinate facts about human beings is that they operate in and respond to traditions and especially to such traditions as are offered to them by the crafts they follow. Tradition grips them, shapes them, limits them, guides them; not for nothing do we speak of *ingrained* ways of work or thought, of men *experienced* or case-hardened, of *habits* of mind. Tradition, moreover, wreaks these things upon human beings notwithstanding that in a very real degree men also make use of the tradition, reshape it in the very use, sometimes manipulate it to the point of artifice or actual evasion if need, duty, or both, seem so to require.[77]

The habits that constrain a judge as he goes about the business of deciding cases include, first, those that shape and direct the use he makes of the various techniques or "tools" available for the interpretation of ambiguous and contested precedents. In most appeals, both parties will be able to cite arguably relevant precedents, and the variety of techniques that a judge may use to extract a rule for the case at hand from these earlier opinions gives him considerable "leeway" to decide the case as he sees fit. But not every interpretation of the precedents will seem equally plausible or attractive to the professionally habituated judge. Some interpretations, though logically possible, will have no plausibility at all. Some will seem more reasonable than others. And some will by virtue of their straightforwardness and common sense be clearly preferable to their competitors. In every case that he confronts, Llewellyn claims, a judge's habits guide his "choice and use" of methods of interpretation, in much the same way that a carpenter's habits guide him in selecting the appropriate tools for different jobs.

A judge's habits direct his behavior at an even deeper level, however. For they not only guide his reflections as he analyses the legal issues that the case at hand presents, but shape, as well, his perception of the facts as forming a dispute that falls under one doctrinal heading rather than another. Llewellyn, like Frank, rejects the idea that the meaning of a case and its location in the field of legal norms are fixed in advance by the nature of the facts themselves. These features of a case, he says, are as much a product of judicial creativity as the legal judgment that decides it. But unlike Frank, Llewellyn claims that even at the most basic level of case-construction—where irrelevant facts are distinguished from relevant ones and the latter organized into a controversy with a recognizable legal shape—widely shared professional habits incline judges not merely to think alike, but to see alike, and thus to concur in their perceptual judgments:

> [A]s he meets the facts of a fresh case, or, once the facts are semiclear, as he approaches an authority for guidance toward decision, he is engaged in human questing for a diagnosis and an organization of the problem, and in lawyer questing for a *legal* way to see and to pose the issue, and for a *legal* line along which to puzzle. The conclusion is indeed not yet given, but the quest and urge for a satisfying picture, and for a satisfying answer: they are given. The mind therefore sorts, arranges, turns, rearranges the facts in one tryout after another, in search for some firm shape that fits, that poses and sharpens a problem, perhaps even suggests a solution. The mind thus almost of itself spots and highlights in an authority the available facet which feels as if it may give a lead.[78]

Llewellyn acknowledges that the process by which the mind does this is usually unconscious and thus "hard to get into daylight," coming into view only when there is a serious problem or "hitch." But it is at this elementary perceptual level that "the Law controls the Law-Official; and it controls in good part by molding in advance his sense of 'what is sense.'" To appreciate the constraints that their professional habits impose on appellate judges, one must therefore "get an understanding of this 'automatic' type of control of thought, judgment, action, which just happens as you go."[79]

Of course, control of this sort works "by degrees" and varies from one person to another. Most significant, perhaps, it also increases with experience:

> The sure-footed have more of it than the clumsy. The quick-witted can, but need not, have more of it than the dull. The trained always have more of it than the untrained or the recruits. The experienced always have more of it than the green, but at the end of a wise career an experienced man may be working more free of it, becoming its master rather than its creature.[80]

The habits that constrain a judge as he goes about his work are not the product of thought but of experience, and no amount of abstract theorizing can ever be a substitute for them, much less bring them into being in the first place. These habits take time to develop, and to acquire them one must have lived in the law and grown accustomed to its routines. By the time they are appointed to the bench, most judges, in the Anglo-American system at least, have already had extensive professional experience and possess the habits of mind that Llewellyn describes. Just for that reason, he suggests, they know how to extend and revise the traditions of their craft in ways that are faithful to the meaning and spirit of these traditions themselves. By contrast, the new "recruit," the "green" lawyer who lacks the habits of a seasoned professional,[81] also lacks the stability of judgment and the disciplined inventiveness of his more senior counterpart. The constrained creativity of the experienced lawyer—which is not to be confused with the wild freedom of the beginner who declares himself emancipated from the dead traditions of his craft—comes only with time and experience, and hence with age, and thus constitutes a species of wisdom that the young and inexperienced cannot possess.

Llewellyn's emphasis on the connected notions of craft, habit, and experience marks one important similarity between his view of law and Aristotle's account of the nature and aims of political education generally. But their accounts are alike in another respect as well. For Llewellyn repeatedly says about the subject matter of his own inquiry what Aristotle asserts about the field of politics as a whole: that it is reckonable to a pragmatically significant degree, but not perfectly, and that one should not expect from an examination of it more precision than the subject itself allows.

Llewellyn insists that judges are conditioned by their professional habits to think and see in distinctive ways and occasionally calls these habits "automatic."[82] But this is a misleading term that misrepresents his own considered view. For though judicial habits are often unconscious, Llewellyn does not think they have a completely determining influence or produce the same behavior in all similar situations. An appellate judge, he stresses, "'is not Pavlov's dog,'"[83] and we should not conceive of judicial habit as an inflexible mechanism leading always to the same result, but as a track along which insight and analysis must run, one that leaves room for maneuver and innovation. The professional habits of judges guide their thought and perception and accustom them to see certain things as relatively more important than others, thereby setting in advance the terms in which any debate about the proper decision of a case must be conducted. But they do not eliminate controversy or lead to such a uniformity of result that we can no longer distinguish creative and inspired decisions from those that are merely workmanlike (a distinction we would indeed be unable to draw if a judge's responses were as fully conditioned as those of Pavlov's dog). The field of meaningful controversy is limited by professional habit, and within this field habit helps also to define the sorts of considerations that can be advanced for and against particular positions. But a judge's habits do not determine the decision of specific cases in a mindlessly automatic way. It follows that judicial behavior cannot be perfectly predicted in advance.

The failure to attain "absolute or 100 percent certainty" in making such predictions is not, however, a cause for regret. Llewellyn repeatedly states that he is interested only in establishing a degree of reckonability sufficient to meet the needs of practicing lawyers, "a reckonability equivalent to that of a good business risk."[84] To demand more than this, he says, is to ask for something we do not require of "any other human group ever set up for the making of difficult and responsible decisions."[85] The "type of knowledge we are after," Llewellyn writes, "is not 'scientific.' It is what is sure enough to be moderately reliable for use in practice and to offer sound leads for further refinement"—refinement, he stresses in a later passage, that "must not go into analysis for professional students of behavior, but into communicable knowhow for practical application by the men of law."[86]

It might seem to follow that academic lawyers can make no special contribution to the better understanding or improvement of the law (in contrast to the view of the scientific realists, who disparaged the handicraft techniques of practicing lawyers and placed their hopes in the emergence of a rigorously trained professoriate instead). This might appear to follow, in fact, from the very idea of habit itself, the central idea in Llewellyn's argument for the modest but pragmatically sufficient reckonability of appellate judging. A habit is a behavioral routine that involves something more than the self-conscious application of a rule. Indeed, it is just this extra, unself-conscious element that gives the routine in question its habitual character. From this one might infer that reflection and habit are sharply opposed and conclude that any effort to intellectualize a habit must either destroy it— turn the habit into something else—or fail to have any effect on it at all. And this may in turn cause one to question whether a habit-based craft like appellate judging can "without destruction of its fineness, its sureness, its soul be subjected by its practitioners to self-conscious intellectual analysis . . . whether articulate principles or rules for doing, phrasings for the inculcation or transmission of knowhow, will not cripple or kill, rather than further or better the doing of the job." This is the question, Llewellyn observes, that is posed by "the old tale of the centipede who, once set to ponder how he managed the coordination of his regiment of legs, discovered in panic that he no longer could." If we assume that the special function of the academic lawyer is to subject the law to "self-conscious intellectual analysis" and to develop more-articulate "principles or rules" for the decision of cases, we may therefore wonder whether he has anything to contribute to the perfection of those judicial habits that give the law its reckonability and ask ourselves if he might not be instead, so far as these habits are concerned, a force of a purely destructive kind, as the tale of centipede suggests.[87]

But having raised this question and explained its plausibility, Llewellyn answers it with an emphatic no. The work of "the cold intellect"—the kind of work in which academic lawyers might be thought to specialize—can never, he admits, replace the practical know-how on which the craft of appellate judging rests. "[M]uch of the most vital part [of the work of appellate judges], the part that puts flesh, blood, and nerves upon the bones, tends still simply to happen; some of that most vital part must always do so." Still, Llewellyn insists, intellectual analysis can make two related and important contributions to the craft of judging. First, because it brings "out for observation lines of function and method in the craft" whose understanding "sharpens the eye for the work," analysis of this sort can help the practitioner of the craft, as well as the detached observer, to distinguish good work from bad and to solve problems in a way that draws upon and amplifies "the lovelier and less tangible currents" of judicial craftsmanship. "[H]ard-eyed analysis has no call to be denied or rejected merely because it cannot hope to compass the whole . . . here—as indeed everywhere when the goals of institutions are rightly kept in mind—the cold intellect can be made an excellent servant to advance a whole which without it risks internal cross-purposing waste or ineffectiveness."[88] Without displacing the practical know-how that constitutes the core of the craft of judging, critical reflective thought can in this way become an element or ingredient in it, helping to ensure the craft's integrity and increasing its effectiveness.

Intellectual analysis of the kind that academic lawyers seem best suited to provide can also contribute to the craft that judges practice in a second way: by clarifying its goal or purpose, something that must be done, Llewellyn claims, if practitioners are to recover their sense of the dignity of judging, and with that, of their own work too. "The inarticulateness of the vast body of appellate judges about how they do their work and why" has, he says, encouraged a mistaken view of the goal of adjudication. Today many lawyers wrongly believe that the aim of the craft of judging is the achievement of justice between "the particular parties who happen to be in hand" on the basis of what Llewellyn dismissively calls "fireside" considerations, that is, considerations unique to the litigants and their specific controversy.[89] Without denying that such "fireside stuff"[90] properly plays some limited role in appellate adjudication, Llewellyn maintains that heavy reliance on it "is for all that a half-baked technique and one which strains toward both discontinuity and unwisdom." By contrast, he argues, "[t]he wise place to search thoroughly for what is a right and fair solution [to any particular dispute] is the recurrent problem-situation of which the instant case is typical."[91] On Llewellyn's view, the main aim of appellate judging is "to locate and explore the significant situation-type" exemplified by the case at hand, devise a rule "to uncover and to implement [that situation's] imminent law," and fit the rule in question into a larger body of evolving doctrine. This is the goal that law as a whole seeks to achieve, and according to

Llewellyn it constitutes the standard for assessing the rightness of particular decisions.[92] He elaborates this claim in the following famous and often-cited passage:

> [F]or purposes of analysis and for purposes of the best appellate judging we need to keep the type-situation facts clear as a peculiar kind of facts with a peculiar message, nay, mission. I doubt if the matter has ever been better put than by that amazing legal historian and commercial lawyer, Levin Goldschmidt: "Every fact-pattern of common life, so far as the legal order can take it in, carries within itself its appropriate, natural rules, its right law. This is a natural law which is real, not imaginary; it is not a creature of mere reason, but rests on the solid foundation of what reason can recognize in the nature of man and of the life conditions of the time and place; it is thus not eternal nor changeless nor everywhere the same, but is indwelling in the very circumstances of life."[93]

Appellate judges, who are required to decide cases one by one in the unplanned order in which they come, will sometimes, Llewellyn suggests, have difficulty discerning the appropriate situation-type to which a particular case belongs. Seeing, perhaps, only a few cases of a certain sort or seeing them in an order that tends to frustrate rather than facilitate an understanding of the deeper pattern they present may force a judge to rely more heavily than he should either on fireside considerations or—at the opposite extreme—on vague generalities whose very abstraction makes it possible for them to be invoked in any setting. Here, Llewellyn argues, the legal scholar has something special to contribute to the development of the law and to the perfection of the craft of judging. An academic lawyer can sometimes take a wider and more leisurely view of a problem than a sitting judge is able to, ranging over different jurisdictions and surveying the problem from a historical perspective longer than may seem useful or appropriate to the judge who must resolve it. For this reason, legal scholars are often able to pursue "a type of general inquiry, comparative study, diagnosis, and analysis which develops a depth and a perspective hard for judicial case-by-case experience to rival." The point of this exercise is to identify what sitting judges may be too close to their materials to see: the "type-situation facts" that, according to Llewellyn, must guide the adjudicative process if it is to avoid "discontinuity and unwisdom." Academic lawyers, viewing their subject from a more detached perspective, are particularly well situated to grasp these facts and to articulate their meaning, and thus to make a distinctive contribution to the work of adjudication in which judges are engaged.

But the academic lawyer who hopes to do so must keep a check on his tendency toward abstraction and detachment from the world. As he proceeds to define the pattern exhibited by a given line of cases and to elaborate that pattern's normative implications, he needs to remember that "such words [as 'right' and 'fair'] and the idea they carry can hardly reach and register unless they come all impregnated with a *relatively* concrete *going* life-situation seen as a *type*." More-general notions of rightness and justice—of the sort that play such a large role in Lasswell and McDougal's policy science—have, according to Lewellyn, only "infrequent direct effect" on appellate judging and in their "actual impact" are "almost utterly vague except for some few ideas well gathered for our lawyers under such heads as 'due process.'" The "recurrent problem situation" whose immanent law constitutes the standard of rightness in common-law adjudication must thus be seen as an intermediate abstraction standing midway between the particular case in all its nonduplicable uniqueness and a comprehensive theory of justice and due process. Only by focusing on this intermediate category can academic lawyers make a real contribution to the craft of judging and help its practitioners meet their two basic but conflicting duties: their responsibility, on the one hand, to treat the parties in each case fairly by looking to "past practice" and the expectations it has engendered, and their obligation, on the other, to promote the future harmony of those in similar settings by encouraging "good practice" characterized by the attainment of what Llewellyn calls "felt net values in and for the type of situation."[94]

The satisfaction of these two conflicting duties is the goal of appellate judging and of legal scholarship to the extent that it seeks to assist in the development of law. This goal is embodied in something Llewellyn describes as "the rule with a singing reason," the rule "which wears both a right situation-reason and a clear scope-criterion on its face."[95] He compares the judge endeavoring to articulate such rules to a woodcarver who, working "in accordance with [his] material as well as within it," seeks to "reveal the latent rather than to impose new form, much less to obtrude an outside will."[96] Success in this enterprise requires a gradual but creative reshaping of "the body of doctrine as that body has been received and as it is to be handed on," in accordance with the immanent requirements of the various life-situations to which it corresponds. Only in this way can a judge meet his "high responsibility to the law" while simultaneously fulfilling his "duty to justice and adjustment." When these "twin duties" have been met and their requirements fulfilled in a "rule with a singing reason," legal doctrine and the "natural law" of the situation that it governs converge and lend each other mutual support, joined, as Llewellyn lyrically declares, "in a choir like the fabled music of the stars." By "reducing the strain between authority and sense," rules of this sort yield "regularity, reckonability and justice all together."[97] They increase at once the rightness of decisions and their predictability, indeed making the first a component of the second rather than a hindrance to it.

What is above all required in the judge who would pursue this goal, and in the academic lawyer who would help him, is an ability to see beyond the details of the case at hand coupled with a resistance to the kind of theoretical extravagance that leads only to abstractions of unhelpful generality. Those who possess these qualities in combination have what Llewellyn calls "horse-sense"—that "extraordinary and uncommon kind of experience, sense and intuition which was characteristic of an old-fashioned skilled horse trader in his dealings either with horses or with other horse traders."[98] The judge with horse-sense, the judge who possesses "the balanced shrewdness of the expert" in his art, will be better able than others to "live his way into an understanding and empathy" that permits him "to *recognize . . .* the immanent law" of a given situation-type, and will thus see with special clarity what decision in any particular case is most likely to comport with, and provide support for, the emerging though still undeveloped *ethos* of the situation that the case in question illustrates.[99]

The capacity to make discriminating judgments of this sort (which Lasswell and McDougal deride as hopelessly unsystematic and imprecise) is for Llewellyn the soul of judicial wisdom. A judge's decisions are good, he says, when they display the quality of horse-sense and bad when they do not. But horse-sense, like soundness of judgment in other areas of life, is not reducible to a method. No analytical description of it can therefore be complete. To explain what he means by it, Llewellyn is thus forced to adopt a different approach, one that relies more heavily on examples instead.

Most of *The Common Law Tradition* in fact consists of examples—

dozens of examples of how judges have succeeded or failed in bringing legal doctrine into line with the evolving requirements of different situation-types. There are, it is true, passages of a more
philosophical sort in which Llewellyn describes the nature and function of horse-sense in general terms. But it is only in his examples—
in his detailed discussion not just of single cases but of whole lines of
decision—that Llewellyn's general ideas, and the notion of horse-
sense in particular, take on real substance and depth. It would therefore be a mistake to think that these examples are merely illustrative
and can be eliminated without loss, leaving a meaningful residue behind. For only examples can tell us what we need to know about the
judge's art. What they offer is a composite picture of the wise judge
at work, a portrait of his habits and qualities. Given Llewellyn's conception of adjudication, no other method of exposition seems appropriate or even possible—particularly not the abstract one that Lasswell and McDougal use to defend their new policy science of law.
To understand the nature of good judgment in political affairs, Aristotle tells us, we must go and look at those who have it and listen to
what they say.[100] Llewellyn makes the same point about the craft of
judging. Proponents of legal science will find this view circular and
unilluminating. But those who, like Aristotle and Llewellyn, believe
in the virtue of practical wisdom are likely to think it the best view
of all and in any case the only really helpful one.

Working within a tradition that provides adequately reliable guidance for the task at hand but is sufficiently open-textured to allow,
indeed to require, continual refinement, the true judicial craftsman,
the judge endowed with horse-sense, knows that his work is constrained even in its most creative aspects and regards the iconoclastic
bogey of an utterly free judicial prerogative as a fantasy or myth. He
knows that his craft is not a science and cannot be made into one,
that it must be learned through experience and requires a form of
practical wisdom irreducible to rules. But he knows also that his craft
is not blind habit, and that invention is ingredient in it, though his
thinking is at every step guided by professional dispositions that pre-
cede and shape it. Any view of law, like Lasswell and McDougal's,
that depreciates the role of practical wisdom will lack appeal for such
a judge and seem to him to give only a distorted and incomplete
picture of the adjudicative process. Confident that his craft provides
tolerable guidance and reckonability, and that it does so not because

it rests upon a rationally transparent science of law but upon an educated sensibility—a soundness of judgment that more closely resembles aesthetic taste and style than scientific understanding—the enlightened judicial craftsman will be neither frightened by the specter of Frank's personalistic nihilism nor tempted by the false ideal of a legal science. The enlightened judge, as Llewellyn portrays him, is a person of prudence, and his philosophy of law, to the extent that he gives it a self-conscious formulation, will be a celebration of the ancient Aristotelian virtue of practical wisdom.

LAW AND ECONOMICS

The common-law tradition to which Karl Llewellyn was so passionately loyal has few defenders in the American legal academy today. Of course it is not entirely without friends. There has recently been, for example, a modest revival of interest in Llewellyn's work (which is otherwise now largely forgotten), and there are several writers who, though not explicitly identifying with him, have argued for the return to what they call a more pragmatic view of law.[101] The notions of craft, habit, and experience on which Llewellyn's defense of the common law is based continue, moreover, to play an important role in the work of those like James Boyd White and Stanley Fish who emphasize the cultural dimension of law and legal education.[102] And a small number of American law teachers are now urging the selective reintroduction of Aristotelian concepts into legal studies.[103] There are significant differences among these various theorists. Still, in a broad sense, all may be said to belong to the prudentialist tradition that Llewellyn championed and of which he provided the richest account.

Taken as a whole, however, prudentialism is a marginal force in contemporary American legal scholarship. Its allies are few and scattered. They do not clearly recognize their common concerns. And, most important, the two movements that have had the greatest influence on American legal thought during the past quarter-century have both been hostile toward the concept of prudence on which the common-law tradition depends. Both the law-and-economics and the critical legal studies movements are descendants of scientific realism, and each displays in its own way the same aversion to the Aristotlian view of practical wisdom which that earlier movement exhibited. The contempt for prudence that the leading proponents of these two movements share is an important, though unnoticed, link between them, which their rhetorical battles have largely obscured. Indeed, so powerful is the disdain for the claims of practical wisdom that writers as different as Richard Posner and Roberto Unger share that I am tempted to describe it as the central, if unrecognized, orthodoxy of American legal scholarship today. Slowly but steadily this concealed orthodoxy has spread within the legal professoriate, and its effect has been to push the prudentialist tradition of which Llewellyn spoke with such fierce pride to the margins of intellectual respectability and to ensure that those who still defend it remain isolated figures with a diminishing influence on the work and self-understanding of academic lawyers as a group.

A hostility toward the main claims of this tradition is particularly evident in the law-and-economics movement, the most powerful current in American law teaching today. Law and economics now completely dominates some fields and is a significant presence in most others. No responsible law teacher, however sympathetic or mistrustful, can ignore it. And when we examine its assumptions and goals, we discover the same antiprudentialist spirit that marked the scientific branch of legal realism and Langdellianism before it.

The starting point of all law-and-economics scholarship is the distinction between "is" and "ought," and though their views concerning the contribution that economics can make to the normative study of law are more varied, most of those in the movement understand its descriptive aims in basically similar terms. Broadly speaking, they see these as being to uncover and explain the behavioral regularities that lie hidden beneath the surface of the law. On its surface the law appears confused and sometimes even contradictory. This superficial confusion may at first seem explicable on no grounds other than historically contingent ones. If that were the case, we could not understand anything about the law except the brute facts of its genealogy, and some knowledge of its accidental origins would be all that academic lawyers could hope to attain. But proponents of law and economics assume that the law has a deeper structure, though one that cannot be understood in its own language, that is, in the working vocabulary of lawyers and judges themselves. By uncovering its latent order—concealed beneath the law's chaotic surface and inexpressible in its own terms—they seek to show that the law has a greater intelligibility than it appears to, and that the historical accidents to which it seems to owe its shape are in reality the product of actions that conform to certain timeless laws of human behavior.

In this respect, of course, law and economics shares the rationalizing ambition of every social science. Every such science seeks to uncover hidden patterns of behavior and to explain them by means of concepts different from those employed by the participants in the field of conduct it is studying. But advocates of law and economics insist that only economics can achieve this goal in a rigorous and comprehensive way—as Karl Llewellyn also claimed, more than sixty years ago, in his early articles calling for a new, descriptive science of law.

The special promise of economics as a descriptive social science is to be explained by the spareness and universality of its most basic premises. Human beings pursue all sorts of ends and do what they do for many different reasons, but according to the economist their actions all display two general characteristics. First, every human action requires the use of scarce resources, making competition for these resources unavoidable—competition among different human beings but also among the different ends that any single person may pursue (for which the same resources are often needed). Second, human action is always rational in one important if limited sense of that term: it is always motivated by a desire to eliminate waste. All human beings want to minimize the cost of attaining their ends, whatever these happen to be, and evaluate different courses of action on this basis. Scarcity is thus, on the economist's view, a basic fact of life, and rationality—the elimination of waste—the equally basic human response to it.

An individual action is explained, from an economic point of view, when its rationality (in the sense indicated) becomes apparent—something that requires an understanding of the end the actor is attempting to achieve, the possible pathways to it, and their comparative cost. And a social practice or institution is explained when it is shown to be a product of the actions of many individuals each acting rationally in the pursuit of his or her own separate goals, the classic example being the economic explanation of markets. The search for such explanations is not limited, however, to market phenomena or indeed to any particular sphere of human life. For it makes no restrictive assumptions about the substance or content of the ends toward which the actions that it studies are directed—in contrast, for example, to the sociology of religion or psychoanalytic theory, which seek to explain human conduct from the point of view of certain specific interests or motivations and thus have more limited applicability.

It is therefore the abstractness of economics, its indifference to the content of human interests, that explains the lawyer-economists' claim that economics can be usefully applied not just to market transactions (with which the founders of the discipline were primarily concerned) but to other phenomena as well, including those of a specifically legal kind. Some legal phenomena may not at first seem amenable to economic explanations of this sort. But no legal rule or institution is in principle off-limits for an economist, beyond the explanatory reach of his or her discipline. For there is no area of human life, and hence none of legal life, in which individuals act in any way other than the economist assumes, pursuing their interests with scarce resources and a desire to minimize waste. Some phenomena, including legal ones, may, it is true, be inexplicable from an economic point of view. But to the extent that they are, they will be inexplicable from the perspective of every other social science too. For no other social science can succeed in explaining human behavior where economics fails. That is because every such science assumes some link between the intentions or motives of human beings, on the one hand, and the consequences of their actions, on the other, and any link of this sort will necessarily include, as one of its elements, the single connection that economics presupposes. If human action is to be intelligible on any terms other than those provided by the natural sciences, we must be able to see it as the outcome of the pursuit of certain interests, whether conscious or unconscious, and whatever the content of these interests—even if they are altruistic or otherworldly—the person whose interests they are must be presumed to pursue them economically. For to the extent that he does not, his actions will be arbitrary and thus incapable of being understood at all. Economic explanation must therefore reach as far as social scientific explanation as a whole. Its limits are the limits of rationality itself, and there is nothing that another social science can explain that cannot also be explained in economic terms. Other social sciences make more-substantive assumptions about the nature of human interests and are thus able to provide additional explanations of certain sorts of human actions. But these explanations are consistent with those that economics offers. They are a supplement and not a challenge to the economist's account. Because it makes no assumptions of this kind, economics has a more formal character than other social sciences, and its formality gives it a wider application than their limiting suppositions about the content of human interests will permit.

The formality of economics, which justifies its claim to be the most comprehensive social science, also explains why it is the most exact. Economists assume that whatever a person wants, he or she will want to acquire or retain it at least cost. The qualitative differences among human wants are, from this perspective, irrelevant. The only thing that matters from an economic point of view is the quantitative distinction between more costly actions or strategies and less costly ones. Abstracting from the content of human wants, the economist focuses attention instead on the comparative costliness of the different pathways to their fulfillment, and the purely quantitative nature of this question permits one to ask and answer it in mathematical terms, hence with a maximum of rigor and precision. The costs of any given action may, of course, assume a variety of different forms (transaction costs, administrative costs, externalities, and so on). But economics makes them all commensurable by treating each as an expenditure of a single universal good called wealth—just as it makes all satisfactions comparable by defining each as an addition to wealth (which is simply another way of stating that economics ignores the qualitative differences among wants in its investigation of human behavior). By ignoring these differences, economics makes it possible to compare all human actions in strictly quantitative terms, despite the diversity of ends toward which they are directed, and thus provides a scheme of understanding that is broader than that of any other social science and, in principle at least, as exact as mathematics. When Richard Posner asserts that of all the social sciences whose methods have been used "to explain the legal system," the discipline of economics is "the most promising, simply because [it] is the most advanced," it is these two features of the discipline—its universality and exactness—that he has in mind.[104] Posner's views have often been controversial, even within the law-and-economics movement, but on this particular point it is fair to say, I think, that he speaks for the movement as a whole.

According to Posner, the social scientific study of legal phenomena—for so long a "seemingly hopeless aspiration"—has at last been made "feasible" by the economic analysis of law.[105] To that extent, the law-and-economics movement, on its descriptive side at least, represents not just a continuation of scientific realism but its fulfillment. For it has finally made good on that earlier movement's promise to provide an exact account of the behavioral regularities that underlie the law's rules and institutions (something the realists themselves, whose understanding of economics was less complete, did not succeed in doing). Indeed, the progress that practitioners of law and economics have made toward the achievement of this goal has been so rapid, Posner suggests, that we are now justified in insisting on the observance of genuinely scientific standards of analysis and proof in the descriptive study of law—standards as demanding as those routinely applied in natural sciences such as biology and astronomy.[106]

As the law-and-economics movement has become more scientifically respectable, however, there has been an increasingly visible tendency for the language and argumentative techniques of its practitioners to diverge from those employed by the human beings who are actually engaged in the various activities that law and economics studies (adjudication, legislation, settlement, and so on)—a tendency that is in general characteristic of every maturing social science. The actors whose behavior the lawyer-economist studies do not themselves talk, or even think, in economic terms, except in certain very special situations. In pressing their own claims (if they are lawyers) and in assessing the claims of others (if they are judges), they employ, instead, a repertoire of methods, strategies, and argument forms that is quite unsystematic and inexact. This, of course, does not itself impeach the scientific status of law and economics or show its methods to be misconceived, any more than the fact that the members of a primitive tribe are unacquainted with the conceptual schemes of anthropology undermines that discipline's claim to be a genuine social science. It does mean, however, that any scholar who adopts an economic approach to the study of legal phenomena must consider them from a point of view different from that shared by the participants in the particular activity he or she happens to be studying.

Because this difference in perspective is inevitable, it would be a serious "mistake," Posner claims, to "expect social scientific writing about the legal system to resemble the way in which the practicing lawyer, or the academic lawyer who thinks like a practicing lawyer, writes about the legal system" (a claim that again, I think, all lawyer-economists accept).[107] The practicing judge or lawyer, Posner continues, must master "an ambiguous rhetoric of right, justice and fairness" and requires various forensic skills to do his work well. These are the tools of his trade and from his point of view they constitute "genuine virtues."[108] From the standpoint of law and economics or any other social scientific discipline, however, these same virtues appear as vices:

> The goal of science, including economic science, is to explain complex and seemingly unrelated phenomena by reference to a theoretical model or construct, and the power of a scientific explanation can be expressed as the ratio of the different phenomena explained to the number of assumptions in the theory. A simple theory tends to yield more, and more definite, hypotheses than a complex one (a more complex theory is more difficult to falsify— and hence to confirm); if these hypotheses survive their confrontation with the test data, the power of the theory to organize diverse phenomena is confirmed. Abstraction is thus the essence of scientific theory, and a successful theory is bound to ignore a good deal of the apparent differences between phenomena—for example, in Galileo's law of falling bodies, the differences between apples and oranges, or stones and bricks.[109]

Practicing lawyers and judges and law professors who share their outlook see their work differently and in particular take a different view of the value of abstraction. In contrast to the lawyer-economist, a practitioner of law "is not oriented toward finding a simple theoretical structure, economic or otherwise, beneath 'a complex and disorderly jumble of legal rules.' He may note and deplore logical inconsistencies within the jumble, but the idea that it might conceal an inner, and simple, economic logic is unlikely to occur or to appeal to him, and the proposal of such an idea may strike him as 'pretentious and immodest.'"[110]

By the same token, however, the lawyer-economist whose aim is to uncover the simple inner logic of the law will be concerned to avoid in his own research the use of those deliberative techniques that play such a large role in the work of practicing lawyers and judges. What Posner calls "sound judgment" is for this latter group a centrally important value. But the lawyer-economist's goal is not to cultivate or display sound judgment. It is to formulate and test the abstract laws of behavior that govern superficially heterogeneous legal phenomena, and in this quite different undertaking the practitioner's arsenal of rhetorical devices is not only unhelpful but disabling. The lawyer-economist is not at all concerned, in short, "with being thought sound by judges and practicing lawyers; nor is he concerned with writing in a language they will understand or with using concepts familiar to them. He is not one of them. He is part of the scholarly rather than the legal community."[111] To the extent that he sees himself in this way—as a member of the scholarly community of social scientists—the lawyer-economist will, in his descriptive work at least, give no weight to the claims of practical wisdom and be strongly disposed to deny the scientific worth of any theory, like Llewellyn's, that assigns these claims a central place.

Normative law and economics is colored by a similar hostility to prudentialism, though here the picture is more complex, for the differences of opinion among those in the movement concerning the ethical significance of economic analysis are deeper than their disagreements regarding its descriptive power. But beneath these differences one can discern the same antipathy toward the claims of practical wisdom that animates the law-and-economics movement on its descriptive side.

At a minimum, every lawyer-economist accepts what I shall call the "weak" view of the normative role of economic theory. Many assign it a much larger role, but the weak view represents a common baseline for all those in the movement and is therefore the appropriate place to begin a discussion of its normative claims.

The weak view asserts that an economist can always make a limited contribution to moral and political debates by identifying the cost of pursuing different goals and by establishing that some means to a given goal are more costly than others. Thus even if we assume, as defenders of the weak view do, that economics cannot tell us which ends to adopt, we must acknowledge that there is at least one substantive moral judgment that its methods do permit, the judgment that a particular course of action is better than some other if, all things considered, it has the same results—achieves the same ends to the same degree—but requires fewer resources to do so. Waste is a bad thing, and if two actions are identical in every other respect, the fact that one of them is wasteful is itself a reason for judging that action inferior from a normative point of view. The other action is the one we *ought* to take. All economists agree that where these conditions are satisfied, the descriptive judgments of their discipline are morally compelling too, even if we assume that economics provides no criterion for choosing among the different and competing ends we might pursue. It was on this basis that Posner, for example, first sought to defend the claim that the economic study of law has normative significance.[112]

Of course, if two actions are directed at different ends, their relative moral value cannot be determined merely by comparing the costs associated with them, for even if one action is more costly than the other, the additional resources it requires may be justified by the end at which it aims. To decide whether the more costly action is nevertheless the better one, it is necessary in all cases of this sort—the most common sort by far—to evaluate the actions' ends and make a choice between them. The weak view holds that the economist, as such, enjoys no special advantage in this regard and must make the choice in question on the same noneconomic grounds as everyone else. But this is to concede that economics has only a limited role to play in the sphere of normative argument. To many in the law-and-economics movement this limited role has seemed inadequate, and in recent years there has been a tendency for lawyer-economists to argue that the principle of efficiency has greater moral potency than the weak view would allow. Efficiency, many have claimed, provides a criterion for determining which actions are right, not just in those rare instances when the *ceteris paribus* conditions of the weak view are satisfied, but often even when they are not. Those who hold this view maintain that rightness and efficiency are in fact equivalent across a wide range of cases, and that within this range the economist's determination that one action is more efficient than another settles the question of their relative moral worth (even though the actions being compared are directed at different ends). This I shall call the "strong" view of the normative significance of economic analysis.

Some who hold the strong view claim that rightness and efficiency are the same in every case, and others take the more qualified position that they are equivalent in certain situations only. But both of these positions—the modest as well as the more far-reaching one—imply that efficiency is not just one value to be weighed along with others in a scale that economics itself cannot provide. Both imply that in some cases (and perhaps in all) the rightness of an action is determined by its efficiency and nothing else. To adopt this view is no longer to think of economics as making a contribution *to* ethics. For if rightness and efficiency are indeed equivalent across some range of cases, however wide, then to that extent economics *is* ethics and differs from more-traditional types of normative analysis only in the rigor and exactness of its methods.

This last claim may be defended in different ways. Some in the law-and-economics movement, for example, have adopted what might be called a welfarist view, arguing that one action is preferable to another if, all things considered, it produces greater welfare or well-being, economics providing the methods for measuring the effects of different actions in this regard.[113] Proponents of this view differ as to how the basic concept of welfare should be understood, some defining it simply as utility, and others equating it with the more complex notion of wealth. But all welfarists agree that in any given situation the right action is the one that creates the greatest sum of well-being—of utility or wealth—and argue that this will always be the most efficient action among the feasible alternatives (so long, at least, as efficiency is understood in terms of the so-called Kaldor-Hicks test, which states that one action is more efficient than another if it produces a greater amount of welfare overall and the beneficiaries of the action could compensate those disadvantaged by it while still realizing some increase in welfare themselves).

Others in the law-and-economics movement defend a strong view of their work's normative significance on libertarian rather than welfarist grounds.[114] In comparing two actions or policies, they say, the proper question to ask is not whether one produces greater welfare than the other, but whether it extends the range or enhances the value of human freedom to a greater degree, the enhancement of freedom being on this view the highest good and the one by which all others must be measured. But like their welfarist opponents, lawyer-economists who hold this view also assign the principle of efficiency a determinative role in moral argument, though for different reasons. If we can imagine a state of the world more efficient than the present one, they argue, that must be because those in the present state are prevented for some reason from transacting with one another, since if they could, they presumably would all agree to move to the more efficient state so long as the gains from moving exceeded the costs (including the cost of distributing the gains in a way that will leave each individual better off than before). The reasons why people may be prevented from transacting are various. They may be prohibited by the state from doing so, or be paralyzed by some structural feature of their situation (of the sort, for example, that the so-called prisoners' dilemma describes). But whatever the reason, libertarians argue, the inability of people to transact when they would if they were able constitutes a restriction on their freedom. In some cases, the restriction can be removed merely by lifting an existing prohibition. In other cases, its removal requires that the structure of the situation be altered in some way (for example, through a regulatory scheme designed to undo the prisoners' dilemma that prevents them from transacting). Regardless of the nature of the obstacle, however, and of the cure that is required to remove it, its elimination may be said in each case to enhance the freedom of those involved by bringing the world more closely into line with the world they would choose for themselves had they the ability to do so. And if the claim that one rule, policy, or institutional arrangement is more efficient than another is understood in paretian terms to mean that the first makes everyone better off (which may of course require actual compensatory transfers of a sort the Kaldor-Hicks test does not), then on the libertarian view I am describing it will also by definition enhance the parties' freedom and thus be the better rule, policy, or arrangement from a moral point of view. The coincidence of rightness and efficiency—and with it a strong view of the normative authority of economics—can therefore be explained not only on welfarist grounds but on libertarian ones too, though the explanations differ and indeed draw upon conflicting interpretations of the meaning of efficiency itself.

How the concept of efficiency is to be understood and its use as a normative standard explained are questions that in recent years have been fiercely debated by lawyer-economists.[115] There has been considerable disagreement among them too as to whether the morally correct course of action is always, or only sometimes, the most efficient one (some contending, for example, that the principle of efficiency may be properly applied only within the limits set by norms of justice, and others replying that these same norms are best explained by an appeal to efficiency itself).[116] It is fair to say that none of these disputed questions has been definitively resolved and that there is no orthodox answer to them that everyone in the movement now accepts. But all the participants in this debate nevertheless share two assumptions. These represent the undisputed common ground on which their disagreements rest and give normative law and economics as a whole its strongly antiprudentialist cast.

The first assumption is that disagreements about the normative significance of the efficiency principle must themselves be resolved by abstract arguments of the kind that professional philosophers employ but that most practicing lawyers and judges are likely to find unintelligible. Posner has observed that some writers who purport to analyze the law from a normative point of view show "a tendency to 'rhetorize' their arguments" by substituting "verbal ingenuity—the redefining of terms and the appropriation of connotations from conventional uses of language to novel ones—for logic and evidence."[117] He suggests that this tendency may be explained by the fact that "lawyer-philosophers" share with practicing lawyers a normative orientation that social scientists do not, but insists that it is as much to be avoided in normative debates, including debates about the ethical significance of the efficiency principle, as in purely descriptive research. If the normative analysis of law is ever to amount to anything more than "conjuring with a vague and powerful symbol," it must, Posner maintains, keep its distance from the modes of discourse and argument employed by practitioners of law, just as the positive analysis of law must. The gap between theory and practice, between the scholarly community and the legal one, is equally wide in both kinds of inquiry, and it is therefore as much a condition of serious work in normative law and economics as in its descriptive counterpart that the work in question be conducted in a language and spirit foreign to the world of practice.

A second shared assumption concerns the nature of the contribution that economics as a discipline can make to the field of normative philosophy in general. Neither those who defend the equation of rightness and efficiency on welfarist grounds nor those who do so for libertarian reasons maintain that economics, as such, introduces a new standard of evaluation that moral philosophers have previously failed to discern. The claim that the morally right action in a given situation is the one that maximizes welfare or, alternatively, the claim that it is the one that extends the range of human freedom furthest both antedate the modern discipline of economics, and to their philo-sophical defense economics makes no special contribution of its own. What economics can do, however, is reformulate these claims with a previously unattainable precision. Thus, for example, though economics offers no new reasons for adopting the maximization of welfare as one's highest moral standard, its methods do make it possible to apply this standard, once adopted, with a systematic exactness that noneconomic methods cannot equal. Similarly, though it provides no new grounds for accepting the libertarian claim that human freedom is the highest good, economics does provide a technique for turning this very general claim into a precise test that can be used to decide which of various complex actions or arrangements is morally prefer-able. In each case, the lawyer-economist who takes what I have called the strong view, asserting the equivalence of rightness and efficiency across some specified range of normative disputes, is able to justify his or her position only by piggybacking on a moral principle for which economics adds no fresh support. But what economics does provide is the means to formulate and apply the principle in question with unprecedented rigor.

In this sense we might say that what economics contributes to moral philosophy is rigor itself. The discipline of economics intro-duces no new and substantively different standard of evaluation into the sphere of normative debate. It supplies only a method for express-ing the foundational claims of other moral theories (like welfarism and libertarianism) in a form that is more exact. Economics is not, in truth, a morality at all. It is a means for making morality, whatever morality one has, into a science. The most distinctive feature of nor-mative law and economics is thus not its dependence upon a particu-lar moral theory—for its defenders do not all think the same theory is the right one—but its scientific ambition, its insistence that the problems of morality can be described and decided as problems of efficiency (however that ambiguous concept is construed), and hence with a precision that ordinary moral discourse cannot attain, and does not even try to.

The whole of normative law and economics is to that extent shaped by an ideal of clarity in moral argument, and by a confidence in the resolving power of certain methical techniques, that are an-tithetical to the prudentialist tradition and to the claims of practical wisdom. The claim that there is no clean-edged method for resolving

moral disputes and that many questions of this kind have no principled answer at all has its roots in the experience of incommensurability as a fact of moral life. It is the phenomenon of incommensurability that most forcefully suggests the need for practical wisdom in
deliberation, and that compels us to ask what prudence is. But the
phenomenon of incommensurability is invisible from an economic
point of view. For the assertion that all moral controversies can be
resolved by applying to them the single standard of efficiency (whatever the philosophical justification for doing so may be) implies that
real incommensurabilities do not exist and, where they seem to,
should be treated as illusions that clear thinking will dissolve. The
methodical rigor of economics, which represents its special contribution to normative debate, can therefore be attained only by denying
the reality of the phenomenon with whose acknowledgment an acceptance of the claims of practical wisdom begins. Anyone who
maintains that the right solution to a moral dilemma is in general
the efficient one sees things from a point of view that is blind to
incommensurability, as blind as it must be to tragedy, the most telling
sort of incommensurability, whose reality the deeply untragic discipline of economics also necessarily denies. It is this blindness that
gives the normative side of law and economics an antiprudentialist
bias as strong as the one that shapes its descriptive program.

To this it may be objected that there is, in truth, no tension of the
sort I have described between normative economics, which seeks to
resolve moral controversies by an appeal to the principle of efficiency
alone, and prudentialism, which accepts the plurality of human goods
and seeks only a pragmatically tolerable accommodation among
them. There is no tension between these two perspectives, it may be
said, because the first quite self-consciously provides a place for the
second and a justification for its continuing cultivation. Arguments
of this sort have been familiar at least since Henry Sidgwick, who
suggested that the goal of maximizing utility is most likely to be
achieved if people do not aim at it directly, but instead follow cus-
tomary norms of a nonutilitarian kind.[118] Similarly, one might argue,
the global goal of efficiency is best attained by indirection in the law
as well, with judges and lawyers performing their tasks in a common-
sensical way that relies more on experience than on scientific method
and demands only a moderate precision of result. The science of economics is able on this view to explain in its own terms why a noneco-

nomic approach that acknowledges the need for practical wisdom is the best approach for legal professionals to take. Posner himself makes an argument of this sort, concluding that law schools should continue to emphasize the nonscientific skills that lawyers and judges have traditionally employed and, while making room in the curriculum for law and economics, ought not to give it too large a place.[119]

Posner's argument does provide a justification for prudentialism and, by implication, for the common-law tradition associated with it. But it is important to emphasize that it does so from a point of view antagonistic to the claims of this tradition itself, and that the justification it provides is therefore importantly different from the one that genuine prudentialists like Llewellyn offer. The suggestion that efficiency is most likely to be achieved in the realm of law by training lawyers to behave prudentially depends, for its persuasive force, on the adoption of a point of view that must itself be muted or suppressed in prudential deliberation. By contrast, Aristotle's classical defense of prudentialism, which Llewellyn repeats in its essentials, assumes no disjunction between the standpoint of practical wisdom and the point of view from which its worth may be established.

Any attempt to justify prudence from the very different standpoint of economics creates two special difficulties. First, those to whom the truth about morality has on this view been revealed, which today includes most law students, will by virtue of their training possess an esoteric knowledge not shared by the uninitiated. The privileged possessors of this knowledge may have difficulty adopting for any length of time a prudentialist attitude themselves and are likely to view with condescension those who do, for they know that this attitude misrepresents the truth about morality (conceiving it to be less unitary and exact than it actually is).

Second, any justification for prudentialism that rests on considerations of efficiency permits—indeed, encourages—its proponents to reexamine these considerations as circumstances change, prompting them to ask if prudential indirection is still required and whether it might not now be better to approach the problem in question more directly, under the rubric of efficiency itself. As the techniques of economic analysis become more refined, it is reasonable to think that they will capture, only with greater precision and therefore better, more of what the discipline of economics now delegates to prudence. It follows that there will be a tendency, over time, for economics to expand at the expense of practical wisdom, and for the moral jurisdiction of one to grow as that of the other shrinks.

Posner appears to have reached this conclusion himself. For he claims that the economic analysis of law is ultimately continuous with more-traditional forms of legal scholarship—which must be true if we view the law from a perspective that treats every unscientific practice or technique as an indirect way of pursuing the goals that legal science sets. Thus, Posner asserts, "someone who uses economics to expose the inner logic of the common law or to propose reforms designed to make the law more efficient" is simply "taking up where Ames and Prosser left off," though "modern advances in economic thinking" make it possible for him to pursue their projects more directly.[120] As the new generation of lawyer-economists refines our understanding of the law, however, the space that economics concedes to practical wisdom is bound to contract. Posner's suggestion that prudence has a place in law and legal education conceals the tension between the economic point of view from which this claim must be defended, on the one hand, and the deliberative habits that it authorizes, on the other. But it cannot eliminate this tension or prevent it from becoming more visible as the discipline of economics increases in sophistication. That these two perspectives appear to be compatible is an illusion. Normative law and economics and prudentialism are in reality at war, and those economically minded lawyers who claim to give practical wisdom its due only mask their hostility toward it.

CRITICAL LEGAL STUDIES

That the modern law-and-economics movement is the heir of scientific realism seems clear enough. Indeed, the proponents of law and economics acknowledge this themselves. But that the critical legal studies movement is also linked to the scientific branch of legal realism is much less obvious. There is, of course, one broad connection between critical legal studies and realism generally that has been widely noted. Like the realists before them, those in the critical legal studies movement have been especially concerned to discredit the idea that the law has an internal logic that compels the decision of cases in the way Langdell assumed. They stress, as Frank did, the volitional element in law—the necessity in every process of legal decisionmaking for choices that the law's own substantive and procedural requirements leave open. And from this they draw the conclusion that judges and other lawmakers arrive at their decisions on the basis, in part, of extralegal considerations, which is of course the same conclusion that Frank and those who followed him reached too.

This does not, however, establish a link between the critical legal studies movement and scientific realism in particular nor suggest a hostility toward the common-law tradition and its prudentialist values. For even Karl Llewellyn, who was devoted to this tradition, accepted Frank's criticisms of Langdell and acknowledged the role of choice in judging. And there are other reasons too for thinking that critical legal studies is more congenial to prudentialism than scientific realism was. One finds, for example, in certain of the movement's central texts an explicit recognition of the value of practical wisdom; Roberto Unger's first book, *Knowledge and Politics,* contains an especially clear statement to this effect, and Duncan Kennedy's emphasis on the need for sound but nonrationalizable intuitions in judging strikes a similar note.[121] Kennedy's insistence that conflicts in the legal order may be traced back to a more basic and ultimately irresolvable difference between two competing "visions of the universe" also bears, superficially at least, a resemblance to the acceptance of moral incommensurability that plays an important role in my own account of practical wisdom and that law and economics completely suppresses. And some of those in the critical legal studies movement—I am thinking of Robert Gordon and William Simon in particular— have presented a picture of the professionally responsible lawyer that in certain ways parallels the one I sketched in Chapter 3 (particularly in its emphasis on the untenability of the narrow view of law practice and on the lawyer's duty to promote the good of the law as a whole). In all these respects the critical legal studies movement is importantly distinguishable from scientific realism and seems even to embrace elements of the prudentialist tradition that scientific realists such as Lasswell and McDougal so violently rejected.

Critical legal studies thus has a more ambivalent relationship to prudentialism than does law and economics, and it would indeed be a mistake to think that the former is as uniformly hostile as the latter to any view of law that makes the virtue of practical wisdom central to its account of what lawyers and judges do. Such hostility is nonetheless a powerful presence in it, particularly in the writings of Duncan Kennedy and Roberto Unger, the movement's two leading theoreticians, who more than anyone else have defined its methods and aims. In the eclectic body of work that may be gathered under the heading of critical legal studies, one finds many expressions of doubt concerning the usefulness of large-scale philosophical theories of law. Still, in its search for an identity the movement has needed some theoretical self-definition, and Kennedy and Unger have been the main ones to supply it. When we examine their ideas—which many in the movement have relied upon for intellectual support—an important link to the antiprudentialist program of scientific realism emerges.

The critical legal studies movement begins, for all practical purposes, in 1976 with the publication in the *Harvard Law Review* of Duncan Kennedy's justly celebrated article "Form and Substance in Private Law Adjudication." Unger's *Knowledge and Politics* had been published the year before, and Morton Horwitz's influential book *The Transformation of American Law* would be published the year after.[122] The Conference on Critical Legal Studies would be founded in 1977 too. But it was Kennedy's article that first introduced the academic legal community to the ideas and style of argument that were to be most representative of the critical legal studies movement in the decade and a half that followed. Even today, if one were asked to pick a single writing to convey some sense of the substance and spirit of critical legal studies, Kennedy's article would, I think, be the choice of many.

"Form and Substance" begins by reexamining the familiar debate between those who think that judges ought to use sharp-edged rules to define the legal rights and responsibilities of individuals and those who favor more-flexible standards instead. Kennedy first observes that this debate has a certain rhetorical structure. The arguments for and against both rules and standards exhibit, he says, a discernible pattern. Those who favor the use of rules appeal to a set of values that are anchored in a morality of self-reliance—in the idea that each of us is separately responsible for our own fate and that we have no one to praise or blame but ourselves when things go badly or well (an idea that Kennedy also calls individualism and that he broadly associates with the liberal tradition in political thought). By contrast, those who favor the use of standards in adjudication invoke a morality of altruism or sharing, one that emphasizes the interdependence of human lives and projects and the value of our mutual concern for one another's welfare (a position he describes as communitarian and identifies with organicist political philosophies). The conflict between these two moralities is a substantive conflict, a conflict between two competing "visions of humanity and society." Hence the debate over whether to use rules or standards is not a formalistic or procedural one, a disagreement merely about means. Rather, it is a disagreement about ends, one expression (of many) of a fundamental quarrel regarding the meaning of morality itself.

This is Kennedy's first point. His second is that the substantive conflict between the ethics of self-reliance and the ethics of sharing is pervasive in the law and reappears in every field, public as well as private. There is no area of law in which it can be avoided, nor can the conflict between these two moralities be moderated by assigning one to the core and the other to the periphery of concern, for in each branch of law both claim with some credibility to occupy a central place. Hence everywhere we turn in the law we encounter with undiminished force the same basic contest of ideals. Nor—and this is Kennedy's third point—can we ever hope to settle this contest in a final way. "The opposed rhetorical modes lawyers use reflect a deeper level of contradiction. At this deeper level, we are divided, among ourselves and also within ourselves, between irreconcilable visions of humanity and society, and between radically different aspirations for our common future."[123] This "conflict among our *own* values and ways of understanding the world is here to stay."[124] It can never be overcome by an appeal to "metaprinciples" that transcend it, for no such principles exist. The conflict between individualism and communitarianism, self-reliance and sharing, liberal and organicist philosophies of government, is thus a permanent as well as pervasive feature of our human condition, and we can no more escape it— in the law or anywhere else—than we can escape that condition itself.

This may seem, Kennedy admits, a "pessimistic" or "defeatist" conclusion.[125] But he mentions two considerations that soften somewhat the disturbing implications of his argument. First, though the conflict between self-reliance and sharing cannot be overcome, the very permanence and ubiquity of that conflict gives us a powerful tool for analyzing the structure of legal argument, which we can now understand to be simply the replaying in one form or another of this basic conflict itself. We are thus able to find "order and meaning" in the law "even within the sense of contradiction."[126] This order is dialectical but highly regular, and its discovery therefore makes the law more intelligible to us.

Second, although there are no metaprinciples that tell us how to choose between individualism and communitarianism, "we find that we are able," Kennedy reassuringly observes, "to distinguish particular fact situations in which one side is much more plausible than the other."[127] We draw these distinctions intuitively and cannot justify them in rational terms. But despite their inexplicability, intuitive judgments of this sort are often, he suggests, a sound guide to action, and the very possibility of making them is enough to give us confidence that we need not be paralyzed by the conflict between our basic values nor fear that when we prefer one to the other we are always acting arbitrarily. The ideal judge, for Kennedy, is thus a kind of intuitive genius. He has good intuitions (which in Kennedy's view means those that tilt in favor of altruistic reform) and the courage to act on them, for he knows that in the end arguments run out and only intuitions remain. Kennedy concludes his article with praise for Skelly Wright, the model of such a judge and an example, he implies, of how we all should live with the "fundamental contradiction" between our wish to be apart from others and our need for their company and support.[128]

"For several generations," Kennedy points out, legal scholars have assumed "that it is impossible to construct an autonomous logic of legal rules" of the sort Langdell envisioned.[129] Students of the law, he says, now universally agree that judicial decisions are not determined by doctrine alone but rest on extralegal factors too, on a variety of nondoctrinal concerns that are often generically described as considerations of "policy." This was of course one of Frank's main points. Kennedy acknowledges that there is "nothing innovative" in his own reaffirmation of it and in his rejection of the idea that legal disputes can be resolved on "neutral" doctrinal grounds purged of policy preferences. But from this assumption Frank drew the antinomian conclusion that no rigorously organized account of judicial behavior can be given, and it is just at this point that Kennedy's argument takes a different turn. For, like the scientific realists, Kennedy claims that it is indeed possible to find an "orderliness" in the adjudicative process despite the indeterminacy of legal doctrine and to describe this order with a measure of comprehensiveness and precision that others have so far failed to achieve. This, he says, is what is "new" in his article—"the attempt to show an orderliness to the debates about 'policy' with which we are left after abandonment of the claim of neutrality."[130]

In one respect, of course, the order that Kennedy describes is different from that which the scientific realists hoped to demonstrate. The latter were primarily interested in questions of causation. They sought to identify the factors, legal and otherwise, that cause judges to decide cases as they do and aspired to create a new science of law that would produce causal generalizations of an empirically testable kind like those of the other social sciences. Kennedy, by contrast, is largely uninterested in issues of causation. His focus is on the structure of legal rhetoric instead. What he wants to understand are the recurrent argument forms that give judicial rhetoric its order and predictability. Kennedy is concerned with patterns of meaning or signification rather than causation and therefore tends to draw inspiration not from the social sciences but from disciplines such as philosophy and literary criticism that address issues of interpretation more directly. Because of this he admits that his own generalities do not lend themselves to empirical verification in the way those of the behavioral sciences do.[131]

Despite this difference in the kind of order he is seeking to describe, however, Kennedy's approach shares two features with the scientific realists' and with that of law and economics too. First, if we look at the sorts of policies "lawyers use in justifying particular rules," what we find, Kennedy asserts, is a "chaotic mass" of arguments, formless and confused. If we are to grasp the hidden order in these arguments, we must look through them to the organizing conceptions of political morality that lie beneath their surface. This requires that we break, as the lawyer-economist must, with the discourse of practicing lawyers and judges. For the "visions of the universe" that give their arguments a hidden structure cannot be systematically elaborated in the practical and particularistic terms lawyers and judges themselves employ. These visions make their way into legal discourse only in an incomplete and broken form. To see them whole—to grasp the simple inner unity of each and to understand the depth of the difference between them—we must substitute the methods and vocabulary of philosophy for those of law. We must learn to see the arguments of lawyers and judges in the same way a lawyer-economist does, as the distorted reflection of some more systematic truth that can be adequately stated only if we abandon their practical point of view for one considerably more abstract. Those who follow Richard Posner of course have a different conception of the abstractions we need to unlock the secret structure of the law from that of Duncan Kennedy's followers. But all insist—as did the scientific realists of the 1930s—that the categories of the law are too muddled and confused, too much concerned with the particular case, too unsystematic to provide a basis for understanding the deep structure of the law and what it is "really" about. For that, they all agree, some far simpler and more comprehensive set of abstractions is required.

Second, when Kennedy looks through the multiplicity of arguments that lawyers use to debate the desirability of rules and standards, what he sees is a single conflict between individualism and altruism, repeated over and over again. In the end, for Kennedy, there is only one conflict in the law, and it is this one; the appearance of variety is an illusion. Borrowing Tolstoy's famous image, we might say that on the surface the law looks like a fox, full of different tricks and strategies.[132] But underneath, according to Kennedy, it is a hedgehog, singlemindedly preoccupied with just one thing. For in every branch of law, he claims, we find the same grand contradiction between the claims of self-reliance and those of communal concern, and all other "formal and substantive dichotomies" are in reality merely expressions of this one.[133] Despite the superficial appearance of disorder in the law, it is therefore possible to construct an account of it that is both simple and comprehensive after all, a reductive account that explains the basic structure of the legal system with a single pair of philosophical terms. "Form and Substance" gives the clear impression that it is Kennedy's ambition to construct an account of this sort.

Kennedy himself now appears to have abandoned the effort to do so, or at least to have given up the idea of a fundamental contradiction on which it crucially depends.[134] But many others in the critical legal studies movement have followed him in his original assumptions, taking the argument of "Form and Substance" as a model.[135] Their work, which shares Kennedy's earlier ambition, has done as much as any to define the goals of the critical legal studies movement as a whole. Kennedy's article, with its emphasis on order and abstraction and its relentless reduction of every human conflict to a single elementary contradiction, belongs to the tradition of scientific realism and shares its antiprudentialist bias. The many who have since imitated him have helped to spread this bias within critical legal studies and thus to make their movement—like law and economics—a potent force for antiprudentialism in legal scholarship generally.

There is one theme in "Form and Substance," however, that seems to push in the opposite direction and has no analogue in law and economics. This is Kennedy's emphasis on the irreconcilability of the conflict between individualism and altruism, and his suggestion that we must rely on intuition to help us decide which value to prefer in particular cases. Kennedy insists that this conflict lacks an intellectual solution. "There is no metasystem that would, if only we could find it, key us into one mode or the other as circumstances 'required.'" Nor is it possible for us to "balance" the values in question except, Kennedy says, "in the tautological sense that we can, as a matter of fact, decide if we have to." The philosophy that best "conveys" the process by which we make and abandon our commitments to these competing values is thus that of existentialism, for only it fully acknowledges the irrationality of our choices and the "terror" they involve.[136] These turn ultimately not upon reason but upon a "change in attitude" that is extremely "elusive of analysis."[137] In the end, the good judge is therefore simply the one who has the right attitude, which in the current state of things means for Kennedy the inclination to favor the claims of altruism over those of individualist self-reliance "in spite of the arbitrariness of values." Kennedy describes the work of such a judge as protorevolutionary—a "dramatic production ancillary" to a real political conflict that would be truly revolutionary—and ends by wishing "the enterprise what success is possible short of the overcoming of its contradictions."[138]

Prudentialism too accepts the incommensurability of human goods, and Kennedy's acknowledgment of a division "among ourselves and also within ourselves, between irreconcilable visions of humanity and society," seems close to this, though his own revolutionary zeal is far removed from the cautionary stoicism of the prudentialist tradition. But the similarity is less substantial than it appears. Throughout his article Kennedy insists that all moral, political, and even psychological conflicts are merely local expressions of the universal confrontation between self-reliance and solidarity. The implication is that there is only one basic question human beings ever face. And more important there is the suggestion, in his concluding praise for the "nobility" of judges like Skelly Wright who "work on the indispensable task of imagining an altruistic order" despite the rational inexplicability of their commitment to it, that this single question has a single proper answer too.[139] Kennedy only hints at this, but one is left with the impression that he believes there is, in fact, a politically correct way of grappling with the fundamental contradiction—which helps explain the implicit call for revolution in his essay's final paragraph.

This contradiction cannot be abolished, nor can anyone's response to it be justified on rational grounds. Still, Kennedy seems to say, there is a right response that the right-minded will intuit. As the basis for a political program such rationally inarticulable confidence carries familiar risks. But that is not the point I want to stress. What I want to emphasize is how remote Kennedy's dialectical structuralism is from the kind of moral pluralism prudentialists embrace. Their pluralism sees many different conflicts not all reducible to one titanic struggle and accepts that there is often no proper solution to these conflicts, not even one that can only be intuited. Those who hold this view maintain that human beings pursue a variety of worthwhile but incommensurable ends, and believe that in many cases neither reason nor intuition can rank their competing claims. They are made uneasy by revolutionary ideals, including the ironic sort that Kennedy espouses, for in all such ideals they detect the utopian desire to give certain values a final preeminence over others. Instead they incline, for reasons I have explained, toward gradualism and a respect for the fragile conditions of fraternity on which all political societies depend. These sentiments, which encourage a conservative view of politics, are at the opposite extreme from those that color Kennedy's influential essay. For the latter is suffused with an optimism about the powers of moral intuition that prudentialism does not share and as a result tends toward a more Manichaean view of politics—with the revolutionary hope that typically accompanies such views—than any real pluralism will allow.

The same antiprudentialist tendency is even more pronounced in the work of Roberto Unger. Unger is the leading philosophical figure in the critical legal studies movement, and his short but densely argued account of it (which was originally published as an article in the *Harvard Law Review* and later as a book) is widely regarded as a kind of manifesto.[140] No one has made as sustained an effort to explain the movement's aims and assumptions. For this reason Unger's book deserves particularly close study, and those who read it carefully will find that his defense of critical legal studies is animated by the same ideal that gave the normative branch of scientific realism its distinctive character—by a devotion to the philosophical rationalization of all legal norms within a comprehensive scheme of values based upon nonlegal principles of a highly abstract sort. In this respect Unger's book shows a striking similarity to Lasswell and McDougal's earlier manifesto, differing only in its insistence on carrying the search for normative foundations even beyond the point that they did. His program is in essence a radicalized version of the one that Lasswell and McDougal outline in their famous article, and like their scheme Unger's own reflects a profound hostility to the claims of practical wisdom. This comparison may seem fanciful, and only a detailed commentary on Unger's argument can support it. But the labor this entails is unavoidable. For to be convinced that his program does indeed belong to the tradition of scientific realism and is imbued with its antiprudentialist spirit, we must follow Unger's argument step by step to its startling conclusion that lawyers who share his view have a duty to abolish the profession as we know it.

Unger begins his book on the critical legal studies movement by observing that the spirit of "contemporary law and legal doctrine" is in general one of disenchanted skepticism, a skepticism that reflects "the ever more advanced dissolution of the project of the classical, nineteenth-century jurists conceived in a certain way." That project, Unger claims, has been completely discredited, and the first aim of critical legal studies is merely to carry the "received critique" of it to an "unprecedented extreme." Others, he says, have been unwilling to do this because of their fear that an all-out attack on the classical conception of law "would leave nothing standing" and might destroy "the very possibility of legal doctrine, and perhaps even of normative argument generally." But Unger insists that his movement's radicalized assault on the classical view leads not to nihilism but to "a constructive program" of analysis and reform instead, and the principal aim of his book is to show how and why this is so.[141]

The classical project was founded, Unger claims, on two connected concepts. The first of these he calls formalism and the second objectivism. Formalism is the belief that legal analysis—the analysis of cases and other authoritative materials—can and should be free from contaminating political or ideological elements. Unger defines formalism as a "commitment to, and therefore also a belief in the possibility of, a method of legal justification that contrasts with open-ended disputes about the basic terms of social life, disputes that people call ideological, philosophical or visionary."[142] In the view of a committed formalist, only the existence of a distinct justificatory method of this kind can ensure that legal analysis retains its certainty and objectivity, properties (it is claimed) that are lost once the line between law and politics is dissolved.

Objectivism (the second defining feature of the classical view of law) is the belief that "authoritative legal materials—the system of statutes, cases, and accepted legal ideas—embody and sustain a defensible scheme of human association."[143] A corollary assumption, which Unger describes as a "more specific brand of objectivism," is the belief in "a system of social types with a built-in institutional [including legal] structure." It is this particular version of objectivism that those in the critical legal studies movement have been most anxious to refute. "The critique of objectivism that we have undertaken," Unger asserts, "is essentially the critique of the idea of types of social organization with a built-in legal structure and of the more subtle but still powerful successors of this idea in current conceptions of substantive law and doctrine."[144]

To believe in what Unger calls the "logic of social types" is to assume that for every form of social organization there is one, and only one, set of institutions capable of embodying that society's most basic principles—institutions whose shape and content can be deduced in an uncontroversial way from the basic character of the society itself. On this view, once a choice has been made as to the foundational principles on which a particular society is to be based, the details of its organization, including its legal organization, can be inferred from these principles as their "built-in" or "intrinsic" content. Thus in America, for example, a commitment was made at what Unger calls our "Lycurgan moment" to a specific type of society—to "a democratic republic and to a market system as a necessary part of that republic"—and the classical jurists of the nineteenth century, who believed in the logic of social types, saw their task as being simply to articulate the one system of laws that would adequately express in concrete terms the abstract principles to which the nation had already committed itself. Believing as they did in the logic of social types, they felt justified in thinking that the controversy surrounding our Lycurgan choice of a regime could be kept out of the search for a "universal legal language" in which to express the institutional implications of that choice, and so were able to conceive their own project as one untouched by political debate.[145]

Specifically, Unger tells us, the ambition of classical jurisprudence was to discover and systematize the legal norms entailed by our national commitment to republican democracy, on the one hand, and to free-market capitalism, on the other. Thus, "[t]he general theory of contract and property provided the core domain for the [classicists'] attempt to disclose the built-in legal content of the market, just as the theory of protected institutional interests and of the legitimate ends of state action was designed to reveal the intrinsic legal structure of a democratic republic." But in each case the effort to elaborate and refine these elementary ideas produced "contradictory implications," "counterprinciples," and "clashing conceptions" that could not be reconciled by any "system of meta-principles."[146] What this revealed, according to Unger, was the inescapable indeterminacy of the foundational commitments whose intrinsic content the classicists were attempting to expound. But if the concepts of market and democracy are indeed indeterminate, as this suggests, then no specific system of laws follows automatically from their adoption as foundational premises. Any particular scheme of rights and obligations that is said to be uncontroversially entailed by these concepts must therefore actually be based, whether its defenders recognize this or not, on an interpretation of what the concepts in question mean. And every such interpretation, Unger argues, is shaped by political or ideological considerations of the same sort that must be weighed in a "foundational moment" when choosing a basic framework for the organization of society as a whole.

The kind of interpretive argument that is needed to support the choice of a particular legal scheme as the appropriate embodiment of certain basic social norms should therefore be viewed as an argument continuous with those offered for the adoption of these norms in the first place. It is, Unger says, essentially the same sort of argument even though it appears to deal with uncontroversial matters of detail only. To accept this conclusion, however, is to acknowledge the falsity of formalism, which asserts the existence of an impermeable barrier between the domain of legal argument, on the one hand, and that of political or philosophical argument, on the other. Discrediting the objectivist belief in a logic of social types thus necessarily undermines the belief in formalism too, wrecking the entire project of classical legal theory as Unger portrays it.

What the classical jurists failed to understand, according to Unger, is that every claim that a given principle of social organization requires the adoption of a specific legal system for its implementation rests upon an interpretation of that principle itself—an interpretation that in turn relies "tacitly if not explicitly upon some picture of the forms of human association that are right and realistic in the areas of social life with which it deals." To make progress in our understanding of the law, he says, we must recognize the role that some such picture always plays in legal thought and choose the one that is best. It is possible, of course, for a legal analyst to deny that his conclusions depend upon his acceptance of a controversial picture of this sort, and, while acknowledging that the law is full of inconsistent and competing doctrines, to insist that he can construct arguments for preferring one doctrinal position to another without relying upon any abstract philosophical theory, or "guiding vision," as Unger calls it. This theoretically agnostic view is indeed the one that defenders of the common-law tradition from Coke to Llewellyn have generally espoused. But it is a view that Unger rejects. If the analysis of legal doctrine is not to be standardless and arbitrary, he insists, it must be informed by "a background prescriptive theory" of some sort, by a systematic and self-conscious philosophy of politics.[147] The modest goals of a legal analyst who wishes only to understand the law and to be in a position to assess it can therefore not be met unless he first becomes a political philosopher:

> Without . . . [a] guiding vision, legal reasoning seems condemned to a game of easy analogies [or "rhetorical posturing," as Unger elsewhere calls it]. It will always be possible to find, retrospectively, more or less convincing ways to make a set of distinctions, or failures to distinguish, look credible. A common experience testifies to this possibility; every thoughtful law student or lawyer has had the disquieting sense of being able to argue too well or too easily for too many conflicting solutions. Because everything can be de-

fended, nothing can; the analogy-mongering must be brought to a halt. It must be possible to reject some of the received understandings and decisions as mistaken and to do so by appealing to a background normative theory of the branch of law in question, or of the realism of social practice governed by that part of the law.[148]

Let us pause at this point to observe the ways in which Unger's argument, as I have presented it so far, resembles the one that Lasswell and McDougal offer in defense of their proposed reforms. To begin with, both arguments start by emphasizing the indeterminacy of legal doctrine and the impossibility of ever eliminating such indeterminacy by an appeal to higher-order rules of law. From this Unger draws the conclusion, as do Lasswell and McDougal, that legal disputes can be resolved only on the basis of extralegal concepts—what they call "extrinsic" criteria of judgment—and like them he insists that a coherent approach to the problems of legal analysis is impossible unless one starts at an elementary level with a well-defined philosophy of politics. There are, he insists, only two alternatives to this approach: on the one hand, despair at "the very possibility of legal doctrine," and on the other, a self-deluding belief in the coherence and vitality of traditional forms of legal argument, "the specific, problem-oriented arguments of practical lawyers and judges" constrained by "a more or less tacit professsional consensus about the rightful limits of institutional roles" (the kind of consensus that Llewellyn emphasizes and Unger claims does not exist).[149] Like Lasswell and McDougal, who also define their project in opposition to these same two alternatives, Unger rejects both in favor of a third: the elaboration of a general theory of value capable of settling specific legal controversies in a systematic way, in short, the construction of a normative science of law.

There is, however, a sense in which Unger may be said to pursue the project of establishing such a science even beyond the point that Lasswell and McDougal did. Lasswell and McDougal's goal is to articulate "the democratic values that constitute the professed ends of [the] American polity" and to develop a scheme for bringing these values to bear, in a methodical way, on various concrete problems of legal administration. But in their famous 1943 article, they simply equate America's most basic values with a specific set of institutional arrangements (roughly speaking, the existing division of constitutional powers, together with the system of free market capitalism modified by the federal income tax and various other regulatory programs designed to improve the market's fairness and efficiency). This equation is not defended but simply made. As a result Lasswell and McDougal never consider the possibility that the value of individual dignity might be better served by an institutional arrangement radically different from the one we now have. On Unger's view, however, their identification of democratic individualism with a specific set of legal rules and institutions can no more be accepted without a supporting argument than any similar equation, and since Lasswell and McDougal proceed as if no such argument were needed, they are as much to be criticized for their objectivism as the legal classicists of the nineteenth century.

By demonstrating "the institutional specificity of the established forms of markets and democracies," Unger claims, the critical legal studies movement has discredited any philosophical theory (like Lasswell and McDougal's) that simply identifies these established forms with the abstract concepts they embody.[150] Any theory of law that hopes to escape this criticism must therefore begin at an even more primitive level of analysis than Lasswell and McDougal did. It must take nothing for granted, but start instead by asking the most basic question imaginable: the question of what it means to be a human being and to live in society with others. This is the point at which Unger begins his own effort to construct a background theory of the sort that he insists is needed to evaluate the law, and the elemental nature of the questions with which he starts gives his whole inquiry a radical appearance.

Unger's theory rests on three connected claims. The first is a claim about the nature of human beings. According to Unger, man is "a being whose most remarkable quality is precisely the power to overcome and revise, with time, every social or mental structure in which he moves." Each person is a "context-transcending agent" who, though in the world, is never "entirely of it." This conception has sometimes been given a paradoxical formulation by saying that what we human beings essentially are "is nothing in particular." This conception of man, which assigns central importance to what Unger calls his "negative capability," represents "a generalized or radicalized version" of the conception broadly shared "by the great secular doctrines of emancipation of the recent past—liberalism, socialism and communism—and by the social theories that supported them."[151]

The second claim on which Unger's constructive theory rests is a claim about the nature of social life. The experience of individuals in society, he says, always has a "shaped quality": "[a]t any given time, related sets of preconceptions and institutional arrangements shape a large part of the routine practical and conceptual activities that take place while remaining themselves unaffected by the ordinary disturbances that these activities produce." These informing structures and ideas Unger calls "formative contexts"[152]—the "practical and imaginative structures that help shape ordinary political and economic activity while remaining stable in the midst of the normal disturbances that this activity causes."[153] The idea that political and economic activity can take place outside of any formative context whatsoever is, Unger claims, literally unthinkable. It is only within some formative context that human actions can be political or economic, that is, have the specific meaning these terms imply.

Unger's third claim (which combines his first two and is merely an extension of them) is that the essential human power to transcend every imaginable context can itself be recognized for what it is, even by human agents themselves, only within a social world that is shaped, as every social world must be, by a formative context. To call an action free is to offer an interpretation of it or to ascribe a specific meaning to it, and every ascription of this kind presupposes an interpretive community of some sort as its condition. Outside of any such community—outside of society—freedom could not exist (any more than slavery could). Consequently, the existentialists who see only "the pure and purely negative experience of freedom itself" and whose "aim becomes to assert that self as freedom and to live in freedom as rebellion against whatever is partial and factitious in the established social or mental structures" of the world fail to understand that if freedom is to be real, it "must exist in lasting social practices and institutions" and "cannot merely exhaust itself in temporary acts of context smashing."[154]

Thus, according to Unger, man's essence is freedom; freedom is social; and every social situation is shaped by a formative context that provides the relatively stable framework for the dynamic actions occurring within it. It does not follow, however, that every formative context is equally conducive to or supportive of freedom. In fact, "enduring social and mental orders may differ from one another in the extent to which they display the truth about human freedom." A "crucial premise" of his constructive program, Unger tells us, is that "social and mental worlds differ, among other ways, in the manner and the extent to which they enable the self to experience in ordinary life its true freedom." To be sure, there will always be a "divergence" between the "transcending capabilities" of the individual person and the "limitation of the structures in which he lives," but this divergence or "gap" may be wider or narrower. In particular, the gap will be narrower the more the formative context of social life "makes available, in the course of ordinary politics and existence, the instruments of its own revision and thereby overcomes the contrast between activities within its structure (the reproduction of society) and activities about its structure (the transformation of society)."[155] To the extent that the formative context of society is viewed by those living within it as something "merely given in a self-generating process" that operates independently of "the [human] will and the imagination," the individuals in question will not think of themselves as possessing any power to revise the elementary terms of their common social life.[156] Here, we may speak of a formative context that has only limited powers of self-revision, if any.

In a social world of this sort, human freedom will be sharply limited, for no one will believe it possible to alter in a deliberate and methodical way the formative context of society. But since human freedom, according to Unger, is in reality limitless, such a society constitutes a lie (or, less dramatically, rests upon a self-misunderstanding, a form of false consciousness). We can contrast this world with one in which society is conceived, by its members, as "made and imagined," as possessing what Unger calls an "artifactual character."[157] To the extent that it is viewed as an artifact, the formative context of society cannot possess a natural or divine sanctity that insulates it from further revision. Even in such a society, of course, the power that individuals possess to remake its basic features may be limited. But the idea that society is made, not given, is, Unger claims, a necessary condition for the ongoing and self-conscious revision of the formative context it provides.

"[R]ecognition that societies differ in the extent to which they lay themselves open to self-revision" thus gives us a principled basis for distinguishing, in purely descriptive terms, between different forms of social life (between, for example, the liberal democracies of the modern world and the traditional, hierarchical societies that preceded them). But this same distinction also functions, Unger says, as a "regulative ideal" guiding our evaluation of different institutional arrangements and programs of reform.[158] The more it opens itself to revision, the more it breaks down "the fixed order of society" and makes itself "vulnerable to collective conflict and deliberation"—the more it frees the "life chances" of the individual from "the tyranny of abstract social categories" and emancipates his powers of forming novel relations with others—the more, according to Unger, the formative context of society will do "justice" to man's true nature as a being whose "capabilities of human connection" are not exhausted by all "the social and mental forms . . . that have ever been produced."[159] The best society will, on this view, be the one whose formative context permits a maximum of self-revision consistent with the counterbalancing requirement (about which Unger has little to say) that it possess sufficient durability to prevent the society's perpetual reconstruction from degenerating into meaningless acts of "context smashing." In such a society, all "unnecessary and unjustifiable constraints" on the power of individuals to revise the formative contexts of social life will have been eliminated and "collective empowerment made possible by the disentrenchment" of those structures that acquire an "immunity to challenge and revision in the course of ordinary social activity." To be sure, formative structures will remain, but they will be structures "with particular qualities." They will be "structure-revising structures" that "turn the occasions for their reproduction into opportunities for their correction," thereby promoting the development of "negative capability"—the "practical and spiritual individual and collective empowerment made possible by the disentrenchment of formative structures."[160]

This extraordinarily abstract ideal entails, Unger claims, a more specific "conception of law and its desirable relation to society." In the best of all societies, he says, it will be the function of law to actively destablilize existing social hierarchies and distinctions—a conclusion that follows from his basic criterion for judging the goodness of different political systems. On this view, which Unger terms the "superliberal" view of law, "[t]he ideal aim of the system of rights, taken as a whole and in each of its branches, is to serve as a counterprogram to the maintenance or reemergence of any scheme of social roles and ranks that can become effectively insulated against the ordinarily available forms of challenge."[161] The proper function of law, on this view of it, is neither to reaffirm the existing system of "abstract social categories" (whatever they may be) nor to establish a framework of rules that is neutral with respect to them, but to unsettle these categories and prevent their reestablishment in any other form.

From this superliberal view of law, Unger draws a series of further implications that brings us closer to the concrete problems with which legal analysis is typically concerned. Thus, for example, he claims that the superliberal view implies the need for certain fundamental changes in the legal organization of economic activity as it now exists. Today, he says, the market "works through the assignment [to individuals] of more or less absolute claims to divisible portions of social capital." But this arrangement is itself, he insists, an entrenched structure that sharply limits the possibilities for combining the human and material resources we possess. To expand the range of our economic possibilities, we must break down the distinction (today accepted as an unalterable fact) between "task-defining" and "task-executing" activities, encourage decentralization beyond the limits currently thought possible, and democratize the process by which decisions are made regarding the direction and magnitude of capital investment—all of which require a redefinition of the legal rights that individuals can claim to the exercise of economic power.[162]

The superliberal view of law has specific implications for the system of political rights as well. Here, too, a number of changes must be made to achieve the basic goal of law as this view conceives it. Unger emphasizes two in particular. First, if man's negative capability is to be fully realized, we must create "solidarity rights" that give "legal force to many of the expectations" arising from "relations of mutual reliance and vulnerability," relations that—because they are at present unprotected by the law—tend to be forgotten in our thinking about the kinds of social relations open to us, and whose legal invisibility thus creates an artificial limitation on our powers of imagination and reform.[163] Second, we must create what Unger calls "destabilization rights"—rights that give individuals "a claim upon governmental power obliging government to disrupt those forms of division and hierarchy that, contrary to the spirit of the [new superliberal] constitution, manage to achieve stability only by distancing themselves from the transformative conflicts that might disturb them."[164] For rights of this latter sort are an essential prophylactic, Unger argues, against the dangers of entrenchment generally.

Unger's proposals for reforming the existing system of economic and political rights follow from his understanding of the proper relationship between law and society, which itself is entailed by his view of human nature. These proposals in turn provide a framework for deciding doctrinal questions of even greater specificity. This framework allows Unger to connect his guiding philosophical ideal to detailed judgments regarding the desirability of particular legal rules and institutions. Unger offers two examples to show that his ideal does indeed have a resolving power of this sort even at the lowest levels of doctrinal analysis, and it will be useful to look briefly at the first of these. For it illustrates, in an especially vivid way, his confident belief that answers to technical legal questions can be derived from broad philosophical ideas through a process of analysis alone.

The example I want to consider is drawn from the law of contracts. Contract law, Unger tells us, has traditionally been thought to revolve around a concept of individualism (associated with the market) and a communitarian counterconcept (associated with the family or household), each concept being assigned a natural and fixed domain of its own. The traditional view of course recognizes that these two concepts occasionally intrude into each other's spheres. But to the traditionalist, Unger says, such intrusions appear accidental and *ad hoc,* hence not explicable in any systematic fashion.

In reality, however, the rigid separation of domains that the traditional view of contract law takes for granted is entirely artificial and harmful to boot. Specifically, Unger claims, the separation of spheres that this view endorses has had two bad effects. First, it has confirmed the identification of community and trust (the communitarian counterconcept) "with the personalistic authority and dependence that often characterize family life." And second, it has discouraged the recognition of, and the provision of support for, those "subtle interdependencies of social life that flourish outside the narrow zone of recognized community," particularly in the sphere of commercial exchange.[165] In different though related ways, Unger maintains, these attitudes unnecessarily constrain the range of options that we are able to conceive as desirable or even possible in social life, and thus impede the development of our capacity for self-transcendence, our negative capability. Only when we cease to take for granted the conceptual division that contract law today assumes—cease to regard it as a natural fact that places certain inexorable limits on the sorts of relationships, and features of relationships, that contract law may properly address—will we be able to approach the task of accommodating the claims of individualism and community uninhibited by the formative context that the law of contracts now imposes.

The truth, according to Unger, is that both autonomy and dependence are features of every social relationship, though their relative importance may vary from one setting to another. Family and market are therefore not distinct spheres of life, but poles of a continuum, each exhibiting, to some degree, the characteristics most prominent in the other. It follows that trust and reciprocity ought not to be denied legal protection when they appear outside the family circle merely on the grounds that they have no place in the domain of market relationships. Once it is acknowledged that trust plays an important role in this latter sphere as well, the way will be open, Unger argues, to the construction of a new doctrinal order that takes this fact into account by giving weight to trust in all sorts of situations where its existence is today ignored (employing, among other things, the concept of a solidarity right to do so). And conversely, the acknowledgment that autonomy deserves protection even within the sphere of family life—traditionally conceived as a realm of solidarity and trust—must lead to a complementary refinement of doctrine. Together, he says, these two doctrinal reforms will produce a new law of contracts that is more rational and unified—less disfigured by *ad hoc* arguments and arbitrary distinctions—than the one we now possess.

Indeed, Unger goes still further. For he suggests that the reformation of contract law along these lines can even help us to resolve such highly technical problems as those posed in cases dealing with the creation of contracts by correspondence and the consequences of unilateral mistake.[166] Our present law of contracts cannot address these problems in a rational and organized way, he says, because it draws too stark a contrast between the realms of market and of family. Rejecting this contrast in favor of a view that emphasizes the "subtle and continuous shading" of autonomy and trust will bring neglected features of social life into view and make it possible to treat them more consistently. Today, considerations of fairness in commercial dealings and of autonomy in family life are occasionally acknowledged but only, Unger claims, in a haphazard and unsystematic way, and the cases that do recognize them seem like arbitrary exceptions to the principles that define these two domains. The doctrinal reorientation he recommends would, he insists, permit these exceptions to be rationalized and thus give the whole of contract law, down to its smallest detail, a normative coherence it currently lacks.

Unger's philosophically inspired rationalization of contract law dramatizes the ambitiousness of his theoretical program and illustrates, again, its similarity to Lasswell and McDougal's. Lasswell and McDougal claim that traditional forms of legal analysis, unsupported by a comprehensive moral theory based on premises extrinsic to the law, cannot provide a rational foundation for the solution of doctrinal problems arising within the legal order itself. For analysis of this sort, they say, we must substitute a methodically structured system of norms and express confidence that within such a system even the most technical legal issues can be resolved. Their approach is thus marked by an insistence on the need for some Archimedean moral theory external to the law; by a scornful rejection of traditional forms of legal analysis and argument; and by an emphasis on the idea of a comprehensive normative scheme linking the most basic principles of political life to the assessment of specific legal rules and institutions.

Unger's theory shares these characteristics too. There are, of course, differences between his background theory and theirs. But his project is motivated by the same ambition and rests upon similar beliefs. Indeed, its rationalizing drive is if anything more extreme. For he not only attempts to provide a deeper ground for his own ultimate values but—as his discussion of contract law makes clear— is prepared to pursue the implications of these values to an even lower level of doctrinal detail, extending the search for an embracing moral scheme in both directions. Unger's theory is more comprehensive than Lasswell and McDougal's. It evidences greater confidence in the power of philosophical ideas to illuminate legal doctrine and guide its construction. It aspires to a higher overall degree of legal rationalization. And it reflects an even more profound contempt for the familiar forms of analogical reasoning that characterize most legal argument. In each of these respects Unger embraces, and exaggerates, the premises of scientific realism.

The depth of Unger's hostility to prudentialism is reflected with particular clarity in some remarks that he makes, toward the end of his essay, on the nature of law practice and the future of the legal profession. These remarks not only reveal his contempt for the inex-

act "analogy-mongering"[167] of lawyers—for their pluralism and reliance on precedent and experience—but demonstrate that an acceptance of his own more scientific approach must lead to the
dismantlement of the profession as we know it.

A rational reconstruction of the legal order is possible, Unger
claims, only if the problems to which specific legal doctrines are addressed are reconceived from the perspective of a background theory
that is based upon a philosophical account of the most basic features
of human personality and society. The rationalization of the law thus
requires, he insists, the effacement of precisely that distinction between law, on the one hand, and politics or philosophy, on the other,
that formalism seeks to maintain. But the idea of a distinctive legal
expertise presupposes the existence of some such boundary. For if law
necessarily shades into ideology or philosophy and if there are no
experts in these latter fields—which seems to be the case—it is
difficult to see what meaning legal expertise, and the related distinction between lawyers and laypeople, can have:

> If legal doctrine is acknowledged to be continuous with other
> modes of normative argument, if the institutional plan that decrees
> the existence of a distinct judiciary alongside only one or two other
> branches of government is reconstructed, and if long before this
> reconstruction the belief in a logic of inherent institutional roles is
> abandoned, legal expertise can survive only as a loose collection of
> different types of insight and responsibility. Each type would com-
> bine elements of current legal professionalism with allegedly non-
> legal forms of special knowledge and experience as well as with
> varieties of political representation. This *disintegration of the bar*
> might serve as a model for what would happen, in a more demo-
> cratic and less superstitious society, to all claims to monopolize in
> the name of expert knowledge an instrument of power.[168]

The destruction of formalism, Unger claims, forces us to recognize
that philosophical issues are latent in all doctrinal disputes, and by
discrediting every "superstitious" belief in the integrity and independence of a distinctive legal expertise makes it clear that the lawyer's
professional knowledge—what Hobbes's student calls the artificial
reason of the law—gives him no special advantage in addressing these
issues as they arise in the search for an appropriate background theory.[169] Thus Unger's assault on formalism (the negative part of his

program) and his effort to construct a new normative science of law from philosophical premises outside the doctrinal framework whose mastery has traditionally been thought to constitute the core of professional legal knowledge (the positive part of his program) both lead to the conclusion that if the law is to be rationalized, our belief in a distinctive legal expertise, the basis of the lawyer's sense of professional identity, must be abandoned.

The antiprofessional implications of Unger's insistence on eliminating the distinction between the technical analysis of legal problems, on the one hand, and the philosophical examination of political ideals, on the other, are aggravated by the content of the specific ideal he defends. According to Unger, "[t]he received view presents the practice of law as the defense of individual or group interests within an institutional and imaginative framework that, at least for the specific purposes of this defense, must be taken as a given."[170] This view of law practice presupposes a sharp distinction between a lawyer's routine activities and the formative contexts that establish the framework within which these activities take place. But it is the existence of this very distinction that Unger's own vision of a society more adequate to man's true essence challenges. To achieve such a society, the distinction between shaped routine and shaping context must be weakened in both theory and practice. It follows that lawyers who share Unger's ideal will see their practice in a different light from the traditional one, conceiving their chief responsibility to be the "defense of individual or group interests by methods that reveal the specificity of the underlying institutional and imaginative order, that subject it to a series of petty disturbances capable of escalating at any moment, and that suggest alternative ways of defining collective interests, collective identities, and assumptions about the possible."[171]

Traditionally, Unger says, the lawyer has been thought of as someone whose work tends to strengthen the existing order because it takes that order for granted. On this view, it is the lawyer's job to make sure that plans get executed and disputes resolved in the way existing arrangements require. By contrast, a lawyer who adopts the "distinctive approach to law practice" implied by Unger's ideal will understand his basic task to be the disruption or destabilization of the existing "institutional and imaginative framework."[172] Seizing his opportunities where he finds them, a lawyer inspired by Unger's vision will seek to turn low-level disputes that arise against a familiar and unquestioned background into controversies about that background itself—to politicize the law by doing everything he can to ensure that "focused disputes of legal doctrine repeatedly threaten to escalate into struggles over the basic imaginative structure of social existence."[173] For the traditional view of the lawyer as someone who preserves order by helping to maintain the distinction between legal and political questions—however difficult that distinction may be to sustain in an ultimate theoretical sense—Unger substitutes a view of the lawyer as someone who meets his professional responsibilities by deliberately turning one kind of question into the other whenever circumstances permit.

The inevitable result of this escalatory process is the collapse of any notion of a separate legal expertise and, with that, the destruction of the very idea of a legal profession. The lawyer who feels that his deepest responsibility is to politicize whatever doctrinal dispute he happens to find himself involved in at the moment is committing professional suicide out of his devotion to a higher ideal. Unger's book draws this conclusion and applauds it. In fact, however, the notion that lawyers have distinctive skills and belong to a special profession is threatened not only by Unger's new critical science of law, but by every program that seeks to replace traditional forms of legal understanding with a comprehensive moral theory systematically built up from elementary philosophical ideas. The concept of a legal profession is threatened, that is to say, by every program of policy science, and the fact that Unger not only recognizes the antiprofessional implications of his theory but enthusiastically embraces them is one more sign that his own work belongs to the tradition of scientific realism and is guided by its inner spirit.

A PATHOLOGICAL DIVISION

Broadly speaking, most law teachers divide their time between two activities, teaching and writing, like their counterparts in other fields. But in one important respect the situation of a law teacher differs from that of graduate-level instructors in many other disciplines. The person who teaches graduate students in history or philosophy, for example, is preparing them for a life similar to his or her own—a university life devoted in significant part to scholarly research and writing. For such teachers there is thus an essential continuity between the pedagogical and the scholarly sides of their work, since in the one activity their aim is to train students for eventual participation in the other. In the case of the law teacher, however, a similar continuity does not exist. Every law teacher belongs to the community of university scholars, and it is to this community that his or her research and writing are primarily addressed. But the objective in teaching law is not to prepare students for membership in the same community. The aim is to equip them not for a life essentially like the teacher's own, but for a different kind of life, one of practical involvements that requires skills other than those a scholar needs. Most law students do not expect to work in universities. In teaching law, one must accept this fact and help to prepare students for a life lived in the world of affairs and not, like the teacher's, at a contemplative distance from it. Hence there is a division—indeed, a tension—between the aims of legal scholarship and the requirements of law teaching that has no analogue in disciplines such as history and philosophy.

This division is a permanent feature of law teaching and can never be entirely removed. That is not necessarily a bad thing, however, for the tension it creates may be a source of fruitful provocation. Indeed, many law teachers undoubtedly find it stimulating and prefer their divided existence to one more purely practical or academic. But the tension between law teaching and legal scholarship is today far greater than it has been in the past and greater than is healthy. It has reached a point, in fact, that may aptly be described as pathological.

The explanation for this lies not in the mild schizophrenia that is a permanent part of the law teacher's situation. More specifically it lies in the antiprudentialist outlook that the law-and-economics and critical legal studies movements share and have helped to promote in the field of legal scholarship during the past twenty years. For two decades these movements—the heirs of scientific realism—have been the best organized and most influential ones in American legal thought. That may now be changing as other schools arise and begin to compete for followers. But whatever the future fate of these two movements, their twenty-year-long dominance has left a lasting impression on the attitudes and values of American law teachers by communicating to them a contempt for the claims of practical wisdom within the domain of scholarly work. As this contempt has deepened in the area of scholarship, its effect has been to widen the gap that separates law teaching and research. To understand why, it will be helpful to compare the present situation in law teaching with the one that existed thirty years ago, before the law-and-economics and critical legal studies movements had emerged.

Most law teachers a generation ago accepted the idea that they were training practicing lawyers and understood the aim of their classroom teaching to be the cultivation of those qualities that a lawyer needs to succeed in practice. This in turn was understood to mean, above all else, training students in the art of handling cases. To master this art, a student had to learn how to draw convincing generalizations from particular decisions—how to formulate what Mark Kelman calls appropriate "covering rules."[174] But to most law teachers thirty years ago the art of case analysis implied more than this. In addition it implied an appreciation of the complexity of cases and of the limited usefulness of any system of abstractions in analyzing them, along with a preference for local solutions arrived at by an admittedly unsystematic arsenal of different and sometimes conflicting methods or techniques. To learn to think about cases in the way a lawyer must meant on this view to become less simpleminded, less enamored of comprehensive solutions, more accepting of complexity and moral pluralism—while continuing to search for reasonable solutions to particular problems. It meant, specifically, to become skilled in the many contradictory techniques of interpretation that provide the flexibility needed to achieve sensible local results within the accidental limits set by precedent. Conceived in this way, the process of legal education might be described, in Llewellyn's terms, as one in which students are introduced to the craft traditions of their profession and helped to acquire the habits they will later need in practice. This conception of the aims of legal education was the dominant one among law teachers thirty years ago.

The then-dominant view of legal scholarship could also be described in Llewellynian fashion. Thirty years ago, most law teachers who engaged in serious scholarly work conceived the goal of their research to be the clarification of doctrine in a particular field and the improvement of its capacity to deal with a certain range or type of human conflict. This, of course, implied a measure of rationalization, for the point of such doctrinal scholarship was to increase the law's orderliness and power. But the rationalizing ambitions of those who pursued scholarly projects of this kind were constrained by a respect for the differences among the various branches of legal doctrine and by a preference for local answers over comprehensive ones, the same preference that they sought to encourage in their students. In this regard it is significant that the great doctrinalists of the last generation (Gilmore, Bittker, and Areeda are good examples)[175] typically wrote not just for other academics but for practicing lawyers too, and understood their own research to be continuous with the work of their more thoughtful counterparts in practice. To be sure, they recognized that an academic lawyer can pursue doctrinal questions with a freedom that most practitioners cannot and may therefore be able to address such questions from a broader point of view. But they pursued their own more leisurely lines of thought in a practical spirit and had no difficulty seeing how their research might contribute to the work of lawyers and judges or to the education of their students.

The connectedness of teaching to scholarship—which thirty years ago most academic lawyers took for granted—encouraged the belief that a law professor's two main tasks, though clearly different, are reconcilable. Today that belief is less widely shared and far more fragile. Many of those now teaching law would still, I think, accept Llewellyn's account of legal method as the one that best describes their objectives in the classroom. But in the area of scholarship this same account has been under attack for a generation. For twenty years, American legal thought has been dominated by two movements inspired by an ideal of legal science that is antagonistic to the common-law tradition and to the claims of practical wisdom which that tradition has always honored. These claims must be brushed aside as superstitions by the academic lawyer who judges the value of research according to the criteria that law and economics and critical legal studies both endorse. Today, any law teacher who wants to do scholarly work of a kind that will be respected by his or her peers is increasingly likely to view the claims of practical wisdom in this light. Even the teacher who rejects the substantive dogmas of both movements will have difficulty escaping the broader climate of opinion they have helped to create. And to the extent that law teachers come to share the antiprudentialist outlook of these movements, even in a general way, they will find themselves as scholars feeling a hostility toward the very values on which their conception of their own role as teachers still depends.

As a result, law teachers now confront a dilemma that their counterparts thirty years ago did not. The two sides of law teaching—always somewhat in tension but previously viewed as parts of a common endeavor—are today more widely separated, and the relationship between them has become one of mistrust. It is possible, of course, to ignore this dilemma and pretend it does not exist. But that is a difficult position to sustain, both intellectually and psychologically, and at some point most self-reflective law teachers are likely to feel the need to confront the growing division that now exists between their scholarly and their pedagogical work. Those that do will find there are three responses open to them.

The first is to accept the priority of the prudentialist attitude that still informs much classroom teaching and to try to accommodate one's scholarly writing and research to it. But it is unlikely that most law teachers will consider this the best response to their divided situation. For the scholarly side of law teaching is now widely regarded as more important than the teaching side—a view reflected in the hiring and promotion policies of many law schools—and if one is to be given priority over the other, many academic lawyers would probably choose to subordinate their teaching to their scholarship rather than the other way around.

A second and more cynical response is simply to admit that law teaching rests upon prudentialist assumptions that cannot be defended from a theoretical point of view, and to accept the fact that it is an unpleasant chore that must be performed if one is to have the time and money needed to pursue the really worthwhile ends of scholarship. Law teachers who take this view see their teaching as a burden, an unavoidable distraction; hence they are likely to teach in a desultory and dispirited fashion, communicating to their students, subtly perhaps but quite effectively, the intellectual contempt they feel for the common-law tradition and its prudential methods.

The third response, in contrast to the first, affirms the priority of the scholarly point of view, but unlike the second refuses to accept the prudentialism of the classroom as a given. Those law teachers who respond in this way to the tension that exists between their scholarship and teaching take the rationalizing ideals of legal science as their guide. But they insist that these ideals, which now dominate the realm of scholarship, can be imported into the field of teaching too and used to reconstruct the professional training of law students along more-scientific lines. To a considerable degree, that is what appears to be happening in our law schools today. Committed to the aims of scientific realism in one or another of its contemporary forms but hoping, understandably, to achieve a greater unity of outlook in their work, many law teachers now urge that legal education be reformed in the image of their scholarly ideals, and are developing new methods and materials to bring this reform about.[176] There are others, of course, who continue to think that the aim of legal education is the cultivation of practical wisdom. But their numbers are declining and the authority of their position weakens year by year. The future lies with their adversaries, with those who want to make law teaching an adjunct of legal scholarship and to define its goals in similar terms.

The legal scientist who conceives his task as a teacher to be the presentation and defense of the same theories he employs as a scholar to describe and evaluate the law will not feel divided in his work or see a tension between his scholarly and his pedagogical roles. These will be, for him, more or less continuous, as they were for his predecessor thirty years ago (though for very different reasons). For the law teacher who wants to restore a sense of wholeness to his work, this conception of teaching, which views it as a continuation of scholarship by other means, is therefore likely to have great appeal. But for his students it represents a professional disaster.

For whatever those in law teaching think, practicing lawyers still need the intellectual and affective powers whose combination constitutes the virtue of practical wisdom. Later in their professional lives, many lawyers come to appreciate the value of practical wisdom and to understand that it is not just a skill but a trait of character. The recognition that this is so will have difficulty taking root and growing into a confident sense of professional identity, however, when it is contradicted by the attitudes to which a lawyer is exposed at the very start of his or her career. It is in the law school classroom that lawyers are introduced to the culture of the profession and here that their professional self-conception first takes shape. If the claims of practical wisdom are repudiated here—which the penetration into the classroom of a neo-Langdellian ideal of scholarship makes increasingly likely—it will be harder to retrieve them later and hence more difficult to understand, let alone embrace, any ideal of professional excellence in which the virtue of prudence occupies a central place. For those entering a profession in which this virtue is still needed, the tendency to dismiss it as a source of obscurantism that will eventually be eliminated by the spreading light of legal science is therefore ultimately self-destructive and amounts—as Unger candidly admits—to a form of professional suicide. And when those who have the responsibility for inducting new recruits into the legal profession themselves actively encourage this suicidal attitude, we may with some justification describe the situation as pathological. Karl Llewellyn knew what was needed to combat this particular disorder. But the path he pointed out has been rejected and the disease he sought to cure has grown much worse. So much so, indeed, that we may now reasonably wonder whether it is too advanced to be reversed.

5

Law Firms

Much academic legal writing in America today is marked by a contempt for the claims of practical wisdom. This attitude is not a new one. It may be found already forcefully expressed in Hobbes's vigorous attack on the common law and its defenders. But during the past quarter-century its influence among American legal scholars has dramatically increased and is now at an unprecedented level. In Chapter 4 I recounted the long and complex course by which this disparaging view of practical wisdom has spread so widely and acquired such prestige. My aim was to expose the connections among the ideas and scholarly programs that have dominated American jurisprudence over the last hundred years and in particular to trace the evolution and eventual triumph within it of the centuries-old Hobbesian ambition to establish a rigorous science of law. Chapter 4 was an essay in the history of ideas, limited to the largely self-contained world of legal thought.

The builders of this world have for the most part been university professors, and it is on them and their self-image that the antiprudentialist spirit of contemporary legal scholarship has had the greatest effect. But today it is having a growing influence on others outside the academy as well. Theoretically minded law teachers who introduce this scholarship into their teaching in an effort to give it added intellectual weight inevitably communicate to a wider audience of nonacademic lawyers some measure of the antiprudentialism that now colors the work of many of America's leading legal scholars. They signal by their choice of topics and methods of analysis a disdain for practical wisdom, which students in turn absorb, at least in a diluted form. In this way, the antiprudentialist outlook so prominent in contemporary legal thought spreads through the culture of the profession as a whole and comes to have a broader influence on lawyers generally.

The implications of this for the fate of the lawyer-statesman ideal are disturbing enough. But the situation is in fact far worse. For at the same time that legal scholarship has been moving in the direction I have indicated, other developments outside the academy have transformed the actual practice of law in ways that put this ideal under pressure as well. These developments have occurred independently of those described earlier. Their effects have nevertheless been similar and reinforcing. For they too have weakened the ideal of the lawyer-statesman and made it less credible to practicing lawyers themselves, subverting its authority in the realm of action while the law-and-economics and critical legal studies movements subvert it in that of thought.

In this chapter I explore the nature and meaning of these changes in law practice. I shall not attempt, however, to survey the field of modern practice as a whole—a vast and nearly formless subject. Instead I intend to concentrate on a single important aspect of it, the practice of law in large corporate firms. I have two reasons for limiting my account in this way. First, these firms are elite institutions. They attract the best law school graduates, have the most powerful clients, and possess the greatest clout within the profession. They also make the most money. As a result, they exert a disproportionate influence on the practicing bar as a whole. Any basic change in the culture of the corporate firm, such as has occurred in the last twenty years, is therefore certain to have repercussions far beyond these firms themselves and to be felt in some measure by all those that stand below them in the hierarchy of power and prestige. If we want to know what conception of professional excellence is likely to guide the next generation of practicing lawyers, we thus have reason to examine with special care the one our large firms have recently come to embrace. In an analogous way, if we wish to understand what is now happening in American legal education, we must pay particular attention to scholarly trends at the country's leading schools. For these not only exhibit with special clarity the main currents of contemporary legal thought but also act as accelerators that speed the communication of new ideas to other institutions. The large corporate law firm occupies a similar position in the world of practice and exerts a comparable influence on the evolution of professional ideals.

Second, the country's corporate firms have for a century produced a steady stream of lawyer-statesmen. Many of our leading diplomats, negotiators, cabinet officers, and political advisers have been drawn from their ranks, and countless other lawyers in these firms have spent some part of their careers in public service. Lawyers from large corporate firms played a significant role in shaping New Deal policy. They led the country's war efforts against Germany and Japan. They were the principal architects of the new world order that followed. They managed the Kennedy administration's campaign for civil rights. And they led the country into Vietnam and out again. Of course not everyone who might be called a lawyer-statesman has been a member of a corporate firm. Some (like Robert Jackson) have come from small-town practices and others (like Archibald Cox) from the academy instead. But a large number of the country's lawyer-statesmen have in this century been associated with such firms, whose internal culture has until quite recently assigned a high value to the virtues of practical wisdom and public service these figures represent. For a hundred years the large corporate firm has been the principal standard-bearer of the lawyer-statesman ideal in the sphere of private practice. If one wants to examine the current status of this ideal within the practicing bar, it therefore makes sense to take an especially close look at the changing culture of those firms that in the past have been its primary carrier.

The Revolution in Large-Firm Practice

Today, as in the past, only a small percentage of lawyers practice in large corporate firms (those, let us say, with one hundred or more attorneys and a predominantly business clientele). Indeed, data collected in 1980 indicate that roughly three-quarters of all the lawyers in private practice "either practice alone or in firms having ten members or less."[1] But the large corporate firm continues to exercise an influence, both within the profession and outside it, that far exceeds its numerical strength.[2] However influence and power are measured—whether in raw economic terms or in subtler, political ones—these firms remain the leaders of the bar. In that respect, their position is little different from what it was a generation ago, or even earlier.

Although these firms still possess great power and prestige, in the past twenty years their institutional character has changed dramatically. Indeed, so great have the speed and magnitude of this change been that we may properly describe it as a revolution.[3] The slowing economy of the 1990s has of course caused many large firms to postpone plans for expansion and even to reduce somewhat their existing scale of operations.[4] But no matter how much trimming these firms now do, the revolutionary change in the nature of their practice that has taken place over the last two decades cannot be undone. It is the product of deep forces that have altered the structure and culture of America's large firms in ways that now seem irreversible.

The most obvious symptom of this change is the sharp increase in firm size itself. In 1978 there were 15 firms in the United States with 200 or more lawyers, and approximately 3500 lawyers practicing in them. Ten years later there were 115 firms of this size, with 35,000 lawyers.[5] According to the *National Law Journal,* there were 251 American firms with more than 100 lawyers in 1986, as opposed to less than a dozen such firms in 1960. In 1968 the largest firm in the country had 169 lawyers. In 1988 the largest firm had 962 lawyers, and there were 149 firms larger than the largest firm twenty years before.[6] It would appear, moreover, not only that the largest firms in the country have been growing in absolute terms, but that their rate of growth has been increasing as well. A detailed study of law firm growth by Marc Galanter and Thomas Palay—the most comprehensive of its kind to date—reports that a sample of 50 of the largest firms in the country (as of 1986) grew at an annual rate of 8 percent during the preceding ten-year period, as opposed to 5.3 percent for the same firms in the period between 1955 and 1965.[7]

Another development, closely related to the recent rapid growth in firm size, has been the increasing number of firms with branch offices, and the appearance of what Galanter and Palay call the genuine multicity firm.[8] In 1960 the branch office was a relative rarity, and the few that did exist were almost all concentrated in Washington, D.C. It is true that Washington has continued to be "the favorite site for branches"; in 1980 there were 178 non-Washington firms that had branch offices there.[9] But the recent increase in firm branching has by no means been restricted to that city. By 1980, 24 percent of all the law firms in the country with fifty or more lawyers had an established presence in *three* or more locations. At the largest firms this development has been even more pronounced. In an effort to capture "the dynamic of multicity growth," Galanter and Palay studied twenty of the largest law firms in New York City and twenty of the largest firms elsewhere in the county. The first group, they report, "had a total of 70 branch offices in 1980 and 99 branches in 1987," a 41 percent increase in seven years. The second group had 61 branch offices in 1980 and 124 branches seven years later, an increase of 103 percent. During this same period, the average size of the branch offices of the New York firms increased from 8 to 17, and that of the non–New York firms from 15 to 30, an increase of 100 percent or more in each case.[10]

Large corporate firms are thus getting bigger—much bigger—and geographically more diversified. At the same time that these outward changes have been taking place, there has also been a change—subtler and more difficult to document but equally important—in the nature of the work that lawyers at these large firms do. In a word, their work has become more specialized.

In his recent study of large-firm practice in Chicago, Robert Nelson reports that of the "major events" on which the lawyers in his survey worked, only 4.9 percent of those that occurred between 1977 and 1980 involved "a phase of general research or practice," as opposed to 10.5 percent of reported events occurring before 1968. Nelson's survey also reveals a concomitant increase, during the same period, in the percentage of reported events representing specialized and subspecialized forms of legal practice.[11] On the basis of his data Nelson concludes that "[t]here is some evidence for a transformation of the work process in the large firm," a transformation marked by "the declining incidence of general practice and client responsibility and the increasing frequency of subspecialization and big cases."[12]

Though this increase in specialization does not, as Nelson is careful to point out, necessarily imply "a 'deskilling' of professional work," it does suggest that large firms have made a conscious effort "to cultivate the specialized skill base" needed to attract corporate clients.[13] They have done this, according to Nelson, in two ways: by encouraging their lawyers to acquire greater expertise in narrower fields, and by developing what he calls "a set of structured relationships between specialists in different fields and with different client bases"—coordinated teams that permit these firms to offer their corporate clients a wider range of increasingly specialized services. Extrapolating from his own quite similar account of the changing nature of large-firm practice, Steven Brill, the editor-in-chief of *The American Lawyer,* concludes that the corporate law firm most likely to prosper in the 1990s, and to emerge as a leader in the profession, will not be "a large group of people doing general practice," but "a cluster of marvelously stocked boutiques," a condominium of specialists. To have a "large enough stock of specialists" to achieve this goal, Brill predicts, a firm "will have to be over 500 lawyers."[14]

Commentators agree that one important cause of this shift toward greater specialization has been the growing size and sophistication of the in-house law departments that many corporations now possess, a development that has altered the nature of the relationship between these companies and the firms that serve as their outside legal counsel. That corporate in-house law departments have been getting bigger, and are handling a larger proportion of their companies' legal work, is confirmed by a number of recent studies, which indicate that the phenomenon is an economywide one.[15] Galanter and Palay report that there is also some evidence to suggest that corporate law departments have been growing in "budget, functions and authority" as well as size,[16] and taking on legal matters of a more complex sort that "once would have gone to outside lawyers."[17]

One important consequence of this has been that many large companies, whose in-house law departments now possess the resources to handle a larger share of their own legal work, have become more-discriminating consumers of outside legal services—more inclined to shop around and to compare the costs and benefits of contracting such work out before deciding which (if any) outside firm to hire.[18] And this in turn has caused outside firms to concentrate their energies in areas of law that it does not pay their corporate clients to master on their own, generally because the areas in question are highly technical and present legal problems that any given company is likely to encounter only at rare intervals (mergers, takeovers, complex litigations, reorganizations, and so forth).

The more specialized character of large-firm practice, on which Nelson and others have remarked, is to that extent a predictable, perhaps inevitable, response to the new and more competitive conditions in the market for legal services that the growth of in-house corporate law departments has produced. Changes in this market have brought about a fundamental shift in the nature of the relationship between the large firm and its clients, a shift, in Galanter and Palay's words, from "comprehensive and enduring retainer relationships toward less exclusive and more task-specific ad hoc engagements."[19] Thirty years ago most corporate law firms had a relatively stable set of clients and represented them in matters both ordinary and exceptional. Today their clientele tends to be more fluid and relations with individual clients less continuous—restricted, for the most part, to extraordinary events that demand a form of specialized legal knowledge that even very large companies often find it uneconomical to develop on their own. Except for their vastly greater size, nothing distinguishes today's corporate law firms from their predecessors more dramatically than this shift in the client-firm relationship.

Another recent change in the character of large-firm practice has been a weakening of the ties that once bound the individual members of a given firm to the firm itself, and that made the movement of lawyers from one firm to another a relative rarity. In his classic study of large-firm practice in New York City in the 1950s, Erwin Smigel describes the lateral movement of lawyers among elite firms as an extremely uncommon occurrence.[20] Having made the decision to join a particular firm, Smigel reports, a lawyer was expected to remain with that firm for the whole of his career, and typically did so unless, of course, he failed to become a partner, in which case he would leave, but for a job at a smaller firm, or in the law department of a corporation, and only rarely for a position at another firm of comparable size and stature. Today such lateral movement is no longer exceptional; indeed, it is rapidly becoming the norm. According to Galanter and Palay, "[a] 1988 survey of the 500 largest law firms found that over a quarter reported that more than half of their new partners were not promoted from within but came from other firms," and "[t]he same survey found that one quarter of the responding firms reported that more than half their associates were hired laterally" as well.[21] Another recent survey, conducted by the *New York Law Journal,* reports that "at 23 of the thirty largest firms in New York, an average of 24% of the associates coming up for partnership were laterals."[22] The growing number of large and mid-sized firms that have in recent years either split up or merged with other firms is another sign of this increase in mobility and of the breakdown in the pattern of stability that typified the relationship between large firms and their members in the era of Smigel's study.[23]

The causes of this breakdown in all likelihood include the recent increase in firm size, which inevitably makes it more difficult for lawyers to identify in a personal way with the firms to which they belong; the realignment of the client-firm relationship, one of whose consequences has been to shift the primary allegiance of corporate clients from firms to individual lawyers, who as a result now find it easier to change firms and take their practices with them; and the large amount of information that is at present available concerning compensation practices at the country's leading firms, information that enables lawyers to compare their opportunities at different firms in a manner that was impossible twenty or thirty years ago. Whatever its causes, the situation that now exists is strikingly different from the one that obtained a generation ago. The loyalty and inertia that once characterized the world of large-firm practice have largely disappeared. Today lawyers change firms, and firms recruit from other firms, with a casualness that would have shocked the lawyers Smigel studied. In short, just as there has been a loosening of the external ties that bind the large firm to its clients, so too has there been a similar loosening of the internal bonds that link the members of each firm to one another, and hence a weakening of the large firm's institutional solidarity. Internally as well as externally, the nature of large-firm practice has been transformed by the emergence of competitive markets that twenty years ago barely existed, and by the increased fluidity of attachments that the creation of a market always entails.

A further consequence of this loss of solidarity has been the attenuation, at many firms, of the so-called up-or-out system of promotion, and the emergence, in its place, of a more differentiated hierarchy of statuses than existed at the time of Smigel's study. With only a few exceptions, the lawyers in the firms that Smigel described fell into one of two clearly defined groups: partners and partner-candidates (associates who might or might not be promoted to partnership when the time came for them to be considered). Today things are no longer nearly so neat. Some firms, for example, have introduced a two-track associate system in which only some of the associates working for the firm are partner-candidates, the rest being ineligible for consideration from the start. At many firms the part-time associate (who works fixed hours but is also typically ineligible for partnership) and the senior attorney (who has been passed over for partnership but indefinitely retained by the firm on a salaried basis) are increasingly common phenomena.[24] Thus in place of the simple two-tiered hierarchy that Smigel describes, contemporary large-firm practice is characterized by a softening of the up-or-out rule, which ensured that every lawyer in the firm was either a partner or a partner-candidate, and by a proliferation of new statuses that do not fit in either category.

The main causes of this development have undoubtedly been economic. That, in any case, is the premise of every serious attempt that has so far been made to explain the demise of the up-or-out rule and the emergence in large firms of what one particularly enthusiastic proponent calls new staffing hierarchies.[25] What is less often discussed are the consequences of this development. One in particular is worth emphasizing. Most of the new statuses that large firms have created share an important feature: the lawyers who occupy these positions are salaried employees of their firms, but unlike associates under the up-or-out rule, they are for the most part permanently or temporarily ineligible for partnership. One may have sound, even admirable reasons for accepting such a position, just as a firm may have good reasons for creating it in the first place. But a person who is an employee of a firm and has no prospect of ever being anything else is likely to have a different and on the whole less intimate relation to the firm than those who are, or have the chance of becoming, partners in it. That is not to say that such a person will be unhappy in his or her work, or view the firm in a negative light. It seems reasonable to assume, however, that the employee's relationship to the firm will be a more remote one and therefore more easily exchanged for a comparable position elsewhere. As the number of such persons in a given firm increases, it also seems likely that their relative detachment from the firm will have an effect on what Oliver Williamson calls its atmosphere,[26] and thus indirectly influence the attitudes even of partners and partner-candidates, reinforcing the tendency toward a loosening of the ties of institutional solidarity that the increased mobility of lawyers has already brought about. The proliferation of new positions off the partnership track ought in any case to be seen as another symptom of this same tendency and of the rapidly expanding market for lawyers associated with it.

This market is the internal counterpart of the external market for legal services that has emerged as a result of changes in the nature of the large firm's relationship to its corporate clientele, and the growth of each market has been accompanied by a variety of new and openly commercial practices that were unheard of thirty years ago. Thus, for example, many firms today employ marketing directors to help them find buyers for their services. According to Galanter and Palay, the position of marketing director was "unknown in 1980."[27] Only nine years later, nearly two hundred law firms had marketing directors of their own.[28] Numerous seminars are now offered every year to help law firms improve their management techniques and increase their capacity for client development.[29] Some large firms, in an effort to attract new business, have even brought in nonlawyers—engineers, economists, business consultants, and others—in order to provide a wider range of client services.[30] Other firms "have established coordinate 'non-legal' businesses (investment advice, economic consulting, real-estate development, consulting on personnel management, marketing newsletters, etc.)" to achieve the same objective.[31] In short, law firms are now selling their services with an energy and a determination that only a few years ago would have been thought either unnecessary or inappropriate, or both.

Something quite similar has happened in the market for lawyers, where law firms appear not as sellers but as buyers. One striking indication of this is the rapid growth in the number of so-called head-hunter firms, whose sole function is to help law firms meet their personnel needs by identifying and wooing suitable lawyers already in practice elsewhere. Once a marginal and even somewhat disreputable phenomenon, by 1989, 244 such firms existed nationwide; just five years before, there had been only a third as many.[32] The effort to recruit qualified law students has also intensified. More firms now visit more schools; summer programs have become more elaborate and are carefully rated in the legal press;[33] and the use of brochures and other advertising techniques that would have been considered unprofessional a generation ago are now viewed as legitimate recruiting devices.[34]

Most significant, perhaps, a large amount of previously unavailable information regarding the compensation practices of different firms—their overall revenues, partnership shares, and associate salaries—is today a matter of public knowledge.[35] The availability of such information makes it easier for firms to compare themselves with one another and reinforces their tendency to compete openly for clients.

At the same time, it gives individual lawyers a more solid basis on which to assess their opportunities at different firms, and to bargain for additional advantages. This "new information order," as Galanter and Palay call it,[36] which specialized trade publications such as the *National Law Journal* and *The American Lawyer* have helped to create, has been a significant factor in the transformation of the market for lawyers, or more precisely, in the creation of such a market characterized by the same arm's-length relationships and mobility of attachments that typify markets in other areas of commercial life.

There is one last fact that even a brief survey of contemporary large-firm practice ought to mention, and that is the lengthening of the working day of the lawyers practicing in such firms. The data here are thin, but they all point toward the same conclusion: that lawyers in large firms are on average working longer hours than they used to. Thus, for example, in 1987 the *National Law Journal* reported the results of a nationwide study indicating that in the seven hundred large firms surveyed (firms with seventy-five or more lawyers each), average hours billed per lawyer rose by 8 percent between 1976 and 1986, to 1685 hours per year.[37] As one would expect, the number of hours that lawyers in large firms bill varies considerably from one region to another, but the tendency everywhere is upward, most dramatically in large cities such as New York, Chicago, Los Angeles, and Washington.[38] Here, too, as in most other respects, New York is clearly the leader. Anecdotal evidence suggests that average hours billed per year in New York's most prestigious firms declined somewhat in the late 1960s and early 1970s,[39] but in the last decade the average has risen steadily and is now in the neighborhood of 2000 hours per year, and even higher at some firms.[40]

The causes of this development are not entirely clear. Contributing factors undoubtedly include the changing focus of corporate law practice generally (away from repetitive matters of a relatively nonurgent sort toward extraordinary high-pressure events); the introduction of computer and other technologies that have reduced delays in document revision and made possible a real-time response to many client demands (something that firms are likely to feel they must provide in today's more competitive market for legal services); and the decision by many large firms to operate around-the-clock with a twenty-four-hour secretarial staff. However it is to be explained, the lengthening of the working day at large firms across the country is a remarkable phenomenon and must be counted among the most significant changes that have taken place in recent years in the nature of large-firm practice.

More surprising, perhaps, there is also some evidence to suggest that whereas the working day of lawyers in large firms has been increasing, their compensation, measured in real-dollar terms, has actually gone down. To be sure, the nominal income of most large-firm lawyers has risen sharply in recent years. The starting salary at many prominent New York City firms, for example, is now about $80,000, up from $53,000 in 1985,[41] and partnership shares are commensurably larger as well.[42] But while a few lawyers at the very top firms may be earning more than they did five or ten years ago, even after discounting for inflation, that does not appear to be the case in large firms generally. Thus, for example, the same *National Law Journal* survey to which I referred a moment ago also found that the median earnings of the partners in the seven hundred firms surveyed increased by only 78 percent between 1976 and 1986—a loss of earnings in fixed-dollar terms, since inflation rose by 93 percent during the same ten-year period.[43] And in 1989 *The American Lawyer* reported the results of a Price Waterhouse survey indicating "that while revenue per lawyer at midsize and large firms has almost doubled since 1978, costs have also nearly doubled, leaving partner earnings up only 1 percent against inflation,"[44] a smaller percentage increase than that in hours billed. Thus even if we assume that the total inflation-adjusted earnings of lawyers in large firms have increased during this period (which itself seems doubtful), it is almost certain that their hourly income has declined.

In sum, the large corporate law firm is today much bigger than its counterpart a generation ago and more likely to have offices in several cities. Its relationship to its clients is more fluid and openly market-oriented, as is its relationship to its own lawyers, who now move easily from one firm to the next. The work it does is more specialized, and the lawyers who do it more likely to be organized into a hierarchy of staff positions that includes a large number of permanent salaried employees who are neither partners nor partner-candidates. And the average working day of those now practicing in large firms is longer than it was ten years ago, and is continuing to lengthen, although the lawyers' real income, measured in hourly terms, appears to have gone down.

No one disputes that these changes have occurred or denies they have transformed the nature of large-firm practice. But what do they imply for the ideal of the lawyer-statesman and the values it represents? Does the large corporate law firm today offer a professional environment supportive of this ideal?

THE LARGE FIRM AND ITS CLIENTS

Thirty or forty years ago one might have answered with a qualified yes. Among the leading figures in these firms were many who then embodied this ideal: lawyers such as Lloyd Garrison, Orville Schell, John McCloy, William Rogers, Adlai Stevenson, and Cyrus Vance.[45] Often these lawyers were the dominant personalities in their firms, to whom others looked as models of professional success—lawyers with a demonstrated commitment to public service and a reputation for sound judgment in matters both public and private. Of course most of those working in large firms thirty or forty years ago were not lawyer-statesmen of similar accomplishment or talent. Most were practitioners absorbed in the routine details of their work with little opportunity to practice the art of statesmanship except in modest ways. Yet even their careers often displayed, on a smaller scale, a pattern similar to that of their more famous partners, a fact which led Smigel to conclude that the most distinguished lawyer-statesmen of the 1950s merely embodied to a striking degree norms and expectations that were widespread within the culture of their firms.[46]

By comparison, today's large firm offers an environment much less hospitable to the lawyer-statesman ideal. There are several reasons why. The first and most important concerns the relationship of the large firm to its clients, which in recent years has changed dramatically. Among the many consequences of this change has been the narrowing of opportunities that lawyers in these firms enjoy to develop the capacity for judgment on which the art of statesmanship depends.

A generation ago, most large firms handled a significant percentage of their corporate clients' routine legal business. To be sure, their clients also sometimes needed help with extraordinary matters, and undoubtedly attached particular importance to the guidance they received in these uncommon situations. But a sizable share of the work that large firms performed for their clients consisted of relatively routine services punctuated occasionally by less familiar problems. Today, by contrast, much of that routine work is handled by the clients' own in-house law departments.

The historical reasons for this transfer of routine legal business from outside firm to inside staff remain a subject of debate. Perhaps, as some have suggested, the avalanche of regulatory laws that were enacted in the 1960s (the Occupational Safety and Health Act, the Clean Air Act, the Civil Rights Act, and so on) increased the number of legal tasks that most corporations were required to perform well beyond what they could delegate at an acceptable cost to outside counsel (especially since much of this work consisted of compliance-monitoring that had to be done on the scene). This stimulated many companies to increase the size and capacity of their in-house law departments, whose members then correctly pointed out that their newly increased powers now enabled them to handle, just as well and far more economically, a large portion of the routine work that had previously been done by outside firms.[47] Whatever its explanation, the simple fact is that many corporations today do more of their own routine legal work than they did before, and increasingly rely on outside firms only for those unusual matters requiring special intellectual or other resources that it would be uneconomical for these companies to acquire on their own.

So clear has this shift in the division of legal labor been that many strategists now claim large firms can survive only by adapting to it, by cultivating the specialties their clients cannot afford to develop for themselves, and leaving to their clients' own internal law departments all legal tasks of a less exotic sort.[48] Large firms that fail to reorganize along these lines are likely, it is said, to fall behind in the competition for corporate clients and eventually to disappear, relics from an older age ill-adapted to the new one.

Broadly speaking, then, the relationship of the large firm to its corporate clients has in the past twenty years become less routine or, as some say, more "transactional," and with this shift has come a greater fluidity in the attachment of firm to client. For the more a company tends to use outside lawyers only episodically to handle special problems rather than continuously to deal with ordinary ones, the less reason it has to choose the same law firm every time. As its relationship to outside counsel becomes more transactional, the main reason that a company has for remaining with a given firm—that firm's familiarity with the company's history and needs—is bound to weaken, so that when outside lawyers must be found to help with some extraordinary matter, old attachments are likely to matter less and the choice be made instead on the basis of an unsentimental calculation of the competing advantages that different law firms have to offer. It would thus be wrong to think of the change that has taken place in the relationship of the large firm to its clients merely as a change of emphasis within a relationship that otherwise continues as before. For the effect of this change has been to demolish the older relationship completely by removing the very reason for the loyalties on which it rested, and to replace these with a shifting set of allegiances based more on expertise than on acquaintance and the special knowledge it affords.

This change in the nature of the lawyer-client relationship has meant a narrowing of the work that large-firm lawyers do, in two related ways. Their attention has narrowed, first, to exceptional events as opposed to more-prosaic ones, and second, to various subject-matter specialties. In broad terms, I believe, each of these restrictions, whose acceptance many now consider essential to the large firm's competitive survival, has made it a less congenial place for the cultivation of deliberative wisdom.

Consider, first, the narrowing of attention to extraordinary problems that for any given client are likely to arise only at rare intervals. Many lawyers, of course, view this as an advantage rather than a defect of large-firm practice. Exceptional problems are generally more exciting and intellectually challenging than routine ones, and if it is a good thing to have some problems of this sort, then (it is claimed) it must be even better to have a steady diet of them. Indeed, lawyers working in large firms often give this as a reason for their choosing such a practice in the first place. There are, however, two important complications that this view of the matter overlooks.

First, and most obviously, it overlooks the fact that even those lawyers in large firms who work exclusively on problems that are exotic from their client's point of view generally do so only as members of large teams on which they themselves are likely for many years to occupy subordinate positions performing repetitive and ministerial tasks—tasks that neither challenge nor excite. Thus even if the relationship of firm to client has become more transactional, so that contacts between them are limited increasingly to unusual events, the tasks that junior lawyers in these firms actually perform have remained, on the whole, as routine as they were before, and one suspects that the growth in firm size which has also taken place during this same period has, if anything, made matters worse.

A second complication that is overlooked by those who view the new transactional style of large-firm practice as a welcome liberation from routine has to do with its effect on the nature of the services these firms are asked and able to provide. The law firm whose assistance is solicited only in extraordinary matters may see many clients with the same exceptional problem, but is likely to have a less intimate relationship with each of them than its counterpart a generation ago did. A transactional law practice will tend to be both broader and shallower than a more routine one—broader because it increases the number of clients serviced by the firm, and shallower because it limits the relationship between each client and the firm to a relatively brief episode whose extraordinary nature must often make it difficult to draw, from that encounter alone, a full and balanced picture of the client's needs and aspirations (which institutions too possess). The more it is limited to extraordinary matters, the more a lawyer's practice is deprived of those common contacts from which such a picture might be reliably constructed. Without these contacts the lawyer will lack a sense of the familiar against which to assess a client's present exceptional predicament. The deliberative context within which the lawyer forms judgments and offers advice must to that extent be a thinner or more abstract one. And that in turn means that the kind of advice such a lawyer is able responsibly to give must be more limited too. For without a context of the sort that long, routine acquaintance provides, it becomes more difficult to advise a client in any but instrumental terms, and in particular to answer the questions of ultimate ends that extraordinary situations often pose for the client's human representatives (for example, whether the incumbent management of a company should resist an unsolicited tender offer on the grounds that it will destroy their company's special identity by undermining various of its goals—which may include more than the maximization of shareholder profit in the crudest dollar terms—or instead welcome the offer as a means of reforming the company along lines that even they, on disinterested reflection, can approve).[49]

An analogy from the sphere of personal life may help to clarify my point. Suppose that someone you do not know asks for your advice at a moment of crisis in his life. Assuming you lack the time to get acquainted, what kind of advice can you give him? One possibility is simply to take as given his own statement of what he believes his present needs to be—however incomplete or contradictory that statement may appear—and then help him frame a plan for meeting these needs in the most efficient way. Alternatively, you can help him devise a strategy that makes sense whatever his interests may be, and whether, in particular, they are what he believes them to be or not: a strategy, for example, of delay, if it seems likely that matters will be clearer later on and there is little cost to waiting. There is one thing, however, that you are likely to find quite difficult to do, and that is to advise the person who has sought your help as to what his interests should be. For advice of this sort generally requires a more extensive knowledge of the person's character, habits, and history—the sort of knowledge that friends often have and that sometimes even makes it plausible for one friend to claim a better understanding of another's interests than that person himself possesses.[50]

Something like this is also true of institutions, including the commercial ones that make up the clientele of most large law firms. It is, of course, a fiction to speak of the aims and interests of an institution, for in reality these can never be anything more than the aims and interests of the individuals who compose it. But that does not make it nonsensical to say that questions can arise concerning an institution's ends. For there may be uncertainty within the minds of the individuals who are responsible for managing it as to what its ends should be, or conflict between different individuals, or groups of individuals, who each have some share in this responsibility. In either case, it may become important to decide which of the conflicting conceptions of an institution's aims and interests is the best one, and this is most likely to happen at extraordinary moments of crisis or disruption, as in the lives of individuals.

The lawyer who is asked to help his corporate client through such a crisis is likely to find, however, that he has little to contribute to this decision if he is meeting the client for the first time and thus lacks a context of routine encounters in which to assess conflicting claims about the client's aims—for the same reason that a stranger will in general have less to contribute than a friend to another person's deliberations concerning his own ends. A lack of familiarity with the person or institution in question prevents one, in each case, from entering as fully as one might into the process of third-personal deliberation, the process of deliberating with and for another about the other's ends. That is not to say that lawyers whose practice is essentially transactional are incapable of offering such help. But the more the relationship to a client approximates a one-time encounter between strangers, the more difficult it becomes for a lawyer to provide deliberative assistance of this kind in a dependable way. And to the extent that is true, the more the help a lawyer does offer is likely to be of an exclusively instrumental sort.

In some cases, to be sure, instrumental help is all, and in every case it is a part, of what a lawyer is expected to provide. To be helpful in this way, moreover, is often both a challenge and (where one succeeds) a satisfaction. But this is not the only kind of help for which lawyers are commonly asked, nor do I think it either the most challenging or most satisfying kind to provide. The most demanding and also most rewarding function that lawyers perform is to help their clients decide what it is they really want, to help them make up their minds as to what their ends should be, a function that differs importantly from the instrumental servicing of preestablished goals. It is this enterprise of codeliberation that the lawyer-statesman ideal places at the center of the lawyer's professional life. The new transactional style of large-firm practice, with its emphasis on the exceptional and its detachment from the routine, makes this enterprise more difficult by narrowing the field within which it can be responsibly pursued. To that extent, the growing dominance of this style, though unavoidable, perhaps, in economic terms, represents a threat to the core of the lawyer-statesman ideal.

The second way in which the work of large-firm lawyers has grown narrower—its increasing restriction to specific subject-matter specialties—has similar implications. The demand for greater specialization is pervasive in the law today, and one sees its effects at every level and in every institutional setting. In the most general sense, this demand is simply a response to the law's growing volume and complexity, to changes in the legal culture that no lawyer can avoid. But at large firms this general pressure is further aggravated by the transformation of the lawyer-client relationship along the lines I have described. For the more transactional this relationship becomes, the more likely it is that any individual lawyer will in his or her practice see only one kind of problem, over and over again, rather than a wide range of problems, as might be expected if dealings with clients were (as they used to be) more continuous and routine.

Even more than most, lawyers in large firms are thus encouraged to become subject-matter specialists by the kind of practice they now have. One important consequence of this is a decrease in the ability of any single lawyer to see a client's problem whole and to address all the issues it presents. To provide their clients with full coverage, therefore, most large firms must now assemble teams of specialists, each of whose members contributes some focal expertise and has responsibility for a discrete part of the client's total situation.

But though a firm can offer its clients full coverage in this sense, there is something that a generalist possesses which a team of specialists does not: the capacity to synthesize, to integrate from a single point of view all the considerations that the client's case presents. The more narrowly specialized his advisers become, the more likely it is that the client will have to provide this point of view himself, and decide what should be made of the various specialized recommendations he receives. In one sense, of course, that decision is always the client's, whatever his lawyers are like, since he must decide, in every case, whether to accept their advice or not. Still, what most clients, including corporate clients, want from their lawyers is not just a string of discrete judgments about various aspects of their problem, but deliberative advice as to what they should do, all things considered. The ability to give such advice is what distinguishes the wise counselor from the technocrat. But to give responsible advice of this sort, a lawyer needs, among other things, an understanding of the client's entire situation, not just some portion of it. And that is precisely what the subject-matter specialization of large-firm practice has made more difficult to attain.

Without a comprehensive understanding of the client's situation, the only advice a lawyer can offer is conditional or hypothetical: "If you wish to do this or that, then I advise you to pursue the following course of action." What one cannot do is recommend, unconditionally, that a client whose ends are conflicting embrace one goal rather than another. To make that sort of recommendation, a lawyer must be able to see the client's predicament from a single integrative point of view, in the same way that the client himself does or at least aspires to. That, however, is just the kind of advice clients often want, and the lawyer who cannot give it because he cannot see a client's problem whole must resign himself to playing the role of a technician: not, of course, an unhelpful role, but a different and more limited one than that of a lawyer-statesman.

The point that I am making can be stated simply. In recent years, large-firm law practice has narrowed in two ways. It has become more episodic or transactional, with contact between firm and client being limited increasingly to extraordinary situations with few routine dealings in between. For many of the lawyers involved, it has become more specialized along subject-matter lines as well. Each of these changes has narrowed the kind of advice that corporate clients are likely to demand from outside firms and that the lawyers in these firms are competent to give. Deliberative advice—advice about the ends a client ought to choose, as opposed to the means for reaching ends already chosen—presupposes a familiarity with the client's past and a breadth of understanding of his or her present situation, which the movement toward a more transactional and specialized form of law practice has gone a long way toward destroying in the country's largest firms. As a result, lawyers in these firms are today less often called upon than they were a generation ago to give advice that requires real prudence as distinct from technical knowledge.

Prudence or practical wisdom is a trait of character that can be acquired, moreover, only through the experience of having to make the sorts of decisions that demand it—only through an extended apprenticeship in judgment. The fewer the occasions on which a lawyer is required to exercise practical wisdom, the less likely he is to develop it. That, I think, is what is happening in the country's large law firms today. The lawyers in these firms are becoming transactional specialists whose narrow relationships with their clients give the clients little reason to ask for the lawyers' deliberative advice, and the lawyers themselves limited experience at providing it. Today, the corporations that constitute the core of the large firm's clientele often look to others for advice of this sort—for example, to investment bankers, who in this generation have assumed many of the general advisory functions that lawyers once performed.[51] The lawyers in these firms have been left, as a result, with a more limited role to play in the transactions on which they work, a largely technical role that demands less practical wisdom and offers fewer opportunities for its development. Eventually, perhaps, the lawyer who sees his professional function in these terms may even begin to wonder whether practical wisdom has any value at all, and openly reject the ideal of the lawyer-statesman—which seems irrelevant to his work—in favor of the very different ideal of the expert with its emphasis on knowledge and technique and its disregard for character.

Of course many lawyers in large firms are not yet prepared to abandon the first of these ideals for the second, at least in a candid and self-conscious way. For they understand, if only viscerally, that such a substitution of ideals would strike at the heart of their own professional self-respect. But the twofold narrowing of the lawyer-client relationship that has reshaped the nature of large-firm practice is nonetheless pushing steadily in this direction and has created an environment in which the lawyer-statesman ideal is less likely to survive, whether its demise be viewed with approval or regret.

A CHANGE OF CLIMATE

The changing character of the large law firm's internal culture, as distinguished from its external relationships with clients, is a second factor that is pressing in the same direction too. By "culture" I mean, broadly speaking, the attitudes and interests that the members of a group share and that define, for them, the point or purpose of their participation in it. Like those engaged in other collaborative activities, the lawyers practicing in large firms share a culture in this sense. But in the last generation their culture has changed quite radically, and while in one respect at least the change has been beneficial, in another it has not. For the cultural milieu that large-firm lawyers now inhabit repudiates not only the worst prejudices of the past but its highest ideals of craftsmanship and character as well. The culture of America's large law firms is today more open and equitable than ever before, but at the same time it is less hospitable to the ideal of the lawyer-statesman. It is a freer culture than its predecessor, but also a less elevated one, a meaner culture, less able to sustain a belief in the value of the virtues that the ideal of the lawyer-statesman represents.

One important distinction between the culture of today's large firm and that of its predecessor a generation ago is the former's comparative openness in a social, economic, and religious sense. Thirty years ago, most of the lawyers practicing in large firms saw their work as a way of making a comfortable living, exactly as their counterparts today do. But they had other things in common too. To begin with the most obvious ones, they were nearly all white males and, in many firms, predominantly Protestant as well. Thirty years ago, only a handful of women and even fewer blacks could be found in the country's largest firms, and though the traditional unwillingness of Protestant firms to hire Jews and Catholics was beginning to break down, most large firms (including the Jewish ones) had a dominant, and often exclusive, religious identity. Beyond these there were other important commonalities—those of social background and education, for example—which together with the ties of race, sex, and religion gave the elite circle of large-firm lawyers thirty years ago a greater degree of solidarity than the mere desire to make a good living could ever by itself produce.[52]

This solidarity was expressed in many ways: in the clubs they joined, the hobbies they pursued, the charities they supported, the schools they sent their children to, and the neighborhoods they chose to live in. There were eccentrics, of course, who did not conform to the pattern. But a pattern certainly existed, and it was sufficiently englobing to define, with some leeway for personal inventiveness, an entire way of life. In short, most of the lawyers working in large firms thirty years ago not only saw their work as a way of making a good living, but agreed, as well, in their conception of what living well implied. The internal culture of the large firm of the preceding generation was to that extent defined by the outlook of a particular socioeconomic class and shared its peculiarities and limitations.

The same cannot be said today. No one will deny that large firms continue, in important ways, to be socially homogeneous institutions, but it is equally obvious that they are far less closed than in the past. The once-clear line, for example, between Jewish and gentile firms has blurred considerably, and Jews now have little reason to fear that they will be discouraged from applying to a particular firm, or rejected for a position in it, on the grounds of their religion (though instances of anti-Semitism still occasionally occur). The position of women is more complicated, but also vastly different from what it was a generation ago. Today women are joining large firms in numbers that are roughly proportionate to their representation in the pool of qualified applicants, and there is little evidence that large firms still discriminate against women on a systematic basis at the initial hiring stage (though here, too, there are occasional instances of overt sexism and allegations of a subtler but more pervasive discrimination in the assignment of work and promotion to partnership).[53] The real challenge that women in large firms now face, and that continues to make their position an uncertain one, is the challenge of finding the time and energy to do their jobs in the way and on the terms their firms demand, while also meeting family responsibilities, in particular those associated with child rearing, which in our society still fall more heavily on women than on men. So long as this continues to be true (and only a shift in certain basic attitudes and practices can change it), women working in large firms will remain at a competitive disadvantage vis-à-vis their male peers.[54] But however great an obstacle to the full professional equality of women these deeply entrenched social roles may be, the fact remains that women are today a presence in large firms in a way and on a scale they have never been before. Indeed, of the various groups that large firms once excluded—women, Jews, blacks, and, to a lesser extent, Catholics—only blacks are still not a significant presence in them, and even here there are some signs of change.[55]

In other respects, too, today's large law firm is more diversified than its predecessor. The lawyers working in such firms are now recruited from a wider ranger of schools, and though lawyers from the top schools still predominate, the number being hired from lesser schools is growing (a fact that may in part be explained by the greater personnel needs generated by recent increases in firm size).[56] There is some evidence as well—though so far very limited—which suggests that the new recruits being hired by large firms today come from a wider range of socioeconomic backgrounds, including, in particular, working-class ones, compared with their counterparts a generation ago.[57] In these ways, too, along with the other more obvious ones that I have mentioned, the large law firm has become a less homogeneous institution, an institution less sharply defined than its predecessor was along specific religious, sexual, racial, educational, and class lines.

The blurring of these lines has necessarily reshaped the large firm's internal culture. As the membership of these firms has become more diverse, the loose consensus that once existed among the lawyers working in them regarding the most appropriate patterns for living has begun to fray and, in certain respects, has broken down completely. There is still, of course, a common interest in material well-being—the shared desire to make a good living—but less agreement on the concrete details of what living well entails. The lawyers in large firms today come to them with a greater diversity of interests and experiences, and though their work itself exerts, to some degree, an homogenizing influence, this diversity inevitably affects the way they choose to live their lives after working hours. A generation ago, there was a strong tendency for lawyers in these firms to converge on a single, relatively well-defined way of life, given their uniformity of background and social position. With increasing diversity that tendency has weakened, and the widespread acceptance of a single common way of life has given way to a variety of "life-styles" (a term that itself emphasizes diversity and personal choice as against custom, tradition, and the habitual acceptance of a settled pattern of living).

One important cause of this has been the opening of the world of large-firm practice to groups that were before unfairly excluded from it. This is a positive change and one we have every reason to approve. Nostalgia for the narrow, nonprofessional solidarity that large-firm practice afforded in the past—the solidarity of a socially, sexually, and religiously closed class—must not obscure the moral gain that this increase in openness represents.

But if the move toward greater openness marks an important positive change in the culture of large firms, it has been accompanied by a second and more ominous change that I can best describe by returning, for a moment, to my earlier starting point. Lawyers working in large firms thirty years ago saw their jobs as a way of making a living just as those working in such firms today do. But they did not see their work in purely instrumental terms, as nothing but a means for making money. Indeed, until quite recently the culture of large-firm practice tended to encourage the different view that whatever its instrumental value, the work of lawyers is also inherently rewarding and offers satisfactions that make the doing of it valuable for its own sake. In the past this view was reflected in and reinforced by the unwillingness of lawyers working in large firms to speak too openly, even among themselves, about their incomes or financial relations—in particular, about the methods employed for determining partnership shares. In the culture of the large firm, money matters of all sorts were traditionally shrouded in a kind of genteel obscurity, as Erwin Smigel discovered, to his frustration, when he attempted to answer the straightforward question of how much money Wall Street lawyers make.[58]

It would be wrong to conclude that at the time of Smigel's study lawyers working in large firms did not care about how much they made or how well off they were compared with others. Many, no doubt, cared about these things intensely. What the general atmosphere of mystery surrounding money matters does suggest, however, is that the lawyers Smigel studied felt it was improper to be too candid or explicit about their interest in money, and viewed expressions of such interest as breaches of an ancient professional ethic rooted in the belief that the law is an honorable calling and not just a commercial enterprise—the source of the lawyer's traditional status pride.[59]

This very old idea has often been expressed, by twentieth-century American lawyers, in terms of the concept of craft, the idea that the law is a craft demanding a cultivated subtlety of judgment whose possession constitutes a valuable trait of character, as distinct from mere technical skill, and which therefore justifies the special sort of pride that the possession of such a trait affords.[60] Refusing to talk too openly about money has in the past been one of the ways in which large-firm lawyers (who of course have always made more money than most others in the profession) have signaled their allegiance to the ideal of character that the notion of craftsmanship implies. Lawyers working in large firms a generation ago may not have cared any less about money than their counterparts today do, but the culture of their firms, which discouraged too open an expression of interest in it, reflected a widespread belief that lawyers *ought* at least to care about other things, and perhaps even assign them a higher value, however much they cared about money in fact. It represented a publicly expressed commitment to a professional ideal that portrayed success in the practice of law as an intrinsic good and not just an instrumental one—a commitment to the good of craftsmanship and to the conception of professional character associated with it. However far short they fell of meeting its demands, this ideal was for large-firm lawyers thirty years ago an important part of their cultural milieu.

By contrast, the culture of today's large firm not only tolerates a degree of candor about money that would have seemed completely unprofessional a generation ago, but actively encourages lawyers to be more and more exclusively preoccupied with it. This new openness about money is visible everywhere: in trade publications, like *The American Lawyer,* which have done so much to make the income of lawyers and firms a matter of public knowledge and whose unembarrassed fascination with moneymaking most large firms, after an initial period of resistance, now endorse and indeed help to sustain (by voluntarily providing these publications with much of the information they request concerning the firms' own internal finances); in the increased number and frequency of conferences designed for large firms and devoted entirely to questions of financial management; in the open use of advertising and other market-oriented techniques to boost firm revenue, and the employment of specialized consultants with training in these fields; and, above all, in the widespread adoption of new fee- and compensation-setting practices that link firm income to client profits and tie the compensation of individual lawyers more exclusively to economic performance than to seniority.[61] In these and other ways, the moneymaking side of large-firm practice is today more visible than in the past, a clearer focus of self-conscious effort and concern.

Some consider this refreshingly honest, the candid acknowledgment of what before was disingenuously concealed, and for that reason view it as a cultural advance.[62] But this view misses something important. A culture that reinforces the idea that the practice of law affords deeper satisfactions than the mere production of income is bound to affect the ideals lawyers share—the standards to which they feel an allegiance whether they live up to them or not—and thus to exert a strong counterpressure against the natural interest that lawyers have always had in making money, an interest that hardly needs to be sustained by artificial means, cultural or otherwise. And if a lawyer's professional ideals have even a slight influence on his or her actions (which only the most jaded cynic will deny), the existence of a cultural norm that portrays success in the practice of law as an intrinsic good of greater importance than the money it produces is bound to have behavioral consequences too. When this norm is relaxed, or reversed, as it has been in recent years, the counterpressure is removed and the interest in moneymaking begins inevitably to play a larger role in defining the aims of professional life, a development whose desirability is not established merely by observing that it represents an increase in candor for the lawyers involved.

What effect has the preoccupation with moneymaking that characterizes today's large firm had on the lawyer-statesman ideal? On the whole, I think, it has helped to make that ideal less credible than before. One way in which it has done this is by putting the idea of a private career punctuated by periods of public service in a less appealing light. If the point of practicing law is to make as much money as one can, a lawyer in a large firm who is earning a substantial income will be understandably reluctant to take time out in the middle of his career, when his earning power is at its peak, to enter public service, where compensation even at the highest levels is certain to be lower. Today the gap between the income of most large-firm lawyers and what they can expect to earn in public service is greater than it was a generation ago, in both absolute and relative terms.[63] This widening gap has itself helped to undermine the traditional pattern of movement back and forth between these spheres. But the disintegration of this pattern has been hastened, too, by the new insistence on the priority of money as a good, for the more one accepts the ranking of values this implies, the more troubling any gap in income, however large, is bound to seem.

Even if we concentrate on just that part of their careers which large-firm lawyers spend in private practice, there are reasons to believe that the preoccupation with moneymaking which is such a striking feature of their present culture is antagonistic to the ideal of the lawyer-statesman. To the extent, for example, that a firm makes the maximization of profit its primary objective, it will naturally tend to choose clients, and to select among areas of practice, on the basis of their financial prospects, which may or may not correspond to the opportunities these offer for the exercise of prudence or practical wisdom. Thus, for example, in the 1980s one area of large-firm practice that grew with spectacular rapidity was the field of mergers and acquisitions, and an area that by contrast shrank quite dramatically was trusts and estates.[64] The reason is not difficult to discern. Mergers and acquisitions is—or at least was—an immensely profitable area of practice, in part because it lends itself more easily than other areas do to different forms of event-based billing that link the compensation of lawyers to the magnitude of a given transaction rather than to the time expended on it. Trusts and estates, by comparison, has become increasingly unprofitable, one reason being the reluctance or inability of lawyers in this field to move away from the traditional practice of hourly compensation.[65] But although a firm's decision to expand the first area and contract the second can therefore easily be justified in economic terms, such a strategy may in the end reduce its lawyers' opportunities for significant third-personal deliberation. For while the field of mergers and acquisitions has an episodic and specialized character that exerts a narrowing influence in the two respects described above, the relation between a trusts and estates lawyer and his clients tends to be both more continuous and more comprehensive—more attuned to the whole of a client's situation—and might indeed be viewed as a model for the kind of third-personal deliberation that genuine counseling of any sort involves. The force of this example will naturally vary from firm to firm. My general point is simply that changes in the practice of a firm may sometimes limit the extent to which its lawyers are called upon to give deliberative advice, and in the culture of today's large firm, with its heavy emphasis on money, such limitations will not be given significant weight.

In this culture, moreover, the lawyers who are most likely to be singled out for special praise are those who have worked on the largest transactions and produced the most income for their firms.[66] More and more these have become predominant considerations in the distribution not only of tangible benefits such as promotion and partnership draw, but of intangible ones as well, such as prestige and professional standing. To be sure, some lawyers who generate a large amount of money for their firms do so because they possess exceptional judgment. But these two things—excellence in deliberation and success in moneymaking—do not always go together, and a lawyer may be an outstanding moneymaker for many unrelated reasons (entrepreneurial skill at marketing a new legal product, ability to administer efficiently a large team of other lawyers, technical expertise, personal contacts, and so on). Indeed, the connection between these skills, on the one hand, and success at making money, on the other, seems on the whole to be a closer and more obvious one than the connection between deliberative wisdom and financial success.

No one will deny that entrepreneurial skill, administrative ability, and the other traits I have just mentioned contribute importantly to a firm's success; in fact, they are vital to it. But the greater the emphasis that is placed on profitability pure and simple, the more these traits, whose contribution to this goal is easier to discern, move to the center of attention and become the dominant virtues in the culture of a firm, displacing the older ones represented by the lawyer-statesman to the margin of cultural regard. The relevance of the lawyer-statesman's virtues to professional success is thereby obscured and his role as a hero figure taken over by the dealmaker, the business-getter, the legal entrepreneur. The outlook of young lawyers, in particular, cannot help but be affected by this substitution of ideals. In the culture of today's large firm, the lawyer-statesman is an anachronistic ornament, and those just entering the culture are encouraged to look elsewhere for their models of success. How these new recruits see themselves, and what they understand the point or purpose of their work to be, must shift as a result.

Finally, and most important, the fascination with moneymaking that pervades large-firm practice today tends, in a subtle but significant way, to unsettle the delicate balance of sympathy and detachment in which practical wisdom consists. It does so in two different, and indeed opposite, ways. First, by encouraging lawyers to pay more-vigilant attention to the financial consequences of their work, a culturally reinforced preoccupation with money makes it more difficult to sustain the kind of self-forgetfulness required to deliberate for and with another person on his or her own behalf. To do so successfully, a lawyer must be able to lose himself in that other person's situation, to see it from within in a way that makes it possible for him not just to name but to appreciate the interests, values, and ambitions that inform it. This demands that he temporarily suspend his own interests, for only by doing so can he clear an affective space in which his client's interests may be entertained with real feeling. But the more preoccupied a lawyer is with money, and hence with his own welfare, the more difficult he will find it to suspend his self-interest in this way. We might say that a preoccupation with money is an obstacle to sympathy. By contrast, a culture that downplays the importance of money, in the way that most large firms did thirty years ago, deploys its normative resources not on behalf of but in opposition to self-interest, and thereby empowers the capacity for sympathy, instead of blocking it as the regnant culture of large firms now tends to do.

If a preoccupation with moneymaking is an obstacle to sympathy, it makes detachment harder to achieve as well. Most clients of large firms are businesses primarily concerned with making money, and like any other passion this one can distort deliberation too—for example, by encouraging a concentration on short-term, easily monetizable considerations to the exclusion of more-ambiguous long-term ones that may have greater importance; or, more significantly, by causing a client to fail to ask whether the course of action that will yield the most money is the best one overall. These sorts of issues do not, of course, arise in every case; indeed, they tend to be exceptional. But it is precisely when they do arise that real deliberative assistance is generally required. The lawyer who shares his client's passionate concern for money may find it difficult, however, to avoid the same distortions in his own deliberations. Every lawyer of course has his own personal interests and desires. But the less congruent these are with those of a given client, the easier it will be for him to explore that client's situation in a spirit of detachment, free of the particular passions in whose grip the client is caught.

So long as the lawyers working in large firms did not think of themselves primarily as moneymakers whose main aim was to produce as much income as they could, a significant gap remained between their outlook and that of their clients, who tended, then as now, to put the goal of moneymaking first. The existence of this gap was an aid to deliberative detachment. But an increasing concern with money has brought the interests of these lawyers more closely into alignment with those of their clients—an alignment symbolized by the percentage-fee arrangements some firms have now begun to use—and this has made detachment more difficult for large-firm lawyers to sustain. Thus viewed from one perspective, an emphasis on money leads to a preoccupation with first-personal concerns that blocks the forgetfulness of self that sympathy requires. It makes it more difficult for a lawyer to get close to his client, to see the client's situation from within. But viewed from another vantage point, the same shift in attitude also makes it harder for a lawyer to give business clients disinterested advice (which is one reason why percentage-fee arrangements have traditionally been disfavored).[67] The shift toward a more aggressively commercial legal culture thus tends, at the same time though in different ways, to stifle each of the two powers in whose union deliberative wisdom consists and thereby to attack the lawyer-statesman ideal at its roots.

THE WORKING DAY

For a lawyer's work to have any point at all, there must be some things that he values for their own sake, to which his work can be related. But if he views his work in instrumental terms, as a means for making money, these intrinsic goods by definition cannot be found within it.

They must therefore be located in the sphere of life that lies beyond the office and begins at the end of the working day.

For the lawyers who are now working in large firms there is a cruel irony in this, for the very process of commercialization that has transformed the culture of these firms and placed the internal goods of craftsmanship in doubt has also led to a significant increase in the time and energy their work demands, and left them with less of both to do the things that make personal life rewarding. The simple fact is that lawyers in large firms today work substantially longer hours than they did ten or fifteen years ago. To be sure, there is still a great deal of variation from one firm to the next and even more among geographical regions. But despite these differences in pace, the general trend everywhere has for some time now been toward a lengthening working day.

Simple economic considerations help in part to explain why this is so. Up to a point, the owners of a firm—the partners who control it—can increase their profits merely by increasing their own hours. The more importance they attach to making money, therefore, the longer the hours they themselves will work. But this strategy has built-in limits, even for those who are able to do without much personal life or sleep. Once these limits have been reached, the only way the owners of a law firm can increase their profits further is by hiring additional legal laborers, called associates, at a fixed salary and then charging a fee for their work in excess of its cost (salary plus allocable overhead). An associate who has been hired at a fixed salary must work a certain number of hours merely to repay the partners of the firm for their investment in him (which increases as starting salaries rise). But every additional hour the associate works beyond that increases the partners' profits. In a legal culture that emphasizes money-making and gives it precedence over other goods, there will therefore be a tendency for the partners of a firm to increase not only their own working day but that of their associates as well, up to a limit defined by the prevailing local norm regarding the number of hours that associates at large firms are generally expected to work.

Instead of remaining stable, however, this conventional limit has steadily increased, and the constraints on what a firm can demand of its associates have substantially weakened as a result. One reason why is that the terms on which associates compete among themselves have changed. The associates in a law firm are in competition, primarily for partnerships but also for prestige within the firm and help in finding positions outside it, if and when they leave. To obtain these goods, an associate must outperform his or her peers in what are collectively understood to be the relevant respects. Various considerations come into play here (technical competence, ability to generate new business, sociability, and the like), but one factor in particular, the number of hours an associate bills, has in the last ten years or so grown in importance relative to the others. The increased emphasis on hours billed as a criterion for measuring associate performance—which reflects in part the cultural devaluation of other attributes less directly connected to the external good of moneymaking and in part the administrative need for a uniform quantitative standard of evaluation in firms whose size makes more-qualitative criteria unworkable—has in turn propelled the competition of associates more and more in this direction. Increasingly, associates at large firms themselves equate success—promotion and prestige—with hours billed. The most competitive associates therefore have reasons of their own to accept a longer working day, indeed actively to promote it, and even those who are less concerned about succeeding must adjust to the heightened expectations raised by these Stakhanovites of law.

Technical developments have also played a role here. For example, the introduction of the computer (and before that, of copying machines) has meant a sharp reduction in the time that lawyers need to wait for the production and revision of legal documents, and that in turn has made it possible for them to work uninterruptedly for longer periods, a tendency reinforced by the decision of many large firms to provide their lawyers with twenty-four-hour secretarial support. In general, whether a lawyer can accomplish anything of value by extending his or her working day depends, among other things, upon the speed with which various ministerial tasks can be performed. For if one's own work requires their completion, as it often does, the longer these tasks take, the more likely one is to go home than to remain in the office waiting for them to be done. In that sense, the limits of a lawyer's productive working day are at any given moment determined by technical conditions as well as by purely physiological ones, and in recent years these technical limits have been pushed further and further back, making it possible for lawyers to extend their working day up to the point that physical endurance will permit: a possibility that the increasing competitiveness of large-firm practice and the commercialism of the firm's own internal culture create powerful incentives to exploit.

My main concern here, however, is not with the causes of the lengthened day that lawyers in large firms now work. These causes are multiple and complex, and reflect changes of a cultural, technical, and economic sort. I am primarily interested instead in the meaning of this change for the individuals involved. What does the lengthening of a lawyer's working day mean in concrete human terms? Suppose (just to fix ideas) that a lawyer's billed hours increase from, say, 1600 to 2000 a year. If we assume a 48-week working year, this represents an increase of over 8 billed hours a week, from a little more than 33 to almost 42. Of course these numbers do not reflect the actual length of the working week, since not all of the time that even the most efficient lawyer spends in the office can be billed to clients. But what I want to focus on now are the consequences of the incremental change that I have postulated. Where will my imaginary lawyer find the additional eight hours each week that I am assuming he or she now works?

Perhaps they will be taken, in one bite, from weekend time, which means the reduction of the weekend to a single day (if that). Or perhaps the eight hours will be spread over the entire week. For most lawyers, who must conform their schedules to those of courts and clients, this means a working day that ends later rather than begins earlier; that, in any case, is how things generally work out. But the difference between leaving the office at, say, six P.M., and leaving two hours later at eight is an enormous one. The lawyer who leaves at six still has time for dinner and an evening's recreation of some kind. For those with small children, there is time to see and play with them before they go to bed. But the lawyer who leaves at eight is in a different situation, especially if he or she is married and has a family. Where, in what remains of the evening, can the time be found to do these things or, more important perhaps, the energy? To gauge accurately the consequences of increasing one's working hours by a few each week—an increase that in fractional terms may seem quite small—it is important to remember that these new hours come on top of an already demanding schedule and have a marginal personal cost that rises with each increment. In its consumption of the time and energy that would otherwise be available for private ends, each additional hour a lawyer works is more costly than the hour worked before. Translating hours added (a quantitative concept) into weekends and evenings lost (a qualitative one) simply makes this point more vivid.

For many lawyers working in large firms, the lengthening of the working day is a cause of personal unhappiness. That is understandable enough. And for those who see the practice of law in the way their professional culture encourages them to—as a means for making money to be spent on other things—it can contribute to a sense of self-defeat as well. But apart from these direct harms, the longer day that lawyers in large firms now work also indirectly threatens the professional ideal of the lawyer-statesman by compounding the pressure that other changes in the nature of their practice have put on it already.

That practical wisdom is a dispositional trait, or combination of such traits, and not a form of expertise, has been a main theme of this book. To have practical wisdom, I have said, a lawyer must be able to combine the opposing qualities of sympathy and detachment, and while some, perhaps, find this easy to do, most learn how only through a process of discipline and training that runs against the grain of other, more primitive feelings. The object of this process is to force the person undergoing it to entertain the widest possible diversity of points of view, and to explore these in a mood of deepening sympathy, while retaining the spirit of aloofness on which sound judgment also critically depends. Breadth of experience, real or vicarious, is an essential component of this process. Hence the narrower a lawyer's experience—before law school, in it, or afterward—the less developed his or her capacity for joining these two attitudes is likely to be. That is why the increasing narrowness of large-firm practice must itself be viewed as a threat to the lawyer-statesman ideal. Yet even if the professional experience of those working in large firms has narrowed, and therefore lost much of its value as a training ground for judgment, there is more to life than work, and experiences other than professional ones. Even the lawyer whose practice is most technical and narrowly confined, and therefore least likely to afford the broad acquaintance with suffering and ambition on which sound judgment generally depends, has a private life and personal experiences, and it is possible, at least, that these provide a substitute for what is missing in his work. If so, he may acquire good judgment after all, and to the extent that his work allows, employ it there as well. But it is just this possibility that the lengthening of the working day increasingly rules out.

There are many ways to broaden one's experience other than through work. One may broaden it, for example, through travel or vicariously by reading, and there is no reason to think that lawyers travel or read less than their counterparts in other professions. But there are different ways in which a person can do these things. Thus both traveling and reading may be done for entertainment or, in a more serious spirit, for the sake of education, in order to expand one's horizon of knowledge and experience. Often, of course, one's motives will be mixed: a person may want both to be amused and to learn something from the experience. Indeed, it is rare to want one or the other of these exclusively. But though they frequently appear in combination, and may in any given case be difficult to disentangle, these attitudes are not identical, and it is possible to perform the same act—to take the same trip or read the same book—more in the spirit of one than of the other.

Entertainment is passive; the expression "to be entertained" itself reflects this. Learning, by contrast, is active, and the expression "to be learned" can be meaningfully applied only to the object of a learning experience and not to the person undergoing it. There is clearly something paradoxical about this, for the person who seeks education rather than amusement is attempting to open himself up to an experience or an idea, to put himself in a position to receive and comprehend it: a position of passivity. But the kind of passivity that learning entails can itself be achieved only through discipline and effort. To learn something, to put myself in a position to encounter something new, I must suspend certain, at least, of my existing prejudices, and though the goal of this exercise might be described as a state of passive openness, I need to expend some energy to reach it. The passivity that is involved in being entertained is a different, indeed nearly opposite, condition. I achieve this condition not by detaching myself from my existing attitudes and feelings but by abandoning myself to them more completely. In entertainment, I give myself over to my prejudices instead of making an effort to suspend them, as I must to extend my understanding of how other people live and what they care about. And that is why the more a person devotes himself, outside his work, to entertainment—the more he travels and reads and does whatever else he does for the sake of amusement alone—the less likely his experience of human life is to widen as a result.

The longer a lawyer's working day, however, the less energy he or she will have at the end of it for anything but entertainment. How many lawyers, after twelve hours in the office, have enough energy left to read or do anything else in a spirit of self-education, to summon the discipline and stamina that every effort of this sort requires? Most are likely to find that all they can do is replenish their exhausted reserves of energy. Replenishment means consumption: of food and sleep, most obviously, but also of entertainment, which is a kind of consumption too. Entertainment is restorative in the same way that food and sleep are. It is a way of taking one's mind "off" things, of giving the mind a rest so that its exhausted powers can restore themselves. Perhaps a few heroically endowed individuals will be capable of more—of reading, for example, not to give their powers of perception a reprieve but to sharpen and extend them. But the longer a lawyer's working day, the less likely this becomes, for lawyers are subject to the same physiological laws that affect everyone else. The more a lawyer works, the more he will want, at the end of the day, merely to be entertained: to be restored, to be passive, to consume. And hence the more he will be drawn to unchallenging activities that put no pressure on him to extend the limits of his experience, but that allow him to sink down comfortably within these limits instead.

I do not mean to imply that there is anything wrong with entertainment. It is a good, like food, and like food its preparation and presentation is an art. Indeed, life seems to me unthinkable without it. But its passivity makes entertainment a poor vehicle for the broadening of experience on which the cultivation of practical wisdom depends. And that is why the lengthening of the working day, which encourages such passivity, makes it ever more implausible to think that what a lawyer does outside the office can compensate for the narrowness of the work he does within it by prodding him to develop his powers of judgment in other ways.

Recent changes in large-firm practice—greater size, a more detailed division of labor, and a shift toward transactional relationships with clients—have tended to narrow the professional experience of the lawyers working in these firms, and put pressure on the lawyer-statesman ideal from within. The lengthening of the working day intensifies this pressure and makes it less reasonable to hope for a compensatory widening of experience outside the realm of work. But that is not the worst of it. For the extension of the working day also subtly reshapes the internal culture of the firm itself. Working a sixty- or seventy-hour week can be physically and mentally grueling under the best of circumstances. The lawyers who will find it easiest to adapt, however, are likely to be those whose personal lives are the least demanding in time and energy—who have no extraprofessional interests or involvements for which they feel they must reserve some portion of their strength. These are the lawyers most likely to succeed under the working conditions that prevail in many large firms today and to emerge, within their own professional culture, as its heroes. But the reduction of energy-consuming extraprofessional involvements that makes it easier for them to maintain the stamina their lengthened working day requires makes them shallower people too, whose imaginative powers shrink as the boundaries of their experience do. Instead of being viewed with alarm, however, these very limitations are today increasingly perceived as strengths or virtues, and held up as part of a new professional ideal: the ideal of the lawyer who cares about nothing but work and is prepared to sacrifice all of his or her personal energies to it, regardless of how narrow and dull the work becomes. In addition to its other consequences, then, the lengthening of the working day has also had a reactive effect on the internal culture of the large law firm itself, and the new ideal of success that it encourages, which depicts narrowness of interests and absence of attachments as advantages from a professional point of view, not only differs from the ideal of the lawyer-statesman, but inverts it.

ALTERNATIVES

The environment of large-firm practice is today less supportive of the lawyer-statesman ideal than it was a generation ago. Just how much less is debatable and in any case impossible to quantify. But the overall direction of change is clear. In part the change is due to a shift in the pattern of firm-client relationships, in part to a more deliberate emphasis on moneymaking, and in part simply to the lengthening of the working day. Other factors, including technological ones, have also played a role. And these developments have all been mutually reinforcing. Together, they have put the lawyer-statesman ideal under stress by making it more difficult for those working in large firms to cultivate the virtues this ideal celebrates or even to see that they are virtues at all. Thirty years ago these firms played an important role in sustaining the credibility of this ideal within the profession as a whole. In many ways, they were its standard-bearers and representatives. Today that is no longer the case.

But even if large-firm practice is no longer supportive of the lawyer-statesman ideal, there may be other institutions that are. And if that is true, there may still be a home within the profession for those lawyers who view the development and exercise of deliberative wisdom as an important good.

Where, more concretely, might one look for such alternatives? Are there, in fact, institutional settings that today are more congenial to the lawyer-statesman ideal which could conceivably replace the large firm as its carrier? Two possibilities are sometimes mentioned in this regard. One is the in-house corporate law department, whose own growth and increased professional capacity have importantly affected the work that large firms do. The other is the small-to-mid-sized firm, the firm large enough to have an interestingly diverse practice well beyond the range of the merely ministerial, yet not so big as to be burdened with the problems of its larger competitors. In each case, there is something to be said for the view that the institution in question offers a more hospitable environment than most large firms now do for those drawn to the professional values I have defended in this book. But there are other reasons for doubting whether either can provide a stable home for these values or secure their place in the profession as a whole.

Consider, first, the in-house law department. The work that in-house lawyers do has in the past had less prestige than law firm practice, at least among students at the best schools, where corporations have traditionally found it difficult to recruit. That seems still to be true, despite the recent growth of corporate law departments and their increased responsibilities.[68] But this may change, as differences in compensation shrink and in-house legal work becomes more challenging. Should a defender of the lawyer-statesman ideal be encouraged by such a shift and work to bring it about? Can one reasonably expect the corporate law department to become a setting in which that ideal is nourished and sustained?

Two considerations weigh in favor of this view. First, instead of an intermittent relationship with their client, lawyers working in-house are more likely to have a relationship that involves them in the client's day-to-day affairs and therefore gives them the contextual knowledge on which real deliberative counseling depends. Lawyers on the outside, who lack such knowledge, can only give their clients technical advice. Those on the inside, who possess it, may be in a better position to do more, and it is arguable that their greater familiarity with their client's situation creates opportunities for the exercise and refinement of deliberative judgment that a more transactional practice precludes.

Second, in-house lawyers typically work shorter hours than do their counterparts in outside firms.[69] Most lawyers working in the law department of a corporation feel a sense of solidarity with lawyers elsewhere, a sense of professional identity that sets them apart from the nonlawyers in their company. But their own attitudes and habits are also bound to be influenced by the corporate culture in which they work, in particular by the expectations it engenders regarding the length of the working day. While different companies have different cultures, most encourage a working day for their upper-level employees, including in-house lawyers, that is shorter and more regular than that of lawyers at large firms (partners and associates alike). Lawyers working in-house thus in general have more time and energy for extraprofessional pursuits than those in most large firms do, and so are better able to combat the narrowing of experience that the specialization of legal work today encourages. Or so one might plausibly contend.

Nevertheless, there are several reasons for thinking that an in-house practice may be less congenial to the lawyer-statesman ideal than the preceding might suggest. First, even if the work that in-house lawyers do is more continuous and routine than that of their counterparts in private practice, it all comes from a single client, which represents another kind of narrowing or specialization. Of course the larger and more diversified a company becomes, the greater the variety of legal tasks it is likely to generate for its in-house legal staff. But the fact that lawyers practicing in-house have only one client, rather than many, means that at least in this respect—in the range and diversity of *client* experience—their work is necessarily more limited than that of lawyers in outside firms.

Second, the lawyers on a company's in-house staff, though familiar with its day-to-day activities, are unlikely to be involved in the handling of their employer's most extraordinary problems, which today as in the past are frequently assigned to outside specialists instead. This may not be true, perhaps, of a company's top lawyers—its general counsel and his or her immediate assistants. Indeed, there is some reason to believe that the participation of the highest echelon of in-house lawyers in exceptional matters is today greater than before. (One piece of evidence for this is the fact that more high-ranking in-house lawyers are former law firm partners, who see themselves as equal in status and ability to the outside specialists with whom they must collaborate in matters of this sort.)[70] But below the highest level of the in-house hierarchy, which includes only a handful of lawyers, a division of labor continues to exist between routine legal business, on the one hand, and extraordinary matters, on the other, the former staying inside and the latter going out. This division has, if anything, hardened in recent years, with the increasing specialization of outside firms. I have already described the effect of this division on outside lawyers, whose growing separation from their clients' everyday affairs deprives them of the context they need to give prudential as opposed to merely technical advice. But this same division also deprives the in-house lawyer of something he needs to develop his deliberative powers too, namely, the opportunity to act as an adviser in those extraordinary situations where it is clearest that the client's choice is among ends and not just means. The more limited such opportunities become for in-house lawyers, the less likely they are to develop these powers, which can generally be acquired only with exercise and practice. Like the outside lawyer who encounters nothing but extraordinary matters, the in-house lawyer who works on few or none at all is therefore equally unlikely to develop the deliberative judgment that the ideal of the lawyer-statesman honors.

Third, and most important, working in-house for a single client puts a special strain on a lawyer's independence, a strain that lawyers in outside firms with many clients feel less acutely.[71] The difference is one of degree, and there are obviously some firms that, though nominally independent, in fact rely so heavily on the business of a single client as to be functionally indistinguishable from in-house law departments. I assume, moreover, that most in-house lawyers are able to maintain a strong sense of professional independence despite their sole allegiance to one client, and if necessary to tell their employer things it may not want to hear. Still, the fewer the clients on whom a lawyer must depend for his livelihood, the greater the pressure on him will be, in any given case, to conform his opinions to those of his client despite the fact that his professional judgment recommends another view. However successful any individual lawyer may be in resisting this pressure, it is bound to grow as the number of his clients shrinks, and the in-house lawyer, who has only a single client, is in this respect in a position of maximum vulnerability, particularly if his other opportunities for professional employment are limited (because of the length of time he has spent working for one company or the adaptation of his legal skills to its special requirements). And to the extent that his independence is weakened in this way, a lawyer's capacity for deliberative wisdom will be compromised as well, for deliberation requires not only sympathetic engagement but detachment too, and the more a lawyer depends on a given client for material support, the harder it becomes to preserve the distance that every real counselor must keep.

In addition to the reasons I have mentioned, the mere growth in size of in-house law departments also makes it less plausible to think that they will, in the long run, provide an environment in which the lawyer-statesman ideal can be sustained. The decline of this ideal in the realm of large-firm practice has, to a considerable degree, been a result of the increased size of these firms and of the specialization and narrowing of professional experience such growth entails, and there is no reason to believe that in-house departments will be exempt from these same consequences as they, too, grow in size. Can a four-hundred-person in-house law department be that different from a four-hundred-person legal staff of any other kind? To the extent that greater size alone tends to produce an institutional and cultural milieu that stunts the development of practical wisdom and depreciates its worth, there is reason to doubt whether the immense in-house law departments that many corporations now possess can provide a new and more enduring home for the lawyer-statesman ideal. I do not say this is impossible, but it is dubious at best.

There is, however, another possibility. Some lawyers, attracted by the challenge of a sophisticated commercial practice, but dissatisfied with the comparatively low value that most large firms now place on the inherent satisfactions of legal craftsmanship itself, have left the world of large-firm practice to establish new firms of their own, firms

committed to remaining small and to preserving a better balance between moneymaking, on the one hand, and professional fulfillment,
on the other.[72] Here, perhaps, one might think, there is a reasonable
chance that the ideal of the lawyer-statesman will survive, even as it
disappears in other areas of practice.

Yet the fate of many of these firms makes it difficult to have much
confidence in this regard. After hopeful beginnings and a brief career,
most firms of this sort fail and either disintegrate or lose their identity
by merging into larger ones.[73] However laudable the ambitions of the
lawyers who create them, small "boutique" firms that limit growth
and even revenue for the sake of other, instrinsic professional goods
tend generally to be unstable and short-lived. There are two reasons
why this is so.

First, for such a firm to succeed, on the terms that it sets out to, it
must create and then sustain an ethos of professional idealism among
its members that supports their individual willingness to make material sacrifices for the sake of achieving a greater measure of intrinsic
satisfaction in their work. In the cultural world of large-firm practice,
that ethos is now largely gone, and a boutique firm whose members
have either come from large firms or may at any moment be hired
away by them must therefore not only establish its own internal culture of idealism but do so in an environment increasingly hostile to
the values it affirms.

Thirty years ago, large firms rarely hired laterally and the lawyers
in them seldom moved from one firm to another. If they did, it was
generally to a smaller firm or in-house law department. Their relative
immobility made it easier for the lawyers in these firms to identify
with them. Or, to put the same point negatively, it made it harder
for individual lawyers to think of themselves as having a professional
persona distinct from their membership in a particular firm; and that
helped firms to sustain a sense of solidarity among their members.
The current situation is quite different. Lawyers in large firms are far
more mobile than before, and one consequence of this is that these
firms are now finding it more difficult to sustain a distinctive culture
of any sort against the disintegrative forces of an increasingly volatile
market for legal personnel. To the extent that they draw their lawyers
from this market, and are threatened by these forces too, boutique
firms will have as hard a time establishing a stable culture of their
own as the large firms to which they self-consciously oppose them-

selves. And because the culture they aim to create is, to some extent at least, defined in opposition to the commercialism that today permeates the environment in which even boutique firms must find, and hold, their personnel, the effort to establish and sustain a culture of this special counteractive sort is bound to be more difficult still.

If the increasing competitiveness of the market for lawyers makes the survival of countercultural boutique firms doubtful for one reason, the growing competitiveness of the market for legal services makes it doubtful for another. The lawyers in these firms must compete with other, larger firms for business, and whether they specialize or not, they are likely to be at a disadvantage in this regard. Suppose, for example, that the founders of a small firm make a deliberate decision not to specialize—motivated, let us assume, by a desire to avoid the technocratic narrowing of professional experience that seems to them such an objectionable feature of large-firm practice. In attracting and servicing its clients, the firm they establish must nevertheless compete with larger ones, no matter how much it abhors their methods of organization, and its smallness makes it less able to respond with the speed that today's transactional practice requires, or to offer the kind of round-the-clock team staffing that larger firms provide. To compete effectively, it must offer its clients the same speed and coverage its competitors do, and that in turn means it must grow, which is likely to alter the firm's character in just the ways its founders hoped to avoid.

Anticipating this, they may decide instead to specialize at the outset in the hope of securing a market niche that will make them less vulnerable to competition from firms with greater resources. But apart from the fact that they now risk losing the very breadth of professional function they initially sought to achieve, specialization is always a risky strategy for small firms to pursue. It exposes them to the danger of what economists call underdiversification, the danger that their practice as a whole will be too closely tied to specific economic conditions that may change—a risk that larger firms are able to avoid by developing a broader range of specialties. That is why many small boutique firms are simply taken over, root and branch, by larger ones. From the standpoint of the larger firm, mergers of this sort almost always represent a welcome bit of additional diversification, and from the perspective of the smaller firm, they offer the kind of security that only a variety of specialties can provide. From both points of view, therefore, such mergers often make economic sense. But they also mark the end of the experiment in professional values that the small firm represented, and the reincorporation of its members into the world of large-firm practice from which they had originally sought to escape.

So whether a small firm chooses to specialize or not, the competitiveness of the market for legal services makes it difficult for the firm to survive in the form its founders wish. The competitiveness of the market for lawyers makes this difficult as well. For both these reasons, the self-limiting boutique firm—dedicated to remaining small and to cultivating among its members a renewed appreciation of the internal goods of practice—is unlikely to achieve its goal in a secure and lasting way. However admirable its aims, this kind of firm thus offers little hope of providing a stable environment to which the lawyer-statesman ideal, now all but dead in large-firm practice, can be successfully transplanted.

This last conclusion is particularly sobering. For it implies that the market forces which today determine the nature and content of large-firm corporate practice—for a century the main carrier in the American legal profession of the lawyer-statesman ideal—are so powerful as to nullify even the most deliberate efforts of those who set themselves against the current to create an environment in which some elements of this ideal can be preserved. If even they cannot succeed, what reason do we have to think that the lawyer-statesman ideal, now repudiated by the most prestigious and powerful segment of the bar, can be saved in any area of practice at all?

6

Courts

THE JUDGE'S SPECIAL ROLE

In the last quarter-century, vast changes have transformed the teaching and practice of law in the United States. The intellectual and institutional developments that have reshaped these two branches of the profession have produced in the upper reaches of each a new culture of shared attitudes and expectations that is less hospitable than its predecessor was to the ideal of the lawyer-statesman. The causes of these changes are complex, and different in each case. But, broadly speaking, their effects have been the same, for the main tendency of each has been to weaken the authority of the lawyer-statesman ideal by attacking the beliefs and practices on which it rests.

In both areas of professional life there are, however, counterpressures that make the declining prestige of this ideal more understandable. In the case of law teaching, for example, the fact that nearly all of those who do it work in universities and are directly exposed to the special attitudes that flourish in university communities might itself be thought to create a counterpressure of this sort. Universities are by their nature unworldly places, and it is generally not the man or woman of affairs, but of theory—of science in the broad sense—whose virtues predominate in them, in the double sense of being both more visible and more highly valued. In the last century, as law schools have become fully integrated university departments with an equal (if sometimes anxiously defended) claim to intellectual respectability, those teaching in them have been influenced by this broader university ethos and have as a result come more and more to view themselves as theoreticians whose special subject matter simply hap-

315

pens to be law, rather than as practitioners primarily allied to their profession and only accidentally connected to the universities in which they work.

Unsurprisingly, as this shift in outlook has occurred, the ideal of the lawyer-statesman has lost much of its appeal to academic lawyers. For this older conception of the lawyer's role is not only different from but antagonistic to the ideal of the scientist-scholar. The more openly law teachers have embraced the latter ideal, the more they have come to see the former one, with its deep distrust of theory and theoreticians, as an embarrassment to be avoided. If the lawyer-statesman ideal is at present in decline in our law schools, one might therefore attribute its demise to the growing influence on academic lawyers of a counterideal embedded in the very culture of university life itself and view this development as the realization of a possibility that has been present since the fateful step was taken, more than a century ago, from a system of legal education based on apprenticeship to one founded on formal university training instead.

Something similar might be said, with even greater reason, about the changes that have taken place in large-firm practice in the last twenty-five years. The corporate law firm has existed as an institution for about a century and during most of this time has been an important carrier of the lawyer-statesman ideal. But it has also obviously been, from the start, a moneymaking enterprise too. Like other lawyers, those practicing in large firms make a living from their craft. They are in the business of selling their time and expertise, and there must inevitably be a tension between this aspect of law practice—its commercial side—and the demands of a professional ideal that emphasizes the value of public service and the intrinsic satisfactions of the craft.

A balance needs to be struck, therefore, in large firms as in any area of private practice, between the requirements of commerce, on the one hand, and the claims of professional idealism, on the other. Where this balance is struck at any given moment depends on how much time and energy a firm needs to devote to protecting the economic livelihood of its members. The more competitive the environment in which a firm must operate—the more it must scramble to attract new clients and hold on to old ones—the greater the human and material resources it will have to devote to the business of making money, and hence the stronger the tendency will be for its members to view themselves as participants in what is primarily, perhaps even exclusively, a moneymaking venture.

In the last two decades, changes in the market for legal services have made the world of large-firm practice enormously more competitive, and this has produced a dramatic shift within these firms in the previous balance between business and professionalism—more and more explicitly in the direction of commercial concerns. In the process, the lawyer-statesman ideal, which embodies the central values of professionalism as these were traditionally conceived, has lost much of its prestige. But since law firms, and large ones in particular, are commercial businesses engaged in making money and not charitable societies for the support of professional values, the possibility of such a shift has been present all along. The only novel feature of contemporary large-firm practice, one might conclude, is the extent to which it has realized this possibility (or, more cynically expressed, the extent to which it has stripped the pretense and puffery from law practice and revealed its true economic aims).

Thus if the ideal of the lawyer-statesman has lost much of its authority in our law schools and large firms, that is, perhaps, not so puzzling after all. For in each there is a built-in conflict between this ideal and other forces, intellectual or material, that challenge it directly. But there is another branch of the legal profession that is free from these same conflicts and therefore more likely, one would think, to provide a hospitable environment for the values embodied in the figure of the lawyer-statesman. I have in mind the adjudicative branch of law, by which I mean the work that judges do deciding disputes in those formal institutional settings we call courts.

Of course not all legal "dispute resolution" (as it is now fashionable to call it) is done by judges or occurs in courts.[1] Today much of this work is done by mediators, arbitrators, special masters, and others, and takes place outside the courthouse in less formal settings. But though these alternative forms of dispute resolution have in recent years grown in number and popularity, the judicial form continues to enjoy a decided priority over them. In part this is a cultural phenomenon that reflects the extraordinary prestige that courts and judges have always enjoyed in America, as Tocqueville long ago observed.[2] But even more obviously, the priority of the judicial form of dispute resolution is a function of the fact that it is judges who must ultimately define the authority that mediators, arbitrators, and special masters exercise—not the other way around—and so long as this remains true, judges and the work they do are bound to retain the position of dominant importance they have occupied in our legal culture from the start.

Indeed, judges occupy this position not only within their own field of dispute resolution but, indirectly at least, in the teaching and practicing branches of the profession as well. Law students, for example, learn their subject mainly through the medium of judicial decisions and are encouraged not merely to scrutinize these decisions as behavioral clues in order to become more skilled at predicting what judges will do, but to practice adopting the judicial point of view from which the decisions were rendered. They are encouraged to learn the habits that define this point of view—to become judicious themselves—and to accept the judge's perspective as the central and defining one for the profession as a whole.

Practicing lawyers need these habits too. For even if we understand the service they provide in narrow terms, as the giving of expert advice about the probable future course of judicial behavior, success in providing such advice requires more than anthropological knowledge unaccompanied by any commitment to the good of the law itself, the commitment that defines the judge's point of view. Even practicing lawyers must to some degree share this concern if they are to give clients the advice they need and to argue effectively on their behalf.

The work that judges do is therefore not only of supreme importance within the sphere of dispute resolution itself. It internally shapes the outlook of those engaged in the very different activities of law teaching and practice as well. Significantly, however, judges are almost entirely free from the pressures that threaten the lawyer-statesman ideal in these other fields.

Thus judges are not—and within the confines of their official work must never allow themselves to become—theoreticians of the sort that many academic lawyers now aspire to be. The decisions that a judge renders, and the opinions that he or she writes, are of course informed by reasoned argument and often have a complex theoretical structure. But the theorizing in which a judge may responsibly engage is always constrained by the need to resolve a specific dispute whose peculiarities place inescapable limits on the kind and degree of abstract generalization that is needed or desirable, limits to which academic lawyers are not subject and which they may choose to disregard. Judges are disciplined by the specificity of the cases they must decide, and this discipline not only puts a limit to the speculative theorizing in which they may engage, but is also bound to remind them, as they go about their work, of the value of deliberative wisdom—the wisdom that consists in a knowledge of particulars and that no general theory can provide. Because of this, one would expect the professional experience of judges to make them more respectful of the virtue of practical wisdom and of the character type associated with it than their counterparts in teaching tend to be.

Even more obviously, judging is not a vehicle for making money in the way the craft of law is for those engaged in private practice. As a result, judges do not need to worry about balancing commercial success against professional idealism—against the requirement that they serve the public good and look for compensation in the intrinsic pleasure of a job well done. Judges are free to pursue the latter goods wholeheartedly in a way practicing lawyers are not. Indeed, any failure on their part to do so is generally considered a breach of trust. The commercialism that is an ineliminable feature of all private practice, and whose recent increase has contributed to the weakening of the lawyer-statesman ideal within the upper reaches of the bar, thus has no counterpart in the field of adjudication, which in this way too is protected against the pressures that now jeopardize the ideal in other areas of professional life.

Given the role that adjudication plays in defining the professional habits of lawyers generally, it seems especially important to identify the values judges respect. And since judges are neither constrained by the need to make money from their work nor encouraged to turn their opinions in specific cases into academic theories, one might expect them to place a higher value on practical wisdom than law teachers and practitioners do. Judging, after all, is a deliberative activity that always starts from and returns to the specific facts of a concrete controversy, requires a combination of sympathy and detachment, and often presents the person engaged in it with conflicts between incommensurable goods, while nevertheless requiring him or her to pursue what I have termed the good of political fraternity. These are the characteristics of deliberation generally, and the work of adjudication exhibits them all in an especially pure form. Judging is a paradigm of deliberation, and so here if anywhere in the legal profession practical wisdom ought to be a well-understood and valued trait, especially given the absence, within the judicial sphere, of those intellectual and material forces that have helped to put this virtue on the defensive elsewhere.

But anyone who today inquires into the working habits of the American judiciary with this expectation in mind is likely to be disappointed. I do not mean the ordinary kind of disappointment that comes from discovering that some group of human beings falls short of its ideals (or one's estimate of what their ideals ought to be). There have always been judges of whom this might be said. What is new in the situation of American judges today is not the failure of some, or even many, to live up to their ideals, but the redefinition of these ideals themselves—the reorientation of the entire professional culture in which our judges work. In recent years there has occurred, within the sphere of adjudication, a depreciation of the lawyer-statesman ideal similar to the one that has taken place in the areas of teaching and practice as well. This shift in values represents a change in the culture of judging that even in isolation would be a cause for concern. But when we consider the central role that judges play in the profession as a whole, its implications become more ominous still.

COPING WITH THE CASELOAD

The most significant fact about our courts today is the enormous number of cases they must handle. In the last twenty-five years, American courts of all sorts—state and federal, trial and appellate—have experienced a steep increase in the number of matters they must attend to and decide. The increase has not, of course, been uniform across the judicial system as a whole. And so far as we can tell, the caseload of the federal courts (for which the best statistics are available) has been growing continuously for a century or more.[3] But though the rate of growth has differed from one court to another, it has been in the same positive direction everywhere and much greater in recent years than previously. Indeed, so great has the increase been that most commentators now routinely speak of a "caseload crisis" to emphasize their sense that the accelerating demands on our courts have transformed the nature of their work in fundamental ways and made them different sorts of institutions from what they were a quarter-century ago.[4] In this respect, the rapid surge in the caseload of the nation's courts has had the same effect on their institutional character as the equally dramatic growth in the size of our leading corporate law firms has had on theirs. Just as the recent explosive increase in firm size is the elementary fact from which any examination of their contemporary culture must begin, so, too, the growing caseload of our courts must be the starting point for any inquiry into the culture—the habits, values, and outlook—of the judges now working in them.

The causes of the caseload crisis have been widely debated. Undoubtedly they include the multiplication of statutorily and judicially created rights and the relaxation of traditional restrictions on the definition of the class of persons eligible to enforce them; the increase in crime (especially drug-related offenses) and hence of criminal prosecution; the decreasing cost of some sorts and certain aspects of litigation; and the growing size and diversity of the American population, which may help to explain what some believe is the most important, if diffuse, cause of the caseload crisis: an apparent increase in the willingness of Americans to use the formal, state-sponsored apparatus of the law, rather than other, more relaxed approaches, to settle their disputes.[5] All these factors, and others too, have contributed to the growing volume of judicial business, though the relative importance of their different roles is highly controversial (and given the inherently vague nature of some of them, will probably remain so). What institutional responses—what changes in the structure, tempo, and style of adjudication—has this development provoked, and with what consequences for the culture of judging?

We may begin with an observation that Richard Posner makes in *The Federal Courts: Crisis and Reform,* a book largely devoted to the caseload crisis and the federal courts' response (or lack of response) to it. Posner's book is in part concerned with problems unique to this particular judicial system (for example, the appropriate scope of the federal courts' diversity jurisdiction). But much of what he has to say, though nominally addressed to the federal courts alone, applies with equal force to state courts too, where (all the available evidence suggests) a caseload crisis of equal or greater proportions has provoked a similar response.[6]

Posner describes this crisis in economic terms, as a problem of supply and demand.[7] In recent years, he says, the demand for judicial services has risen sharply, for a variety of reasons, but the supply of such services has not increased commensurately, resulting in a larger average workload for each judge and the need for some method of rationing (essentially a queue that operates on a first-come, first-served basis) to allocate available judicial time and energy. It is this excess of demand over supply, and not the sheer magnitude of demand itself, that has made the present situation of our courts so critical.

There are obviously only two ways, Posner continues, to bring the supply of judicial services back into balance with the demand for them. This can be done, first, by limiting demand, and second, by expanding supply. The demand for judicial services might be reduced, for example, by deliberately increasing the costs of litigation or, more simply, by eliminating certain classes of entitlement, thereby making the grievances associated with them nonlitigable. This approach, Posner observes, has for the most part not been pursued, largely for political reasons (though it is worth noting that a committee created by Congress in 1988 to study the federal courts has recently made a number of proposals for their reform, some of which, at least, might be described as demand-limiting).[8] The only other way to meet the caseload crisis is by expanding the output of judicial services, and to the extent that the crisis has been met at all, this is the main form the response to it has taken.

First, the supply of judicial services has been expanded by increasing the number of judges themselves and, in both our state and federal courts, by enlarging the staff of assistants working under each judge's supervision—"elbow" clerks, staff clerks, and secretaries, whose productive efforts augment the judge's own, enabling him to produce a larger volume of decisions than he could working by himself. In addition to these general measures, other more specialized ones have been adopted by both trial and appellate courts. Many appellate courts, for example, have relaxed their rules regarding the publication of opinions and have restricted opportunities for oral argument, in order, essentially, to save judicial time.[9] At the trial level, there have been a number of developments whose object is the same, including, for example, the increased use in complex litigation of special masters, magistrates, and others charged with the initial responsibility for deciding certain aspects of the case, and the greater involvement of judges themselves in the pretrial phase of litigation.[10] All of these measures have essentially one aim: to enable judges, both trial and appellate, to dispose of a larger number of cases and thereby close the gap between supply and demand that has created the caseload crisis.

Many of these supply-side adjustments have been controversial. Some critics, for example, have argued that increasing the number of judgeships, especially in the federal system, is likely to dilute the prestige of the office, making it more difficult in the long run to recruit men and women of the highest ability to it, a problem compounded by the growing discrepancy between judicial salaries and the incomes of practicing lawyers.[11] Of course not everyone accepts this view, and at least with respect to the federal judiciary it would appear, as Posner notes, that there are built-in limits to further increases in size. The requirement that there be a single Supreme Court and the practical need to limit its membership to a number capable of joint deliberation; the widely accepted assumption that every federal circuit should include more than a single state; and the need to limit the size of the individual courts of appeal to permit meaningful *en banc* review all suggest that the number of federal judges cannot increase (and the prestige of their office decrease) indefinitely.[12] But even with this qualification, the belief that a substantial increase in the number of federal judges (such as has already occurred) will make their work appear less special and therefore lower its prestige cannot be summarily dismissed. Nor, for that matter, can a similar concern about the growing number of state court judges, even if their work is considered less prestigious on the whole.

Other concerns raised by recent efforts to expand the output of judicial services touch a deeper chord, however. For they suggest that these have had a harmful effect not only on the stature of the judge's office but on the soundness of the adjudicative process itself—on the way in which judges do their work, however many of them there may be. These deeper concerns all rest on the belief that judging is an activity with distinctive aims and responsibilities, which, it is claimed, recent changes in American judicial practice have weakened or obscured.

Judith Resnick, for example, has warned of the dangers that the increased involvement of judges in the pretrial management of cases poses to the integrity of the judicial process as it has traditionally been conceived.[13] The dangers of what she calls "managerial judging" are two. First, a deeper involvement in the pretrial manoeuvering of the parties and the need to form an opinion about the merits of their positions at an earlier stage of the proceedings are likely, she claims, to compromise a judge's independence and transform him prematurely into a partisan of one of the positions involved. Of course, the judge in any legal proceeding must become a partisan at some point merely by virtue of the requirement that he decide the case in someone's favor. But for the managerial judge, the moment of commitment is accelerated, and by making it more difficult for him to postpone taking sides in a case, his pretrial participation in it impairs the quality of his deliberations.

Second, Resnick argues, the growing use by judges of various pretrial management techniques has weakened the salutary discipline imposed upon them by the requirement that they act in public and formally record their reasons for doing what they do. Much of what a judge does in the course of managing a case is done privately and informally, and is thus not conditioned by the knowledge that it may be subject to later scrutiny or review. This means, most obviously, a greater risk of undetected bias, but also an increased danger that the judge will rely more heavily than he or she should on first impressions in a case—impressions that sometimes lose their plausibility when put to the test of a public defense. However understandable as a response to the caseload crisis, managerial judging thus tends to encourage decisions that are more precipitous and prone to personal bias and so to compromise the work of judging at its core.

Similar concerns have been raised by Owen Fiss and Joseph Vining with regard to what they call the bureaucratization of the judiciary, by which they mean the great increase in ancillary staff (elbow clerks, staff attorneys, special masters, and so on) that has occurred in recent years—most visibly in our federal courts, but in many state court systems too.[14] The term "bureaucratization" is not entirely appropriate, perhaps, for even with their greatly expanded support staffs, American judges still possess more independence and initiative than any hierarchically structured corps of bureaucrats organized along European lines.[15] But the phenomenon that Fiss and Vining have in mind is clear enough, as are their reasons for believing it destructive of judicial values.

Both claim that the growth of support staff has diminished the sense of personal responsibility judges feel for their decisions and led to greater anonymity in judging—to what Fiss, borrowing from

Hannah Arendt, calls the "rule of no one."[16] This in turn has resulted, Vining says, in a weakening of the sense among those who read judicial opinions that they have been written by individuals with recognizable identities of their own, and in the growing feeling, instead, that they are the product of impersonal institutions with which it is impossible to converse in a meaningful way (since genuine conversation requires that one's interlocutor take personal responsibility for what he or she says).

In explaining this development, Fiss and Vining emphasize two aspects of judicial bureaucratization: first, its tendency to increase the remoteness of judges from the circumstances of the cases they decide by delegating responsibility for the initial assessment of each case to someone else, thereby depriving the judge of those "critical educational experiences"[17] that a more intimate relation to the case might furnish; and second, its creation of a division of labor that distributes the task of judgment among a number of agents, whose decisions need only be collated or combined, and not actually made, by a single person. Together, Fiss and Vining say, these tendencies have weakened the sense of personal responsibility that has always been considered an essential condition of judicial integrity in the Anglo-American system of law. And they insist that the loss of this sense is today increasingly visible in the products of adjudication themselves—in the opinions that judges nominally write but for the most part merely edit, in which it has become more and more difficult to detect the authentic voice of any person willing to take responsibility for what these opinions say.

THE MONOCULAR JUDGE

With these concerns I am largely sympathetic. For I too believe that the bureaucratization of the judiciary and the rise of the managerial judge are developments that threaten to transform the activity of judging in essential ways. But the accounts that Resnick, Fiss, and Vining offer of these developments are incomplete and fail to identify their most disturbing consequence: the stifling of deliberative imagination on which the work of judging centrally depends. In addition to the consequences these three critics stress, the changes in adjudicative practice they describe have all made it less deliberative in character. They have all caused adjudication to become, in Resnick's helpful phrase, a more managerial activity in which deliberative imagination is neither as needed nor as valued as before. To understand why, let us begin by looking more closely at the phenomenon of judicial bureaucratization.

The most important consequence of increasing the number of subordinates working under a judge is, as Fiss points out, to shift the initial responsibility for resolving disputes to someone other than the judge, making the judge's own task essentially one of review (a phenomenon that Resnick calls tiering—the creation of new levels of primary decisionmaking and the coincidental transformation of those who used to occupy this position into *de facto* appellate judges).[18] Rarely, of course, is the shift complete. Thus even though a trial judge employs a special master to decide certain aspects of a case, he is likely to reserve for himself the initial decision of the other questions it presents. And an appellate judge will often form an independent view of a case, based on his own reading of the parties' briefs, and then use his clerk's assessment of it simply as a sounding board to test whatever decision he has reached. But these are only important qualifications and do not change the basic fact that as a judge's staff of clerks and other deputized assistants grows, his work is likely to consist, increasingly, of reviewing the decisions they have made instead of making these decisions himself. And that is a fateful change, for however sensible it appears from an administrative point of view as a device for conserving judicial energy, it also entails a reduction in the demand that his or her own work makes on the judge's imaginative powers and the consequent enfeeblement of these powers themselves.

Deliberative imagination is the capacity to entertain a point of view defined by interests, attitudes, and values different from one's own without actually endorsing it. Every deliberative process in which a choice must be made among alternatives that cannot be arranged in a clear rank order of better and worse demands imagination in this sense. That is true whether the choice in question is first-personal (a choice concerning the direction and content of one's own life), third-personal (a choice that must be made by someone else, whom one is helping to advise), or adjudicative (where the point of deliberating is to choose among the conflicting claims of other persons). In each case deliberation requires a combination of sympathy and detachment, and those who lack these traits will display a charac-

teristic deficiency of imagination. Such a union of conflicting dispositions is difficult to achieve. It takes time, and even once attained
needs continual exercise to remain supple and strong. But without it,
none of these three sorts of choices—first-personal, third-personal,
or adjudicative—can be deliberative in the fullest sense.

Whoever is responsible for making the initial decision in a legal
controversy must directly consider two or more conflicting claims.
These compete for his allegiance, and to engage them, to entertain
them, he must exercise his deliberative imagination, whether his decision is subject to review or not. But the person reviewing the decision is in a different position. For he is not faced, directly at least,
with a plurality of points of view but only one—the point of view
expressed in the judgment of his subordinate. Of course, behind this
judgment there still stands the original plurality of claims, and anyone
reviewing the decision continues to have contact with them through
the judgment itself. But this contact is now indirect. The judge doing
the reviewing is no longer in immediate touch with these claims.
What he directly confronts, instead, is the opinion of his subordinate
and this, unlike the parties' opinions, has no competitors of its own.

In that sense, we might say, the vantage point of a reviewing judge
is essentially monocular. For he sees the conflict that a case presents
from a perspective that has already acquired a certain unity through
his subordinate's prior judgment, whose main function is to impose
a harmonizing order on the parties' conflicting claims. An important
stimulus to the judge's deliberative imagination is weakened as a result. The more directly he confronts a plurality of claims, the more
strongly a judge is likely to feel the need to empathically engage each
on its own terms while making a commitment to none. When claims
compete directly in this way, they produce a kind of friction that
arouses the imagination and makes the need for it quite clear. But
when a judge encounters the disputes that come before him from the
point of view of an earlier decision that has already arranged and
ranked the claims of those involved, this friction is weaker and less
likely to provoke his imaginative powers.

It is of course always open to a reviewing judge to put himself
directly back in contact with the conflict his subordinate has provisionally settled. But the further he goes in this direction, the less value
his subordinate's judgment will have as a time-and-labor-saving device. So if he is to get the expected benefit of the delegation of deci-

sionmaking power he has made, a reviewing judge must, to some degree, defer to the judgment of his deputy or delegate. He must make a presumption in favor of that judgment and not treat the question to which it is addressed as one deserving entirely fresh consideration. There is, of course, a wide range of possibilities here, and judges differ in the nature and extent of the deference they show to the judgments of those employed by them in various subordinate positions. But every relationship of this sort requires some deference to achieve its basic aim, and the more he defers, the further a judge moves away from the original plurality of viewpoints that gives each case its controversial character and toward the monocular perspective of his subordinate's unifying judgment.

Owen Fiss has criticized the bureaucratization of the judiciary on the grounds that it increases the dependence of judges on the perceptions of their staff. Clerks, magistrates, and others have become, he says, the eyes and ears of the judiciary, the sense organs by which the facts of cases are conveyed to the judges who decide them, thereby depriving judges of the education that a more direct acquaintance with the facts might yield.[19] That is true, but I would emphasize a somewhat different point. Judicial bureaucratization increases the dependence of judges not only on the perceptions of their subordinates but on the judgments they form too, on the preliminary evaluation staff members make of the claims before the court. This means that when a case comes to the judge who must (in a formal sense at least) decide it, the conflict it presents has already been subdued. For instead of the original clash of as-yet unranked claims, all making an equal bid for recognition, what he now confronts is an opinion that gives certain of these claims precedence over others and imposes a unifying structure on the conflict between them. The judge of course knows this conflict exists. But he experiences it only indirectly, from the vantage point of his subordinate's assessment of the case—a perspective defined not by conflict but its opposite, by harmony and order. The interposition of his subordinate's judgment and his deference to it thus change fundamentally the nature of the judge's situation and give his whole outlook on a case a singularity of focus that suppresses the original clash of claims from which it grew. In the process, an important spur to imagination is lost and deliberation replaced by the deference on which every system of tiered review depends.

APPELLATE COURTS

There is an obvious and plausible objection to this argument. I have said that the growth of judicial staff and the increased reliance of judges on the opinions of subordinates have a discouraging effect on their deliberative imagination. But one may reasonably reply that every appellate judge is by definition in this position, and hence vulnerable to the danger I have described. Yet we do not view this as a serious impediment to deliberation in and of itself. The effect of an increase in judicial staff is simply to turn trial judges into appellate judges, and appellate judges, at any given level, into higher-tiered ones. Why should that be of any serious concern if we have no general reason to doubt that appellate judging can be, and often is, a fully deliberative activity?

What gives this objection its plausibility is the fact that appellate judges do necessarily view the disputes that come before them through the lens of a prior decision. An appellate judge's relationship to the claims in any given case is therefore always indirect, and the earlier judgment that mediates his relationship to them is one to which he must defer to some degree. Appellate judges are therefore more than ordinarily vulnerable to the dangers of monocularity simply in virtue of the position they occupy. But this objection misses something too. It overlooks the fact that the work of appellate judges has traditionally been surrounded, in American courts at least, by safeguards intended to offset these very dangers, and it ignores the extent to which these same safeguards have been compromised by various institutional reforms aimed at increasing the output of our appellate courts, including, in particular, the expansion of judicial staff.

Thus, for example, both the submission of written briefs by the parties and the opportunity they are given, in most appeals, to present their claims directly to the court in oral argument help to put appellate judges back in touch with the conflict the case presents and to experience for themselves, in a more immediate way, some of the tension that accompanied it before the case was settled by the court below. These practices disrupt the insularity of appellate judging and offset its dampening of deliberative imagination. Indeed, one might reasonably maintain this is their primary goal. But in the last decade a number of appellate courts have limited the availability of oral argument on the grounds that it takes too much time. And there is evidence to suggest that appellate judges as a group now devote less attention than before to the parties' briefs, preferring instead to read a summary of their arguments set out in a memorandum prepared by a clerk.[20] Each of these developments represents the weakening of an important counterweight to the monocularity of appellate judging.

Another such counterweight—more important than the two I have just mentioned—is the requirement that appellate decisions be accompanied by written opinions explaining and defending their conclusions. A trial judge makes many decisions in the course of his or her work, some quite complex, but most of these are not supported by a written opinion. The judgments that appellate courts render are more often accompanied by an opinion of this sort. Indeed, opinion-writing is the norm in appellate adjudication. One explanation for this is that written opinions increase the visibility of a court's decisions and thereby enhance the sense of responsibility that its members feel for them—though if that were the only explanation, it would be hard to see why trial judges should not be subject to the same norm too.

A second justification, which has special force in the context of appellate adjudication, is that opinion-writing disciplines the imagination. It is one thing to reach a tentative conclusion in a case, but something very different to write an opinion defending it. The search for the right words to support a judgment one has provisionally formed often stirs up new objections and compels the reexamination of earlier beliefs. A judge may feel that he has decided a case and is finished with it. But when he attempts to justify his decision in writing, he will be forced to reenact the drama of the original conflict in his imagination, taking first one side and then the other in an effort to anticipate the strongest arguments that might be made against his own earlier position and the best responses to them. Writing judicial opinions imposes on the writer a duty of responsiveness that can be met only by giving each side to a dispute its due, by entertaining every claim in its most attractive light, and that in turn demands a special effort of imagination. The discipline of opinion-writing is thus a goad to the imagination, and the greater the distance of the writer from the original conflict in a case, the more valuable this discipline becomes as a guard against the relaxation of his imaginative powers: which is why it is especially needed at the appellate level.

In many appellate courts, however, this discipline is weaker today than it has been in the past. In part this is due to procedural changes in court practice that permit more cases to be decided with no opinion or only an unpublished one—changes intended to increase the number of disputes that a court can decide in a given period of time.[21] But a more important cause of the weakening of this discipline has been the growing tendency of appellate judges to work by editing draft opinions prepared for them by their clerks instead of writing opinions themselves.

To be sure, the practice of judges varies in this regard, and there are some who still write their own opinions. The line between writing and editing, moreover, is an indistinct one, and editorial work itself can be highly original. Still, editing does not in general make as strong a demand on the imagination as original composition.[22] The diminished responsibility that editors commonly feel for the writings they produce (even when it is their name the writings bear); the increased tendency to defer to the judgment of the original author; and the temptation, to which every editor is liable, to view his primary task as one of stylistic improvement only—all these changes in self-perception are predictable consequences of a shift in the role of appellate judges from author to editor, and all degrade the effectiveness of the safeguard that opinion-writing establishes against the dangers of monocularity.

Appellate judges are peculiarly subject to these dangers. That is why they have a special need for more protection from them. But in the last twenty-five years, the protection they once enjoyed has substantially eroded, and one important reason why is the extraordinary increase in the support staff they employ. For this has enabled appellate judges to delegate the writing of opinions to their clerks and thereby to escape a challenge of incomparable value as a forcing-ground for the imagination.

Maximizing Justice

The bureaucratization of the judiciary—the growing number of clerks and other subordinates on whom judges now rely—has made the activity of judging less deliberative than before. But can the same be said of what Judy Resnick calls managerial judging, the increased involvement of judges in the pretrial management of cases as a strategy for reducing court delay? Let us begin by considering more closely the aims of this strategy itself.

The order in which cases are decided in American trial courts depends, to a large degree, upon the order in which they are docketed, and that is a matter not subject to court control. Those waiting for their cases to be heard form a queue, and the position of any particular case in the queue is generally not a function of its size, importance, difficulty, or even (except in certain circumstances) urgency. The inevitable result, many have claimed, is a misallocation of judicial resources, including, in particular, the time and energy of judges themselves. For whenever any scarce commodity is distributed by means of a queue, there is no reason to believe that those receiving it are the ones that need and value it the most. When a good is distributed through a system of market exchange, concerns about misallocation are less serious. But no such market exists for the distribution of dispute resolution (the good that courts provide to those who appear before them). It follows that judges must make special efforts to mitigate, so far as they are able, the misallocation of this good that the existing queue-based system of distribution entails. One way they can do this is by policing the queue itself—by making sure that it moves along at a rapid pace and that cases which can be settled without a trial are settled as quickly as possible. That is the goal of managerial judging, which is in essence a strategy for economizing on judicial resources, for increasing the efficiency with which judges distribute their time and energy to the parties in the queue.

The attitude of a judge who adopts this point of view and begins to manage the cases that come before him in the spirit it recommends resembles that of a manufacturer engaged in the business of producing a certain commodity for sale—pencils, for example. Clearly, different factors go into the production of pencils. There is, first of all, the material of which pencils are composed (lead, wood, rubber, and so on). Then there is the equipment needed to assemble these materials, the labor required to operate the equipment, and the workspace in which the equipment must be housed. All of these cost money, and the basic problem a manufacturer of pencils faces is that of deciding how much to spend on each of these different elements in order to maximize profit (the excess of revenues over costs). The elements in question can be combined in different ratios, and for any given ratio the total level of investment may be more or less. What the manufacturer wants to know is which ratio of elements and level of investment will produce the greatest profit. He wants to identify what economists call his optimal production function. The judge who adopts a managerial approach to his work faces a similar challenge. For like the manufacturer, he too sees himself as the superintendent of a complex process of production in which various ingredients (including, most importantly, his own time and energy) are combined to produce a particular good, namely, dispute resolution. And like the manufacturer, he is above all concerned to discover the combination of ingredients that will enable him to produce the most of this good in a given period of time.

There are, of course, certain notable differences between the situation of a factory owner, on the one hand, and that of even a determinedly managerial judge, on the other, and these may tempt one to conclude—wrongly, I believe—that the latter's outlook is not essentially economic after all. The most striking difference concerns the relative clarity of their goals. Whereas it is clear what the manufacturer wants to maximize, it is less obvious what the judge does. The manufacturer wants to maximize profits, which for any ratio of inputs and at any level of investment will be a determinate amount of money. Because he knows what his maximand is, and can measure it precisely, a manufacturer is able to search in a meaningful way for an optimizing production strategy. But what is it that a managerial judge is attempting to maximize? The suggestion that his outlook is an economic one just like the manufacturer's implies that he must be searching for an optimum too. But what can the maximand that defines the judge's optimum be?

I shall not consider at any length Posner's suggestion that what judges seek to maximize is their personal influence and prestige.[23] Perhaps this is so, at least at an unconscious level. But if the analogy I have drawn between the managerial judge and the manufacturer of pencils is to have any force at all, the judge's goal must be something he or she labors to achieve in a deliberate and self-conscious way. Psychology and sociobiology have shown us that unconscious processes can be understood in economic terms.[24] But activities that are economic in an ordinary sense—the manufacturer's search for an optimal production function, the householder's attempt to maximize the utility of his family's consumption decisions, and so on—are distinguished from the unconscious processes these disciplines describe by their intentionality, their self-conscious orientation toward the end of maximizing some determinate good. If the attitude of the managerial judge is economic in this ordinary sense, and not just the wider one that sociobiologists and psychologists employ, then it too must be characterized by a self-conscious orientation toward such an end. But no judge will acknowledge that what he wants to maximize is his own personal welfare, even when it is described in flatteringly nonmaterial terms (in contrast to the manufacturer of pencils, who is happy to admit that his goal is the maximization of profit). If the managerial judge's outlook is an economic one in the same sense as the manufacturer's, it must therefore have a different maximand from the judge's own influence and prestige.

Perhaps we should say that the maximand of the managerial judge is social peace. Every legal contest represents a disruption of the peace, and no one will deny that it is the function of adjudication to restore the peace by deciding which party should prevail. So perhaps we should think of the managerial judge's goal as the production of as much peace as possible. But this, too, is not a very satisfactory view, as a moment's reflection makes clear. For many of the things that judges do are inconsistent with the adoption of such a goal. Why, for example, if a judge wanted to terminate as many disputes as quickly as he could, would he ever give any weight to precedent or take the time to write opinions, rather than deciding the cases that come before him *in camera* and on the basis of whatever considerations he happens to think appropriate? And why, if this were his goal, would a judge ever protect the rights of individuals, when their protection tends to impede the achievement of social peace, for example, by slowing the law's adjustment to changed circumstances or conferring respectability on dissident and unsettling ideas?

One might respond that protecting rights, deferring to precedent, and writing opinions are all practices that promote social peace in the long run, even if they slow its attainment now. But this view raises the same problem as the claim that what judges seek to maximize is their own stature and influence. For if the maximization of social peace is an end that judges can achieve only by aiming at other ones, which on their face seem inconsistent with it, and if this strategy of indirection requires that judges learn to think of these other ends as valuable in their own right and not merely as a means to the attainment of social peace, then the judge's ultimate goal will again lack the self-consciousness that the manufacturer's possesses and that makes his attitude an economic one in the ordinary sense.

But if the good a managerial judge is seeking to maximize is neither his own personal welfare nor social peace, crudely conceived, what can it be? The best answer, I think, and the one most consistent with the understanding of judges themselves, is that the maximand of judging is justice. Doing justice to the parties that appear before one means honoring the rights and enforcing the duties that the law assigns them; and treating justice as a maximand simply means doing as much of this as can be done with the resources at one's command. This ancient and powerful idea rests on a picture of the law as a distributive order that allots different rights and responsibilities to different individuals. The judge's job, on this view, is to ensure that the distributive scheme established by the law is properly maintained—that those subject to it receive the benefits and burdens the law distributes to them. Justice is the name we give to the condition that results when these distributional requirements are satisfied, and the goal of judging, as the managerial judge sees it, is to bring this condition about to the greatest extent that available resources permit.

If we think of the law as a distributive scheme, there are two things that a judge must do in any individual case in order to decide it. First, he must determine what the dispute is about (something that is not always clear even to the parties themselves). And second, he must identify the particular distribution of rights and duties that the law prescribes in controversies of this sort. These two tasks are the main ones judges perform, and it is clear that the time and energy they have to perform them are limited.

A managerial judge will therefore feel it important to deploy these resources in such a way as to produce the greatest amount of justice overall. With this goal in mind, he will decide which cases to spend time on and which to resolve summarily or encourage the parties to settle on their own. If spending an additional hour on one case, for example, will substantially increase the likelihood that justice will be done between the parties to it, but spending the same hour on another is likely to produce only a small improvement in this regard— because it is obvious what justice requires in the latter case or else very difficult to say—a judge who views his work in a managerial spirit and has only an hour to spend will spend it on the second case rather than the first, just as the owner of a pencil factory will devote each dollar that he has to its marginally most profitable use.

To be sure, even on this view important differences remain between factory owner and judge. In the first place, though each has a maximand, the factory owner's is more easily measurable than the judge's. A manufacturer can determine, with relative ease, how much money he has made or lost in a given accounting period, and competitive pressures prevent him from indulging the false belief that a certain amount of profit is the most he can produce when a reorganization of his production process would yield more. A judge, by contrast, is likely to find it difficult to say, at any moment, whether he is producing more justice than he might by reallocating his time and energy—most importantly because the very nature of the good he is producing is itself controversial in a way that the nature of profit is not. (We debate what justice is, and the different answers we give influence our estimate of how much of it is being produced by a particular judge or by the legal system as a whole.) And the relatively less competitive relationship between courts makes it easy for judges to lapse into the lazy habit of thinking they are producing all the justice they can, when in reality they are using their resources inefficiently and could produce more if they chose to.

Second, the factory owner's maximand—the profitability of his enterprise—not only provides him with a criterion for determining the ratio in which he should employ his productive inputs at any given level of investment, but enables him to decide how large his overall investment should be as well. Generally speaking, a manufacturer can increase his revenues by increasing his expenditures. But whether he should depends upon the profitability of doing so, and since profit is by definition the surplus of revenue over expenditure, it provides a standard by which to evaluate different levels of investment as well as different combinations of inputs at any particular level. Justice, like profit, may be treated as a maximand and used as a measure for making evaluations of the latter sort. But unlike profit, it cannot be defined as a surplus and therefore does not provide a criterion for deciding how large an amount should be invested in the production of justice overall. That requires a collective decision to spend a certain amount on justice as opposed to other social goods (like schools and bridges), a substantive judgment that cannot be made in the same calculative fashion that a factory owner determines his optimal level of investment.

A judge's ability to identify with precision which allocation of time and energy will produce the greatest amount of justice at any particular level of expenditure is therefore limited; and he also lacks the means for deciding in a purely calculative way how large his total justice budget ought to be. But this only means that the power of economic analysis is greater in other productive activities than it is in that of judging. It does not mean that the economic point of view is inappropriate in this setting, or that those judges who adopt it and apply its teachings in a systematic way are unable to produce more justice with the same resources than their less economically minded colleagues. Within limits, it *is* possible for judges to view their work in this light and to improve their performance by doing so. And if that is the case, then however restricted the opportunities for economic rationalization may be within the field of adjudication, it seems irresponsible for a judge not to pursue them as far as he can.

That, in any case, is what the champions of managerial judging maintain. Theirs is essentially a program of economic reform, premised on the belief that a reallocation of judicial effort from the courtroom to the conference table can mitigate the inefficiencies of our present queue-based system of adjudication and thereby increase the amount of justice that our courts are able to produce with the resources committed to them. It is the duty of judges, they say, to allocate their time and energy as productively as possible, and under the historically evolved conditions that exist in the American court system today, this requires, they insist, a relatively heavier concentration of effort during the pretrial phase of cases when the queue for justice can be most easily policed. That is the economizing strategy of the managerial judge. What is it about this plausible—indeed, almost banally reasonable—approach that makes it so deeply threatening to the deliberative imagination?

THE TRAGIC SENSE

It would be foolish to suggest that the economic point of view has no place in the work that judges do, that judges ought to be completely unconcerned with the way in which the allocation of their time affects the amount of justice they produce. Surely, up to a point, a concern of this sort is salutary and in any case inevitable. But it also carries with it a concealed threat to the deliberative imagination. For when it becomes sufficiently dominant (as in the outlook of the managerial judge), the tendency to view the aim of judging in economic terms—to see its goal as the production of a maximum of justice, subject to existing budgetary constraints—obscures the deliberative nature of adjudication and promotes a false understanding of the judge's task and of the capacities needed to do it well. The rise of managerial judging is disturbing, therefore, not because it introduces into the process of adjudication an attitude that has no place in it at all, but because it gives that attitude a prominence which encourages, and eventually legitimates, a distorted picture of the nature and requirements of adjudication itself.

The distortion I have in mind is a consequence of the commensurating drive of economics. If a factory owner wants to determine how different inputs must be combined to produce the greatest profit, what will be of dominant interest to him is a characteristic these inputs share in common, namely, their cost in dollar terms. Rubber, wood, and lead are different materials, but a manufacturer of pencils who is concerned to maximize his profits will not be concentrating on the qualitative differences among these things. Rather, he will focus on the property they all possess of costing money and on the purely quantitative gradations that distinguish them in this regard.[25] His view of these and the other factors involved in the production of pencils (capital, labor, and so on) will be a homogeneous one. He will evaluate all of them along one single axis of comparison. Indeed, at a basic level, that is simply what it means to approach the business of making pencils in an economic spirit. For the decision to address from an economic point of view the task of using scarce resources to produce a maximum of any valued good always entails their commensuration in just this sense, and to the extent that a person is unwilling or unable to evaluate the resources in question from the uniform perspective of cost, the discipline of economics can offer no guidance at all.

This is true of every economic program, including that of the managerial judge. The managerial judge wants to produce a maximum of justice with the resources at his disposal. To do this he must decide which of the cases lined up in the queue before his court can be settled expeditiously and which should be allowed to come to trial, and how his own interventions in the pretrial process can best promote these results. That in turn requires that he form some preliminary view of what these cases are about—of what the parties to them are claiming and where the core of their disagreement lies—for only after forming such an opinion can a judge say whether justice will be better served by spending more time on one case rather than another. But if he approaches the parties' claims in this spirit, a judge will mainly be concerned with a property they share in common—with the fact that every legal claim, regardless of its nature, requires a certain amount of time to review and assess (more or less depending on its novelty, complexity, and so forth). In this respect, all legal claims are alike and differ only in the length of time their evaluation takes. To view these claims in a managerial perspective is thus analogous to viewing the factors involved in the production of pencils from the standpoint of their dollar cost. Of course, the claims that a judge must provisionally weigh before deciding how his own scarce time can most efficiently be spent do not become the same just because his survey of them is made with an eye to determining how much time the adjudication of each will require—any more than rubber, wood, and lead become the same when a pencil manufacturer asks how much he should spend on each. But in the first case, as in the second, the adoption of an economic point of view highlights the similarities and downplays the differences among the items being compared, and encourages the person who takes it to see them in an essentially uniform light. Wherever this commensurating attitude prevails, the idea that there are ways in which some of these items may be incomparably different ceases to be an interesting one and is eventually forgotten.

But why should this be thought to threaten the deliberative process in which judges are expected to engage? Commensuration, after all, is hardly foreign to adjudication. The chief responsibility of a judge is to decide the cases that come before him in a reasoned way, and any decision that gives reasons for favoring the position of one party over that of another assumes these can be evaluated from some common point of view. In other words, it assumes the parties' positions are commensurable. To that extent, it would appear that rationality in judging demands commensurability, or rather presupposes it.

There is much truth in this view, which reflects one of our most deeply held beliefs about the adjudicative process. We all believe that judges must give reasons for their decisions, and not just declare them, kadi-style. And to rationalize their decisions, they must bring the competing claims before them into alignment along some common axis of evaluation. They must make these claims commensurable.

Behind this basic truth, however, there lies another equally important one, and that is that the claims which compete for judicial endorsement cannot always be commensurated without recharacterizing them in a way that alters their essential meaning for the parties involved. Often, to be sure, the interests and values of the parties will be sufficiently alike to permit their comparison without wrenching them out of the perspective in which they are viewed by the parties themselves. But sometimes it is necessary to do exactly that in order to make these interests and values comparable. The likelihood of this increases as we move from legal disputes that involve only a struggle for money to those that represent a fight over basic norms of personal and political morality (like the death penalty and abortion battles that have occupied our courts in recent years). Of course, we require judges to decide the latter class of cases in the same way they decide all others. But the fact that they do does not actually make the claims in question commensurable from the parties' point of view. In cases of this sort, the rationalizing opinion that arranges the parties' claims along some common axis of comparison is a fiction that is powerless to change the underlying situation: one of conflict between incommensurable values. And while there may be utility to the fiction—so much so that we would think it inappropriate for the judge in such a case to be too candid about the true nature of the conflict involved—there is also a utility (if one wants to call it that) to keeping this truth in view and not forgetting that the values in question are incommensurable when seen through the parties' own eyes.

Why is the judge's appreciation of this latter fact important? Why isn't his awareness of the incommensurability of the claims before him a pointless and futile sort of knowledge if in the opinions he writes he is bound to treat these claims as though they were commensurable after all? What makes this knowledge so important is that aspect of the judge's job that constitutes the core of statesmanship in all its different guises, including the judicial one: his obligation to preserve the bonds of political fraternity, to strengthen the willingness of opposing groups to continue as members of a common enterprise even when there is no shared standard to resolve their disputes. This is a goal that judges too must keep in view. It is not their only goal, but it is an important part of what they do.

Of course, for a judge to achieve this goal he must constantly be searching for the common points of agreement that the parties before him share. More important, where agreement of this sort does not exist, he must make an effort to create it, and the commensurating opinion, which treats the parties' claims as if they could be adequately assessed from some common point of view, is perhaps the most important way that judges have of doing this. But as he struggles to meet the enormous responsibility this entails, it is crucial that a judge keep in mind the nature of the problem that he faces and of the good he is attempting to secure. For if he loses sight of these things, he is likely to forget the real complexity of his predicament, to allow himself to believe that it is simpler than it is, and in the end, through a slackening of imaginative effort, to lose even the capacity to understand the values and interests of those who appear before him from any but a falsifyingly common point of view. The strength and alertness of imagination on which all statesmanship depends demand an unflinching acceptance of the depth of human disagreement, and as a judge's sense of this wanes—as these disagreements come more and more to seem fully intelligible in terms of some set of universally shared interests and values—the more his or her own imaginative capacities are likely to decay.

I can express this same idea in a different way. Some moral and political conflicts are tragic ones in the sense that there is no common standard to resolve them. The knowledge that this is so Miguel de Unamuno called the tragic sense of life.[26] But statesmen, judges included, have an obligation to pursue political fraternity even in the presence of such conflicts, and the knowledge of which Unamuno speaks is essential to the imaginative effort this entails. Without it the import and weightiness of the statesman's obligation vanish. A judge cannot do without Unamuno's tragic sense—without an awareness of the gulf that separates those on opposing sides of many moral and political debates. To be sure, he must often conceal it in the opinions that he writes. But he must never lose it, for a judge who lacks the tragic sense will be blind to the incommensurabilities from which the deepest human conflicts flow. He will fail to understand the depth of his dilemma and the full meaning of his responsibilities. He will be unmoved to make the extraordinary effort that one must to engage incommensurable claims in a way that is faithful to each. He will perceive the moral world to be flatter than it is, and his own role in it less demanding and complex. In the end statesmanship will become, for him, the same as administration.

My concern about managerial judging thus comes to this. By encouraging judges to see their own work in an economic light—to see their task as one of resource allocation in a production process of a certain sort—managerial judging reinforces the tendency of judges to view the claims before them as commensurable. In that way, it dulls the tragic sense whose preservation is essential to judicial statesmanship. The rise of the managerial judge, and of the attitude he represents, contributes to the weakening of this sense and thus undermines the deliberative imagination on which statesmanship depends. The effects of managerial judging are to that extent congruent with those of judicial bureaucratization. For in different but complementary ways, these two developments have impoverished the imagination of judges and transformed the work they do—both in reality and in the judges' own perception of it—from an activity that calls for statesmanship to one requiring only administrative skill instead.

COLLEAGUESHIP

The change in outlook these developments have caused is reflected in the shifting fashions of judicial style too. Even a casual reader of opinions must be struck by the different style of opinion-writing that prevails today, as compared with the one that did twenty-five or thirty years ago. In saying this, I have in mind mainly our appellate courts, and more specifically our federal ones, but this new style can be detected in the work of other courts as well. It is rapidly becoming the dominant judicial style of the period, and it gives us an important clue to the culture judges now inhabit, one that sees the managerial excellences in an increasingly favorable light and those of the lawyer-statesman hardly at all.[27]

Two features of contemporary opinion-writing are of particular significance in this regard. The first is the increased tendency of individual judges sitting on appellate panels to issue separate opinions of their own, either concurring with or dissenting from the opinion of the court. The result has been a dramatic splintering of appellate opinions—their division into many separate overlapping and conflicting parts. A generation ago, most appellate courts spoke with a single, recognizable voice. In a growing number of cases, that voice is no longer identifiable. In its place we hear instead a plurality of voices competing for attention in what sounds, at times, like the cacophonous babble of a meeting in which everyone speaks at once.

This tendency has been especially noticeable in the opinions of the Supreme Court.[28] But the decisions of the other federal appellate courts have become increasingly splintered too, as Judge Posner emphasizes in his illuminating discussion of the problem.[29] In Posner's view, this tendency reflects a weakening of institutional morale, of the appellate judge's sense that he belongs to an institution with certain responsibilities toward the people that it serves—in particular, a responsibility to produce clear opinions with relatively unambiguous messages that will be informative and helpful to their intended readers (mainly practicing lawyers, but in the case of the Supreme Court, the educated public as well). In recent years, Posner says, many federal appellate judges have defaulted on this responsibility by indulging, beyond reasonable limits, their personal desire to elaborate a distinctive jurisprudence of their own in a series of separate concurrences and dissents, sacrificing the wholeness and integrity of their court's collective voice for the refinement of their individual ones instead. To some extent, of course, every judge ought to be concerned about the coherence and appeal of the pattern that emerges from his or her votes in different cases. But there is a point beyond which such concern becomes mere selfishness, and disserves the judge's readers, who are more interested, after all, in the behavior of courts than in that of their individual members. Against such selfishness Posner counsels self-restraint, collegial deference, and attention to the responsibility of clear opinion-writing. These are good suggestions, which judges ought to follow, but the real vice of the fractionated opinion lies at a deeper level.

One of the responsibilities of courts is to preserve the political order when it is threatened by conflicts between passionately held and profoundly divergent points of view. This is not their only task nor do they alone perform it. But there is no institution in our system of government that is more visibly responsible for pursuing the good of political fraternity than our courts, and our federal ones in particular.

Where it exists, political fraternity is a property of the entire social order. But as Frank Michelman has stressed, there is a miniaturized analogue of it that may be present in or missing from smaller communities, including the one that is constituted by a multimember court.[30] This is the property of colleagueship, as I shall call it, and its presence in a court is as much a good for it as the spirit of political fraternity is for society at large.

Within a court, as in any reasonably complex community, disagreements periodically arise for which there is no agreed-upon criterion the disputants can apply to determine who is right. Sometimes, of course, the differences from which these disagreements stem must be allowed to stand, with each side being represented in the court's opinion. But this is not always the case. Sometimes it is better for the judges to avoid open disagreement by recharacterizing the problem before them in such a way that the cause of their dispute disappears (or at least becomes more manageable). And sometimes it is appropriate for one side simply to yield. Knowing when to do which of these things—when to stand on principle, when to put a matter off, and when to concede—is an important part of judicial statesmanship, one of whose aims is to preserve the institution of the court itself by cultivating a spirit of colleagueship among its members.

Why is such colleagueship a good? Most importantly, because it is a condition of the court's authority, which to a considerable degree derives from the perception of it as an institution rather than a collection of individuals held together by a voting rule. As it moves (or is perceived to move) in the latter direction, a court loses authority in the eyes of those for whom it is making law, and to allow such a loss of authority is irresponsible for the judges sitting on it. They must therefore do what they can to preserve the court's authority, including strengthening the spirit of colleagueship that knits its members together into a community. To that extent, the exercise of statesmanship within a court—an internal form of judicial statesmanship—is just as important an aspect of judging as the external statesmanship courts use to preserve the integrity of the larger political communities from which their authority derives.

Indeed, these two communities—the court, on the one hand, and society, on the other—are connected in several ways. The first is, to begin with, an instrument for attaining the second. For the more a court is perceived as a community, the more authoritative its decisions become, and the more authoritative, the more effective in promoting political fraternity within the society at large. Alternatively, one might say—as Michelman has—that the first community is an image of the second and provides the larger society with a model toward which it can aspire.[31] Or, perhaps, these two communities should be thought of as parts of a single whole, complementing and reinforcing each other in different ways. Each of these characterizations has something to recommend it, and we need not choose among them. But whatever the nature of their connection, it is clear that the judicial community and the larger political one are importantly linked, so that a weakening of the first is likely to cause a weakening of the second as well. The extent to which a court is able to achieve the external aims of statesmanship, or even takes an interest in them, therefore depends, among other things, on the strength of the spirit of colleagueship that informs its own internal life.

It is the weakening of this spirit in our appellate courts that the increased splintering of their opinions reflects—the weakening of the sense that there are institutional values that must be weighed against the desire to preserve one's own individual jurisprudential identity in as clear and uncontaminated a form as possible, values that sometimes require a judge to submerge his personal identity or even to sacrifice it for the sake of the court to which he belongs. The increasing division of appellate opinions into a series of separate concurrences and dissents reflects the growing importance that judges now attach to creative self-expression and fidelity to personal principle, on the one hand, and the correspondingly decreased weight they give to colleagueship and the good of institutional integrity, on the other. This represents a significant shift in judicial motivation, whose result has been a steady deterioration in what I have called the internal branch of judicial statesmanship, the branch that is concerned with the collegial integrity of courts, the "little platoons," in Burke's phrase, to which judges immediately belong.[32] And as this branch has decayed, the external branch, whose aim is to promote political fraternity in the community at large, has weakened as well. For the good at which each aims is essentially the same, so that as the value of one has become less obvious to judges, it is natural that the other should have come to seem less valuable too and the art of statesmanship that serves both ends have lost prestige among judges generally.

What has brought about this change in outlook? Many factors have no doubt played a part. One, which Posner emphasizes, is the grow-ing number of judges on each federal court of appeals—a develop-ment that has weakened their institutional cohesion and diluted the loyalty individual judges feel to them. Another is the increasingly ideological nature of the judicial appointments process, which changed dramatically during the Reagan years. Traditionally, senators belonging to the president's political party recommended candidates to fill the federal judgeships in their states. But in the Reagan admin-istration this role was taken over by the Justice Department, which began to apply a strict "litmus test" in evaluating potential appointees, to approve or disapprove them depending upon the firmness of their adherence to a small set of well-defined substantive views.[33] Predict-ably, the judges who emerged from this new screening process were men and women of more doctrinaire outlook than those appointed under the old regime—more inclined to insist on intellectual clarity, on the brightness of the line between truth and error, and hence less likely to tolerate compromise and ambiguity. The spirit of separatism reflected in the splintering of judicial opinions is also, in part, a conse-quence of this.

But more important than either of these factors is a third—the growth of judicial staff, and of law clerks in particular, which has contributed to the fractionation of opinions in two ways. First, and most obviously, the greater the number of clerks working for a judge, the more opinions he can produce (at least if he does not insist, as few now do, on writing all his opinions himself). The existence of a corps of clerks makes the proliferation of judicial opinions possible. But clerks not only facilitate proliferation. Second, and more subtly, they encourage it. The primary attachment of most law clerks is to the judge for whom they work and not the court on which he sits. And because their own time at the court is much shorter than his— he is appointed for life, and they only for a year or two—they are less likely to be interested in issues of long-term collegiality and more likely to want, instead, to see their judge stand out in his opinions as an individual with distinctive views of his own. For that is the only way in which they can realistically expect to make an impression on the law during their brief tenure as clerks. If they are to make such an impression, law clerks must do it through their judge, whose voice cannot be heard if it is drowned in a majority opinion issued in some other judge's name.

Eager that their judge's views be heard (since that is the only way their own can be), and unmoved by considerations of collegiality (in which they have no real stake), law clerks therefore tend to exert a steady pressure on the judges for whom they work to issue separate concurrences and dissents. Of course, no judge can be manipulated at will by his clerks, and most are able to resist this pressure if they want. But resistance, too, takes time and energy—more so as a judge's staff expands and his dependence on it grows—so that even a self-effacing judge who values collegiality may be pressured by his clerks to express himself with greater independence. For the judge who begins by assuming that collegiality is less important than the clean elaboration of his own distinctive philosophy of law, the existence of a staff that not only makes the latter aspiration easier to achieve but is temperamentally disposed to share it too can only reinforce the judge's separatist inclinations and further weaken his sense of the value of judicial colleagueship and of the statesmanship that is needed to sustain it.

THE CULTURE OF CLERKS

These last remarks bring me to the second of the changes in judicial style on which I want to comment. This change is harder to define than the first, and more difficult to document, yet apparent to most readers of opinions. Like the first, it is to a large degree a consequence of the increasingly important role that law clerks play in the process of opinion-writing. The change I have in mind has several facets, but each reflects the culture and condition of these clerks themselves— above all, their immaturity and own self-conscious lack of judgment. These are the qualities one sees most clearly reflected in the style of what has become the model opinion in our federal courts: the long and excessively footnoted decision that moves, in a stiffly mechanical way, through a recitation of the different factors bearing on the case at hand to the generally uninformative conclusion that a balancing of them yields a certain result. If there is a norm in opinion-writing today, this is it, and its stylistic features reflect the combination of hubris and self-doubt that is the mark of the culture of clerks, a culture whose influence on the form and substance of judicial thought has grown enormously in recent years.

In his book on the federal courts, Judge Posner offers an insightful account of the effects that the rise of the law clerk has had on the style of judicial opinions.[34] To begin with, he observes, it is clerks who are largely responsible for the increasing length of opinions. Opinions written by law clerks tend to be longer because their authors have not yet acquired the conciseness that comes with experience and practice. Being new to the law, moreover, they lack confidence in their own insight and judgment, and therefore tend to include every conceivable argument for their position in any opinion they write.

This same timidity, Posner suggests, also accounts for the obsessive footnoting and heavy use of legal jargon that are hallmarks of contemporary opinion-writing. Too insecure to speak in their own voices, law clerks tend to speak through the words and opinions of others instead and to express themselves by means of conventional phrases for which they need take no personal responsibility—an attitude of self-effacement that contrasts strikingly with the personal assertiveness reflected in the splintering of opinions into separate concurrences and dissents.

To these stylistic expressions of the law clerk mentality two more may be added: the growing use of carefully structured multipart tests for the resolution of legal disputes (modern equal-protection doctrine being a particularly good example of this),[35] and—what is closely related—an increasing reliance on the rhetoric of balancing to describe and legitimate the deliberative procedure by which decisions are arrived at in particular cases. The first of these, Posner maintains, is a product of youthful timidity too. For what it reflects is an anxious desire to constrain one's judgment with a scheme of detailed rules and to make the final outcome in a case look (perhaps even feel) as mechanical as possible, like something that more closely resembles the last step in a formal proof than an act of deliberative judgment. Law clerks, who are unsure of their judgments, are particularly drawn to such schemes.

The rhetoric of balancing reflects a similar unease.[36] Everyone—judges, clerks, and the readers of opinions—knows that the decision in a case never emerges mechanically from the application of a test, no matter how complex. The most a test can do is identify the factors that must be considered and indicate their relative weight. In any particular case, it always remains to do the actual weighing. The image of a balance reminds us that this is so, and to that extent might be thought a useful corrective to an overly mechanical conception of the judicial process. At the same time, however, it conceals in obscurity the act of judgment that the weighing of different factors involves. The rhetoric of balancing ("These are the factors that bear upon the case. Balancing them, we find . . .") can make the decision of a case seem reasonable while not mechanically compelled. But when one probes beneath the surface of those opinions that employ this rhetoric most deliberately—that use the image of a balance as if it could confer legitimacy on the court's decision in the case—one often finds no account of the process of deliberation that the word "balance" summarily describes. In these cases, the act of balancing remains obscure despite its central importance in the court's own statement of what it has done. We cannot say what this act is or how it was performed. As a rhetorical device, therefore, the image of the balance—a dominant image in the opinions of the Supreme Court and, increasingly, of other appellate courts as well—is likely to be particularly attractive to those who by virtue of their inexperience feel unable to articulate the bases of their judgments, or who simply lack confidence in them and are therefore afraid to expose their own deliberations too nakedly.

Like the use of complex multipart tests and similar analytic schemes, to which it is in fact a perfect complement, the rhetoric of balancing is thus a strategy of insecurity. Along with the increasing length of judicial opinions and the heavy use of footnotes to support them, the growing reliance on these complementary techniques is a feature of the new style of opinion-writing that has emerged from what it would not be too farfetched to call the law clerk revolution: the rise, to a position of previously unimaginable influence, of law clerks and the mentality they share. At bottom this is the mentality of youth, an outlook at once anxious and domineering, made insecure by the lack of practiced judgment but buoyed by a confidence in the power of ideas and by a belief in the importance of being true to oneself regardless of the institutional costs.

Being young (professionally if not always chronologically), most law clerks lack what Karl Llewellyn called horse-sense: the ability of those who have mastered an activity to pursue it with subtlety and grace, employing powers of discernment irreducible to rules. Generally speaking, the beginners in any activity lack the sort of judgment it requires, or have less than those who have been engaged in it for a longer period of time. Because of this they have no choice but to rely on the opinions of their seniors, to which they often attach themselves uncritically, and on general rules and principles, which even a beginner with intelligence but no experience can comprehend. The less developed one's own powers of discernment in an activity—the less assured one's craftsmanship in Llewellyn's sense—the more one will need to rely on strategies like these, which in essence provide a kind of substitute or surrogate for judgment and thereby help to compensate for its absence.

This is how we should view the stylistic changes in opinion-writing that Posner describes: as the natural expression of an approach to judging that does not rely upon the exercise of judgment but rather tries to make up for its lack. The prolixity, the excessive use of footnotes, the jargon, the complicated multipart tests, the endless talk about balancing (which sounds, on the surface at least, so sensibly mature)—these are the habits of beginners, of smart young lawyers with great intelligence but little experience who are not yet the masters of their craft and must therefore of necessity rely on something other than their own undeveloped judgment. In this respect, the law is like every complex discipline, and those who have just entered it are in the same position, and labor under the same burden of inexperience, as beginners everywhere. The outlook of the law clerk is simply a local expression of this general human fact.

Should we be concerned about the growing prominence of this outlook in the work of our appellate courts? No one will deny that an exposure to young lawyers, with their enthusiasm and fresh ideas, is a good thing for aging judges, at least in moderate doses. It helps to keep them alert and up-to-date, establishes an important line of communication between our law schools and our courts, and for many judges is undoubtedly a pleasure in its own right. But beyond a certain point—one I think we have already passed—the answer must be yes. For as the youthful outlook of the law clerk becomes increasingly embedded in the practice of opinion-writing, as its stylistic expressions come more and more to be perceived as the normal ones that any sound opinion must display, judges will grow used to this attitude and be encouraged to adopt it themselves. They will come to see their own work through the eyes of their clerks, who today set the standards in opinion-writing. And as this happens, the older person's virtue of practical wisdom will lose its meaning for judges too and be replaced by other, more youthful traits such as cleverness and dialectical agility, redefining the qualities judges admire in a practitioner of their craft and in the opinions he or she writes. Subtly perhaps, but steadily and effectively, the increasing influence of law clerks and their antiprudential culture thus brings about a shift in judicial values, contributing to the decline of the lawyer-statesman ideal in the minds of judges themselves by making the beginner in the craft of judging the measure of the master's art.

The most important fact about our courts today is neither, as some maintain, that they are too activist nor, as others claim, that they are insufficiently so. The most important fact about our courts is that the judges serving on them now work in an environment that in many reinforcing ways undermines the values of the lawyer-statesman ideal and promotes opposing ones instead. And the most important fact about the increase in the number of law clerks working in our courts is that it has helped to bring this situation about: by distancing judges from the pathos of conflict in a way that enervates their imagination; by encouraging the spirit of separatism that is reflected in the splintering of judicial opinions; and, above all, by promoting the idea that the length of an opinion, the number of its footnotes, and the variety of factors it marshals for balancing can be a substitute for wisdom— a young person's idea whose strange triumph in our courts has transformed what used to be the preeminent example of an older person's art.

A VICIOUS CIRCLE

In every craftlike activity, of which Llewellyn was surely right to say the law is one, it is the rule that the old teach the young. The obvious justification for this is the greater experience and superior judgment of those long steeped in the activity. Thus in the law, young people have traditionally been educated into its culture by being made to study the opinions of judges, older people whose opinions tend to reflect the habits and values of older people, including an appreciation of the place of prudence in the law. But increasingly today, the opinions that law students read have been written by clerks, that is, by other beginners like themselves, and the qualities these opinions exemplify tend to be the very qualities of the students who are reading them. What they see reflected in these opinions, therefore, is essentially an image of themselves, clothed in the trappings of authority.

Contemporary legal theory has a strong antiprudentialist bias that has begun to seep into the classroom too. So long as law students continued to read cases written by older judges who understood the importance of prudence in their work, this bias was counterbalanced or offset. But that counterbalance no longer exists. Indeed, in the opinions they study today, law students are more likely to find the outlook of their teachers confirmed and strengthened than opposed. For these opinions, with their elaborate analytical tests and other surrogates for judgment, are shaped by the same antiprudentialist spirit that now informs the work of many academic lawyers and in a similar way are leading the newest recruits to the profession farther and farther away from the lawyer-statesman ideal. In this sense one might say that in America today the normal process of legal education—of the old teaching the young—has been interrupted, or more precisely, that it never even begins.

This brings me back to the point from which I started at the beginning of Chapter 4. In that chapter and the two that have followed, I have given an account of certain recent changes in American law teaching, practice, and adjudication. These changes, which have transformed the legal profession, have all had the same result. They have all helped to disconnect the profession from the ideal of the lawyer-statesman that shaped the self-understanding of American lawyers for the better part of two centuries but has collapsed in the last generation. In each of these three areas one may now speak of a crisis in professional values. These separate crises, moreover, are merely facets of a single larger one, and only when they are seen as such can the present condition of our law schools, firms, and courts be fully grasped. By examining its different parts in turn, I have sought to make the magnitude and meaning of this wider crisis clear.

For nearly two centuries the lawyer-statesman ideal sustained the legal profession in America and gave it moral depth. It is a noble ideal, and around it generations of lawyers were able to build professional lives with personal meaning. But that ideal is now failing throughout the profession as a whole. What will become of the legal profession if it fails? And is its failure something we can still prevent?

7

Honesty and Hope

A TROUBLING INHERITANCE

The lawyers of my generation now find themselves in positions of authority and power. Twenty years after graduating from law school, we stand near the top of our profession. We are partners in our firms and senior professors on our faculties. And we are beginning to be appointed in large numbers to the courts. To a significant degree, the stewardship of these institutions, and of the legal profession generally, is in our hands. When we came to the law, it seemed mysterious and remote. Yet after an impossibly short time we find that it is we who are the guardians of our profession and responsible for its well-being. We have come, in the normal course of succession, to the authority and influence that every generation enjoys at its maturity, and the responsibilities that go with this authority are now ours, for the time being at least, until we are relieved by the next generation of lawyers that is following behind. This is our hour in the sun.

But the profession we have inherited is not the one we joined twenty years ago. In many outward ways it is remarkably different. Its schools now encourage a style of scholarly work that is increasingly remote from—even hostile to—the concerns of practicing lawyers. Its leading firms have become giant industries, marked by an extreme division of labor and aggressive commercial tactics, that bear only a fading resemblance to their predecessors. And the caseload crisis has transformed our courts and made the work of judging a more managerial and less deliberative activity.

These changes in the profession are dramatic and important. But it is with the inward change they all reflect that I have been mainly

concerned in this book. For each of these developments points to a
shift in the way lawyers understand themselves and their work—in
the professional self-consciousness of lawyers. This inward change is
subtle and hard to describe. It belongs to the inherently ambiguous
realm of attitudes and beliefs. Yet it is the key to understanding all
the more visible changes in the profession that have taken place in
the last twenty years. It connects these changes and gives them a
common meaning. It is the source of the professionwide crisis of
which they are merely the local signs.

The inward change of which I am speaking has been brought
about by the collapse of the lawyer-statesman ideal. For more than a
century and a half that ideal helped to shape the collective aspirations
of lawyers, to define the things they cared about and thought important to achieve. Even thirty years ago, it was still a potent force in
the profession. But in the years since, as my generation has risen to
power, the ideal of the lawyer-statesman has all but passed from view.
Law teachers no longer respect it. The most prestigious law firms
have ceased to cultivate it. And judges can no longer find the time,
amid the press of cases, to give its claims their due.

The ideal of the lawyer-statesman offered an answer to the question of what a life in the law should be. It provided a foundation on
which a sense of professional identity might be built. And because
the foundation it provided was rich in human values, this ideal was
appealing at a personal level too. The decline of the lawyer-statesman
ideal has undermined that foundation, throwing the professional
identity of lawyers into doubt. It has ceased to be clear what that
identity is and why its attainment should be a reason for personal
pride. This is the great inward change that has overtaken the legal
profession in my generation, and its outward manifestations, which
are visible in every branch of professional life, all point to a collective
identity crisis of immense—if largely unacknowledged—proportions.

A New Ideal for Lawyers?

The lawyer-statesman ideal, which shaped the moral ambitions of the
American legal profession for so long, is now in full retreat. It is losing
its hold on lawyers everywhere. But there are some who view its
collapse in a positive light. These are the modern proponents of pol-

icy science, the heirs of Lasswell and McDougal and the tradition they represent. In their eyes the ideal of the lawyer-statesman is an anachronism, a vestige from an earlier phase of the profession's development, unrelated to its present needs. They see it as an obstacle to the rational reconstruction of the law. They say that American lawyers have outgrown this ideal and must now adopt a new one—and a new identity—instead. The profession's present crisis is, for them, merely the birth-passage from an old, outworn conception of the lawyer's calling to a fresh and more responsive one, a development to be greeted with elation, not dismay. While acknowledging the depth of this crisis, and the seriousness of its consequences for the profession, they thus place an opposite value on its outcome from the one that I do, and deride those who share my concern as romantics, nostalgics, or worse. Among the legal writers of my generation, Bruce Ackerman has been the most outspoken defender of this view.[1] But many others, encouraged by the antiprudentialism of the law-and-economics and critical legal studies movements, have been drawn to it as well.

Those who hold this view maintain that today's lawyers must make two basic adjustments to meet the needs of the times. First, they must give up their ancient habit of proceeding case by case, of viewing the complex structures of the legal and political world from the incomplete and often misleading perspective of individual disputes. Instead, they must study these structures directly and systematically. Traditionally, lawyers have proceeded in an *ad hoc* fashion, constructing their arguments from whatever bits of rhetoric they could find to meet the needs of the case at hand. But this will no longer do. If lawyers are to understand, let alone be in a position to manipulate, the complexities of late-twentieth-century society, they must replace their old undisciplined techniques, well-suited to the pointillism of the common law, with other, more methodical ones—with the systematic study of the structures and patterns that inform these complexities themselves. They must become students of the social order and learn to approach cases from this comprehensive point of view rather than the other way around.

Second, today's lawyers must also become fluent in several other fields: economics, statistics, political science, and philosophy, for a start. The keys to understanding the structure of society lie mainly here. The law is by comparison an intellectually backward discipline, and those working in it must depend, to a large degree, on methods and insights drawn from other areas. In the past, lawyers thought of their craft as an "autonomous" discipline, that is, as a self-contained activity with materials and methods uniquely its own.[2] But they can no longer afford to do so, at least if they wish to make any progress toward a truly rigorous understanding of the law. For that, a knowledge of many other subjects is required. Good law today is necessarily "law and."[3]

Implicit in these requirements is a new ideal for lawyers. This ideal has its roots in the nineteenth-century movement for scientific law reform. It was sharpened by the scientific realists and is now a dominant presence in American legal thought. From the beginning it has stood in opposition to the ideal of the lawyer-statesman, and as this older ideal fades from the consciousness of the profession, supporters of the new one put theirs forward to fill the gap it leaves behind. After a century of struggle, they sense victory close at hand.

But is their new model of professional excellence an appealing substitute for the ideal of the lawyer-statesman? Can it in fact fill the gap created by latter's demise? There are three reasons to think it cannot. First, even at the highest levels of private practice there is still little need for the kind of multidisciplinary social science whose value defenders of this model stress. Second, whatever its application in practice, the ideal of the lawyer as an omnicompetent social engineer puts the value and distinctiveness of the lawyer's craft in doubt. And third, this new ideal lacks the depth and human meaning that the ideal of the lawyer-statesman possessed. For the concept of character, which gave the latter great personal appeal, has no place in it at all.

I can elaborate the first point with an example. Consider the work of a lawyer specializing in securities regulation, a field dominated by statutes and addressed to structural problems of an explicitly economic kind. Here if anywhere we might expect a policy-scientific approach to have value for the private practitioner. But in fact it has almost none at all. To begin with, even in this densely statutory field the practitioner's work remains largely case-centered. A securities lawyer must of course have a detailed knowledge of the statutes that provide the foundation for his subject. But beyond this he needs to know the case law that has grown around these statutes, whose key provisions are often brief and formulaic. Indeed, he is likely to view the latter knowledge as the more demanding and important of the two. For not only are the cases in his field harder to decipher than the laconic language of the securities statutes themselves. They are also, at any given moment, the repository of the complex legal meanings these statutes have been given by the courts, and therefore of special interest to a lawyer who needs to know precisely what they permit, forbid, and require.

In one obvious sense, a securities lawyer must pay attention to the overall structure of his field. He must keep in mind the relations among the various cases and statutes with which he is concerned and not treat them as if they were free-floating atoms of law. He must understand the links that bind them into an organized whole. But what a securities lawyer needs to comprehend this whole is not advanced training in economics or other nonlegal disciplines. There are, of course, academic writers who have analyzed our securities laws from an economic point of view, and a practitioner in the field may take an interest in their work and will almost certainly cite it when he thinks it useful to do so.[4] But the broad knowledge of his subject that he requires to do his own work well depends more on the practitioner's traditional techniques of analogy and distinction than on the scientific methods of his academic counterparts. For it is these lawyerly techniques that remain most useful in deciding which interpretations of a statute can in good faith be sustained and which (though not illogical or silly) run with the grain of earlier decisions rather than against it—the core questions that a securities lawyer faces in attempting to make sense of his field. What Guido Calabresi called the statutorification of the law has no doubt transformed the quality of private practice, especially in large firms, and made the work of lawyers there more mechanical and routine.[5] But however fateful for the culture of these firms, the growth of statutory law has not as yet compelled the lawyers in them to exchange their old professional habits for newer, more scientific ones. Even in the most nontraditional fields lawyers still get by, for the most part, with a repertoire of unscientific techniques that continue to seem adequate to the task at hand.[6]

But this is not the strongest reason for thinking that a worthy successor to the lawyer-statesman ideal cannot be found in the concept of a policy science of law. A much stronger reason is that this concept itself obscures the nature of the lawyer's role and hence professional identity. It leaves in doubt whether lawyers possess a valuable expertise, different from that of those in other fields, and thus fails to provide a foundation on which the professional pride of lawyers may be rebuilt.

It is now widely assumed that a lawyer's education should include a sustained exposure to several other disciplines as well—most importantly, to philosophy and economics. Indeed, some claim that without a working knowledge of these subjects a lawyer can no longer perform his or her professional tasks in an adequate way. The world has grown too complex, they say, for lawyers to make do without the more systematic forms of understanding that philosophy and economics provide. This is the main idea behind the call for a new policy science of law and the suggestion that the work of lawyers be reconceived in its light. But it immediately raises a basic question about the identity of the legal profession. For if lawyers are to have a distinct professional persona of their own, they must possess some special set of skills that philosophers and economists (and statisticians and political scientists and sociologists) do not, and it is unclear where in this mélange of disciplines—in the ever richer blendings of "law and"—these skills are to be found. If a lawyer must become a jack-of-all-trades with a knowledge of many fields, how in the end will he differ from the experts in these fields themselves? What special role will he perform and distinctive qualities bring to it? Is it, perhaps, that at the end of his multidisciplinary education a lawyer will be familiar with many different modes of thought and therefore in a position to mediate between them—in contrast to philosophers, economists, and others who are commonly at home in just one field? Or is there some special technique, distinct from those that experts in these other disciplines employ, that lawyers alone possess and that it is the object of their legal training to impart?

On the first view, the lawyer is a kind of dilettante, familiar with many fields but expert in none. Within any specialty, of course, it is the expert's opinion that governs. The lawyer—who is merely an amateur—must therefore be prepared to defer to the judgment of specialists whenever the question is one that belongs to their own field. Here he can never be anything more than a second-class citizen.

Nor does it increase the lawyer's stature much to be portrayed as a generalist with a broad, if amateurish, knowledge of several subjects who is better able than most specialists to say which questions should be allocated to which fields. For even if we assume that lawyers alone possess this general kind of knowledge (itself an implausible assumption), that hardly justifies assigning them a role equal in dignity to the one real experts play in their own home disciplines. Within their chosen specialty, experts need not defer to the judgments of anyone else. Indeed, in one sense they cannot, since it is their opinions that constitute the standard by which all others in the field are assessed. By contrast, if the lawyer's job is merely to distribute different questions to different groups of experts (in which he has no standing himself), his whole outlook must in essence be deferential and subservient. For the final answer to these questions can then only be given by someone who possesses an expertise the lawyer lacks. Of course, if we begin by assuming that many legal disputes are not decidable by experts—by professional philosophers, economists, and other specialists—the lawyer's function appears in a different and more favorable light. But the more one insists on the role that expertise should play in the resolution of such disputes, the less elevated the lawyer's job is likely to seem, so long, at least, as lawyers are assumed to possess no substantive expertise of their own but merely to direct the flow of controversy toward other nonlegal specialists who do.

Let us consider, then, the second possibility: that lawyers do possess a distinctive expertise that specialists in other fields lack. In fact, this seems like a reasonable assumption. When a lawyer sits down with an economist and a philosopher to discuss a legal problem, it is clear he has something to add beyond the suggestion that his two companions divide the problem between them in a certain way. In addition the lawyer can contribute—will be expected to contribute—his expert knowledge of the law.

What does this knowledge come to? Negatively we can say that it does not consist, mainly at least, in a knowledge of legal rules, of prescriptions and prohibitions written down in books that lawyers are (by virtue of their training) better able to recall. For legal rules invite and often require interpretation. A knowledge of the law must therefore include an understanding of the methods to be used in interpreting these rules, and it is the possession of this understanding that represents the lawyer's chief expertise.

We may pursue this train of thought a step further. When a lawyer offers an interpretation of a novel or debated question of law, he always does so from a particular point of view, one defined by the law's own aims and purposes. It is in light of these that he constructs his interpretation of contested rules and principles. But the purposes of the law are notoriously controversial and frequently require an interpretive exposition of their own. So a lawyer's expertise cannot be just an aptitude for interpreting the law from the standpoint of certain already agreed-upon goals. More important, it must include the ability to construct the interpretive arguments that are needed to define these goals themselves.

If the lawyer's ability to do this is to be in any way distinctive, however, it cannot be just an amalgam of techniques from other fields. It cannot be made up entirely from the methods and insights of other, nonlegal disciplines like philosophy and economics. For if that were the case, it would be the experts in these fields, and not the lawyer, who should have the final word in debates about the purposes of law (and therefore in disputes about the meaning of specific legal rules as well). Naturally, a lawyer may make use of other disciplines in his work. These often provide him with valuable material. But there must be some special approach, uniquely his own, that he employs to integrate these materials and to assess their relevance in particular disputes—at least if his discipline is to be anything more than an amateurish composite of theirs.

The distinctiveness of the lawyer's approach may be brought out concretely in the following way. Suppose that Congress is considering whether to enact a statute regulating some important aspect of corporate or commercial life (insider trading, for example). It empanels a committee to discuss the matter and to prepare a draft of the statute in question. The committee consists of a philosopher, an economist, and a lawyer. What special contribution can the lawyer make to the work of the committee, and what distinctive skills should we expect him or her to display in making it?

Clearly, there are questions of a broad philosophical kind the committee may want to consider. To what extent, for example, should the statute that Congress is contemplating be used as an instrument for the promotion of distributive justice, and how ought a regime of fair distribution be defined? And there will undoubtedly also be specialized issues of an economic sort the committee feels it must examine. As regards these matters, the lawyer possesses no expertise, and it is appropriate that the views of the committee's other members carry the most weight in any discussion of them.

But at some point the committee will need to find the right words to express its conclusions in statutory form. Here the philosopher and the economist are likely to turn to the lawyer for help and to assign him the leading role in preparing a draft of the statute.

Statutory drafting is not, however, a merely mechanical process— the transcription of ordinary words into arcane legal terminology. It is in fact a complex art, and the skills it requires go well beyond a simple knowledge of legal rules and the esoteric language in which they are expressed. Above all, it requires imagination. For if the lawyer who has taken the lead in drafting the statute is to have a clear idea of what its scope and contours ought to be, he must imagine in advance a wide range of possible cases that may arise within its orbit and ask how each should be resolved. Only by imaginatively testing their consequences in this way can the merits of different phrasings be compared and an informed choice made among them.

Of course, no one can anticipate all the cases to which a statute may one day be applied. The later history of even the most carefully drafted statute is bound to contain some surprises. But if it is the lawyer on my imaginary committee who takes the lead in the drafting process—if it is his opinion about the superiority of one phrase to another that the philosopher and the economist accept as the expert view—that is because he is better able than they to imagine future cases, to see their latent possibilities and give them, in advance, a vividly concrete form.

The contributions that the different members of the committee make to its work are obviously interdependent. The philosopher, for example, does not simply offer an opinion about the meaning of distributive justice and then ask the lawyer to give it a suitable legal form. Their functions are more closely linked than this. For the imaginary cases the lawyer conjures up in his drafting help to test the philosopher's opinion and often provide reasons to revise it. If he is to participate in this process of revision, the lawyer too must have some understanding of the philosophical issues at stake, and the same is obviously true when the question involved is of a technical economic sort. To collaborate effectively with the other members of the committee, it is therefore necessary that the lawyer have some familiarity with their disciplines in addition to a mastery of his own.

But even if an acquaintance with other fields like philosophy and economics is sometimes needed in their work, the special expertise of lawyers—including the one on my committee—lies elsewhere. What lawyers are particularly trained to do and can generally do better than philosophers and economists is think about cases—imaginary future cases, as in my example, but real past ones too. The ability to fashion hypothetical cases and empathically to explore both real and invented ones is the lawyer's professional forte. It is what his case-centered education and experience give him special competence at doing—unlike philosophers and economists, whose disciplines are on the whole more concerned with the construction of abstract systems of thought. And it is what defines the distinctive vantage point from which lawyers tend to see things: the point of view of those who see the world through the lens of individual cases and are temperamentally inclined to assess the abstract claims of philosophy and economics from the particularistic standpoint they afford.

If lawyers have a distinctive expertise of their own, it thus consists in the art of handling cases. There is, in fact, no other candidate for the position. For this art is the only one in which lawyers have a professional advantage over experts in the various nonlegal fields on whose relevance to law the advocates of policy science insist. A philosopher or an economist may of course have some facility in deliberating about cases, just as a lawyer may have some understanding of the concepts and methods they employ. But if he is an amateur in their fields, they are amateurs in his, and when it comes to the imaginative probing of specific cases, it is the lawyer who is best equipped, by training and temperament, to lead the way. A well-educated lawyer will be aware of the theories circulating in other disciplines and, in general terms at least, will understand their application to the law. But it is not his knowledge of these theories that defines the lawyer's expertise or the core of his professional persona. That is to be found, instead, in his ability to deliberate well about cases—a valued trait and one the law promotes in special measure.

Thus if we think of the lawyer as a jack-of-all-trades with a dilettante's understanding of many fields but no expertise of his own, whose special function is to serve as an intermediary between other disciplines like philosophy and economics, his position will be a subordinate one marked by deference toward the real experts in these areas—not a very elevated or inspiring ideal for lawyers to embrace. If, on the other hand, we start with the assumption that lawyers do possess a distinctive expertise equal in dignity to that of those in other fields, and then inquire what this expertise may be, the best answer remains the old one: that lawyers are experts at dealing with cases and possess to an exceptional degree the special imaginative powers this requires. But that is of course precisely the answer the decaying ideal of the lawyer-statesman has always given.

Those who maintain that the lawyer of the future must be a multi-disciplinary social engineer and who claim that this new model of professional excellence offers an appealing alternative to the lawyer-statesman ideal are thus mistaken, whichever of these two views we adopt. For on the first there is nothing appealing to lawyers in the model they propose. And on the second their alternative to the ideal of the lawyer-statesman proves in the end to be indistinguishable from it. On neither view, therefore, is it plausible to think that the concept of a policy science of law can provide a new rallying-point for the profession—a new and satisfying foundation on which the identity of lawyers may once again be based. For if it is not an elevated conception, no one will rally to it. And if at its heart it is simply a modified version of the lawyer-statesman ideal, it offers no more hope than that ideal does of surviving the identity crisis in which the profession is now caught.

There is one final reason for doubting whether the void left by the collapse of the lawyer-statesman ideal can be filled by even the most visionary program of policy science—perhaps the most important reason of all.

The lawyer-statesman ideal is an ideal of character. It calls upon the lawyer who adopts it not just to acquire a set of intellectual skills, but to develop certain character traits as well. It engages his affects along with his intellect and forces him to feel as well as think in certain ways. The lawyer-statesman ideal poses a challenge to the whole person, and this helps to explain why it is capable of offering such deep personal meaning to those who view their professional responsibilities in its light.

The ideal set up by the proponents of policy science is by contrast narrowly intellectual. It is an ideal directed at the thinking part of the soul only. To achieve the mastery of other disciplines that this ideal so highly values is a purely intellectual feat that a person can perform without undergoing the more elementary change in affect that every ideal of character contemplates. Learning a subject like philosophy or economics is of course bound to produce a legitimate sense of accomplishment. But an understanding of even the most complex intellectual discipline cannot by itself convey the deeper satisfaction that comes with the attainment of a valued trait of character like practical wisdom. For this does more than increase a person's knowledge of the world. It alters one's dispositional attitude toward it and thereby modifies one's personality in an essential way. The ideal of the lawyer-statesman made it easy for lawyers to identify with their role because it promised a deeper satisfaction of this kind. No program of policy science can do the same. And that is the most important reason why it is incapable in the end of offering a really fulfilling alternative to the lawyer-statesman ideal, however well suited to the conditions of our age such a program appears to be.

AN OLD IDEAL RESTORED?

If the ideal of the lawyer-statesman cannot be replaced, perhaps its central values, at least, may be restored. That is the hopeful suggestion implicit in the new republicanism and one that Robert Gordon, in particular, has advanced with considerable force.[7] Those who hold this view do not share the enthusiasm for policy science that many contemporary legal writers display; indeed, they tend to be quite skeptical of its claims. They trace their intellectual roots instead to the federalist-republican culture of the early nineteenth century and its historical successors (progressivism in particular). At the core of this tradition, they say, is the simple but potent idea that lawyers have an obligation to serve the public good—consciously to promote not only their clients' private interests but also the integrity of the rules and institutions that form the framework within which these interests exist. On their view, for a lawyer to lead a responsible professional life, he must keep one eye on the legal arrangements that define the broad background of his everyday work. He must take an active interest in the betterment of these arrangements and be prepared to contribute to their improvement and repair. Failing this, the practice of law loses its status as a calling and degenerates into a tool with no more inherent moral dignity than a hammer or a gun.

Through all its permutations, they maintain, the republican tradition has adhered to this idea, which today remains as valid as before. To be sure, various intellectual and institutional developments have placed its relevance in doubt. The declining independence of lawyers and the acceptance by many of a view of advocacy that depreciates all direct concern for the public good have been especially important in this regard. But there is no reason to believe these doubts cannot be overcome. The advocacy model of law practice that in its strong form is so dismissive of the need for public-spiritedness has been substantially weakened by recent criticisms of it.[8] And while it is true that some lawyers are in certain ways today more dependent on their clients, in others they are freer than before.[9] One should not despair, therefore, about the possibility of reviving the legal profession's ethic of public service. The conditions for doing so exist. What is mainly needed is will—a renewed commitment to this ethic and the courage to make the sacrifices it demands. The key to restoring the profession's failing sense of identity is thus not some new set of refined intellectual techniques (as the proponents of policy science suggest). The crucial factor is resolve: the ability to make and stand by a commitment to serve the public good. That is not easy to do, even under the best of circumstances. And the forces that conspire against it— including, most importantly, the ethos of commercialism that now dominates the country's leading firms—are exceptionally strong. But the republican revival that has been so influential in the world of legal scholarship has inspired some to hope that even at this late hour the ethic of public service may be restored to a central place in the consciousness of practicing lawyers and, with encouragement from the organized bar, renew the sense of moral purpose that dignified their work in the past.

This hopeful view is clearly right in two respects. First, unless the practice of law is tempered by a concern for the public good, it can never be anything but an amoral tool for the satisfaction of private needs. And second, the level of public-spiritedness within the profession is today dismally low and needs to be increased. Lawyers should spend more time on law reform and the *pro bono* representation of worthy causes and clients. Whether they will or not is largely a question—as this view also rightly suggests—of courage and resolve.

But is such a change in outlook, however desirable, capable of restoring to lawyers the confident sense that their professional role is an intrinsically fulfilling one, as the lawyer-statesman ideal implied? Not, I think, by itself. Although a devotion to the public good is essential to the law's standing as a morally honorable calling, it is not enough to ensure that even those lawyers who feel this devotion most deeply will find intrinsic satisfaction in their work. For that, something more is required.

Suppose, for example, that a lawyer takes an interest in the public good and works with determination to advance it, making significant material sacrifices along the way. Suppose, even, that this interest is the dominant one in his professional life. It is what motivates him to go to law school and then afterward to pursue the particular career he does. Such a lawyer certainly lives up to the highest standards of public-spiritedness. But he may still view his own professional role in narrowly instrumental terms. For it is entirely possible that he sees his legal skills merely as an asset to be used in the campaign for a better world and judges the soundness of his investment in them strictly in terms of how much betterment they produce. The lawyer who views his work in this way resembles the one who sees the practice of law merely as a means for making money. The ends the public-spirited lawyer pursues may be more praiseworthy than those of his selfish counterpart. These two are not on a moral par in every way. But the attitude they take toward their work is in one respect the same, for its value to each derives from a goal external to the work itself.

There is, of course, no necessity that a public-spirited lawyer see things in this way. He may, indeed, view his role in a very different light, as possessing an intrinsic value of its own. Thus, though committed to the public good, he may believe that disputes about its meaning often raise questions to which no clear answer exists; that the settlement of these disputes requires prudence as well as public-spiritedness; that the exercise of prudence is a component of good politics and not just a prelude to it; and that the practice of law is an activity that fosters the development of deliberative wisdom to an exceptional degree. The lawyer who believes these things will be public-spirited too, but he is less likely to view his professional role in strictly instrumental terms. He is less likely to see it as a means to an external goal than as a part of the good he is seeking, and thus more likely to find some measure of intrinsic satisfaction in his work.

But if he is to do so, two conditions must be met. First, his work must require certain powers or capacities whose exercise he values for their own sake and not just because they produce an independently desirable outcome, even of a morally praiseworthy kind.[10] And second, these powers must figure importantly in his conception of himself. They cannot be mere skills he may acquire or discard without changing in a significant way.[11] They must be part of his identity—elements in his personality—that bear on who he is as well as what he does. They must be traits of character.

The lawyer-statesman ideal satisfied these two conditions and therefore gave its adherents reason to hope they might find intrinsic fulfillment in their work. But the neorepublican ethic of public service does not. For this ethic is, in essence, an abbreviated version of the lawyer-statesman ideal from which everything but the latter's emphasis on civic duty has been stripped. In particular, the new republicans give no weight to the character-virtue of practical wisdom, which the ideal of the lawyer-statesman stressed. That is because of their strongly egalitarian outlook. Deliberative wisdom is a virtue that people possess to different degrees, making the distinction between excellence and mediocrity unavoidably relevant to it. Devotion to the public good, by contrast, requires only an act of will that every citizen is in principle able to perform. Given their commitment to a will-based conception of equality, it is unsurprising that the new republicans should emphasize the second element of the lawyer-statesman ideal while ignoring the first entirely. But if we eliminate this aspect of the ideal and reduce it to the element of public service alone, we are left with a conception of the lawyer's role that is too thin to explain why it is an inherently fulfilling one to play.

Only this narrowing of the lawyer-statesman ideal, moreover, gives us any grounds to hope for its revival. Even today, a lawyer working in a large firm or other complex organization may be a dedicated activist if his or her will is strong and steady.[12] The demand that lawyers in such settings devote more time and energy to the pursuit of the public good is therefore not an unreasonable one to make. But the barriers these same institutions put in the way of restoring other elements of the lawyer-statesman ideal—those the new republicans reject—are far more difficult to surmount. For their very size and structure make these institutions deeply inhospitable to the cultivation of deliberative judgment. A really serious revival of public-spiritedness in the country's leading firms would be hard enough to achieve, but far easier than the structural reforms now needed to provide a supportive setting for the broader version of the lawyer-statesman ideal I have defended in this book.

The new republicans offer an ideal that is too narrow to explain what makes the practice of law an intrinsically fulfilling activity. But it stands at least a modest chance of revival. By contrast, the older ideal of the lawyer-statesman, which did provide an explanation of this sort, is today so besieged by hostile forces—in our schools and firms and courts—that its restoration now seems nearly hopeless. In each of these areas of professional life it may be possible to increase the public-spiritedness of lawyers. This badly needs to be done. But no matter how successful any such campaign, it cannot by itself restore the virtue of practical wisdom to a position of respect in the profession—something that must occur if lawyers, even public-spirited ones, are again to see their role in noninstrumental terms, as a calling or vocation. Only the reestablishment of the lawyer-statesman ideal could do this, and the likelihood of that happening grows smaller every year.

HONESTY

The collapse of the lawyer-statesman ideal has created a crisis of identity in the legal profession. It has raised doubts about whether the practice of law can continue to be an intrinsically satisfying pursuit that offers deep personal meaning to those in it. Neither policy science nor neorepublicanism offers an adequate response to these troubling concerns. Perhaps lawyers should simply admit, then, that they can no longer find the elements of a personally fulfilling identity in the realm of work, and resign themselves to the fact that they must look for these outside that realm in their private lives instead. This is a particularly sobering conclusion, and nowhere is the train of thought leading to it more forcefully expressed than in Max Weber's famous essay "Science as a Vocation." "The fate of our times," Weber writes near the end of that essay,

> is characterized by rationalization and intellectualization and, above all, by the disenchantment of the world. Precisely the ultimate and most sublime values have retreated from public life either into the transcendental realm of mystic life or into the brotherliness of direct and personal human relations. It is not accidental that our greatest art is intimate and not monumental, nor is it accidental that today only within the smallest and intimate circles, in personal human situations, in *pianissimo,* that something is pulsating that corresponds to the prophetic *pneuma,* which in former times swept

through the great communities like a firebrand welding them together.[13]

The institutions of public life once had the power to convey a
sense of purpose to the human beings who lived according to their
routines. In doing so, one's life took on meaning. One acquired an
identity, a place in the world, and with that the strength to meet life's
suffering and the senselessness of death. But that is no longer true.
All that gave the public world its meaning-giving power—the gods
that inhabited it, the ancient traditions that sustained it, the prophe-
cies that from time to time inflamed it—has vanished. Today as in
the past, of course, human beings need to believe that their lives are
worth living. But for us disenchanted moderns, this need can be met
only in the realm of personal relations, of brotherly and erotic love,
in the sphere of private life. It is to this sphere that the gods of the
public world have retreated and here that each of us must now search
for his or her salvation, for a sense of meaningful location in the
world, in short, for an identity.

This general point applies, in particular, to the field of professional
work. "Science as a Vocation" is, indeed, mainly about the nature
and meaning of one sort of professional work, that of the university
scholar. Weber begins by describing the material prospects "of a graduate student who is resolved to dedicate himself professionally" to
academic life and then goes on to consider the spiritual implications
of such a choice. What he tells his audience is that they must not
look for the satisfaction of their yearning to believe their lives have
meaning in the realm of professional work. "Science today is a 'vocation' organized in special disciplines in the service of self-clarification
and knowledge of interrelated facts. It is not the gift of grace of seers
and prophets dispensing sacred values and revelations, nor does it
partake of the contemplation of sages and philosophers about the
meaning of the universe."[14] The career of the modern scholar is an
utterly prosaic affair, devoid of all religious or philosophical significance, whose demands must be met in a simple and unassuming way,
and without the hope that its routines can by themselves provide
answers to the ultimate questions of life. For these, Weber insists, the
person who chooses an academic career must, like everyone else,
look beyond his or her professional work to "the direct and personal
human relations" in which the demand for meaning may still be met.

The implications for the legal profession seem clear enough. So long as lawyers shared a common professional ideal founded on a conception of character-virtue, their work offered them an identity and hence a meaningful place in the world. But this ideal has disappeared. The law has become a business like any other, a workaday way of making a living, and as this has happened, those in it have experienced the same disenchantment as workers in other fields. As a result, they too have been forced to look for their salvation outside the realm of work, after hours, in the intimacies of private life. To the ultimate question of life's meaning, it is now unthinkable that one can find even the smallest part of an answer by choosing a legal career. This must be sought, instead, *in pianissimo,* in the world of love and friendship that begins where the world of work leaves off. Nothing can be done about this, for the older professional culture that encouraged lawyers to believe they might find part of the answer to life's riddle in their work is now irrevocably gone. The loss of this culture is final, and the only choice that lawyers now have is whether to struggle futilely against their fate or accept it with a measure of dignity and grace.

Historically speaking, the idea that a person can find life's meaning in his or her work is a relatively new one. It plays no role, for example, in the writings of the ancient moralists, who would have thought it absurd. Indeed, it is only in the seventeenth century that the idea of a calling—of work as a path to salvation—emerges with any clarity. Many forces contributed to this development. None did so more powerfully, however, than the inner-worldly asceticism of the early modern Protestant sects (a phenomenon that Weber himself brilliantly analyzed, and that Charles Taylor has recently reexamined in an illuminating way).[15]

Behind the original Protestant idea of a calling there lay a whole complex of religious ideas (the inscrutability of God's will, the need for human beings to help complete the work of creation through their own productive labor, and so on). This religious background is now gone. But the idea of a calling, of salvation through work, did not disappear with the religious beliefs that brought it into being. For a time at least, it outlived them as a secular ideal that could survive without religious supports.

Once the religious foundations of this ideal had collapsed, however, it became necessary to redefine the concept of a calling. If work were still to be viewed as a path to salvation—as an activity capable of conferring meaning on the whole of a person's life—that view had now to be justified in terms of some intrinsic feature of the work rather than its external relation to a divinely ordered project of creation. But not every kind of work is rich enough in human values to sustain an internal justification of this sort. Some kinds are just too undemanding and routine. Of course, in the original Protestant conception of a calling, these distinctions were unimportant. All forms of work were assumed to stand on the same plane because all were equally dedicated to the service of God, even the most lowly. But the demise of this latter belief destroyed the basis on which the democratic outlook of ascetic Protestantism rested, and by focusing attention on the intrinsic attributes of work in a way it had not been before, inevitably gave new importance to the qualitative distinctions among different lines of work. Work might still be a path to salvation, in purely secular terms, but anyone who accepted this view was forced to acknowledge that not every kind of work was equally up to the task.

One way of marking this distinction, which assumed great importance in the second half of the nineteenth century, is with the idea of a profession and the line that it implies between two different sorts of work. The idea of a profession is an old one and serves many purposes, some crudely material. And the question of which jobs are to be counted as professions has been, and remains, controversial. But one important element in a group's claim to professional status has very often been the belief that the work its members do engages a sufficiently broad range of human capabilities to have a transformative effect on the members' personalities, to shape their identities in a lasting way by promoting the development of a distinctive professional character.[16] The culture of professionalism, which acquired such influence in the latter part of the nineteenth century, was predicated on the belief that only certain sorts of work have this effect and hence offer their practitioners the kind of personal fulfillment that makes it possible for them to find the meaning of their lives in their careers. The ideal of professionalism of course had other elements as well. But in this one respect, at least, it was a secular successor to the concept of salvation in a calling that appeared, with such enormous consequences for the whole of modern culture, in the writings of the great seventeenth-century divines.

It is in this context that the rise and fall of the lawyer-statesman ideal must be understood. While its influence lasted, that ideal helped lawyers to believe they were professionals in the sense I have described. It did so because it defined the qualities of the outstanding lawyer in dispositional terms—because it was an ideal of character. The ideal of the lawyer-statesman touches the springs of personality more deeply than any notion of expertise can do. And this made it possible for those who subscribed to the ideal to think that living in the law might be a pathway to salvation, to a certitude about the worth of their existence and of life itself, even in a world from which the *pneuma* of religious feeling had largely disappeared.

For lawyers, therefore, the loss of this ideal represents a dramatic narrowing of the possibilities of salvation within the realm of work. Like nonprofessional workers, they too must now find these possibilities outside their jobs, in the sphere of private life. Of course this is not their fate alone. The present crisis in the professional self-understanding of lawyers is merely one expression of a broader development in which all the great professions of the nineteenth century have lost their saving power. Today, in fact, the whole ethos of professionalism seems like a doomed attempt to sustain the idea of a calling within certain traditionally prestigious lines of work—an attempt that has now clearly failed, leaving those in the professions in the same position as their nonprofessional counterparts. At the end of the twentieth century we have returned, then, to a democratic regime like that which existed in the seventeenth-century Puritan's imagination, but with one important difference. For while the Puritan's vocational democracy rested on the equal capacity of every kind of work to bring salvation, ours is based upon the equal incapacity of all to offer any.

This view has an appealing candor. It acknowledges the enormity of the forces that have drained the ideal of the lawyer-statesman of its original meaning. It does not pretend these forces are reversible or even containable, but accepts their triumph as the fate of what Weber called our "godless and prophetless time."[17] It is a painfully honest view, and those lawyers who accept it are likely to conclude they have no choice but to abandon any claim to a meaning-giving professional identity and to accept the need to search for the point or purpose of their lives in the sphere of private relations just like everyone else. For why should lawyers think they can escape the disenchantment of the public world that has engulfed us all?

But however honest this conclusion seems, it underestimates the difficulty that lawyers (and I suspect other professionals too) have in giving up the demand for fulfillment in their work. Let us grant that what lawyers do is increasingly incapable of satisfying their need for a meaningful identity. This does not mean they will stop insisting that the need be met, in part at least, within the sphere of their professional pursuits. Clearly, the more routine and unchallenging legal work becomes, the less likely a lawyer is to see it as anything but a means of making a living, and many lawyers today undoubtedly view their jobs in this disenchanted light. But there are several reasons why lawyers in general find this a hard view to accept and continue to demand fulfillment from their work even as it offers less and less.

First, there is the sheer quantity of time that the practice of law requires. The more time one spends in an activity, the harder it becomes to view it in strictly instrumental terms. The large amount of time that lawyers devote to their work thus itself gives them one reason to hope they can discover some inherent meaning in it.

Second, the line between a lawyer's job and his or her personal life is often very fluid, shifting as the job itself demands. Few lawyers punch a timeclock. The nature of their work requires more flexibility than such a rigid schedule would allow. Indeed, for many lawyers the fluidity of their working day—the fact that its limits must be set by the internal demands of the work itself—is a source of professional pride. They would think less well of their jobs if their hours were fixed, even if fixing them meant a shorter working day overall. This attitude reflects a disinclination on the part of lawyers to view their jobs in instrumental terms, which a timeclock would make harder to avoid. And that disinclination is itself, I think, a protective response to the extra hardships an unpredictable work schedule imposes on those who must accommodate their lives to it. The fluidity of the lawyer's working day imposes special burdens on him. The causes of this fluidity, moreover, are largely beyond his power to control. One natural response is to recharacterize these burdens as benefits by insisting that the very features of law practice that account for its fluidity also account for the richness and complexity that make it more fulfilling than other, less variable sorts of work. The irregular hours that lawyers must keep thus give them a second reason to hope that what they do during these hours will have intrinsic and not just instrumental value for them.

Third, and most important, the idea that the law is a calling continues to be powerfully affirmed in our law schools, where the attitudes of lawyers are first formed. Our law schools have done much to undermine the lawyer-statesman ideal by bringing the virtue of practical wisdom into intellectual disrepute. But they have also continued to reinforce the belief that choosing a career in the law means choosing a professional identity and not just an occupation or a trade. There are other ways in which the profession encourages this belief—for example, by promulgating its own internal code of ethics. But the country's law schools have played an especially important role in sustaining the idea that the law is a calling, while simultaneously helping to destroy the conception of the profession on which that idea was based. However deep their hostility to the traditional sources of professional pride, law teachers hate the suggestion that theirs is a trade-school operation, for the status of their own work depends upon the status of the work they are training their students to do. Law professors thus have a selfish interest in perpetuating the belief that the law is more than a technique for making money, and many law students come to accept this belief, even though their teachers, who have encouraged them, have also done their part to destroy the older ideal of law practice on which its content and credibility depended.

In any case, many of those now coming to law school still view their choice of career in these terms. They hope to find a professional identity and with that a measure of personal fulfillment in their work. In the future, this hope will be difficult to satisfy. The changing nature of the profession has put great obstacles in its way. But it will also be difficult to root out, for powerful forces still work to keep it alive. Honesty requires that we acknowledge this fact too. And when we do, the Weberian view looks less realistic than before. For the suggestion that lawyers renounce the ambition to be saved through work and look for salvation in the realm of private life instead misgauges the hold that this (perhaps unattainable) ambition still has on those in the profession today.

The crisis of self-understanding through which the legal profession is now passing is as deep and troubling as it is in part because the profession continues to encourage an ambition that it is no longer able to satisfy. If lawyers could either find personal fulfillment in their work, on the one hand, or give up the hope of finding it there, on the other, their predicament would be less demoralizing than it is.

But both possibilities seem at the moment quite remote, and any view, like the Weberian, that stresses only the first horn of this dilemma is bound to miss part of its essential pathos. To that extent we might say—however odd it sounds—that the Weberian view of the profession's current crisis is in the end a falsely optimistic one as well. For despite its honesty and sober realism, it too offers lawyers more consolation than their present predicament warrants.

HOPE

What should a lawyer who insists on honestly confronting this predicament do?

If he is a law teacher, he should attempt to convey to his students some feeling for the values I have defended in this book. At an individual level, this is a reasonable goal to pursue. In contrast to both judges and practitioners, law teachers have a great deal of control over their own work. Generally speaking, they are free to write about what they wish, and have substantial freedom too in defining the content and character of the courses they teach. This means that law teachers who share my point of view will find in the classroom considerable opportunity to act on their beliefs. They will use this freedom to combat the idea that the law becomes interesting or intelligible only when seen from the standpoint of another field; to discredit the claim that one cannot participate in its culture without having first mastered the idiom and techniques of some more rigorous nonlegal discipline, such as philosophy or economics; and, above all, to discourage the belief that behind the surface chaos of the law there are simple organizing structures that it is the chief object of law study to describe in an abstract way.

More positively, they will use the freedom of the classroom to stress the importance of individual cases. They will try to show that the analysis of cases is challenging and fun and, though it cannot be reduced to a method, that there are better and worse ways of doing it. They may make use, from time to time, of other disciplines. But if they do, they will be sure to emphasize that the role these disciplines play in the analysis of cases is a subordinate one whose scope is a matter of judgment that the disciplines in question cannot settle on their own. They will insist on the peculiarity of cases, on their idiosyncrasies, and on the complexity of the world—on its factual complexity, but more important, on its moral and spiritual complexity, on the plurality of incommensurable values that fight for recognition in the law as in other spheres of life. They will encourage their students to think of the law as an independent discipline, with demands and satisfactions of its own, and not merely as the action arm of some more comprehensive policy science. Of course they will stress the need for lawyers to serve the public good and will remind their students that they have a responsibility to take an interest in the well-being of the legal system as a whole. But they will also make it clear that they believe no technique is sufficient to fulfill this trust, that wisdom is required too, and that wisdom is a trait of character and not of intellect alone. All of this they will teach their students, sometimes explicitly but more often by the way they approach their subject and what they emphasize in it. The freedom of the classroom gives them an opportunity to make these points, and if the question is whether a teacher who cares about the values affirmed by the ideal of the lawyer-statesman can seize this opportunity and use it to good effect, I am confident that the answer is yes, for I have seen some of my own teachers do it.

But if one asks whether there is at present much reason to hope that this style of teaching will again become dominant in our law schools, I think the answer is probably no. There is much that individuals can do, in their own teaching, to promote the deliberative ideal of the lawyer-statesman. But the currently most influential forms of legal scholarship, with their strong antiprudentialist cast, make it likely, I think, that the main tendency will be in the opposite direction: toward an ever more theoretical style of teaching that encourages a simplifying view of law and the substitution of method for character. The law teacher who stands by the view of the profession that I have set out in this book will in years to come be increasingly isolated from his peers. He will feel more and more like a relic separated from the main current of his time, and if he is to continue doing what (in a formal sense at least) he is free to do, he must learn to do it without the hope that his branch of the profession can be brought to share his old-fashioned views again.

As for judges, the difficulty of sustaining a commitment to the lawyer-statesman ideal is greater still. That is because judges are constrained in their work to a degree law professors are not. I do not mean constrained merely by their role, which requires that judges be more circumspect in what they do and say. I mean constrained by the conditions under which the craft of judging must now be practiced. Foremost among these is the enormous number of cases that judges are required to decide. So long as the caseload in our courts remains at its present level, there is no realistic alternative to the bureaucratized system of adjudication that has been devised to meet it: a system hostile, in its essence, to the deliberative values of the lawyer-statesman ideal. In theory, of course, the workload at least of our federal courts could be substantially reduced—for example, by abolishing their diversity jurisdiction, as has sometimes been proposed. But even such a large step would be insufficient to restore the conditions under which our federal judges worked a half-century ago. To achieve that goal it would be necessary to remove whole classes of entitlement from the protection of the federal courts, a morally dubious and politically impossible measure. And it must be remembered, too, than any reduction in the federal caseload is likely to produce a commensurate increase in the work of the country's state courts, increasing the pressures for bureaucratization in one sphere while lessening them in another.

A judge who wants to fight these pressures and make his own work more deliberative must begin by writing his opinions with only minimal assistance from his clerks. That is not enough, by itself, to restore the deliberative imagination to a central place in the activity of judging, but it is, I think, a necessary first step, and today even this first step has become impossibly hard for many judges to take. There are still a few virtuosi who can produce enough opinions by themselves to meet their caseload quotas. But many judges cannot keep up on their own even now, and are bound to fall farther behind as their caseloads grow. On the whole, those coming to the bench today have less writing experience than their counterparts fifty years ago did.[18] And as the failed nomination of Robert Bork and the next three successful ones suggest, those who have written nothing at all now stand the best chance of being appointed to our highest courts, for purely political reasons. Together with these developments, the enormous workload that judges must now carry makes any suggestion that they return to the practice of writing their opinions themselves, instead of depending on their clerks to do the writing for them, appear utopian. But if he cannot do even this much, it is difficult to see how a judge can honor the deliberative ideal of the lawyer-statesman in his own work, let alone campaign for its restoration at an institutional level.

Finally, what about practicing lawyers, who constitute the great majority of the profession? If he takes the ideal of the lawyer-statesman seriously, what should a practitioner do?

The first thing he should do is stay clear of the sort of large-firm practice I described in Chapter 5. To be sure, there is reason to think these firms will not continue to grow as rapidly as they have in recent years and that some may even shrink a bit in size. But even those that have let some lawyers go are still enormous, and there is little prospect of their shrinking to pre-1970 levels. Nor does the harshly economizing spirit in which these reductions have been made give one much reason to hope that the increasingly commercial culture of these firms is going to change—indeed, just the opposite.[19] In fact, I think it highly unlikely that the country's largest firms will ever regain their earlier respect for the lawyer-statesman ideal. A lawyer who wants a practice in which this ideal still has a place must therefore look elsewhere to find it.

One might look, first, to the smaller firms that have been created by unhappy refugees from larger ones, eager to establish an environment in which the intrinsic pleasures of law practice are more highly valued. I have no doubt that, on the whole, these firms are today more likely to offer the lawyers working in them a satisfying professional life. The division of labor in them is less extensive. The spirit of commercialism is less advanced. And some, at least, encourage a commitment to public service that few large firms now do, except in the most begrudging and mechanical way.

But however attractive the inward culture of these firms may be, their outward position remains vulnerable. For the most part, they operate in the same urban market as their larger counterparts, and this means that to survive economically they must often either specialize or grow, reproducing on a smaller scale the conditions that today make most large firms such deadening places to work. And even when the economic pressure to expand is light, it is often hard for those who have left large firms—despite the fact they were unhappy in them—to escape the pull of the idea that big means great, an idea frequently defended on the grounds that large firms attract the best-paying clients with the most-demanding problems, but whose root appeal is far stronger than this overused and overbroad rationalization can explain.

So the smaller, spin-off firms of which I have been speaking may not represent a secure alternative for those who want to practice law in the spirit of the lawyer-statesman ideal. Nor, I think, do most in-house corporate law departments, despite the hopeful claims that have recently been made by some on their behalf. To begin with, many in-house departments (the larger ones at least) are organized on the basis of a division of labor as intensive as that of their outside counterparts. And, more important, every in-house law office is by definition tied to the interests of the business of which it forms a part—a tie that constrains the independence of the lawyers working in it and compromises their imaginative capacity to hold the interests of the business that employs them at arm's length, as lawyers who wish to give the best advice about the most important matters must. It is true that in recent years the position of in-house general counsel has become a more independent one and taken on some of the attributes that the position of outside counsel once possessed. So there is reason to believe that at the very top, in-house legal work now offers opportunities for the exercise of statesmanship that it traditionally did not. But below this level, concerns about the independence of the in-house lawyer's judgment remain as valid as before.

Beyond these alternatives to large-firm practice, there is one other that a lawyer sympathetic to my views might consider: the general-practice law firm in a small town or city outside the country's largest metropolitan centers. These firms typically serve a local market that is to varying degrees detached from the larger ones in which the biggest firms and their spin-offs operate. They commonly exhibit a lower degree of specialization. They are less influenced by the culture of growth that now dominates most large firms in the country's major cities. And they are often intertwined in complex ways with the communities in which they exist (so that a lawyer entering such a firm comes immediately into an environment in which the spirit of public service is still strong). For the lawyer who wants to live a life centered on the values of the vanishing ideal I have defended in this book, these firms offer, I believe, as supportive an environment as any.

Of course, they have their shortcomings too. The work they offer can be routine and uninspiring, and there are certain areas of law—international law, for example—that they rarely touch at all. And as one moves away from the country's great cosmopolitan centers, the risk of local prejudice and xenophobia increase. But what makes the work of larger firms appear more interesting is often only the fact that their clients are willing to spend more money to have their problems researched, which does not always mean greater opportunities for judgment on the part of the lawyers involved. So far as prejudice and xenophobia are concerned, the danger they present, though real, is substantially less than it was even a quarter-century ago, largely because of the extent to which our egalitarian national culture has reshaped local habits and beliefs (a process that began with the civil rights movement and is continuing today). So on balance there is reason to believe that a small-town or small-city practice may provide a more congenial setting for those who share my view of what a life in the law can be than the other alternatives I have mentioned. Years ago, Justice Robert Jackson wrote movingly of the work of the country lawyer, and of the role he played in an earlier period in preserving his profession's noblest ideals.[20] Perhaps it is in this direction that lawyers who feel as I do about the fate of their profession, and who long to restore its failing sense of mission, ought to look once more.

But I have no illusion that the mass of students at our best law schools—where the leaders of the profession are trained and its institutional self-understanding shaped—will turn back toward the kind of practice Justice Jackson described with such feeling and eloquence. The pressures against their doing so are just too great. There is, first of all, the money and prestige of large-firm practice, and the confidence-sapping conformism of student culture itself. Beyond that there is the fact that most of the active recruiting at our best schools is done by the biggest firms from the largest cities; other sorts of careers in private practice simply disappear from view. How many students will find the courage to buck the tide, to forgo the money, to resist the illusion of power and influence, and to seek out other opportunities on their own when the road to large-firm practice lies so conveniently nearby? I suspect not many. For those who do look, the opportunities are there. But the likelihood that the profession as a whole will awaken to the emptiness of its condition and that there will be a great resurgence of support, at an institutional level, for the vanishing ideal of the lawyer-statesman seems to me quite low.

For the most part, I suspect, things will go on much as before, and the profession will drift more and more in the direction it has been moving this past quarter-century. Of course, each generation of lawyers makes its own contribution to the architecture of the law. The contribution mine has made has been to tear down the old system of ideas and institutions that gave the lawyer-statesman ideal its authority and power. The next, perhaps, will begin the work of rebuilding what we have torn apart. That may happen, and I hope it does, though I doubt in fact it will. But even if it does not, those who see the ideal and seize the opportunity to realize it in their own work will win for themselves a prize of infinite value, like the sailor in a storm who manages, somehow, to save himself and his ship's most precious cargo.

Notes

Introduction

1. Alexis de Tocqueville, *Democracy in America,* ed. J. P. Mayer, trans. George Lawrence (New York: Anchor Press, 1966), p. 268.
2. Dan Quayle, speech to the American Bar Association, reported in *New York Times,* 14 Aug. 1991, p. A1; Derek Bok, "Law and Its Discontents," *The Record,* 38 (1983): 12–33 (a publication of the Association of the Bar of the City of New York).
3. Alexander M. Bickel, *The Least Dangerous Branch: The Supreme Court at the Bar of Politics* (Indianapolis: Bobbs-Merrill, 1962), pp. 65–69; Harry V. Jaffa, *Crisis of the House Divided* (Chicago: University of Chicago Press, 1982), pp. 363–386.
4. Richard Kluger, *Simple Justice* (New York: Knopf, 1976), pp. 678–699.
5. West Virginia State Board of Education v. Barnette, 319 U.S. 624 (1943).
6. Planned Parenthood of Southeastern Pennsylvania v. Casey, 60 U.S.L.W. 4795 (1992).

1. An Embarrassed Virtue

1. William H. Rehnquist, "The Lawyer-Statesman in American History," *Harvard Journal of Law and Public Policy,* 9 (1986): 537–557.
2. See Perry Miller, ed., *The Legal Mind in America from Independence to the Civil War* (Garden City, N.Y.: Doubleday, 1962). Robert A. Ferguson, *Law and Letters in American Culture* (Cambridge, Mass.: Harvard University Press, 1984), contains much useful material and conveys a good sense of the profession's aspirations during this period. See also Robert W. Gordon, "Lawyers as the 'American Aristocracy': A Nineteenth-Century Ideal That May Still Be Relevant," *Stanford Lawyer,* 20 (1985): 2–7, 79–82.
3. The speech that Rufus Choate gave upon the death of Daniel Webster in 1852 is a good example of the genre. See *Addresses and Orations of Rufus Choate* (Boston: Little, Brown, 1891), pp. 222–240. See also Jean V. Matthews, *Rufus Choate, the Law and Civic Virtue* (Philadelphia: Temple University Press, 1980).

4. See, for example, Kathleen Sullivan, "Rainbow Republicanism," *Yale Law Journal,* 97 (1988): 1713–1723; Michael A. Fitts, "Look Before You Leap: Some Cautionary Notes on Civic Republicanism," *Yale Law Journal,* 97 (1988): 1651–1672; Derrick Bell and Preeta Bansal, "The Republican Revival and Racial Politics," *Yale Law Journal,* 97 (1988): 1609–1621; Hendrick Hartog, "Imposing Constitutional Traditions," *William and Mary Law Review,* 29 (1987): 75–82; Joyce Oldham Appleby, *Capitalism and a New Social Order: The Republican Vision of the 1790s* (New York: New York University Press, 1984), pp. 8–19.

5. See Charles Taylor, *Sources of the Self* (Cambridge, Mass.: Harvard University Press, 1989), pp. 91–107.

6. "When philosophy paints its grey in grey, then has a shape of life grown old. By philosophy's grey in grey it cannot be rejuvenated but only understood. The owl of Minerva spreads its wings only with the falling of the dusk." G. W. F. Hegel, *Philosophy of Right,* trans. T. M. Knox (Oxford: Oxford University Press, 1967), p. 13.

7. See Maxwell Bloomfield, "Law and Lawyers in American Popular Culture," in *Law and American Literature,* ed. Carl S. Smith, John P. McWilliams, and Maxwell Bloomfield (New York: Knopf, 1983), pp. 132–143.

8. Robert W. Gordon, "The Ideal and the Actual in the Law: Fantasies and Practices of New York City Lawyers, 1870–1900," in *The New High Priests: Lawyers in Post–Civil War America,* ed. G. W. Gawalt (Westport, Conn.: Greenwood Press, 1984), pp. 53–74.

9. See Herbert Hovencamp, "The First Great Law and Economics Movement," *Stanford Law Review,* 42 (1990): 993–1058.

10. "An impartially administered, scientific legal order would bridge the gulf between the ideal and the actual, the lawyers' high-minded and public-regarding selves, and their activities on behalf of clients . . . The reform instrument of first importance was science; if legal rights could be made *certain* and procedurally *effective,* the advantages accruing from illegitimate tactics would simply disappear, and lawyers could keep their clients within the law." Gordon, "The Ideal and the Actual in the Law," p. 57. See also James C. Carter, "The Ideal and the Actual in the Law: The Annual Address," *Report of the Thirteeth Annual Meeting of the American Bar Association* (Philadelphia: Dando, 1890), pp. 217–245.

11. See R. Kent Newmyer, *Supreme Court Justice Joseph Story: Statesman of the Old Republic* (Chapel Hill: University of North Carolina Press, 1985); Albert J. Beveridge, *The Life of John Marshall,* 4 vols. (Boston: Houghton Mifflin, 1916–1919); James Bradley Thayer, *John Marshall* (New York: Da Capo Press, 1974); Felix Frankfurter, "John Marshall and the Judicial Function," *Harvard Law Review,* 69 (1955), 217–238.

12. On the development of the concept of social engineering, see William Graebner, *The Engineering of Consent: Democracy and Authority in Twentieth-*

Century America (Madison: University of Wisconsin Press, 1987); see also Thomas L. Haskell, *The Emergence of Professional Social Science: The American Social Science Association and the Nineteenth-Century Crisis of Authority* (Urbana: University of Illinois Press, 1977).

13. An illuminating contemporary discussion of the role that literature can play in a person's moral education may be found in Martha C. Nussbaum, *Love's Knowledge: Essays on Philosophy and Literature* (Oxford: Oxford University Press, 1990). See especially chap. 5, "'Finely Aware and Rightly Responsible': Literature and the Moral Imagination," pp. 148–167. See also Ferguson, *Law and Letters in American Culture,* pp. 66–84.

14. See Alpheus Thomas Mason's excellent biography *Brandeis: A Free Man's Life* (New York: Viking Press, 1946), pp. 511–646.

15. Karl Llewellyn, *The Common Law Tradition: Deciding Appeals* (Boston: Little, Brown, 1960), pp. 59–61, 121–122. I discuss Llewellyn's conception of practical wisdom in more detail in Chapter 4.

16. See Anthony Kronman, "Alexander Bickel's Philosophy of Prudence," *Yale Law Journal,* 94 (1985): 1567–1616; John Moeller, "Alexander M. Bickel: Toward a Theory of Politics," *Journal of Politics,* 47 (1985): 113–139. For a sharply contrasting view of Bickel's thought, see Edward A. Purcell, "Alexander M. Bickel and the Post-Realist Constitution," *Harvard Civil Rights–Civil Liberties Law Review,* 11 (1976): 521–564.

17. See Alexander Bickel, *The Least Dangerous Branch: The Supreme Court at the Bar of Politics* (Indianapolis: Bobbs-Merrill, 1962), pp. 235–243.

18. See the title essay in Alexander Bickel, *The Morality of Consent* (New Haven: Yale University Press, 1974).

19. For a discussion of republican theory as it relates to the American constitutional tradition and to contemporary constitutional lawmaking, see Cass R. Sunstein, "Beyond the Republican Revival," *Yale Law Journal,* 97 (1988): 1539–1590; Cass R. Sunstein, "Interest Groups in American Public Law," *Stanford Law Review,* 38 (1985): 29–87; Frank Michelman, "Law's Republic," *Yale Law Journal,* 97 (1988): 1493–1537; Frank Michelman, "Supreme Court, 1985 Term—Foreword: Traces of Self-Government," *Harvard Law Review,* 100 (1986): 4–77; Suzanna Sherry, "Civic Virtue and the Feminine Voice in Constitutional Adjudication," *Virginia Law Review,* 72 (1986): 543–616; Bruce Ackerman, "The Storrs Lectures: Discovering the Constitution," *Yale Law Journal,* 93 (1984): 1013–1072; G. Stone, L. Seidman, C. Sunstein, and M. Tushnet, *Constitutional Law* (Boston: Little, Brown, 1986), pp. 5–13.

The civic republican strain of thought is evident in recent social and political theory as well. See Benjamin R. Barber, *Strong Democracy: Participatory Politics for a New Age* (Berkeley: University of California Press, 1984); R. Bellah, R. Madsen, W. Sullivan, A. Swidler, and S. Tipton, *Habits of the Heart: Individualism and Commitment in American Life* (Berkeley: University of

California Press, 1985); Charles Taylor, "Kant's Theory of Freedom," in *Philosophy and the Human Sciences: Philosophical Papers* (Cambridge: Cambridge University Press, 1985), vol. 2, pp. 318–337; Michael Sandel, "The Procedural Republic and the Unencumbered Self," *Political Theory*, 12 (1984): 81–96.

20. See "Symposium: The Republican Civic Tradition," *Yale Law Journal*, 97 (1988): 1493–1724. See also *William and Mary Law Review*, 29 (1987): 57–99.

21. For an analysis of the opposition between interest-group politics and republicanism, see Michelman, "Law's Republic"; Sunstein, "Interest Groups in American Public Law"; Marvin Meyers, "Beyond the Sum of the Interests," in *The Mind of the Founder: Sources of the Political Thought of James Madison,* ed. Marvin Meyers (Hanover, N.H.: rev. ed. published for Brandeis University Press by University Press of New England, 1981), pp. xxiv–xxxiii. Interest-group theories are defended in Robert Dahl, *A Preface to Democratic Theory* (Chicago: University of Chicago Press, 1956); David Bicknell Truman, *The Governmental Process* (New York: Knopf, 1951); Gary S. Becker, "A Theory of Competition among Pressure Groups for Political Influence," *Quarterly Journal of Economics*, 98 (1983): 371–400; Daniel A. Farber and Philip P. Frickey, "The Jurisprudence of Public Choice," *Texas Law Review*, 65 (1987): 873–927.

22. See J. G. A. Pocock, *The Machiavellian Moment: Florentine Political Thought and the Atlantic Republican Tradition* (Princeton: Princeton University Press, 1975), pp. 506–552.

23. Aristotle, *Politics*, 1252a1–16. See Wolfgang Kullman, "Man as a Political Animal in Aristotle," in *A Companion to Aristotle's Politics,* ed. David Keyt and Fred D. Miller, Jr. (Oxford: Basil Blackwell, 1991), pp. 94–117.

24. The tendency to mix classical republican and Kantian ideas is evident in Michelman, "Supreme Court, 1985 Term"; Sunstein, "Beyond the Republican Revival"; Hanna Fenichel Pitkin, "Justice: On Relating Private and Public," *Political Theory*, 9 (1981): 327–352; Barber, *Strong Democracy.*

25. "Everything in nature works according to laws. Rational beings alone have the faculty of acting according *to the conception* of laws, that is according to principles, *i.e.,* have a *will.*" Immanuel Kant, *Fundamental Principles of the Metaphysic of Morals,* in *Kant's Critique of Practical Reason and Other Works on the Theory of Ethics,* trans. Thomas K. Abbott (London: Longmans, Green, 1873), p. 29.

26. Josiah Royce, *The World and the Individual, Second Series: Nature, Man and the Moral Order* (London: Macmillan, 1901), p. 276. Compare Karl Marx's discussion of the difference between bees and architects in *Capital,* ed. Frederick Engels, trans. Samuel Moore and Edward Aveling (New York: Random House, 1906), vol. 1, p. 198.

27. Aristotle, *Politics*, 1254a20–1255a2; 1277b34–1278b5.

28. See *Nicomachean Ethics*, 1112b. For helpful discussions of Aristotle's account of deliberation and choice, see David Wiggins, "Deliberation and Practical Reason," in *Essays on Aristotle's Ethics*, ed. Amelie Oksenberg Rorty (Berkeley and Los Angeles: University of California Press, 1980), pp. 221–240; G. E. M. Anscombe, "Thought and Action in Aristotle," in *Articles on Aristotle*, ed. Jonathan Barnes, Malcolm Schofield, and Richard Sorabji (London: Duckworth, 1977), vol. 2, pp. 61–71; John M. Cooper, *Reason and Human Good in Aristotle* (Cambridge, Mass.: Harvard University Press, 1975), pp. 1–88; T. H. Irwin, "Aristotle on Reason, Desire and Virtue," *Journal of Philosophy*, 72 (October 1975): 567–578; Nancy Sherman, *The Fabric of Character: Aristotle's Theory of Virtue* (Oxford: Clarendon Press, 1989), pp. 13–55; Sarah Broadie, *Ethics with Aristotle* (Oxford: Oxford University Press, 1991), pp. 179–265; Troels Engberg-Pedersen, *Aristotle's Theory of Moral Insight* (Oxford: Clarendon Press, 1983), pp. 188–222.

29. *Nicomachean Ethics*, 1094b7–12; *Politics*, 1253a19–20.

30. *Nicomachean Ethics*, 1179a32–1181b24; *Politics*, 1277b7–32, 1332b16–1333a15.

31. *Nicomachean Ethics*, 1179b29–30.

32. *Republic*, 457d.

33. *Nicomachean Ethics*, 1145a17. See Norman O. Dahl, *Practical Reason, Aristotle, and Weakness of the Will* (Minneapolis: University of Minnesota Press, 1984); Broadie, *Ethics with Aristotle*, pp. 266–312.

34. Kant, *Fundamental Principles*, p. 9.

35. See Hannah Arendt, *The Life of the Mind* (New York: Harcourt Brace Jovanovich, 1971), vol. 2, pp. 63–73, 84–110; Taylor, *Sources of the Self*, pp. 127–142.

36. Immanuel Kant, *Critique of Pure Reason*, trans. Norman K. Smith (London: Macmillan, 1964), A133/B172.

37. See Hannah Arendt, *Lectures on Kant's Political Philosophy*, ed. Ronald Beiner (Chicago: University of Chicago Press, 1982); Ronald Beiner, *Political Judgment* (Chicago: University of Chicago Press, 1983).

38. Kant, *Fundamental Principles*, p. 10.

39. See Robert Nozick, *Anarchy, State, and Utopia* (New York: Basic Books, 1974), pp. 30–33; John Rawls, *A Theory of Justice* (Cambridge, Mass.: Harvard University Press, 1971), pp. 11–17, 251–257; Bruce Ackerman, *Social Justice in the Liberal State* (New Haven: Yale University Press, 1980), pp. 3–17; Ronald Dworkin, *Taking Rights Seriously* (Cambridge, Mass.: Harvard University Press, 1977), pp. 184–205.

40. See Michelman, "Supreme Court, 1985 Term"; Sunstein, "Beyond the Republican Revival."

41. Kant, *Fundamental Principles*, p. 4.

2. Practical Wisdom and Political Fraternity

1. See Jeremy Bentham, *An Introduction to the Principles of Morals and Legislation* (Oxford: Oxford University Press, 1923), pp. 29–32. The utilitarian commensuration of values is thoughtfully discussed in Martha C. Nussbaum, *The Fragility of Goodness: Luck and Ethics in Greek Tragedy and Philosophy* (Cambridge: Cambridge University Press, 1986), pp. 89–121.

2. Jean-Paul Sartre, *Existentialism and Human Emotions,* trans. Bernard Frectman (New York: Philosophical Library, 1957), pp. 24–25.

3. Max Weber, "The Social Psychology of the World Religions," in *From Max Weber: Essays in Sociology,* ed. H. Gerth and C. Wright Mills (New York: Oxford University Press, 1946), p. 271.

4. Aristotle, *Nicomachean Ethics,* 1111b20–30.

5. Plato, *Republic,* 368c–369b.

6. Immanuel Kant, *Critique of Pure Reason,* trans. Norman K. Smith (London: MacMillan, 1964), A19/B33.

7. Compare Max Scheler, *The Nature of Sympathy,* trans. Peter Heath (London: Routledge and Kegan Paul, 1954), pp. 8–9.

8. See Martha C. Nussbaum, *Love's Knowledge* (Oxford: Oxford University Press, 1990); Nancy Sherman, *The Fabric of Character: Aristotle's Theory of Virtue* (Oxford: Oxford University Press, 1989), pp. 44–50; M. F. Burnyeat, "Aristotle on Learning to Be Good," in *Essays on Aristotle's Ethics,* ed. Amelie Oksenberg Rorty (Berkeley: University of California Press, 1980), pp. 69–92. The same subject is explored from a psychological point of view in *Affect and Cognition: The Seventeenth Annual Carnegie Symposium on Cognition,* ed. Margaret Clark and Susan Fiske (Hillsdale, N.J.: Lawrence Erlbaum Associates, 1982).

9. Aristotle, *Nicomachean Ethics,* 1144b30–34.

10. Stuart Hampshire, *Morality and Conflict* (Cambridge, Mass.: Harvard University Press, 1983), pp. 40–41.

11. Sigmund Freud, *Civilization and Its Discontents,* ed. and trans. James Strachey (New York: Norton, 1939), p. 17.

12. Plato, *Republic,* 430e, 441d.

13. Aristotle, *Nicomachean Ethics,* 1166a1–1166b28; see also *Eudemian Ethics,* 1240a8–1240b37.

14. Plato, *Gorgias,* 506d–508a; *Republic,* 573b.

15. Sigmund Freud, "The Psychotherapy of Hysteria," in *The Standard Edition of the Complete Psychological Works of Sigmund Freud,* ed. and trans. James Strachey (London: Hogarth Press, 1955), vol. 2, p. 305.

16. See Jonathan Lear, *Love and Its Place in Nature* (New York: Farrar, Straus and Giroux, 1990), pp. 156–222.

17. Nietzsche gives a particularly acute account of the strategy of forgetting.

See Friedrich Nietzsche, "On the Uses and Disadvantages of History for Life," in *Untimely Meditations,* trans. R. J. Hollingdale (Cambridge: Cambridge University Press, 1983), pp. 120–121.

18. Weber, "The Social Psychology of the World Religions," pp. 147–148.

19. See Anthony Downs, *An Economic Theory of Democracy* (New York: Harper and Row, 1957); Gordon Tullock, *Private Wants, Public Means* (New York: Basic Books, 1970); James M. Buchanan, *Essays on the Political Economy* (Honolulu: University of Hawaii Press, 1989).

20. Many liberal writers have pointed out that tolerance is necessary only when one begins to feel disgust for what is being tolerated. Joseph Raz has given perhaps the most persuasive and subtle contemporary account of toleration in his important book *The Morality of Freedom* (Oxford: Oxford University Press, 1986), pp. 401–407. Raz notes that "[t]oleration implies the suppression or containment of an inclination to persecute, harass, harm or react in an unwelcome way to an individual" (p. 401). Hence "[o]ne is tolerant only if one inclines or is tempted not to be" (p. 402).

21. Aristotle, *Nicomachean Ethics,* 1167a22–1167b16, 1161a10–1161b11; *Politics,* 1262b5–25, 1295b23–27. See Anthony Kronman, "Aristotle's Idea of Political Fraternity," *The American Journal of Jurisprudence,* 24 (1979): 114–138.

22. See Jonathan Lear, *Aristotle: The Desire to Understand* (Cambridge: Cambridge University Press, 1988), pp. 164–174; Burnyeat, "Aristotle on Learning to Be Good"; Sherman, *The Fabric of Character.* I discuss further the connection between adeptness and pleasure and their relation to connoisseurship in Chapter 3.

23. Stephen Macedo gives a powerful defense of the morality of public justification in *Liberal Virtues: Citizenship, Virtue, and Community in Liberal Constitutionalism* (Oxford: Oxford University Press, 1991), pp. 39–77. "Public justification," he claims, "embodies a complex form of respect for persons." Macedo also links the practice of public reason-giving with the work of judges and in particular with the institution of judicial review (p. 49).

24. Niccolo Machiavelli, *The Prince,* trans. Harvey C. Mansfield, Jr. (Chicago: University of Chicago Press, 1985), p. 61. On the problem of dirty hands see Thomas Nagel, "Ruthlessness in Public Life," in *Public and Private Morality,* ed. Stuart Hampshire (Cambridge: Cambridge University Press, 1978), pp. 75–91; and Bernard Williams, "Politics and Moral Character," in *Public and Private Morality,* pp. 55–73.

25. Nathan Gardels, "Two Concepts of Nationalism: An Interview with Isaiah Berlin," *The New York Review of Books,* 21 Nov. 1991, pp. 19, 21. Berlin says, "At eighty-two, I've lived through virtually the entire century, the worst century that Europe has ever had. In my life, more dreadful things occurred than at any other time in history. Worse, I suspect, even than the days of the Huns." He chillingly concludes, "I am glad to be as old as I am."

See also Isaiah Berlin, "The Pursuit of the Ideal," and "The Decline of Utopian Ideas in the West," in *The Crooked Timber of Humanity,* ed. Henry Hardy (New York: Knopf, 1991), pp. 1–48.

26. Plato, *Republic,* 541a.

27. See Max Weber, "Politics as a Vocation," in *From Max Weber,* p. 126.

28. Sigmund Freud, *Beyond the Pleasure Principle,* ed. and trans. James Strachey (New York: Norton, 1961), pp. 38–58.

29. See Max Weber, "Science as a Vocation," in *From Max Weber,* p. 147.

30. Weber, "Politics as a Vocation," pp. 125–126.

31. Benedict Spinoza, *Ethic,* Part 5, Proposition 42, in *Spinoza Selections,* ed. John Wild (New York: Charles Scribner's Sons, 1930), p. 400.

32. Aristotle, *Politics,* 1276b1–15.

33. Hannah Arendt, *On Revolution* (New York: Viking Press, 1963), pp. 217–285; Robert Mangabeira Unger, *False Necessity: Anti-Necessitarian Social Theory in the Service of Radical Democracy* (Cambridge: Cambridge University Press, 1987).

34. Compare Max Weber's remarks on the routinization of charisma. Max Weber, *Economy and Society,* ed. Guenther Roth and Claus Wittich, trans. Ephraim Fischoff and others (New York: Bedminster Press, 1968), vol. 3, pp. 1121–1123.

3. The Good Lawyer

1. First-hand accounts of the law school experience often express such views. In *One L* (New York: Putnam, 1977) Scott Turow reports a student who complains: "They're making me different . . . It's someone I don't *want* to be. Don't you get the feeling all the time that you're being indoctrinated?" (p. 79). In his preface Turow writes: "It is during the first year, according to a saying, that you learn to think like a lawyer, to develop the habits of mind and world perspective that will stay with you throughout your career. And thus it is during the first year that many law students come to feel, sometimes with deep regret, that they are becoming persons strangely different from the ones who arrived at law school in the fall" (p. 4).

Chris Goodrich, writing about his experience at Yale Law School, wonders during a first-year class: "But this was being a good lawyer? 'Massaging' the facts and the law—that's the word [the professor] used—to suit your client's goals? I had the feeling [the professor] was massaging student minds in the very same way." *Anarchy and Elegance* (Boston: Little, Brown, 1991), p. 39. Goodrich reflects: "No doubt about it—two months of law school had helped me speak better, analyze more deeply, think more logically. But I had a nagging feeling that my outward appearance had become disconnected from my inner self, that my new ability to put a rational veneer on anything had made me a stranger to myself. I felt a consistent low-level pain, at times a sense of being overstuffed to the point of bursting and at others of being achingly hollow, as if life fluids had been drained from me" (p. 105).

See also Karl Llewellyn's masterly account of the first year of legal education in *The Bramble Bush* (New York: Oceana Publications, 1930), p. 116. The most recent addition to the genre is Richard D. Kahlenberg, *Broken Contract: A Memoir of Harvard Law School* (New York: Hill and Wang, 1992).

2. See Hannah Arendt, "What Is Authority?" in *Between Past and Future* (New York: Viking, 1968), p. 123.

3. Lon L. Fuller, "The Forms and Limits of Adjudication," *Harvard Law Review*, 92 (1978): 353–409; Owen M. Fiss, "The Supreme Court, 1978 Term—Forward: The Forms of Justice," *Harvard Law Review*, 93 (1979): 1-58.

4. See Malcolm P. McNair, ed., *The Case Method at the Harvard Business School* (New York: McGraw-Hill, 1954).

5. The term "law jobs" comes from Karl Llewellyn, though he defined the main ones in a slightly different way. See Karl Llewellyn, "The Normative, the Legal and the Law-Jobs: The Problem of Juristic Method," *Yale Law Journal*, 49 (1940): 1355–1400.

6. Ronald Dworkin, *Law's Empire* (Cambridge, Mass.: Harvard University Press, 1986), p. 407.

7. See Max Weber, *Economy and Society*, ed. Guenther Roth and Claus Wittich, trans. Ephraim Fischoff and others (New York: Bedminster Press, 1968), vol. 1, p. 7.

8. The thin line between empathy and identification is illustrated in the two Hannibal Lecter films, *Silence of the Lambs* (Orion Pictures, 1991) and *Manhunter* (DeLaurentis Entertainment Group, 1986).

9. Oliver Wendell Holmes, "The Path of the Law," *Harvard Law Review*, 10 (1897): 457–478.

10. See, for example, Geoffrey Hazard and Susan Koniak, *The Law and Ethics of Lawyering* (Westbury, N.Y.: Foundation Press, 1990); David E. Schraeder, *Ethics and the Practice of Law* (Englewood Cliffs, N.J.: Prentice-Hall, 1988); Michael Davis and Frederick A. Elliston, eds., *Ethics and the Legal Profession* (New York: Prometheus Books, 1986); Geoffrey Hazard and Deborah Rhode, *The Legal Profession: Responsibility and Regulation* (Westbury, N.Y.: Foundation Press, 1988); Geoffrey Hazard, *Ethics in the Practice of Law* (New Haven: Yale University Press, 1978); William H. Simon, "Ethical Discretion in Lawyering," *Harvard Law Review*, 101 (1988): 1083–1145.

11. Charles Fried, "The Lawyer as Friend: The Moral Foundations of the Lawyer-Client Relation," *Yale Law Journal*, 85 (1976): 1060–1089.

12. Ibid., pp. 1080–1086.

13. See Max Weber, "The Meaning of 'Ethical Neutrality' in Sociology and

Economics," in *The Methodology of the Social Sciences,* ed. and trans. Edward Shils and H. A. Finch (New York: Free Press, 1949), pp. 1–47.

14. See Murray L. Schwartz, "The Professionalism and Accountability of Lawyers," *California Law Review,* 66 (1978): 669–697 (noting that nonadvocate functions often are regarded "almost as exceptions to the primary role of lawyers as advocates"). See also William H. Simon, "The Ideology of Advocacy: Procedural Justice and Professional Ethics," *Wisconsin Law Review* 1978: 30–144; Paul Haines, "Restraining the Overly Zealous Advocate: Time for Judicial Intervention," *Indiana Law Journal,* 65 (1990): 445–469; Murray L. Schwartz, "The Zeal of the Civil Advocate," in *The Good Lawyer,* ed. David Luban (Totowa, N.J.: Rowman and Allanheld, 1983), pp. 150–171; William Rich, "The Role of Lawyers: Beyond Advocacy," *Brigham Young University Law Review* 1980: 767–784.

15. See Robert M. Cover, "Violence and the Word," *Yale Law Journal,* 95 (1986): 1601–1629.

16. Plato, *Gorgias,* 513c.

17. See Valerie P. Hans and Neil Vidmar, *Judging the Jury* (New York: Plenum Press, 1986), p. 249.

18. Alexis de Tocqueville, *Democracy in America,* ed. J. P. Mayer, trans. George Lawrence (New York: Anchor Press, 1966), pp. 270–276.

19. See Reid Hastie, Steven D. Penrod, and Nancy Pennington, *Inside the Jury* (Cambridge, Mass.: Harvard University Press, 1990), p. 129; Reid Hastie, "Is Attorney-Conducted Voir Dire an Effective Procedure for the Selection of Impartial Juries?" *The American University Law Review,* 40 (1991): 703–726; Shari Seidman Diamond, "Scientific Jury Selection: What Social Scientists Know and Do Not Know," *Judicature,* 73 (1990): 178–183.

20. See Ron Gilson's discussion of lawyers as transactional engineers in "Value Creation by Business Lawyers: Legal Skills and Asset Pricing," *Yale Law Journal,* 94 (1984): 239–313; Ron Gilson, "The Devolution of the Legal Profession: A Demand Side Perspective," *Maryland Law Review,* 49 (1990): 869–916.

21. Thurman Arnold, "The Criminal Trial as a Symbol of Public Morality," in *Criminal Justice in Our Time,* ed. A. E. Dick Howard (Charlottesville: University Press of Virginia, 1965), pp. 137–161.

22. "I do not claim that *all* lawyers will ever, or that most of them will *always,* prove supporters of order and enemies of change. I do say that in a community in which lawyers hold without question that high rank in society which is naturally their due, their temper will be eminently conservative and will prove antidemocratic." Tocqueville, *Democracy in America,* p. 265. See also Rufus Choate, "The Position and Functions of the American Bar, as an Element of Conservatism in the State: An Address Delivered before the Law School in Cambridge, July 3, 1845," in *The Legal Mind in America from*

Independence to the Civil War, ed. Perry Miller (Garden City, N.Y.: Double-day, 1962), pp. 258–273.

23. Richard Danzig, *The Capability Problem in Contract Law: Further Readings on Well-Known Cases* (Mineola, N.Y.: Foundation Press, 1978).

24. See Richard Posner, *The Problems of Jurisprudence* (Cambridge, Mass.: Harvard University Press, 1990), pp. 454–469.

25. Terrence, *The Self Tormentor,* I, 1, 20.

26. See A. A. Long and D. N. Sedley, *The Hellenistic Philosophers* (Cambridge: Cambridge University Press, 1987), pp. 354–358.

4. Law Schools

1. Robert Cover, "Foreword: Nomos and Narrative," *Harvard Law Review,* 97 (1983): 4–68; Robin West, "Jurisprudence as Narrative: An Aesthetic Analysis of Modern Legal Theory," *New York University Law Review,* 60 (1985): 145–211; Richard Delgado, "Storytelling for Oppositionists and Others: A Plea for Narrative," *Michigan Law Review,* 87 (1989): 2411–2441; Mari J. Matsuda, "Public Response to Racist Speech: Considering the Victim's Story," *Michigan Law Review,* 87 (1989): 2320–2381; Kathryn Abrams, "Hearing the Call of the Stories," *California Law Review,* 79 (1991): 971–1054.

2. Carol Gilligan, *In a Different Voice* (Cambridge, Mass.: Harvard University Press, 1982); Nel Noddings, *Caring: A Feminine Approach to Ethics and Moral Education* (Berkeley: University of California Press, 1984); Martha Nussbaum, *The Fragility of Goodness* (Cambridge: Cambridge University Press, 1986); Ann Scales, "The Emergence of Feminist Jurisprudence," *Yale Law Journal,* 95 (1986): 1373–1403; Suzanna Sherry, "Civic Virtue and the Feminine Voice in Constitutional Adjudication," *Virginia Law Review,* 72 (1986): 543–616; Lynne N. Henderson, "Legality and Empathy," *Michigan Law Review,* 85 (1987): 1574–1653.

3. See William M. Landes and Richard A. Posner, "The Influence of Economics on Law: A Quantitative Study," *Chicago Law and Economics Working Papers,* Second Series, No. 9, Aug. 1992.

4. Founded in February 1991, the association held its first meeting in May of that year. It now has a regular newsletter and approximately four hundred members. Supporting the law-and-economics movement are many specialized journals, such as the *Journal of Law and Economics,* the *Journal of Law, Economics and Organization,* the *Journal of Legal Economics,* the *Journal of Legal Studies,* the *Journal of Research in Law and Economics,* and the *George Washington Journal of International Law and Economics.*

5. Bruce A. Ackerman, ed., *Economic Foundations of Property Law* (Boston: Little, Brown, 1975); Richard A. Posner and William M. Landes, *The Economic*

Structure of Tort Law (Cambridge, Mass.: Harvard University Press, 1987); Victor P. Goldberg, ed., *Readings in the Economics of Contract Law* (Cambridge: Cambridge University Press, 1989); Alan Schwartz and Robert E. Scott, *Commercial Transactions* (Westbury, N.Y.: Foundation Press, 1991); Frank H. Easterbrook and Daniel R. Fischel, *The Economic Structure of Corporate Law* (Cambridge, Mass.: Harvard University Press, 1991).

6. William Lovett, "Economic Analysis and Its Role in Legal Education," *Journal of Legal Education,* 26 (1974): 385–421; "Conference on the Place of Economics in Legal Education," *Journal of Legal Education,* 33 (1983): 183–368. Some law schools, such as Columbia, have made an exposure to law and economics a required part of the first-year curriculum.

7. Robert W. Gordon, "The Independence of Lawyers," *Boston University Law Review,* 68 (1988): 1–83; William H. Simon, "Ethical Discretion in Lawyering," *Harvard Law Review,* 101 (1988): 1083–1145.

8. Roberto Mangabeira Unger, *The Critical Legal Studies Movement* (Cambridge, Mass.: Harvard University Press, 1986); Duncan Kennedy, "Form and Substance in Private Law Adjudication," *Harvard Law Review,* 89 (1976): 1685–1778; Duncan Kennedy, "The Structure of Blackstone's Commentaries," *Buffalo Law Review,* 28 (1979): 205–382.

9. James Boyle, "The Politics of Reason: Critical Legal Theory and Local Social Thought," *University of Pennsylvania Law Review,* 133 (1985): 685–780; James Boyle, "Is Subjectivity Possible? The Postmodern Subject in Legal Theory," *University of Colorado Law Review,* 62 (1991): 489–524; Clare Dalton, "An Essay in the Deconstruction of Contract Doctrine," *Yale Law Journal,* 94 (1985): 997–1114; Gary Peller, "The Metaphysics of American Law," *California Law Review,* 73 (1985): 1151–1290; Jack Balkin, "The Crystalline Structure of Legal Thought," *Rutgers Law Review,* 39 (1986): 1–110, and "Deconstructive Practice and Legal Theory," *Yale Law Journal,* 95 (1987): 743–786.

10. Richard Posner, "The Present Situation in Legal Scholarship," *Yale Law Journal,* 90 (1981): 1113–1130; Note, "'Round and 'Round the Bramble Bush: From Legal Realism to Critical Legal Studies," *Harvard Law Review,* 95 (1982): 1669–1690.

11. Jerome Frank, *Law and the Modern Mind* (Gloucester, Mass.: Peter Smith, 1970), pp. 53–61, 67, 83, 99, 225.

12. Grant Gilmore, *The Ages of American Law* (New Haven: Yale University Press, 1977), pp. 42–48, 57–60; Thomas Grey, "Langdell's Orthodoxy," *University of Pittsburgh Law Review,* 45 (1983): 1–53.

13. Christopher C. Langdell, *A Selection of Cases on the Law of Contracts* (Boston: Little, Brown, 1871), and *Summary of the Law of Contracts* (Boston: Little, Brown, 1880).

14. For Hegel history is a rationally progressive process—one in which reason

gradually works itself pure. Nothing in Darwin's theory of evolution requires this. Evolution, as Darwin conceived it, is an explicable process but not one that necessarily leads to successively higher forms of rationality (though that may be its accidental result).

15. Plato, *Meno,* 82b–85b.

16. See, for example, *The Federalist,* Nos. 9 and 31 (Alexander Hamilton), ed. Clinton Rossiter (New York: New American Library, 1961); *The Complete Works of Benjamin Franklin,* ed. John Bigelow (New York: G.P. Putnam's Sons, 1987); David Hume, "That Politics May Be Reduced to a Science," in *Essays Moral, Political, and Literary,* ed. Eugene F. Miller (Indianapolis: Liberty Classics, 1987), pp. 14–31.

17. Thomas Hobbes, *Leviathan,* ed. Michael Oakeshott (Oxford: Basil Blackwell, 1946), p. 136.

18. Leo Strauss, *The Political Philosophy of Hobbes* (Chicago: University of Chicago Press, 1936), pp. 30–43.

19. Aristotle, *Nichomachean Ethics,* 1142a10–20.

20. Ibid., 1094b19–27 (trans. Martin Ostwald).

21. Thomas Hobbes, *A Dialogue between a Philosopher and a Student of the Common Laws of England,* ed. Joseph Cropsey (Chicago: University of Chicago Press, 1971).

22. S. F. C. Milsom, *Historical Foundations of the Common Law* (London: Butterworths, 1981), pp. 99–239.

23. Hobbes, *Leviathan,* p. 182.

24. Ibid., p. 175.

25. H. L. A. Hart, *Essays on Bentham* (Oxford: Oxford University Press, 1982), p. 47.

26. Hobbes, *Dialogue,* pp. 83–84. On Bentham's assessment of Blackstone, see his famously caustic characterization in "Commonplace Book," *Works of Jeremy Bentham,* ed. John Bowring (1843), vol. 10, p. 141; see also Jeremy Bentham, *A Fragment on Government,* ed. H. L. A. Hart (London: Athlone Press, 1977), p. 394; Gerald Postema, *Bentham and the Common Law Tradition* (Oxford: Oxford University Press, 1986), p. 425. For Austin's attitude toward Blackstone, see John Austin, *The Province of Jurisprudence Determined,* ed. H. L. A. Hart (London: Weidenfeld and Nicolson, 1954), p. 190, and *Lectures on Jurisprudence,* ed. Robert Campbell (New York: James Cockcroft, 1875), pp. 108–116.

27. See Charles M. Cook, *The American Codification Movement: A Study of Antebellum Legal Reform* (Westport, Conn.: Greenwood Press, 1981), pp. 201–210; Henry Hart and Albert Sacks, *The Legal Process,* tent. ed. (1958), p. 781; Alison Reppy, "The Field Codification Concept," in *David Dudley Field Centenary Essays,* ed. Alison Reppy (New York: New York University School of Law, 1949), pp. 44–49; Nathan M. Crystal, "Codification and

the Rise of the Restatement Movement," *Washington Law Review*, 54 (1979): 255–260.

28. Steven J. Gould, *The Panda's Thumb: More Reflections in Natural History* (New York: Norton, 1980), pp. 66–67.

29. See Oliver Wendell Holmes, "The Path of the Law," *Harvard Law Review*, 10 (1897): 457–478, and "The Common Law," in *The Essential Holmes*, ed. Richard Posner (Chicago: University of Chicago Press, 1992).

30. William Twining, *Karl Llewellyn and the Realist Movement* (Norman: University of Oklahoma Press, 1973); Laura Kalman, *Legal Realism at Yale, 1927–1960* (Chapel Hill: University of North Carolina Press, 1986). See also Wilfred E. Rumble, Jr., *American Legal Realism: Skepticism, Reform and the Judicial Process* (Ithaca: Cornell University Press, 1968).

31. The same basic argument can be found, with some important modifications, in Felix Cohen's essay "Transcendental Nonsense and the Functional Approach," *Columbia Law Review*, 35 (1935): 809–849.

32. Frank, *Law and the Modern Mind*, pp. 70–72.

33. "[T]he judge's innumerable unique traits, dispositions, and habits often get in their work in shaping his decisions not only in his determination of what he thinks fair or just with reference to a given set of facts, but in the very processes by which he comes convinced what those facts are." Ibid., p. 119. Also: "The trial court's facts are not 'data,' not something that is 'given'; they are not waiting somewhere, ready made, for the court to discover, to find. More accurately, they are processed by the trial court—are, so to speak, 'made' by it, on the basis of its subjective reactions to the witnesses' stories." Jerome Frank, *Courts on Trial: Myth and Reality in American Justice* (Princeton: Princeton University Press, 1950), pp. 23–24.

34. "The rules and principles of law are one class of such stimuli [that produce the hunches that determine cases]. But there are many others, concealed or unrevealed, not frequently considered in discussions of the character or nature of law." Frank, *Modern Mind*, p. 113.

35. "The decision of a judge after trying a case is the product of a unique experience." Ibid., p. 160. "To know the judge's hunch-producers which make the law we must know thoroughly that complicated congeries we loosely call the judge's personality." Ibid., pp. 119–120. "For the ultimately important influences in the decisions of any judge are the most obscure, and are the least discoverable—by anyone but the judge himself." Ibid., p. 123.

36. "What are the hidden factors in the inferences and opinions of ordinary men? The answer surely is that those factors are multitudinous and complicated, depending often on peculiarly individual traits of the persons whose inferences and opinions are to be explained. These uniquely individual factors are important causes of judgment more than anything which could be

described as political, economic, or moral biases." Ibid., p. 114. "For the ultimately important influences in the decisions of any judge are the most obscure, and are the least easily discoverable—by anyone but the judge himself. They are tied up with intimate experiences which no biographer, however sedulous, is likely to ferret out, and the emotional significance of which no one but the judge, or a psychologist in the closest contact with him, could comprehend." Ibid., p. 123. "The rules a judge announces when publishing his decision are, therefore, intelligible only if one can relive the judge's unique experience while he was trying that case—which, of course, cannot be done." Ibid., p. 161.

37. "The complete liberation of lawyers from the so-called tradition of scholasticism can come only through their liberation, with respect to law—like that of scientists with respect to science—from emotional attitudes of the child." Ibid., pp. 89–90. "What blocks a clearer understanding by lawyers of what they are about is not dull-mindedness. Nor is it, for the most part, inadequacy of educational training. It is, for the most part, an *emotional blocking* due to the very character of law, to the facility with which the law is converted into a substitute for fatherly authority. If any lawyer can measurably prevent himself from making that substitution, his thinking about law will become more realistic, experimental—adult." Ibid., pp. 106–107 (emphasis in original).

38. "By abandoning an infantile hope of absolute legal certainty we may augment markedly the amount of actual legal certainty." Ibid., p. 171. "If and when we have judges trained to observe their own mental processes and such judges with great particularity set forth in their opinions all the factors which they believe led to their conclusions, a judge in passing on a case may perhaps find it possible, to some considerable extent, intelligently to use as a control or guide, the opinion of another judge announced while passing on another case." Ibid., p. 163.

39. Karl Llewellyn, "Some Realism about Realism—Responding to Dean Pound," *Harvard Law Review*, 44 (1931): 1222–1264, and "A Realistic Jurisprudence—The Next Step," *Columbia Law Review*, 30 (1930): 431–465.

40. Llewellyn, "A Realistic Jurisprudence," pp. 439 n. 9, 447, 449–453.

41. Holmes, "The Path of the Law," p. 458.

42. "The third suggestion for general method lies in the *fusion or confusion of the realms of Is and Ought.* This confusion is rooted with dire firmness in our thinking." Karl Llewellyn, "Legal Tradition and Social Science Method—A Realist's Critique," in Karl Llewellyn, *Jurisprudence: Realism in Theory and Practice* (Chicago: University of Chicago Press, 1962), p. 84. "To fuse Is and Ought is to confuse the gradually accumulating semi-permanent data on

which any science must rest with the flux of changing opinion as to social objectives—that welter of objectives any of which a science can be made to serve." Ibid., p. 87.

43. Ibid. See also Karl Llewellyn, "Law and the Modern Mind: A Symposium (Part I, Legal Illusion)," *Columbia Law Review,* 31 (1931): 82–90.

44. Llewellyn, "Legal Tradition and Social Science Method," p. 77.

45. John Henry Schlegel, "American Legal Realism and Empirical Social Science: From the Yale Experience," *Buffalo Law Review,* 28 (1979): 459–586, and "American Legal Realism and Empirical Social Science: The Singular Case of Underhill Moore," 29 *Buffalo Law Review,* 29 (1984): 195–323.

46. One "common point of departure" that realists share is "[t]he temporary divorce of Is and Ought for purposes of study." Llewellyn, "Some Realism about Realism," pp. 1235–1236.

47. Llewellyn, "Legal Tradition and Social Science Method," p. 85.

48. Ibid., p. 86.

49. Ibid., p. 87.

50. Harold D. Lasswell and Myres S. McDougal, "Legal Science and Public Policy: Professional Training in the Public Interest," *Yale Law Journal,* 52 (1943): 203–295.

51. Ibid., pp. 234–35.

52. Ibid., p. 236.

53. Ibid., p. 237.

54. Ibid.

55. Ibid., pp. 237–238.

56. Ibid., p. 242.

57. Ibid., pp. 204–205.

58. Ibid., pp. 242, 244.

59. Ibid., p. 216.

60. Ibid., p. 205.

61. Ibid., pp. 212–213.

62. Ibid., p. 213.

63. Ibid., p. 217.

64. Ibid., p. 265.

65. Ibid., p. 272.

66. Ibid., p. 281.

67. Llewellyn, "Legal Tradition and Social Science Method," p. 97.

68. Ibid., p. 89.

69. Llewellyn, *The Common Law Tradition: Deciding Appeals* (Boston: Little, Brown, 1960), pp. 512–513.

70. Ibid., pp. 3–4.

71. Ibid., p. 11.

72. Ibid.

73. Ibid., pp. 4–5, 12.
74. Ibid., pp. 116, 190.
75. Ibid., p. 214.
76. Ibid., p. 213.
77. Ibid., p. 53.
78. Ibid., p. 119.
79. Ibid., pp. 202–203 (quoting "Law in Our Society," Syllabus, Lecture XIII [mimeo 1949]).
80. Ibid., p. 203.
81. Ibid.
82. Ibid.
83. Ibid., pp. 204, 268.
84. Ibid., pp. 17–18.
85. Ibid., p. 154.
86. Ibid., pp. 57, 516.
87. Ibid., p. 264.
88. Ibid., pp. 266–267.
89. Ibid., p. 43.
90. Ibid., p. 245.
91. Ibid., p. 44 (emphasis omitted).
92. Ibid., pp. 274, 127.
93. Ibid., p. 122.
94. Ibid., p. 60.
95. Ibid., p. 183.
96. Ibid., p. 222.
97. Ibid., pp. 183, 190–191.
98. Ibid., p. 201.
99. Ibid., pp. 121, 261 (emphasis in original).
100. *Nichomachean Ethics*, 1140a.
101. Paul Gewirtz, "Introduction," in Karl Llewellyn, *The Case Law System in America*, ed. Paul Gewirtz (Chicago: University of Chicago Press, 1989), pp. ix–xxiii; reviewed by William Twining, "Book Review," *Yale Law Journal*, 100 (1990): 1093–1102; Dennis M. Patterson, "Book Review: Law's Practice," *Columbia Law Review*, 90 (1990): 575–600. Recent work advancing a prudentialist view of law includes Suzanna Sherry, "Civic Virtue and the Feminine Voice in Constitutional Adjudication," and Daniel Farber, "The Inevitability of Practical Reason: Statutes, Formalism, and the Rule of Law," *Vanderbilt Law Review*, 45 (1992): 533–559. See generally, "Symposium on the Renaissance of Pragmatism in American Legal Thought," *Southern California Law Review*, 63 (1990): 1569–1928.
102. James Boyd White, *Heracles' Bow: Essays on the Rhetoric and Poetics of the Law* (Madison: University of Wisconsin Press, 1985), *When Words Lose Their*

Meaning: Constitutions and Reconstitutions of Language, Character, and Community (Chicago: University of Chicago Press, 1984), and *Justice as Translation: An Essay in Cultural and Legal Criticism* (Chicago: University of Chicago Press, 1990); Stanley Fish, *Doing What Comes Naturally* (Durham: University of North Carolina Press, 1989).

103. See Linda Hirshman, "The Book of 'A,'" *Texas Law Review*, 70 (1992): 971–1012; Lawrence B. Solum, "The Virtues and Vices of a Judge: An Aristotelian Guide to Judicial Selection," *Southern California Law Review*, 61 (1988): 1735–1756.

104. Posner, "The Present Situation in Legal Scholarship," p. 1121.

105. Ibid.

106. "As biology is to living organisms, astronomy to the stars, or economics to the price system, so should legal studies be to the legal system: an endeavor to make precise, objective, and systematic observations of how the legal system operates in fact and to discover and explain the recurrent patterns in the observations—the 'laws' of the system." Richard Posner, "Volume One of the Journal of Legal Studies—An Afterword," *Journal of Legal Studies*, 1 (1972): 437.

107. Richard Posner, "Some Uses and Abuses of Economics in Law," *University of Chicago Law Review*, 46 (1979): 302.

108. Ibid.

109. Ibid., pp. 301–302.

110. Ibid., p. 302.

111. Posner, "The Present Situation in Legal Scholarship," p. 1122.

112. Posner, "Some Uses and Abuses of Economics in Law," p. 302.

113. See Richard Posner, "Utilitarianism, Economics, and Legal Theory," *Journal of Legal Studies*, 8 (1979): 103–140, "The Ethical and Political Basis of the Efficiency Norm in Common Law Adjudication," *Hofstra Law Review*, 8 (1980): 487–507, and "The Value of Wealth: A Reply to Dworkin and Kronman," *Journal of Legal Studies*, 9 (1980): 243–252.

114. Posner himself has also defended the principle of wealth maximization (his version of the efficiency principle) on the libertarian grounds that it is particularly respectful of individual freedom. See Posner, "The Ethical and Political Basis of the Efficiency Norm in Common Law Adjudication," pp. 491–496.

115. See "Symposium on Efficiency as a Legal Concern," *Hofstra Law Review*, 8 (1980): 485–770; "Symposium on Change in the Common Law: Economic and Legal Perspectives," *Journal of Legal Studies*, 9 (1980): 189–427.

116. See Ronald Dworkin, "Why Efficiency?" *Hofstra Law Review*, 8 (1980): 563–590, and "Is Wealth a Value?" *Journal of Legal Studies*, 9 (1980): 191–226; Guido Calabresi, "About Law and Economics: A Letter to Ronald Dworkin," *Hofstra Law Review*, 8 (1980): 553–562; Anthony Kronman,

"Wealth Maximization as a Normative Principle," *Journal of Legal Studies,* 9 (1980): 227–242; Posner, "The Ethical and Political Basis of the Efficiency Norm in Common Law Adjudication," pp. 497–502.

117. Richard Posner, "Lawyers as Philosophers: Ackerman and Others," *American Bar Foundation Research Journal* (1981): 231–249.

118. Henry Sidgwick, *The Methods of Ethics* (London: Macmillan, 1907), pp. 480–484. This same idea is expressed in Bernard Williams, *Ethics and the Limits of Philosophy* (Cambridge, Mass.: Harvard University Press, 1985), pp. 105–109.

119. Posner, "The Present Situation in Legal Scholarship," p. 1113.

120. Ibid., p. 1115.

121. Roberto Mangabeira Unger, *Knowledge and Politics* (New York: Free Press, 1975), pp. 253–259; Duncan Kennedy, "Distributive and Paternalist Motives in Contract and Tort Law, with Special Reference to Compulsory Terms and Unequal Bargaining Power," *Maryland Law Review,* 41 (1982): 563–658.

122. Morton Horwitz, *The Transformation of American Law* (Cambridge, Mass.: Harvard University Press, 1977).

123. Kennedy, "Form and Substance in Private Law Adjudication," p. 1685.

124. Ibid., p. 1712.

125. Ibid.

126. Ibid.

127. Ibid., p. 1724.

128. Ibid., pp. 1777–1778.

129. Ibid., p. 1724.

130. Ibid.

131. Ibid., p. 1723.

132. Isaiah Berlin, *The Hedgehog and the Fox: An Essay on Tolstoy's View of History* (New York: Simon and Schuster, 1970).

133. Kennedy, "Form and Substance in Private Law Adjudication," pp. 1685–1686.

134. Peter Gabel and Duncan Kennedy, "Roll Over Beethoven," *Stanford Law Review,* 36 (1984): 1–55.

135. See Allan C. Hutchinson and Patrick J. Monahan, "Law, Politics, and the Critical Legal Scholars: The Unfolding Drama of American Legal Thought," *Stanford Law Review,* 36 (1984): 199–245; Boyle, "The Politics of Reason"; Robert W. Gordon, "Unfreezing Legal Reality: Critical Approaches to Law," *Florida State University Law Review,* 15 (1987): 195–220; Steven L. Winter, "Indeterminacy and Incommensurability in Constitutional Law," *California Law Review,* 78 (1990): 1441–1541.

136. Kennedy, "Form and Substance in Private Law Adjudication," p. 1775.

137. Ibid., p. 1776.

138. Ibid., p. 1778.

139. Ibid., pp. 1777–1778.
140. Hugh Collins, "Roberto Unger and the Critical Legal Studies Movement," *Journal of Law and Society,* 14 (1987): 387–410; William Ewald, "Unger's Philosophy: A Critical Legal Study," *Yale Law Journal,* 97 (1987): 665–756. See also H. Jefferson Powell, "The Gospel According to Roberto: A Theological Polemic," *Duke Law Journal,* 1988: 1013–1028; Stanley Fish, "Unger and Milton," *Duke Law Journal,* 1988: 975–1012; Richard Rorty, "Unger, Castoriadis and the Romance of a National Future," *Northwestern University Law Review,* 82 (1988): 335–351.

The vision of law and society that Unger first described in his essay on the critical legal studies movement is one he has continued to refine in his subsequent work. The main outlines of this vision have remained substantially unchanged, however. See Roberto Mangabeira Unger, *Social Theory: Its Situation and Its Task (A Critical Introduction to Politics, a Work in Constructive Social Theory)* (New York: Cambridge University Press, 1987). For an extension of the same vision to issues of personal psychology, see Roberto Mangabeira Unger, *Passion: An Essay on Personality* (New York: Free Press, 1984).

141. Unger, *The Critical Legal Studies Movement,* pp. 5, 14.
142. Ibid., p. 1.
143. Ibid., p. 2.
144. Ibid., pp. 7–8, 6.
145. Ibid., pp. 5–6.
146. Ibid., pp. 6–7.
147. Ibid., pp. 8–9.
148. Ibid., p. 8.
149. Ibid., pp. 14, 11, 9–10.
150. Ibid., p. 102.
151. Ibid., pp. 22–23, 93–95.
152. Ibid., p. 106.
153. Ibid., pp. 106, 108.
154. Ibid., p. 104.
155. Ibid., pp. 104–105.
156. Ibid., p. 108.
157. Ibid., p. 24.
158. Ibid., p. 25.
159. Ibid., p. 23.
160. Ibid., pp. 93–94.
161. Ibid., pp. 24, 41.
162. Ibid., pp. 32, 34.
163. Ibid., pp. 39–40.
164. Ibid., pp. 39, 53.

165. Ibid., p. 66.
166. Ibid., pp. 75–80.
167. Ibid., p. 8.
168. Ibid., p. 111 (emphasis added).
169. Ibid.
170. Ibid., p. 110.
171. Ibid., p. 111.
172. Ibid., pp. 111, 110.
173. Ibid., p. 17.
174. Mark Kelman, "Assume Nothing!" *Stanford Lawyer,* 22 (1988): 20.
175. See Grant Gilmore, *Security Interests in Personal Property* (Boston: Little, Brown, 1965); Boris Bittker and James S. Eustice, *Fundamentals of Federal Income Taxation of Corporations and Shareholders,* 3d ed. (Boston: Warren, Gorham and Lamont, 1971); Philip Areeda, *Antitrust Law: An Analysis of Antitrust Principles and Their Application* (Boston: Little, Brown, 1978).
176. See Bruce Ackerman, *Reconstructing American Law* (Cambridge, Mass.: Harvard University Press, 1984). I discuss the weaknesses of this view of legal education at greater length in Chapter 7.

5. Law Firms

1. Justin A. Stanley, "Should Lawyers Stick to Their Last?" *Indiana Law Journal,* 64 (1989): 473 (referring to a study by Barbara Curran, *The Lawyer Statistical Report* [Chicago: American Bar Foundation, 1985], p. 14).
2. Erwin Smigel, *The Wall Street Lawyer: Professional Organization Man?* (Bloomington: University of Indiana Press, 1964), pp. 1–14; James Willard Hurst, *The Growth of American Law: The Law Makers* (Boston: Little, Brown, 1950); Joel B. Grossman, *Lawyers and Judges: The ABA and the Politics of Judicial Selection* (New York: Wiley, 1965); Mark J. Green, *The Other Government: The Unseen Power of Washington Lawyers* (New York: Grossman, 1975); Nelson W. Polsby, "The Washington Community, 1960–1980," in *The New Congress,* ed. Thomas E. Mann and Norman J. Ornstein (Washington, D.C.: American Enterprise Institute for Public Policy Research, 1981); James B. Stewart, *The Partners: Inside America's Most Powerful Law Firms* (New York: Simon and Schuster, 1982).
3. Robert Nelson, *Partners with Power: The Social Transformation of the Large Firm* (Berkeley: University of California Press, 1988); Marc Galanter and Thomas Palay, *Tournament of Lawyers: The Transformation of the Big Law Firm* (Chicago: University of Chicago Press, 1991); Ronald Gilson and Robert Mnookin, "Coming of Age in a Corporate Law Firm: The Economics of Associate Career Patterns," *Stanford Law Review,* 41 (1989): 567–595; "Symposium: The Growth of Large Law Firms and Its Effect on the Legal

Profession and Legal Education," *Indiana Law Journal*, 64 (1989): 423–600. See also Ronald Gilson and Robert Mnookin, "Sharing among the Human Capitalists: An Economic Inquiry into the Corporate Law Firm and How Partners Split Profits," *Stanford Law Review*, 37 (1985): 313–392.

4. Robert M. Greene, "A Strategy for Survival," *The American Lawyer*, March 1992, p. 6; "More Revenues, But Thinner Profits, for Law Firms," *New York Times*, 29 June 1992, p. D1.

5. Steven Brill, "The Law Business in the Year 2000," *The American Lawyer*, June 1989, p. 10.

6. Galanter and Palay, *Tournament of Lawyers*, p. 46.

7. Ibid.

8. Ibid., p. 47.

9. Ibid.

10. Ibid.

11. Nelson, *Partners with Power*, p. 147.

12. Ibid., p. 171.

13. Ibid.

14. Brill, "The Law Business in the Year 2000," p. 14.

15. See Galanter and Palay, *Tournament of Lawyers*, p. 49.

16. Ibid.

17. Ibid., pp. 49–50.

18. Ibid., p. 50, n. 92.

19. Ibid., p. 50.

20. Smigel, *The Wall Street Lawyer*, pp. 86–90, 130–36. See also Galanter and Palay, *Tournament of Lawyers*, p. 54.

21. Galanter and Palay, *Tournament of Lawyers*, pp. 54–55 (referring to Larry Smith, "Notable Gains and Losses Punctuate Another Stable Growth Year," *Of Counsel*, 8 [1989]: 1).

22. Ibid., p. 55.

23. One need only glance at the "Sidebar" page of the *National Law Journal* to appreciate the extent to which law firms have been combining and dividing of late. See, for example, "D.C.'s Dow Lohnes Finds Merger Partner," *National Law Journal*, 6 Nov. 1989, p. 2; "More De-Mergers," *National Law Journal*, 21 Aug. 1989, p. 2; "Robins Kaplan Merges with D.C. Firm," *National Law Journal*, 26 March 1990, p. 2; "Merger in Cleveland," *National Law Journal*, 2 April 1990, p. 2; "Law Firm Tries to Untie Knot for Partner," *National Law Journal*, 4 June 1990, p. 2; "Merger in Seattle," *National Law Journal*, 2 July 1990, p. 2; "All Invited to the Merger?" *National Law Journal*, 16 July 1990, p. 2; "Boston, Chicago Merger Talks Go Differently," *National Law Journal*, 3 Sept. 1990, p. 2. See generally "Lawyers Catch Merger Fever," *New York Times*, 25 Aug. 1987, p. D1.

24. Brill, "The Law Business in the Year 2000," p. 8. See also Steven Brill, "The

Changing Meaning of Partnership," *The American Lawyer,* March 1990, p. 4.

25. Brill, "The Law Business in the Year 2000," p. 6. See also Gilson and Mnookin, "Coming of Age in a Corporate Law Firm," p. 568.

26. Oliver E. Williamson, *Markets and Hierarchies: Analysis and Antitrust Implications (A Study in the Economics of Internal Organization)* (New York: Free Press, 1975), pp. 37–39.

27. Galanter and Palay, *Tournament of Lawyers,* p. 53. See also George R. Snider, "Big Changes Await Firm Marketing," *National Law Journal,* 16 Oct. 1989, p. 24.

28. Galanter and Palay, *Tournament of Lawyers,* p. 53 (quoting Merrilyn Tarlton, former president of the National Association of Law Firm Marketing Administrators, as reported in "New Partner in the Firm: The Marketing Director," *New York Times,* 2 June 1989, p. B6).

29. *The American Lawyer,* for example, sponsors seminars on law firm management techniques, and the *National Law Journal* hosts an annual symposium on law firm marketing.

30. Galanter and Palay, *Tournament of Lawyers,* p. 66.

31. Ibid.

32. Ibid., p. 54.

33. See, for example, "Summer Associates '89," *The American Lawyer,* Oct. 1989 (Pullout Management Report).

34. Arthur S. Hayes, "Brochures: A New Weapon in the Recruiting Wars," *The American Lawyer,* Dec. 1988, p. 28; Mary Ann Galante, "Firms Finding More Value in Marketing," *National Law Journal,* 18 Nov. 1985, pp. 28–29.

35. See, for example, "The Am Law 100," *The American Lawyer,* July/Aug. 1989 (Pullout Supplement); "NLJ 250 Annual Survey of the Nation's Largest Firms," *National Law Journal,* 24 Sept. 1990.

36. Galanter and Palay, *Tournament of Lawyers,* p. 68.

37. Rita Jensen, "Partners Work Harder to Stay Even," *National Law Journal,* 10 Aug. 1987, p. 12.

38. Martin Halstuk, "Rising Tide of Lawyers Who Quit," *San Francisco Chronicle,* 2 Oct. 1989, p. A1; Robert B. McKay, "The Rise of the Justice Industry and the Decline of Legal Ethics," *Washington University Law Quarterly,* 68 (1990): 840 (noting that firms now frequently demand billable hours in the 2000–2200 range); Nelson, *Partners with Power,* p. 185 (number of hours worked at four large Chicago firms averaged 2097); Paul Reidinger, "It's 46.5 Hours a Week in Law," *American Bar Association Journal,* 1 Sept. 1986, p. 44.

39. Paul Hoffman, *Lions in the Street: The Inside Story of the Great Wall Street Firms* (New York: Saturday Review Press, 1973), pp. 130–131.

40. "Law Journal's Legal Highlights in '90's," *New York Law Journal,* 7 Jan. 1991, p. 1. According to one survey of twenty-five large New York firms, the

number of billable hours has risen 29 percent since 1983, up to a median of 2290 hours per year. Some lawyers average 2500 billable hours per year. Nancy Zeldis, "Billables Up," *National Law Journal,* 11 April 1988, p. 2. For more on billable hours in New York City firms, see Erwin Cherovsky, *The Guide to New York Law Firms* (New York: St. Martin's Press, 1991). There is some evidence that the number of billable hours has declined slightly as a result of the recent economic slump. See Michele Galen, "For Law Firms, It's Dog v. Dog Out There," *Business Week,* 6 Aug. 1990, p. 56.

41. Galanter and Palay, *Tournament of Lawyers,* p. 56.

42. See, for example, "The Am Law 100," July/Aug. 1989 (Pullout Supplement, pp. 34–38); Daniel Wise, "It Was a Banner Year for New York Firms," *National Law Journal,* 24 July 1989, p. 2 (per partner profits at 200-plus-lawyer firms in New York increased $75,000 from 1988 to 1989). But see Steven Brill, "Short-Term Pain, Long-Term Gain," *The American Lawyer,* Jan./Feb. 1991, p. 5 (indicating recent dip in partnership profits).

43. Jensen, "Partners Work Harder to Stay Even," p. 36.

44. Brill, "The Law Business in the Year 2000," p. 6.

45. See, for example, Dean Acheson, *Present at the Creation: My Ten Years at the State Department* (New York: Norton, 1969); William H. Harbaugh, *Lawyer's Lawyer: The Life of John W. Davis* (New York: Oxford University Press, 1973); Porter McKeever, *Adlai Stevenson: His Life and Legacy* (New York: William Morrow, 1989); Walter Isaacson and Evan Thomas, *The Wise Men: Six Friends and the World They Made* (New York: Simon and Schuster, 1986); Godfrey Hodgson, *The Colonel: The Life and Wars of Henry Stimson, 1867–1950* (New York: Knopf, 1990); T. A. Schwartz, *America's Germany: John J. McCloy and the Federal Republic of Germany* (Cambridge, Mass.: Harvard University Press, 1991); Kai Bird, *John J. McCloy: The Making of the American Establishment* (New York: Simon and Schuster, 1992).

46. Smigel, *Wall Street Lawyer,* pp. 343–345.

47. Galanter and Palay, *Tournament of Lawyers,* pp. 110–116.

48. Brill, "The Law Business in the Year 2000," p. 14.

49. Martin Lipton, "Truth about Takeovers: Going for Gold Might Just Impoverish Us," *Legal Times,* 22 Jan. 1990, p. 27; Morton Mintz, "Community Dislocations: A Painful Side Effect of Merger," *Washington Post,* 20 April 1980, p. A2; Jack Willoughby, "What a Raider Hath Wrought," *Forbes,* 23 March 1987, p. 56.

50. Michael J. Sandel, *Liberalism and the Limits of Justice* (Cambridge: Cambridge University Press, 1982), p. 181.

51. Joan Karen Willin, "Investment Advisory Services by Banking Organizations," *Banking Expansion Reporter,* 3 Nov. 1986, p. 1; Anne Schwimmer, "Hard Truths about the Restructuring Business," *Investment Dealer's Digest,* 16 Nov. 1990, p. 18.

52. Smigel, *Wall Street Lawyer,* pp. 36–47, 73–74, 102, 120–130.
53. Doreen Weisenhaus, "Still a Long Way to Go for Women, Minorities," *National Law Journal,* 8 Feb. 1988, p. 1 (noting that although women constitute 40 percent of newly hired associates, 90 percent of partners at the largest firms are white males); Joan H. Stern, "Female Talent at Law Firms," *National Law Journal,* 18 March 1991, p. 15 (arguing that "simple economics" should provide firms with reason to "alter their attitude toward women lawyers"); Nina Burleigh and Stephanie B. Goldberg, "Breaking the Silence," *American Bar Association Journal,* Aug. 1989, p. 46 (on sexual harassment). See generally Emily Couric, "Women in the Large Firms: A High Price of Admission," *National Law Journal,* 11 Dec. 1989, p. S2.
54. Gail G. Peschel and Paula S. Linden, "The Gender Gap: Employment and Pay Differences," *National Law Journal,* 27 March 1989, p. 22; Patricia A. Mairs, "Bringing Up Baby," *National Law Journal,* 14 Mar. 1988, p. 1; Jennifer A. Kingson, "Women in the Law Say Path Is Limited by 'Mommy Track,'" *New York Times,* 8 Aug. 1988, p. A1; "Law Firms and Lawyers with Children: An Empirical Analysis of Family/Work Conflict," *Stanford Law Review,* 34 (1982): 1265 ("both law firms and students expect that women will shoulder most of the childrearing responsibilities and that employers will accommodate most of the short-term needs of women with newborn infants, but that employers will only partially accommodate the longer-term needs of lawyers with small children"); Geoffrey Hazard, "Male Culture Still Dominates the Profession," *National Law Journal,* 19 Dec. 1988, p. 10 ("language and internal culture of law still is male").
55. See, for example, Nelson, *Partners with Power,* p. 131; Peter Carbonara, "Blacks Still Haven't Made It," *The American Lawyer,* March 1989, pp. 64–65; Rita Jensen, "Minorities Didn't Share in Firm Growth," *National Law Journal,* 19 Feb. 1990, p. 1; Rosalind Resnick, "Measured Progress," *National Law Journal,* 20 Aug. 1990, p. 1. There are, of course, some notable exceptions. Conrad Harper, a partner at Simpson Thacher & Bartlett and president of the Association of the Bar of the City of New York, is one such. See John Kifner, "Bar Group Ready to Name First Black President," *New York Times,* 12 Dec. 1989, p. B1. See also "Minority Enrollment Efforts Show Gains at Law Schools," *New York Times,* 8 March 1990, p. A20; David Margolick, "35 Law Firms in New York Pledge to Hire More Minorities," *New York Times,* 26 Sept. 1991, p. B1.
56. Nelson, *Partners with Power,* p. 133; Brill, "The Law Business in the Year 2000," p. 8; Terry Carter, "Is Associate Quality Slipping? Maybe," *National Law Journal,* 27 March 1989, p. 1; Rita Jensen, "Firms Gathering Summer's Harvest," *National Law Journal,* 31 July 1989, pp. 25–29; Alex M. Johnson, "Think Like a Lawyer, Work Like a Machine: The Dissonance between Law School and Law Practice," *Southern California Law Review,* 64 (1991):

1244 ("evidence suggests that megafirms and high-prestige firms are recruiting at law schools that they have previously shunned").

57. At Yale, for example, students from primarily working-class backgrounds whose parents did not attend college or professional school have formed an organization, First Generation Professionals, to help their members overcome their lack of professional role models and to promote recruitment at the school. See "Yale Law Students from Poor Backgrounds Unite," *New York Times,* 5 June 1988, p. 47.

58. Smigel, *Wall Street Lawyer,* pp. 18, 26, 92, 260; see also Hoffman, *Lions in the Street,* p. 58.

59. Richard L. Abel, *American Lawyers* (New York: Oxford University Press, 1989), p. 17; Robert Gordon, "The Independence of Lawyers," *Boston University Law Review,* 68 (1988): 11–17; Mark J. Osiel, "Lawyers as Monopolists, Aristocrats, and Entrepreneurs (Review of *Lawyers in Society,* Richard L. Abel and Philip S. C. Lewis, eds.)," *Harvard Law Review,* 103 (1990): 2009–2066.

60. Karl Llewellyn, *The Common Law Tradition: Deciding Appeals* (Boston: Little, Brown, 1960), pp. 213–235.

61. Galanter and Palay, *Tournament of Lawyers,* pp. 52–54; Gilson and Mnookin, "Sharing among the Human Capitalists," pp. 313–319.

62. Brill, "The Law Business in the Year 2000."

63. Jamienne S. Studley, "Financial Sacrifice Outside Private Sector," *National Law Journal,* 27 March 1989, p. 18; Gail G. Peshel and Paula S. Linden, "13 Percent Took Jobs in Government," *National Law Journal,* 27 March 1989, p. 20. According to Abel (*American Lawyers,* p. 302), the mean income for law firm associates in the United States in 1954 was $7786, and the mean income for government attorneys was $7915. The distance has since widened substantially. See, for example, Marcia Coyle and Marianne Lavelle, "1 of 11 Federal Attorneys Quits Each Year," *National Law Journal,* 11 Sept. 1989, p. 5 (noting 72 percent pay gap); "Closing the Gap," *National Law Journal,* 4 Sept. 1989, p. 12 (noting that young associates in firms earn double their government counterparts); Roy A. Schotland, "Government Pay Is the Most Important Issue," *National Law Journal,* 23 Jan. 1989, p. 12.

64. See, for example, "Data Show Which Specialties Thrive, Are Down," *National Law Journal,* 22 Oct. 1990, p. S4. Legal recruiters in the Northeast consistently report that trusts and estates is "not hot." "What's Hot, What's Not in Placement," *National Law Journal,* 27 March 1989, p. 24; see also Margaret Cronin Fisk, "Profiles in Power 100: The Most Influential Lawyers in America," *National Law Journal,* 25 March 1991, p. S2.

65. John H. Langbein, "The Twentieth-Century Revolution in Family Wealth Transmission," *Michigan Law Review,* 86 (1988): 722–751.

66. One particularly striking expression of this is the "Big Deals" column that appears regularly in *The American Lawyer.*

67. See Frederick B. Mackinnon, *Contingent Fees for Legal Services: A Study of Professional Economics and Responsibilities* (Chicago: Aldine, 1964), p. 10; Robert S. Alexander, "The History of the Law as an Independent Profession and the Present English System," in *The Lawyer's Professional Independence: Present Threats/Future Challenges,* ed. American Bar Association (1984), p. 17; Julius H. Cohen, *The Law: Business or Profession?* (New York: G.A. Jennings, 1924), pp. 205–216; Eve Spangler, *Lawyers for Hire* (New Haven: Yale University Press, 1986), p. 175.

68. The percentage of law graduates entering business was 11.3 in 1981. By 1988 it had tapered off to 6.9 percent. National Association for Law Placement, "Nationwide Fifteen-Year Employment Survey Profile, 1974–1988."

69. Even this is no longer as true as it once was. See Jonathan P. Bellis and Rees W. Morrison, "Inside, Looking Out," *National Law Journal,* 2 Dec. 1991, p. 65; Nicholas Varchaver, "Quantity Counts: The Push to Bill More Hours," *The American Lawyer,* Jan./Feb. 1992, p. 50.

70. Anthony Borden, "Ben Heineman's In-House Revolution," *The American Lawyer,* Sept. 1989, p. 100; Alison Frankel, "G.E.'s Baird: Aetna's New Insurance Policy," *The American Lawyer,* July/Aug. 1990, p. 27.

71. Nelson, *Partners with Power,* pp. 56, 231; Robert A. Kagan and Robert Eli Rosen, "On the Social Significance of Large Law Firm Practice," *Stanford Law Review,* 37 (1985): 409 (the outside lawyer "is less likely [than in-house counsel] to be caught up in current management's way of seeing things or habits of deference to the chief executive officer"); Robert Eli Rosen, "The Inside Counsel Movement, Professional Judgment and Organizational Representation," *Indiana Law Journal,* 64 (1989): 479–553.

72. Darrell Preston, "Legal Eagles Plot Solo Practice," *Dallas Business Journal,* 14 (1991): 1; Sam Adler, "The Little Firm That Could," *Manhattan Lawyer,* Jan./Feb. 1991, p. 1; Alexander Stille, "Small Firms in America," *National Law Journal,* 8 July 1985, p. 1; "Hedlund Leaving Latham to Form Own Firm," *Crain's Chicago Business,* 29 April 1991, p. 70.

73. Amy Dockser, "Midsize Law Firms Struggle to Survive," *Wall Street Journal,* 19 Oct. 1988, p. B1; "The Strange Case of the Vanishing Firms," *Wall Street Journal,* 29 July 1988, p. 17; Steven Brill, "After the Revolution," *The American Lawyer,* June 1987, p. 3 (noting that "60% of all midsized firms in Manhattan are considering or have actively considered within the last six months a merger, liquidation, or other restructuring"); Judy Temes, "They're Standing on Firmer Ground," *Crain's New York Business,* 27 Nov. 1989, p. 31 ("while the number of firms with 500 attorneys or more quadrupled in the last five years, those with only 100 or more grew only 36%. And for the first time, in 1987, the ranks of midsized firms—those with 50 to 100 attorneys—declined"); James F. Fitzpatrick, "Legal Future Shock: The Role of Large Law Firms by the End of the Century," *Indiana Law Journal,* 64 (1989): 464.

6. Courts

1. Owen Fiss, "Comment: Against Settlement," *Yale Law Journal*, 93 (1984): 1073–1090; Richard Posner, "The Summary Jury Trial and Other Methods of Alternative Dispute Resolution: Some Cautionary Observations," *University of Chicago Law Review*, 53 (1986): 366–393; Carrie Menkel-Meadow, "Symposium: Pursuing Settlement in an Adversary Culture: A Tale of Innovation Co-opted or 'The Law of ADR,'" *Florida State University Law Review*, 19 (1991): 1–46; Neil Vidmar and Jeffrey Rice, "Symposium: Jury-Determined Settlements and Summary Jury Trials: Observations about Alternative Dispute Resolution in an Adversary Culture," *Florida State University Law Review*, 19 (1991): 89–103.
2. Alexis de Tocqueville, *Democracy in America*, ed. J. P. Mayer, trans. George Lawrence (New York: Anchor Press, 1966), pp. 102, 270.
3. The expansion of the federal courts' caseload can be traced to the growth of federal power during the Civil War and after. This expansion has accelerated dramatically since 1960. Since then the caseload of the federal district courts has tripled; the caseload of the federal appeals courts has increased tenfold. Richard Posner, *The Federal Courts: Crisis and Reform* (Cambridge, Mass.: Harvard University Press, 1985), pp. 51–53; *Report of Federal Courts Study Committee* (1990), pp. 4–5.
4. Macklin Fleming, "Court Survival in the Litigation Explosion," *Judicature*, 54 (1970): 109–113; Daniel Meador, *Appellate Courts: Staff and Process in the Crisis of Volume—An Appellate Justice Project of the National Center for State Courts* (St. Paul, Minn.: West, 1974), pp. 7–9; Robert H. Bork, "Dealing with the Overload in Article III Courts," *Federal Rules Decisions*, 70 (1976): 231–246; Warren E. Burger, "Agenda for 2000 A.D.—A Need for Systematic Anticipation," *Federal Rules Decisions*, 70 (1976): 83–110; Posner, *The Federal Courts*, pp. 59–93; Nancy Levit, "The Caseload Conundrum, Constitutional Restraint and the Manipulation of Jurisdiction," *Notre Dame Law Review*, 64 (1989): 321–366. For an opposing view see Marc Galanter, "Reading the Landscape of Disputes: What We Know and Don't Know (and Think We Know) about Our Allegedly Contentious and Litigious Society," *UCLA Law Review*, 31 (1983): 4–71.
5. Donald Horowitz, *The Courts and Social Policy* (Washington, D.C.: Brookings Institution, 1977); Wade H. McCree, "Bureaucratic Justice: An Early Warning," *University of Pennsylvania Law Review*, 129 (1981): 777, 794–796; Lawrence Friedman, *Total Justice* (New York: Russell Sage Foundation, 1985); Bruce Mann, *Neighbors and Strangers: Law and Community in Early Connecticut* (Chapel Hill: University of North Carolina Press, 1987), pp. 101–136; *Report of Federal Courts Study Committee*, pp. 4–5. See also Bayless Manning, "Hyperlexis: Our National Disease," *Northwestern University*

Law Review, 71 (1977): 767–782 (attributing the caseload crisis to excessive lawmaking).

6. Robert A. Kagan, Bliss Cartwright, Lawrence M. Friedman, and Stanton Wheeler, "The Business of State Supreme Courts, 1870–1970," *Stanford Law Review*, 30 (1977): 121–156; Victor E. Flango and Mary E. Elsner, "Estimating Caseloads: Two Methods Tested in Tulsa," *State Court Journal*, 7 (Spring 1983), pp. 18–24; "An Update: State Caseload Statistics," *State Court Journal*, 7 (Summer 1983), p. 8; Thomas B. Marvell, "State Appellate Court Responses to Caseload Growth," *Judicature*, 72 (1989): 282–291. See also Nicholas L. Demos, "Speedy Trial Judges," *The Judges' Journal*, 22 (Fall 1983): 38–62 (offering suggestions for state court judges on how to deal with the caseload problem). For an opposing view see Marc Galanter, "The Day after the Litigation Explosion," *Maryland Law Review*, 46 (1986): 3–48.

7. Posner, *The Federal Courts*, pp. 7, 77–93.

8. Ibid., pp. 95–96. The Federal Courts Study Committee has made at least two such proposals: first, that limitations be placed on federal diversity jurisdiction, and second, that defendants be barred from removing to the federal courts ERISA actions originally brought in state court. *Report of the Federal Courts Study Committee*, pp. 38–44.

9. Posner, *The Federal Courts*, pp. 119–124. See also William L. Reynolds and William M. Richman, "The Non-Precedential Precedent—Limited Publication and No-Citation Rules in the United States Courts of Appeals," *Columbia Law Review*, 78 (1978): 1167–1206; Pamela Mathy, "Experimentation in Federal Appellate Case Management and the Prehearing Conference Program of the United States Court of Appeals for the Seventh Circuit," *Chicago-Kent Law Review*, 61 (1985): 431–482.

10. Judith Resnik, "Managerial Judges," *Harvard Law Review*, 96 (1982): 374–448. See also the debate between Resnik and Paul Connolly on the efficacy and constitutionality of various forms of judicial case management. Judith Resnik, "Managerial Judges and Court Delay: The Unproven Assumptions," *The Judges' Journal*, 23 (Winter 1984): 8–11, 54–55; Paul R. J. Connolly, "Why We Do Need Managerial Judges," *The Judges' Journal*, 23 (Fall 1984): 34–43; Judith Resnik, "The Assumptions Remain," *The Judges' Journal*, 23 (Fall 1984): 37–40.

11. "Remarks of Justice Antonin Scalia before the Fellows of the American Bar Foundation and the National Conference of Bar Presidents," 15 Feb. 1987, pp. 4–5 (mimeo).

12. Posner, *The Federal Courts*, pp. 97–102.

13. Judith Resnik, "Failing Faith: Adjudicatory Procedure in Decline," *University of Chicago Law Review*, 53 (1986): 494–560.

14. Owen Fiss, "The Bureaucratization of the Judiciary," *Yale Law Journal*, 92

(1983): 1442–1468; Joseph Vining, *The Authoritarian and the Authoritative* (Chicago: University of Chicago Press, 1986), pp. 51–57.

15. Mirjan Damaska, *The Faces of Justice and State Authority: A Comparative Approach to the Legal Process* (New Haven: Yale University Press, 1986), pp. 231–239.

16. Fiss, "The Bureaucratization of the Judiciary," p. 1452.

17. Ibid., p. 1453.

18. Judith Resnik, "Tiers," *Southern California Law Review,* 57 (1984): 837–1035.

19. Fiss, "The Bureaucratization of the Judiciary," pp. 1454–1455.

20. Thomas B. Marvell, *Appellate Courts and Lawyers: Information Gathering in the Adversary System* (Westport, Conn.: Greenwood Press, 1978), p. 96; but see Daniel Meador, *Appellate Courts: Staff and Process in the Crisis of Volume,* p. 42 (reporting results of a survey in which few judges admitted to reading clerks' memoranda in lieu of briefs). Many writers have emphasized the significant responsibilities delegated to law clerks. See generally John Oakley and Robert Thompson, *Law Clerks and the Judicial Process: Perceptions of the Qualities and Functions of Law Clerks in American Courts* (Berkeley: University of California Press, 1980); David Crump, "Law Clerks: Their Roles and Relationships with Their Judges," *Judicature,* 69 (Dec./Jan. 1986): 236–240; William M. Richman and William L. Reynolds, "Appellate Justice Bureaucracy and Scholarship," *University of Michigan Journal of Law Reform,* 21 (1988): 623–646.

21. Posner, *The Federal Courts,* p. 120.

22. See ibid., pp. 102–119; Joseph Vining, "Justice, Bureaucracy, and Legal Method," *Michigan Law Review,* 80 (1981): 248–258. For contrasting views see Patricia M. Wald, "The Problem with the Courts: Black-Robed Bureaucracy or Collegiality under Challenge?" *Maryland Law Review,* 42 (1983): 766–786; Harry T. Edwards, "A Judge's View on 'Justice, Bureaucracy, and Legal Method,'" *Michigan Law Review,* 80 (1981): 259–269, and "The Rising Work Load and Perceived 'Bureaucracy' of the Federal Courts: A Causation-Based Approach to the Search for Appropriate Remedies," *Iowa Law Review,* 68 (1983): 871–936.

23. Richard Posner, *Economic Analysis of Law,* 2d ed. (Boston: Little, Brown, 1977), pp. 415–416.

24. Richard Dawkins, *The Selfish Gene* (New York: Oxford University Press, 1989); Sigmund Freud, "The Economic Problem of Masochism," in *The Standard Edition of the Complete Psychological Works of Sigmund Freud,* ed. and trans. James Strachey (London: Hogarth Press, 1961), vol. 19, pp. 159–170.

25. Karl Marx, *Capital,* ed. Frederick Engels, trans. Samuel Moore and Edward Aveling (New York: Random House, 1906), vol. 1, pp. 61–69; Max Weber, *Economy and Society,* ed. Guenther Roth and Claus Wittich, trans. Ephraim Fischoff and others (New York: Bedminster Press, 1968), vol. 1, pp. 86–90.

26. Miguel de Unamuno, *The Tragic Sense of Life,* trans. J. E. Crawford Flitch (New York: Dover, 1954), pp. 17–18.

27. On the relation between the judicial style of an era and the self-understanding of judges, see Benjamin Cardozo, "Law and Literature," in *Law and Literature and Other Essays* (New York: Harcourt, Brace, 1931), p. 3; Karl Llewllyn, *The Common Law Tradition* (Boston: Little, Brown, 1960), pp. 464–468; J. Gillis Wetter, *The Styles of Appellate Judicial Opinions: A Case Study in Comparative Law* (Leyden: A.M. Sythoff, 1960); James Boyd White, *Heracles' Bow: Essays on the Rhetoric and Poetics of the Law* (Madison: University of Wisconsin Press, 1985), pp. 40–44.

28. Frank Easterbrook, "Ways of Criticizing the Court," *Harvard Law Review,* 95 (1982): 802–832.

29. Posner, *The Federal Courts,* pp. 226–247.

30. Frank Michelman, "Supreme Court, 1985 Term—Foreword: Traces of Self-Government," *Harvard Law Review,* 100 (1986): 4–77.

31. Ibid., p. 74.

32. Edmund Burke, *Reflections on the Revolution in France* (Harmondsworth: Penguin, 1969), p. 135.

33. See Herman Schwartz, *Packing the Courts: The Conservative Campaign to Rewrite the Constitution* (New York: Charles Scribner's Sons, 1988), pp. 3–9, 58–149; William G. Ross, "Participation by the Public in the Federal Judicial Selection Process," *Vanderbilt Law Review,* 43 (1990): 1, 39–45.

34. Posner, *The Federal Courts,* pp. 102–119. See also Paul M. Bator, "The Judicial Universe of Judge Richard Posner," *University of Chicago Law Review,* 52 (1985): 1146, 1149.

35. See Robert F. Nagel, *Constitutional Cultures: The Mentality and Consequences of Judicial Review* (Berkeley: University of California Press, 1989), pp. 121–155.

36. Paul W. Kahn, "The Court, the Community and the Judicial Balance: The Jurisprudence of Justice Powell," *Yale Law Journal,* 97 (1987): 1–60.

7. Honesty and Hope

1. Bruce A. Ackerman, *Reconstructing American Law* (New Haven: Yale University Press, 1983).

2. Richard A. Posner, "The Decline of Law as an Autonomous Discipline," *Harvard Law Review,* 100 (1987): 761–780.

3. The phrase is Arthur Leff's. See Arthur A. Leff, "Law and," *Yale Law Journal,* 87 (1978): 989–1011. Leff himself was profoundly skeptical of the claims of legal science.

4. The literature is immense. For a representative sampling see Roger Cramton and Alan Schwartz, "Using Auction Theory to Inform Takeover Regula-

tion," *Journal of Law, Economics and Organization,* 7 (1991): 27–53; Lucian A. Bebchuk, "A Framework for Analyzing Legal Policy towards Proxy Contests," *California Law Review,* 78 (1990): 1071–1135; Lucian A. Bebchuk, "Toward Undistorted Choice and Equal Treatment in Corporate Takeovers," *Harvard Law Review,* 98 (1985): 1695–1808; Bernard S. Black, "Bidder Overpayment in Takeovers," *Stanford Law Review,* 41 (1989): 597–660; Frank H. Easterbrook and Daniel R. Fischel, "Optimal Damages in Securities Cases," *University of Chicago Law Review,* 52 (1985): 611–652; Daniel R. Fischel, "Insider Trading and Investment Analysts: An Economic Analysis of Dirks v. Securities and Exchange Commission," *Hofstra Law Review,* 13 (1984): 127–146.

5. Guido Calabresi, *A Common Law for the Age of Statutes* (Cambridge, Mass.: Harvard University Press, 1982), p. 1.

6. There are other settings, of course, in which the techniques of certain nonlegal disciplines may be of greater use to the practicing lawyer. A lawyer working at the Environmental Protection Agency, for example, whose job is to draft administrative regulations dealing with smokestack emissions needs to know something about economics and statistics and perhaps epidemiology too. Still, his or her distinctive contribution as a *lawyer* consists in something other than a knowledge of these subjects, as the next section of my argument makes clear.

7. See Robert W. Gordon, "The Independence of Lawyers," *Boston University Law Review,* 68 (1988): 1–83; "Corporate Law Practice as a Public Calling," *Maryland Law Review,* 49 (1990): 255–292.

8. The most forceful by far is David Luban's. See David Luban, *Lawyers and Justice: An Ethical Study* (Princeton: Princeton University Press, 1988), pp. 50–103. Luban gives the adversary system a qualified endorsement, rejecting many of the traditional arguments for it, but finding it better, on balance, than the alternatives.

9. Gordon, "The Independence of Lawyers," pp. 48–68.

10. This is Aristotle's distinction between action and production. See Aristotle, *Nicomachean Ethics,* 1140b5–7.

11. Meir Dan-Cohen draws a similar distinction between two different sorts of roles, which he calls "detached" and "nondetached." The occupant of a nondetached role identifies with it personally; the occupant of a detached role does not. Meir Dan-Cohen, "Law, Community and Communication," *Duke Law Journal,* 1989: 1654–1655. See also Alasdair MacIntyre, *After Virtue* (Notre Dame, Ind.: Notre Dame University Press, 1981), pp. 27–28.

12. Gordon, "Corporate Law Practice as a Public Calling"; William Simon, "Ethical Discretion in Lawyering," *Harvard Law Review,* 101 (1988): 1083–1145.

13. Max Weber, "Science as a Vocation," *From Max Weber: Essays in Sociology,*

ed. Hans Gerth and C. Wright Mills (New York: Oxford, 1946), p. 155.

14. Ibid., p. 152.

15. Charles Taylor, *Sources of the Self* (Cambridge, Mass.: Harvard University Press, 1989), pp. 211–233.

16. In Max Weber's terminology, a profession is not only a "privileged commercial class" with economically valuable rights and opportunities, but a "status group" as well. Weber defines status as "an effective claim to social esteem . . . typically founded on . . . [a] style of life"—the collective equivalent of character—that may be either hereditary or occupational in origin. Max Weber, *Economy and Society,* ed. Guenther Roth and Claus Wittich, trans. Ephraim Fischoff and others (New York: Bedminster Press, 1968), vol. 1, pp. 304–307. A useful survey of different theories of professionalism as applied to the legal profession in particular may be found in Richard Abel, *American Lawyers* (New York: Oxford University Press, 1989), pp. 14–39. The idea of a profession as a "calling" with which one identifies—as opposed to a job one merely performs—is discussed in Wilbert E. Moore, *The Professions: Roles and Rules* (New York: Russell Sage Foundation, 1970), pp. 7–9; Burton J. Bledstein, *The Culture of Professionalism: The Middle Class and the Development of Higher Education in America* (New York: Norton, 1976), pp. 129–202; William J. Goode, "Community within a Community: The Professions," *American Sociological Review,* 22 (1957): 194–200.

17. Weber, "Science as a Vocation," 153.

18. This point is made by Bruce Ackerman in his perceptive tribute to Judge Henry Friendly, "In Memoriam: Henry J. Friendly," *Harvard Law Review,* 99 (1986): 1709–1713.

19. See Steven Brill, "Shattered Dreams," *The American Lawyer,* June 1991, p. 3.

20. Robert H. Jackson, "Tribute to Country Lawyers: A Review," *American Bar Association Journal,* 30 (1944): 136–139.

Index